Medway High School
Library 345
F

DATE DUE

Courts on Trial

"I must say that, as a litigant, I should dread a law suit beyond almost anything else short of sickness and death."

JUDGE LEARNED HAND.

"Nothing so sweet as magic is to him,
Which he prefers before his chiefest bliss:
And this the man that in his study sits."

CHRISTOPHER MARLOWE.

"But the negative truth . . . leads us away from sterile and irreclaimable tracts of thought and emotion, and so inevitably compels the energies which would otherwise have been wasted, to feel after a more profitable direction."

JOHN MORLEY.

"The important thing is to have faith but not illusions, and to risk action on this faith."

HORACE KALLEN.

COURTS ON TRIAL

MYTH AND REALITY IN AMERICAN JUSTICE

BY JEROME FRANK

PRINCETON, NEW JERSEY
PRINCETON UNIVERSITY PRESS

Copyright 1949 by Jerome Frank

L. C. Card: 72-11942
ISBN: 0-691-02755-2 (paperback edn.)
ISBN: 0-691-09205-2 (hardcover edn.)

First Princeton Paperback Edition, 1973
Third Hardcover Printing, 1973

All rights reserved. No part of this book may be reproduced in any form or by any electronic or mechanical means including information storage and retrieval systems without permission in writing from the publisher, except by a reviewer who may quote brief passages in a review.

Printed in the United States of America
by Princeton University Press, Princeton, New Jersey

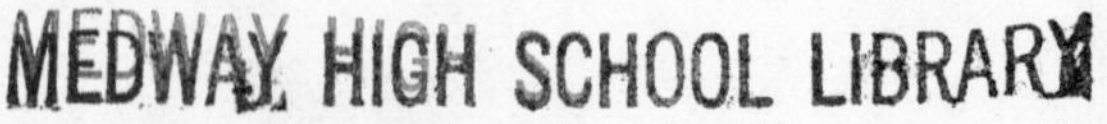

Book No. 10581

TO

LEARNED HAND

OUR WISEST JUDGE

PREFACE

I HAVE tried in this book to tell, with candor, much about the workings of our courts with which the ordinary citizen unfortunately is not acquainted. As the book is intended for intelligent non-lawyers as well as lawyers, I have avoided the use of lawyers' technical jargon.

What I have said in the following pages is a sort of complement to two earlier books, *Law and the Modern Mind* (1930) and *If Men Were Angels* (1942). Overlapping those books in part, and continuing where they left off, this volume centers on the doings of trial courts. My principal aim is to show the major importance of those courts; how they daily affect the lives of thousands of persons; and how, often with tragic results, they do their job in ways that need reform.

The bulk of this volume consists of lectures delivered at Princeton University, on the Stafford Little Foundation, in December 1948. Part of the subject matter, however, had previously been included in lectures given elsewhere and in articles published here and there.

The theme of modern legal magic appears first in Chapters IV and V and recurs in later chapters. For several reasons, I think it well to note these facts about the development of that theme. In 1930, in *Law and the Modern Mind,*[1] I discussed the relation between the magical thinking of the young child and much legal thinking. In the preface to a book published in 1938,[2] I said that that book was a "by-product of some lectures on law and anthropology delivered by the writer in New York at the New School of Social Research in 1931, some talks by the writer at Yale Law School in 1932, and a book then begun, but never completed, entitled 'Wizards and Lawyers.' " I briefly discussed the theme in an article published in 1932,[3] and again in 1942 in *If Men Were Angels.*[4] I set it forth at length, much as it appears in the present volume, in a "course-book" which in 1946 I began to use in teaching at Yale Law School.

In some previous books, I shunned the first-person pronoun, saying "the writer" when I meant "I," on the assumption that the indirect locution signified modesty. That assumption now seems to me a mis-

[1] pp. 60-62, 73-75, 82, 85-92, 181-185.

[2] *Save America First.*

[3] 17 Cornell L.Q. 568, 582.

[4] pp. 114-118.

take. To say "I" removes a false impression of a Jovian aloofness; it means no more than "I think" or "I happen now to believe"; the reader is thus put on his guard. In the following pages, I have often cited or quoted from my own writings. I did so not out of egotism but laziness, for what I had said elsewhere was most readily accessible to me.

I have dwelt on the importance of avoiding, as far as possible, prejudice and dogmatism; but doubtless here and there I have been swayed by my own prejudices and dogmas. I urge the reader to be on the watch for my hidden biases. As I have discussed a large and difficult subject, of course I have made blunders. I shall be grateful to those who point them out, for, if ever there is another edition of this book, I shall try to correct them.

As the reader will see, I am critical of some attitudes of many brilliant legal thinkers. But my criticisms should not be taken as indicating any lack of appreciation of the solid worth of other aspects of their writings to which I am incalculably indebted. Nothing could be more absurd than the notion that, because one finds faults in some ideas of men of genius, he should disregard all the rest.

I have said much in this book of the backwardness of the legal profession in seeking to remove remediable defects in our method of trying law suits. Yet I think the lawyers must not be severely blamed on that account. Inertia is not peculiar to lawyers as a group. Most of those who comprise any profession or trade tend to venerate all its traditions, and are unable detachedly to inspect its customary ways. Moreover, many noted American lawyers, including some leading members of that conservative lawyers' organization, the American Bar Association, have been conspicuous as constructive critics of our legal system, just as they have been foremost in other phases of American life.

Since my position in this book is somewhat novel, I have deliberately used a technique which, as I said in the preface to an earlier book, is reminiscent of the following: Mr. Smith of Denver was introduced to Mr. Jones at a dinner party in Chicago. "Oh," said Jones, "do you know my friend, Mr. Schnicklefritz, who lives in Denver?" "No," answered Smith. Later in the evening, when Smith referred to Denver, Jones again asked whether Smith was acquainted with Schnicklefritz, and again received a negative reply. As the dinner party broke up, Smith remarked that he was leaving that night for Denver, and Jones once more inquired whether Smith knew Schnicklefritz. "Really," came the answer, "his name sounds quite familiar."

I am grateful to the publishers of my former books from which quotation is made in this one—Coward-McCann, *Law and the Modern Mind;* Harper & Brothers, *If Men Were Angels;* and Simon & Schuster, *Fate and Freedom.* I also express my gratitude to the authors and publishers whose works are quoted in this volume:

Appleton-Century-Crofts, Graham Wallas, *Human Nature in Politics,* 1921; Boyd Printing Co., Albert S. Osborn, *The Mind of the Juror,* 1937; Burns, Oates & Washburne, London, Saint Thomas Aquinas, *Summa Theologica* translated by the Fathers of the English Dominican Province, 1929; Cambridge University Press, Lord MacMillan, *Law and Other Things,* 1937; John Day Co., Lin Yutang, *The Importance of Living,* 1937; Jonathan Cape, J. W. N. Sullivan, *Beethoven: His Spiritual Development,* 1927; Cornell University Press, Horace M. Kallen, *The Liberal Spirit,* 1948; Emerson Books, Ranyard West, *Conscience and Society,* 1945; Harcourt Brace & Co., I. A. Richards, *Principles of Literary Criticism,* 4th edn., 1930, and Fred Rodell, *Woe unto You, Lawyers!* 1939; Harper & Brothers, Wendell Johnson, *People in Quandaries,* 1946; Harvard University Press, Suzanne K. Langer, *Philosophy in a New Key,* 1942, and Arthur O. Lovejoy, *The Great Chain of Being,* 1936; Henry Holt & Co., Morris Cohen, *A Preface to Logic,* 1944; George H. Sabine, *A History of Political Theory,* 1937; Houghton Mifflin Co., Henry Adams, *Mont Saint-Michel and Chartres,* 1913, and Ruth Benedict, *Patterns of Culture,* 1939; Alfred A. Knopf, Curtis Bok, *Backbone of the Herring,* 1941, and *I Too, Nicodemus,* 1946, and Franz Kafka, *The Trial,* 1937, translated by Willa and Erwin Muir; J. B. Lippincott Co., Damon Runyon, *Trials and Other Tribulations,* 1947; Little, Brown & Co., Emile Faguet, *Politicians and Moralists of the Nineteenth Century,* 1899; and John H. Wigmore, *The Principles of Judicial Proof,* 1913; The Macmillan Co., Henri Berr and Lucien Febvre, "History and Historiography," in 7 *Encyclopedia of the Social Sciences 357,* 1932 and P. W. Bridgman, *The Intelligent Individual and Society,* 1938, and Abraham Flexner, *Medical Education,* 1925, and John Chipman Gray, *The Nature and Sources of Law,* 1921, and Bronislaw Malinowski, "Magic, Science, and Religion," in *Science, Religion and Reality,* edited by J. Needham, 1925, and Henry W. Taft, *Witnesses in Court,* 1934; Modern Age Books, Margarest Schlauch, *The Gift of Tongues,* 1942; Oxford University Press, Ranyard West, "A Psychological Theory of Law," in *Interpretations of Modern Legal Philosophies,* edited by P. Sayre, 1947; Oxford University Press (Clarendon Press) George W. Paton, *A Text-*

book of Jurisprudence, 1946, and Fritz Schultz, *Roman Legal Science,* 1946; Rinehart & Co., Erich Fromm, *Man for Himself,* 1947; University of Chicago Press, Harold Lasswell, *Psychopathology and Politics,* 1930, and Henri Pirenne, "What Are Historians Trying to Do?" in *Methods in Social Science,* edited by S. A. Rice, 1930; Vernon Law Book Co., Leon Green, *Judge and Jury,* 1930; West Publishing Co., George B. Clementson, *Special Verdicts and Special Findings by Juries,* 1905, and John H. Wigmore, *A Panorama of the World's Legal Systems,* 1928.

Journal of American Judicature Society, 12:166, 1929, John H. Wigmore, A Program for the Trial of Jury Trial; *Records of the Association of the Bar of the City of New York,* 3:331, 1948, Edwin J. Lukas, New York City Children's Courts and Cognate Matters; *Atlantic Monthly,* Sept. 1922, p. 296, George W. Alger, The Letter Law and the Golden Rule; *Commentary,* 1:1, 1946, John Dewey, The Crisis in Human History; *Harvard Law Review,* 12:493, 1899, Oliver Wendell Holmes, Law in Science—Science in Law; *Illinois Law Review,* 32:383, 1937, Harold C. Havighurst, book review; *University of Chicago Law Review,* 4:233, 1937, Walter Wheeler Cook, "Facts" and "Statements of Fact"; also, 15:501, 1948, Edward Levi, An Introduction to Legal Reasoning; *University of Pennsylvania Law Review,* 61:1, 1912, Charles A. Boston, Some Practical Remedies for Existing Deficiencies in the Administration of Justice; *Yale Law Journal,* 40:537, 1931, Underhill Moore and Gilbert Sussman, Legal and Institutional Methods Applied to the Debiting of Direct Discounts; also, 51:537, 1942, Hubert W. Smith, Components of Proof in Legal Proceedings; also, 29:253, 1920, Edson R. Sunderland, Verdicts, General and Special.

June 1949 JEROME FRANK

CONTENTS

Courts on Trial

I. THE NEEDLESS MYSTERY OF COURT-HOUSE GOVERNMENT

About two hundred years ago, a singularly unsuccessful English lawyer gave a series of lectures at Oxford on English courts and legal doctrines. Incorporated in a book, those lectures, Blackstone's *Commentaries,* became a sort of lawyer's Bible, particularly in America. Those lectures, and that book, however, were intended not for lawyers but as an essential part of the education of the young English aristocrats who were to become the rulers of England. Blackstone's lectures and his book have received, of recent years, well-deserved criticism—on the ground that they were insufferably snobbish and badly misdescriptive of judicial realities.[1] They should not, then, be imitated. But Blackstone's purpose should indeed be emulated in America—in American fashion, however. The rulers of America, the numerous John Q. Citizens who have no intention of becoming lawyers, should be taught what their courts do and why.

For alas, they know too little of that subject. American journalism, on the whole, does a poor job of accurately reporting court-doings. Our lawyers have made little effort to explain to the laymen, in intelligible terms, the workings of our judicial system. The resultant public ignorance is deplorable. Our courts are an immensely important part of our government. In a democracy, no portion of government should be a mystery. But what may be called "court-house government" still is mysterious to most of the laity.

To a considerable extent, that is true because too few lawyers and judges have been willing to speak out plainly, even to other lawyers, about the actualities of court-house behavior. In most law-schools, many aspects of that behavior are disregarded. Legends and myths have grown up about the judiciary which serve to obscure the realities. Erle Stanley Gardner's fiction and Judge Curtis Bok's delightful semi-autobiographical novels do disclose some of the behind-the-scenes events. But not enough, because those writers are too reticent, still too much dominated by the traditional hush-policy concerning the courts.

[1] See Frank, "A Sketch of An Influence," in the volume *Interpretations of Modern Legal Philosophies* (1947) 189 for references.

Many lawyers half believe a lot of stork-stories concerning the birth process of judicial decisions. They often repeat those stories at Bar Association meetings. They tell them to the non-lawyers. The latter are by no means wholly convinced of the truth of those tales. As a result, there prevails a needless public cynicism about lawyers and courts. For the observant citizen notes striking discrepancies between the legends and the realities. His skepticism is a puzzled, frustrated, skepticism. As he lacks adequate information, that skepticism cannot become constructive, cannot effectively aid in the improvement, both needed and possible, of the judicial process.

I shall not attempt to be an American Blackstone, for I lack the competence. My intention is more modest. In order to provoke constructive skepticism, I shall try to do a little to help you peer behind the legal myths, to show you something of how court-house government actually operates. I shall do this in no muck-raking spirit, out of no desire, by being unconventional, to titillate and amuse. My purpose is less frivolous. It is to arouse you, to call attention to some court-house government activities which are less adequately performed than they could be, largely because they have been too little publicly discussed.

I am—I make no secret of it—a reformer, one of those persons who (to quote Shaw) "will not take evil good-naturedly." I see grave defects in some of the ways in which courts operate, defects that I believe can be eradicated, but that will never be intelligently dealt with unless they are publicized. On the other hand, I have no fatuous notion that the judicial process can be made perfect. It is a human process, involving inherent human failings and weaknesses. Yet its substantial betterment is nevertheless possible. Indeed, to better it, requires a recognition of its unavoidably human, fallible, character. The illusion that it either is, or can be, super-human constitutes one of the chief hindrances to its substantial reform.

Some persons suggest that candor about court-house ways is unwise, that it is undesirable to let the public know the imperfections, both the curable and the incurable, in our judicial doings. I confess I have little patience with, or respect for, that suggestion. I am unable to conceive, I repeat, that, in a democracy, it can ever be unwise to acquaint the public with the truth about the workings of any branch of government. It is wholly undemocratic to treat the public as children, who are unable to accept the inescapable shortcomings of man-made institutions. The public, I think, can "take it." Our people need not be coddled, and should not be deluded. It is the essence of democracy that the citizens are entitled to know what all their public servants, judges included, are doing, and how well they are doing it. The best way to bring about the elimination of those shortcomings of our judicial system which are capable of being eliminated is to have all our citizens informed as to how that system now functions. It is a mistake, therefore, to try to establish and maintain, through ignorance, public esteem for our courts.

I feel emboldened in my present undertaking by the example of a great American judge, Mr. Justice Holmes. In 1897, in a lecture, he recommended that some high-flown, unrealistic, legal notions be "washed in cynical acid." But he said: "I take it for granted that no hearer of mine will misinterpret what I have to say as the language of cynicism. . . . I trust that no one will understand me to be speaking with disrespect of the law, because I criticize it so freely. I venerate the law, and especially our system of law, as one of the vastest products of the human mind . . . But one may criticize even what one reveres. Law is the business to which my life is devoted, and I should show less than devotion if I did not do what in me lies to improve it. . . ."

In one respect, however, I shall deviate from Holmes. I shall, generally, for reasons I shall explain later, avoid the use of the word "law." Instead, I shall speak, (1) of what courts actually do, (2) of what they are supposed to do, (3) of whether they do what they're supposed to do, and (4) of whether they should do what they're supposed to do.

2

Should you ask the average intelligent lawyer to explain briefly the function of our courts, he would probably tell you something like this: Our legal system is based on legal rules. Those rules state what may and may not be lawfully done. For instance, the legal rules say that murder is a legal wrong; that, if a man makes a contract, he must live up to it; that, by a certain kind of writing, land is lawfully transferred. The legal rules embody or reflect moral norms, social standards, social policies, community ideals or values. Those rules—some of them made by legislatures and some by the courts—are necessarily general in their scope. The major task of the courts is the specific application, in particular law suits, of these general rules to the particular facts of those suits. A court's task thus divides into two parts: First, it finds the facts of a case—whether one man killed another, or drove eighty miles an hour, or paid his rent, or signed a certain paper. Second, it determines what legal rule covers those facts. The court's decision then results.

There are two kinds of courts, the lawyer would continue. One kind, called trial courts (or "lower" or "inferior" courts), performs both parts of the judicial task; they both find the facts and apply the rules. The other kind, called upper courts, appeal courts, usually does little about the facts of cases. These courts devote most of their time to deciding, on appeals, whether or not the lower courts, in particular cases, made mistakes about the rules.

Having, in that manner, described the courts' function, most books by learned lawyers talk as if the chief difficulty in the job of the courts inheres in determining what rules should be applied, what the rules mean, their extent and interpretation. I think those books are grossly misleading. I grant that sometimes such rule-difficulties exist. Otherwise I, as an "upper-court" judge, would have almost nothing to do. But the other part of the job of the courts, that part which is assigned almost entirely to trial courts—the ascertainment of the facts of individual law suits—presents a far more difficult, a far more baffling, problem. That baffling problem, however, has been by-passed by most of those who have written learned treatises about the judicial process. Take, for instance, the numerous invaluable off-the-bench writings of Cardozo. There you will discover only a few fleeting and casual references, in a few short sentences, to fact-finding and trial courts.

Yet trial-court fact-finding is the toughest part of the judicial function. It is there that court-house government is least satisfactory. It is there that most of the very considerable amount of judicial injustice occurs. It is there that reform is most needed.

I say that in no spirit of upper-court-judge snobbishness. Although I sit in an upper court, I do not feel superior to many so-called "inferior" judges. Among them are some of the ablest and most conscientious men on the bench, men much more than my equal. But as, comparatively, the work of the upper courts is simple and easy, these courts discharge their duties fairly well. If the trial courts, having more exacting duties, do not function as well as they might, most trial judges—trained as they are, and with the antiquated tools they are given—should be absolved of responsibility.

American lawyers, in the past few decades, have, with marked effectiveness, spent much time in improving many legal rules. But the legal profession has done next to nothing about the problem of fact-finding. Because of its importance, and because of its neglect, I shall in this book deal chiefly with that subject. I shall, for the most part, concentrate on trials, trial courts and fact-finding.

II. FIGHTS AND RIGHTS

If you visit a trial court during its working hours, what do you see going on? A law-suit. Let us then begin by considering the word we frequently use in describing law-suits—"litigation." What does it mean? "Litigation" derives from two Latin words, *litis* and *ago*. The first, *litis*, means contention, strife, a quarrel. *Ago* means "to go." So, apparently, *litigo*—from which we get our word litigate—originally meant to "go to it" in a quarrel, or to carry on a quarrel, to dispute, to engage in strife, to brawl—and later, "to go to law" in the sense in which that phrase is now popularly used. And *litigiosus,* whence our word "litigious," referred to a person full of strife. Litigation, then is strife. A law-suit is a kind of fight or combat.

Why? Anthropology seems to furnish the answer. Let me give you a brief, crude, superficial sketch of what the anthropologists report.

In every society, quarrels are bound to arise. In some societies, the customs, the mores, the folkways, are moderately well-stabilized, and the social pressures—working through fear, pride, ridicule, a sense of decency, and the like—will not only reduce the sources of friction, but will compel men to settle, by amicable, private adjustment between the disputants, most of the quarrels that do occur.

But in any society there arise some differences that are not adjusted. In some so-called "primitive" or "archaic" societies, when some sorts of disputes were not settled, if a man felt, or said, that he was deeply wronged by another and wanted vengeance, or restitution of his property, he did not "go to law" as we do today. Instead, he relied on "self-help," or self-redress. That is, he did not go to anything resembling a court. He struck at the other man. With a club or axe or knife. He fought to get back property or to avenge what he considered a wrong. He fought, we would say sophisticatedly, for his "legal rights." And, in some groups, the fight spread. It was not confined to the man who felt, or said, that he was wronged, and the man who did the supposed injury. It might involve the whole group. There was a free-for-all. That was bad, for it meant widespread havoc, destruction of things, killing and maiming of those persons who composed the society.

In some social groups, the peacelessness of such a general fracas became unbearable, and the blood-feud, or vendetta, appeared as a substitute. The fighting was now restricted to limited sub-groups, to the clans of men concerned in the original quarrel. The blood-feud, terrible as it was, was far less anarchic than the general brawl. It was a great step forward. It meant a contraction of the fighting area. Less blood was spilled, less disorder resulted, than in the general carnage.

But the blood-feud was bad enough. Wiser societies invented devices designed to prevent mass fighting as the proper way to settle those disputes which the parties did not settle amicably between themselves. A man claimed that another had seized his cattle or carried off his daughter; it came to be the custom that the claimant must not act by force in asserting his rights, without first obtaining the approval of some designated person who represented society, and that the claimant must fight according to set rules. "Self-help," self-redress, was thus socially regulated. Elsewhere we find the development of socially assisted self-help, gradually dissolving into the notion of a socially sanctioned and enforced arbitration of most quarrels. The savage and disruptive blood-feud gave way in some societies to the "composition," a schedule of tariffs of payments for wrongs. At first these compositions were voluntary. Later they became compulsory: The wrongdoer must pay a fine and the wronged man must accept it. He who did not agree to submit to this social arbitration, and to abide by its decision, was in some societies, an "outlaw," guilty of "peacelessness"; he was *caput lupinum*, a wild animal, an enemy of society.

One way or another, modern organized societies have developed the notion that most quarrels must not be allowed to become private pitched battles, that disputes must be settled without privately-inflicted violence. The modern state asserts a virtually complete monopoly of the right to use physical force when controversies between private persons occur.

I have given you an absurdly abbreviated sketch. It calls for qualifications at almost every point. Particularly does it err if it creates the impression of a uniform, or universal, social development, "a single-line advance," or the impression that many social groups ever got along without some devices for peaceably settling at least some disputes. But this over-simplified sketch will do for our present purposes.

For it serves to show what it means to "go to law": "Going to law" is giving up private war as a means of obtaining what we call one's "rights." It is the acceptance of the determination of those "rights" by a socially selected person or persons. Every well organized modern society designates some persons who will settle at least most of the disputes of a kind likely to breed violent strife, who will determine what the parties are entitled to. The disputants look to a social agency, authorized to invoke socially endorsed force to carry out the dispute-decider's decision. Such an official dispute-decider is what we mean by a court. "Going to law," submitting quarrels to a court for decision, is a substitute for private warfare. Force, exercised by officials, force put back of official decisions, takes the place of private violence. If today you look behind the bench, you will find the sheriff, the policemen, indeed the army. Significantly, we symbolize court-house justice by the sword as well as the scales.

Thus considered, what is the primary function of a court in our society today? Its primary function is to render specific decisions of specific disputes, in order to bring about their orderly settlement, so as to prevent brawls which might cause social disruption. The court is thus a peace-preserving device. It stops subversive aggression, keeps the peace, by deciding controversies. It meets crises of maladjustment by peaceable adjustments of conflicts. Just as, in our democracy, we have substituted political elections, peaceful revolutions, for revolutions by force, so we have substituted a sort of judicial or court-room duel for private war.

How important the court device is we can best understand by imagining the conditions which would ensue were we to abolish it. Illuminating is the story of an alleged old Persian custom that whenever a king died there was a five-day period of anarchy in order that the people might perceive the advantages of having rulers and laws. What a court-less nation would be like we may see by regarding the calamitous international situation under which we were recently living—and dying—and from which all sane men hope we will soon forever depart.

To be sure, courts have other functions than that of settling controversies; to some of those functions I shall later call attention. But you will have no adequate comprehension of what our courts do unless you keep constantly in mind that their main business is the trial and decision of specific disputes.

I want, therefore, to stress the fact that litigation in our courts is still a fight. The fighting, to be sure, occurs in a court-room, and is supervised by a government officer known as a judge. Yet, for the most part, a law-suit remains a sort of sublimated, regulated brawl, a private battle conducted in a court-house.

This notion has often been expressed. In 1906, a French judge, De la

Grasserie, said that modern "legal process is another kind of war," that it is "mimic warfare." Perhaps you will think that statement somewhat strained, too much colored by the views of anthropologists, and largely academic. If so, I suggest that you read a little handbook for the practical guidance of practicing lawyers, published, in 1946, under the auspices of the American Bar Association. The author, Leonard Moore, no impractical theorist, but a successful, seasoned, practicing trial lawyer, begins his treatise thus: "Litigation resembles warfare. Opposing counsel are charged with the responsibility of so conducting their campaign that ultimate victory will result." He goes on to say that a law-suit, like a war, is won through "stratagems" and "tactics," resembling "skirmishes and a series of battles," that the effective lawyer uses something like a "scouting party to discover the enemy's position and strength, sometimes to draw his fire," because "if weakness is shown, a strong attack may completely destroy all his opposition."

Let us now observe some of the implications of the fact that a law-suit is a fight. In a society in which most disputes were not submitted to a dispute-decider, when two men disagreed about the ownership of a cow or a wife, if one of them claimed that the other was violating some socially accepted norm, and if the disputants were unable to settle their quarrel amicably, often the claimant could get back what he considered his own only by hurting or killing his adversary in a physical combat. In our modern terminology, as I suggested, the fight concerned a "legal right." The claimant's legal right, we might then say, was settled by the winning or losing of that fight. For all practical purposes, therefore, what we call a "legal right" was a fight won, and a "legal duty," a fight lost. What "rights" and "duties" meant, in such circumstances, you can surmise by watching gangsters in conflict.

Whenever litigation is substituted for private war, the object of the fighting is less direct. In the private out-of-court war, the claimant tried by his own force to make the other man give in. In litigation, the claimant fights for his (so-called) "legal right" by trying to induce a court to put the society's force behind a court-order directing the defendant to yield. The immediate or direct object of the out-of-court combat on the one hand, and the mediate or indirect object of the court-fight on the other, are the same—namely, to make the other man do what you want him to do. But the immediate or direct object of the court-fight is to persuade the court to enter an order. It is a fight for a favorable court decision, for a court-order which will either be obeyed or enforced, and by which you will induce the other man to do what you want him to do. Instead of using your own private violence—your own club or knife or gun or bomb—on your adversary, you try to get a court order which, if not complied with, will, if necessary, call forth the armed forces of the organized community to inflict pain on your opponent until he gives you what you want and what the court said you were entitled to have. The parties to the court fight do not themselves use physical weapons. But such weapons, inflicting physical harm, are nevertheless used, if necessary, at the close of the suit, by officials, the sheriff, the police, or the army. Inside the court-room, however, the weapons are merely verbal, are implements of persuasion, means for swaying the mind of the trial judge or jury so as to obtain a favorable court-order.

But—this must not be forgotten—legal rights, so far as courts are concerned, depend entirely on those decisions, those enforced or potentially enforceable court-orders.[1] In that sense, specific law-suits, taking the place of specific physical combats, are the road to legal rights; a legal right is a law-suit won, and a legal duty, a law suit lost. Tentatively we may say that, in practical terms, with us today, what we call the specific "legal right" of any man means this and nothing more: Either (1) what a court has already ordered in a past law-suit relating to that specific man's rights; or (2)—and this is the usual situation—what some court, somewhere, may order, some day in the future, in a specific law-suit relating to that man's specific rights.

2

What we are accustomed to describe as "legal rights," then, apparently grow out of specific lawsuits and are to be found in specific court-orders, judgments or decrees. If no court-order has as yet been entered with respect to any of your legal rights or mine, then those rights are not yet known, but can only be guessed. Maybe you have some particular right, maybe you haven't. The only way you can find out definitely is to see what a court will do about it.

Let me illustrate. Every day something like this occurs in a lawyer's office: Mr. Eminently Sensible, on December 1, 1946, is about to sign a contract with Mr. Samuel Smart for the purchase of some goods. Sensible calls aside his lawyer, Mr. Sagacious, and asks, "Will

[1] "A judge's sentence is like a particular law regarding some particular fact." Saint Thomas Aquinas, *The Summa Theologica,* Second Part, Question 67, Art. 1. See also, ibid, Question 71, Art. 3, comparing a law-suit with warfare.

this contract fully protect me? If Smart fails to deliver those goods, and the market goes up, can I collect the difference from him?" Let us assume that Sagacious is a highly competent lawyer, and that the contract is in a standard form, well drafted. Mr. Sagacious, of course, knows that a well-settled, precise, legal rule, with which every second-year law student is acquainted, says that, if such a contract is broken by the seller, a court will award the buyer, as damages from the seller, the difference in money between the sales-price and the market-price.

Nevertheless, Mr. Sagacious, if he is a cautious lawyer, will hedge his answer. For Sensible has not asked about any legal rule. He doesn't want a legal treatise, long or short, relating to the legal rules about contracts. He wants to know whether he can collect some money, and how much, in a law-suit he may possibly bring against Smart at some future time. He is therefore asking for a prophecy, a guess, about a court-order in possible litigation not yet begun. What about such a guess? Can it be accurate?

Conventional theory suggests that the answer is "Yes." For it is a fundamental postulate of that theory that, when the legal rules are precise, then legal rights must be correspondingly precise.

I deny the correctness of that theory. I say that Sensible's lawyer cannot tell him with any high degree of certainty what Sensible's legal rights are—that is, what the court will decide. For, in such a suit, which may be tried in 1950, Smart may produce witnesses who will tell the court that Sensible used fraud in inducing Smart to sign the contract in 1946, or that, on October 10, 1947, Smart paid Sensible $2,000 to release Smart of all his obligations, and that they saw Sensible sign the release and give it to Smart, but that it was accidentally burned two weeks later.

How can Sensible's lawyer foresee what sort of lying or mistaken stories will be told by Smart's witnesses, and whether the trial court —a judge or jury—will believe any such stories? How, then, can he prophesy who will win such a future court-battle? No amount of scrutiny of the contract, or looking into legal treatises or reading of court opinions, will tell him.

In short, Sensible's legal rights, and Smart's legal duties, under that contract, are no more and no less than what some court, someday, somewhere, will decide, on the basis of the believed testimony, in a law-suit between those two men, and a law-suit relating to that very contract. Not a law-suit, mind you, between Hennessy and McCarthy about their contract, although it contains the same words as the Sensible-Smart contract. For the decision in the Sensible-Smart case may be that Sensible, the buyer, loses, although in the Hennessy-McCarthy suit, the buyer, Hennessy, may win. Courts, in deciding cases, are engaged in a sort of retail, not a wholesale, job.

Sensible's legal rights, then, mean what will hereafter happen as the result of a specific law-suit, if one is brought. Unless and until that suit has been tried and decided, Sensible's legal rights are unknown.

"Oh, yes," you may say, "perhaps it's true that any asserted legal right can at any time be contested in a law-suit, and, until it is, cannot be definitely known to exist; but the fact remains that most men usually acknowledge, without litigation, that other men have many legal rights. So it's absurd to say that it takes law-suits to create rights." My answer is that such out-of-court acknowledgments, such out-of-court acquiescences, do not prove that those rights, if litigiously tested, would stand up. We all know of instances of alleged rights, undisputed for years, which, when they finally got into litigation, didn't stand up. For example, the owner of a patent has been paid uncontested royalties for over ten years, when suddenly there bobs up someone who challenges the patent and succeeds in having the courts declare it invalid. Most asserted rights go forever unchallenged; but no man has any guaranty that some day a law-suit will not be brought attacking any one of his seemingly secure rights. No person enjoys immunity from litigation.

Most clients do not need lawyers to tell them what will happen if their purported rights go unchallenged in court. Usually they come to lawyers because there are courts, because court-fights may occur, or may have occurred, and because lawyers are deemed to know how the courts will deal with disputed rights. You might conceivably have a lawyerless court. But a court-less, litigation-less, legal profession is unimaginable.

That men do not dispute, in court, most asserted rights is indeed fortunate. For one of the principal factors in maintaining social order is that, happily, most people do not fight with their fists or with weapons—or in court. Most people do not litigate, most of the time. If every potential law-suit became an actual law-suit, society would go to smash. If everyone litigated whenever he could, no one ever could. Anyone who has encountered a litigious paranoiac in action can envision what would happen if all men were incessantly litigious.

If, now, someome were to ask why most men do not "go to law" most of the time, or whenever they can, or why most men obey court orders without any use of state force, he would be asking for an explanation of the phenomenon of social cohesion, asking why societies endure. I shall not here even attempt an explanation, since it would involve, at a minimum, an exhaustive knowledge of ethics, anthropology and psychology. In addition to conscious, moral restraints, one would have to consider such social compulsives as fear of ridicule, desire for public esteem, prestige, social habits—all that J. S. Mill included in "the authority of Conventionalism." Most men are less likely to offend social proprieties than to violate legal rules, less likely, for example, publicly to appear clad only in underwear than to commit theft.

My point is that the habit of not contesting, in court, most asserted legal rights does not show that any particular asserted right actually exists as a so-called legal right when it has not yet been tested by litigation. More important, anyone's rights may, at any time, become the center of a court fight, and every law-suit is a specific law-suit leading to the determination of someone's specific rights.

This includes all readers of this book. Whether it will sometime be decided that any one of you is to go to jail, or to lose or keep your house, or collect the money on a mortgage you hold, or have the custody of your children, or remain the president of your company—any of such matters may be determined by a now unpredictable future court-decision in a case relating specifically to you. Whether any such suit will arise, and how it will be decided, no one now knows. For no one can now prophesy if, or when, or where, any such suit will be brought; or, if one is brought, whether there will be conflicting testimony; or, if so, what it will be; or whether the suit will be tried by a jury or a judge, or what judge, or how the jury or the judge will react to the testimony. Wherefore, until those cases arise and are decided, your legal rights and duties are unknown.

Think of the recent case of Mr. Bertram Campbell. After a trial in New York, he was found guilty of the crime of forgery, and sent to jail for a long period. Years afterwards, another man confessed that he, not Campbell, had committed the crime. A crime had been committed. That is, a clear, simple, legal rule, against forgery, had been violated. But the court had gone wrong on the facts. How many innocent men are now in jail because of such errors about the facts—errors not, as in Campbell's case, later discovered—we don't know. Nor does any one of us know whether someday he will be indicted and mistakenly convicted. If you regard Compbell's case as unique, I suggest that you read Borchard's important book, *Convicting the Innocent,* published in 1932. He reports sixty-five cases, selected from a much larger number, of innocent men sent to jail or sentenced to death by American courts. Of course, there's the other side of the story: We don't know how many guilty men escaped punishment through mistakes in fact-finding. Nor, again, do we know how many men, in non-criminal cases, have been financially ruined by losing their property or their jobs, because of similar court-room factual mistakes.

III. FACTS ARE GUESSES

If you scrutinize a legal rule, you will see that it is a conditional statement referring to facts. Such a rule seems to say, in effect, "If such and such a fact exists, then this or that legal consequence should follow." It seems to say, for example, "If a trustee, for his own purposes, uses money he holds in trust, he must repay it." Or, "If a man, without provocation, kills another, the killer must be punished."[1] In other words, a legal rule directs that (if properly asked to do so) a court should attach knowable consequences to certain facts, if and whenever there are such facts. That is what is meant by the conventional statement, used in describing the decisional process, that courts apply legal rules to the facts of law-suits.[2]

For convenience, let us symbolize a legal rule by the letter *R*, the facts of a case by the letter *F*, and the court's decision of that case by the letter *D*. We can then crudely schematize the conventional theory of how courts operate by saying

$$R \times F = D$$

In other words, according to the conventional theory, a decision is a product of an *R* and an *F*. If, as to any lawsuit, you know the *R* and the *F*, you should, then, know what the *D* will be.[3]

In a simple, stable, society, most of the *R*'s are moderately well stabilized. Which legal rules that society will enforce it is not difficult for men—or at any rate, for the lawyer, the professional court-man—to know in advance of any trial. In such a society, the *R*—one of the two factors in the $R \times F = D$ formula—is usually fixed.

In our society, however, with the rapid changes brought about by

[1] I use the words "*seems* to say" for reasons which I shall later explain. See Chapter XII.

[2] I am here referring to so-called "substantive" rules, which state that certain sorts of out-of-court conduct will, in court, yield certain consequences. There is another kind of rules, rules of "procedure," which relate to the way cases in court should be commenced and tried. I shall discuss those rules later. Suffice it to say here that upper courts, on appeals, deal not only with "substantive" rules, but also try to see that trial courts do not too widely depart from the "procedural" rules.

[3] I suggested this $R \times F = D$ symbolization of the conventional theory of the decisional process in 1932. See Frank, "What Courts Do in Fact," 26 *Ill. L.Rev.* (1932) 645, 761. See also, Frank, *If Men Were Angels* (1942) 77-78, 269-271; In re Fried, 161 F. (2d) 453, 464 (C.C.A. 2).

modern life, many of the *R*'s have become unstable. Accordingly, in our times, legal uncertainty—uncertainty about future decisions and therefore about legal rights—is generally ascribed to the indefiniteness of the *R*'s. The increasing multiplicity of the rules, the conflicts between rules, and the flexibility of some of the rules, have arrested the attention of most legal thinkers. Those thinkers, perceiving the absence of rigidity in some rules, have assumed that the certainty or uncertainty of the *D*'s, in the $R \times F = D$ equation, stems principally from the certainty or uncertainty of the *R*'s.

That assumption leads to a grave miscomprehension of court-house government and to the neglect by most legal scholars of the more difficult part of the courts' undertaking. I refer to the courts' task with respect to the other factor in the $R \times F = D$ formula, the *F*. The courts, as we saw, are supposed to ascertain the facts in the disputes which become law suits. That is, a court is supposed to determine the actual, objective acts of the parties, to find out just what they did or did not do, before the law-suit began, so far as those facts bear on the compliance with, or the violation of, some legal rule. If there is uncertainty as to whether the court will find the true relevant facts—if it is uncertain whether the court's *F* will match the real, objective *F*—then what? Then, since the decision, the *D*, is presumably the joint product of an *R* and an *F*, the *D* is bound to be uncertain. To put it differently: No matter how certain the legal rules may be, the decisions remain at the mercy of the courts' fact-finding. If there is doubt about what a court, in a law-suit, will find were the facts, then there is at least equal doubt about its decision.

Go back now to Mr. Sensible and his lawyer. Suppose that the lawyer knows the pertinent *R*'s, and that they are as fixed as fixed can be, as precise as a table of logarithms. But, I ask again, how can the lawyer in 1946 prophesy what will be the *D* in 1950, unless he also knows the *F* that, in 1950, the trial judge (or jury) will use in the $R \times F = D$?

What is the *F*? Is it what actually happened between Sensible and Smart? Most emphatically not. At best, it is only what the trial court—the trial judge or jury—thinks happened. What the trial court thinks happened may, however, be hopelessly incorrect. But that does not matter—legally speaking. For court purposes, what the court thinks about the facts is all that matters. The actual events, the real objective acts and words of Sensible and Smart, happened in the past. They do not walk into court. The court usually learns about these real, objective, past facts only through the oral testimony of fallible witnesses. Accordingly, the court, from hearing the testimony, must guess at the actual, past facts. Judicially, the facts consist of the reaction of the judge or jury to the testimony. The *F* is merely a guess about the actual facts. There can be no assurance that that *F*, that guess, will coincide with those actual, past facts.

To be sure, this difficulty becomes of no importance when the parties to the suit do not dispute about the facts, when their sole difference concerns the proper *R*. Then the *R* will settle the court fight. In other words, if Smart agrees to the facts as Sensible tells them, then the only question for the court will be whether the *R* is as Sensible claims it to be. With reference to that sort of law-suit, the trained lawyer, as a specialist in the *R*'s, is frequently an excellent predicter of decisions. For often (although not always) the applicable *R* is fairly certain and knowable, or sufficiently so that a competent lawyer can foretell what the court will say it is.

But usually, when men "go to law," the facts are not admitted, and the testimony is oral and in conflict. For convenience, call such suits "contested" cases. It cannot be known in advance which cases will be "contested." To predict a decision in a suit not yet begun, about a dispute which has not yet occurred, requires, then, the most extensive guessing. For whenever there is a question of the credibility of witnesses—of the believability, the reliability, of their testimony—then, unavoidably, the trial judge or jury must make a guess about the facts.[4] The lawyer, accordingly, must make a guess about those guesses. The uncertainty of many "legal rights" corresponds to the correctness or incorrectness of such lawyer-guesses.

2

Let me bring out that point more sharply. When, in 1946, the Sensible-Smart contract is signed, no dispute has yet arisen. The lawyer, in making his guess at that time, must attempt to take into account what may be the future acts of Sensible and Smart, the acts they may

[4] Where the oral testimony consists solely of that of a witness who has not been contradicted, some courts hold that a jury must accept that testimony as true, in the absence of unusual circumstances (such as e.g., that the witness had an "interest" in the outcome of the suit or the improbability of the testimony). Whether all such courts will hold similarly as to a trial judge sitting without a jury is not clear.

In some few kinds of cases, there must be proof of some sorts of facts by at least two witnesses.

do in the interval between 1946 and the date of a future law suit. Patently, that contingency makes the guessing pretty difficult.

Suppose, however, that Sensible consults his lawyer in 1948, after a dispute has arisen, so that all the actual facts have already happened. It may seem to you that if the client, Sensible, accurately reports all those facts to his lawyer, the latter can undoubtedly tell his client just what a court will decide. I'm sorry to say you are wrong. The lawyer must still cope with many elusive, uncontrollable, wayward factors which may upset any prediction. Trials are often full of surprises. The adversary introduces unanticipated testimony. Witnesses, on whom the lawyer relied, change their stories when they take the witness-stand. The facts as they appeared to the lawyer when, before a trial, he conferred with his client and his witnesses, frequently are not at all like the facts as they later show up in the court-room.

But perhaps you believe that the trial judge or jury will surely learn the truth about the facts. If so, you are adopting an axiom, implied in the conventional theory of how courts decide cases, the "Truth-Will-Out axiom." But often that "axiom" does not jibe with reality. For reflect on the following: When a witness testifies, what is he doing? He is reporting his present memory of something he observed in the past, something he saw or heard. A witness is not a photographic plate or phonographic disc. Let us suppose that he is entirely honest. Nevertheless, note these sources of possible error:[5]

(1) The witness may erroneously have observed the past event at the time it occurred. The rankest amateur in psychology knows how faulty observation is, knows that what a man thinks he observes may not accord with what actually happened. Human observation is obviously fallible, subjective. It is affected by defects of sight, or hearing, or by the observer's emotional state or physiological condition, and by his preconceived notions. "Men," say the courts, "often think they see when they did not see, . . . misinterpret what they hear." As hundreds of experiments have demonstrated, two observers of the same happening frequently disagree.

(2) But suppose a witness made no error in his original observation of an event. He may, nevertheless, erroneously remember that correct observation. The faulty, subjective, nature of human memory is notorious. Many a witness has an imaginative memory. "Even a

[5] See, e.g., Wigmore, *Principles of Judicial Proof* (1913); Gross, *Criminal Investigation* (1907); Gross, *Criminal Psychology* (1911); Muensterberg, *On the Witness Stand* (1908); Frank, *Law and the Modern Mind* (1930) 106-109.

conscientious person," said a court, "in trying to narrate a transaction which exists in his memory in a faded or fragmentary state, will, in his effort to make the reproduction seem complete and natural, substitute fancy for fact, or fabricate the missing or forgotten facts."

"When," writes Paton, "a witness makes a simple statement—'the prisoner is the man who drove the car after the robbery'—he is really asserting: (a) that he observed the car; (b) that the impression became fixed in his mind; (c) that the impression has not been confused or obliterated; (d) that the resemblance between the original impression and the prisoner is sufficient to base a judgment not of resemblance but of identity. Scientific research into the nature of the eye has shown how easy it is for vision to be mistaken; lack of observation and faulty memory add to the difficulties. Borchard, in discussing established cases of error in criminal convictions, points out that many of those errors arose from faulty identification and that in eight of the cases there was not the slightest resemblance between the real criminal and the person who was falsely convicted."[6]

(3) Now we come to the stage where the witness reports in the court-room his present recollection of his original observation. Here, again, error may enter. The honest witness, due to a variety of causes, may inadvertently misstate his recollection, may inaccurately report his story. Ram, writing of witnesses, notes that "it happens to all persons occasionally to use one word for another, making the sense very different from what was intended; unconsciously we say what we did not mean to say. . . ."

Sir William Eggleston, a noted lawyer, now Australian Ambassador to this country, expresses the opinion that "no witness can be expected to be more than 50% correct, even if perfectly honest and free from preconception." "In order to know what another person has seen and apprehended, we must first of all know what he thinks—and that is impossible," says Gross. "If we know, at least approximately, the kind of mental process of a person who is close to us in sex, age, culture, position and experience, we lose this knowledge with every step that leads to differences . . . Suppose that in some case, several people of different degrees of education and intelligence have made observations. Suppose all want to tell the truth. Their testimonies, nevertheless, may be very different."

Thus far, I have posited an honest and unprejudiced witness. But many witnesses are neither. Some are downright liars. Aside from

[6] Paton, Jurisprudence (1946) 457.

perjurers, there are the innumerous biased witnesses, whose narratives, although honest, have been markedly affected by their prejudices for or against one of the parties to the suit. A court has said that a biased witness, out of sympathy for a litigant he regards as having been wronged, "with entire innocence may recall things that have never occurred, or forget important instances that have occurred. . . ." "Perhaps the most subtle and prolific of all the 'fallacies of testimony' arises out of unconscious partisanship," writes Wellman. "It is rare that one comes across a witness in court who is so candid and fair that he will testify as fully and favorably for the one side as the other. . . . Witnesses usually feel more or less complimented by the confidence that is placed in them by the party calling them to prove a certain state of facts, and it is human nature to prove worthy of this confidence." Miller, another experienced trial lawyer, says: "When a disinterested person is enlisted as a witness on one side of the case, his sympathies and desires naturally become involved with the person calling him; and when he discovers what things the litigant desires to prove, a witness, especially if the events are distant in time, is apt unconsciously to give a strong coloring to the facts and sometimes to remember things he did not see; and more often innocently to misrepresent things he did see. . . . That fact arises not from an intention deliberately to falsify but from the desire to be an important element in the case." "The liar . . . is far less dangerous than the honest but mistaken witness who draws upon his imagination," Moore remarks. It is difficult to "determine in the case of an honestly intentioned witness how much of his evidence should be discarded as unreliable, and how much accepted as true. . . . Nothing is more deceitful than half the truth, and biased witnesses are much addicted to half-truths and coloring of facts. . . . Such a witness is more dangerous than one who commits a gross perjury. . . ."

A story is told of a trial judge who, after hearing the testimony and the lawyers' arguments, announced: "Gentlemen, if Humphrey, the deceased, said—in the light of these Missouri decisions—'Daughter, if you'll come and live with me, I'll give you this house,' then I'll decide for the plaintiff. Now just what was the testimony?" Unfortunately the court reporter had boggled his notes. The judge impatiently asked if the principal witness, the plaintiff's maid, was present, and, learning that she was in the courtroom, asked her again to take the stand and repeat her testimony. This is what she said: "I remember very well what happened. It was a cold and stormy night. We were all sitting around the fire. Old Mr. Humphrey said to Mrs. Quinn, 'In the light of these Missouri decisions, daughter, if you'll come and live with me, I'll give you this house.'" Of course, in that case it was obvious enough to the judge that the witness had a convenient and partisan recollection. But there are hundreds of cases where that kind of memory and that kind of testimony are not exposed but believed.

The axiom or assumption that, in all or most trials, the truth will out, ignores, then, the several elements of subjectivity and chance. It ignores perjury and bias; ignores the false impression made on the judge or jury by the honest witness who seems untruthful because he is frightened in the court-room or because he is irascible or overscrupulous or given to exaggeration. It ignores the mistaken witness who honestly and convincingly testifies that he remembers acts or conversations that happened quite differently than as he narrates them in court. It neglects, also, the dead or missing witness without whose testimony a crucial fact cannot be brought out, or an important opposing witness cannot be successfully contradicted. Finally it neglects the missing or destroyed letter, or receipt, or cancelled check.

Nor is it true that trial courts will be sure to detect lies or mistakes in testimony. That is clearly not so when a jury tries a case. Many experienced persons believe that of all the possible ways that could be devised to get at the falsity or truth of testimony, none could be conceived that would be more ineffective than trial by jury.[7]

Judges, too, when they try cases without juries, are often fallible in getting at the true facts of a "contested" case. Partly that is due to our faulty way of trying cases in which we hamstring the judge. But even with the best system that could be devised, there would be no way to ensure that the judge will know infallibly which witnesses are accurately reporting the facts. As yet we have no lie-detector for which all responsible psychologists will vouch and which most courts will regard as reliable.[8] But even a perfect lie-detector will not reveal

[7] I shall return to that theme in Chapters VIII and IX.

[8] Loevinger, 33 *Minn. L. Rev.* (1949) 455, 485, lists fourteen "psychometric methods of detecting deception": (1) use of scopalamin; (2) use of sodium amytol; (3) hypnotic sleep; (4) measurement of systolic blood pressure; (5) measurement of rate of respiration; (6) measurement of galvanic reflex; (7) word association tests; (8) observation of pupillary reflex; (9) measurement of pulse rate; (10) recording of eye-movements; (11) recording of unconscious muscle movements; (12) measurement of amplitude and rate of heart beat; (13) analysis of chemical content of blood; (14) change in the brain-wave patterns.

mistakes in a witness' original observation of the facts to which he testifies, and probably will not disclose his mistakes due to his unconscious prejudices.[9]

Lacking any adequate mechanical means of detecting such matters, the courts resort to a common-sense technique: All of us know that, in every-day life, the way a man behaves when he tells a story—his intonations, his fidgetings or composure, his yawns, the use of his eyes, his air of candor or of evasiveness—may furnish valuable clues to his reliability. Such clues are by no means impeccable guides, but they are often immensely helpful. So the courts have concluded. "The appearance and manner of a witness," many courts have said, "is often a complete antidote to what he testifies." The "witness' demeanor," notes Wigmore, "is always . . . in evidence."

Osborn has admirably explained the reasons for giving weight to witness-demeanor:[10] "Let us imagine that every spoken word in a trial is all correctly written out, and then all read by the jury, or read to the jury or the judge. Is there anyone so foolish as to say that a wrong decision would not be more likely in the absence of the living witnesses and speakers. . . . The most skilful official stenographer could not write down all of the varied influences that appeal to [the jury]. The witnesses speak and the lawyers speak but not by words alone. Many of these speakers are eloquent in other ways, sometimes to their detriment and sometimes to their advantage. Their faces and their changing expressions may be pictures that prove the truth of the ancient Chinese saying that a picture is equal to a thousand words. . . . Unconsciously we all tell about ourselves certain things by our actions and our general appearance. This language of others it becomes necessary for the juror to interpret. . . . The task of the juror therefore . . . is to interpret this language without words, as well as he can, and distinguish the true from the false. . . . An important phase of the study of this wordless language is no doubt a scrutiny of everything about a speaker that may indicate sincerity or insincerity. The steps down seem to be unnaturalness, uneasiness, nervousness, hesitation, affectation, concealment and deceit, and the steps up seem to be outspokenness, naturalness, frankness, openness, and properly qualified statements." Osborn wrote about a jury trial, but what he said is true also of a judge trial.

[9] See further, Chapter XIV.
[10] Osborn, *The Mind of the Juror* (1937) 86-98.

3

Having in mind this significance properly attached to close observation of the witnesses, I now must emphasize an element in the decisional process which, curiously, has seldom been considered: Trial judges and juries, in trying to get at the past facts through the witnesses, are themselves witnesses of what goes on in court-rooms. They must determine the facts from what they see and hear, from the gestures and other conduct of the testifying witnesses as well as from their words. Now, as silent witnesses of the witnesses, the trial judges and juries suffer from the same human weaknesses as other witnesses. They, too, are not photographic plates or phonographic discs. If the testifying witnesses make errors of observation, are subject to lapses of memory, or contrive mistaken, imaginative reconstruction of events they observed, in the same way trial judges or juries are subject to defects in their apprehension and their recollection of what the witnesses said and how they behaved.[11]

The facts as they actually happened are therefore twice refracted—first by the witnesses, and second by those who must "find" the facts. The reactions of trial judges or juries to the testimony are shot through with subjectivity. Thus we have subjectivity piled on subjectivity. It is surely proper, then, to say that the facts as "found" by a trial court are subjective.

When Jack Spratt, as a witness, testifies to a fact, he is merely stating his belief or opinion about that past fact. When he says, "I saw McCarthy hit Schmidt," he means, "I believe that is what happened." When a trial judge or jury, after hearing that testimony, finds as a fact that McCarthy hit Schmidt, the finding means no more than the judge's or jury's belief that the belief of the witness Spratt is an honest belief, and that his belief accurately reflects what actually happened. A trial court's findings of fact is, then, at best, its belief or opinion about someone else' belief or opinion.

This aspect of judging seems to have puzzled Plato, who tried to distinguish sharply between "knowledge" and "opinion." "When," he has Socrates say, "judges are justly persuaded about matters which you can only know by seeing them, and not in any other way, and when thus judging them from reports they attain a true opinion about

[11] Suppose a trial judge is so deaf that he cannot hear what the witnesses say, or so near-sighted that he cannot see the facial expressions and other aspects of the witnesses' demeanor. See State ex rel. Shea v. Cocking, 66 Mont. 169, 213 Pac. 594, as to a blind judge; Rhodes v. State, 128 Ind. 189, 27 N.E. 866 as to a juror with defective eyesight.

them, they judge without knowledge, and yet are rightly persuaded, if they have judged well... And yet,.. if true opinion... and knowledge are the same, the perfect judge could not have judged rightly without knowledge; and therefore I must infer that they are not the same."[12] Jowett, commenting on this passage, writes, "The correctness of such an opinion will be purely accidental.... Plato would have done better if he had said that true opinion was a contradiction in terms."[13]

4

And now I come to a major matter, one which most non-lawyers do not understand, and one which puts the trial courts at the heart of our judicial system: An upper court can seldom do anything to correct a trial court's mistaken belief about the facts. Where, as happens in most cases, the testimony at the trial was oral, the upper court usually feels obliged to adopt the trial court's determination of the facts. Why? Because in such a case the trial court heard and saw the witnesses as they testified, but the upper court did not. The upper court has only a typewritten or printed record of the testimony. The trial court alone is in a position to interpret the demeanor-clues, this "language without words."[14] An upper court, to use Judge Kennison's phrase, "has to operate in the partial vacuum of the printed record." A "stenographic transcript," wrote Judge Ulman, "... fails to reproduce tones of voice and hesitations of speech that often make a sentence mean the reverse of what the mere words signify. The best and most accurate record [of oral testimony] is like a dehydrated peach; it has neither the substance nor the flavor of the peach before it was dried." That is why, when testimony is taken in a trial court, an upper court, on appeal, in most instances accepts the facts as found by the trial court, when those findings can be supported by reasonable inferences from some witness's testimony, even if it is flatly contradicted in the testimony of other witnesses.

Considering how a trial court reaches its determination as to the facts, it is most misleading to talk, as we lawyers do, of a trial court "finding" the facts. The trial court's facts are not "data," not something that is "given"; they are not waiting somewhere, ready made, for the court to discover, to "find." More accurately, they are processed

[12] Plato, *Theaetetus,* 201-202.
[13] 4 Jowett, *Dialogues of Plato* (1892) 151.
[14] See Chapter XV as to "talking movies" of trials.

by the trial court—are, so to speak, "made" by it, on the basis of its subjective reactions to the witnesses' stories. Most legal scholars fail to consider that subjectivity, because, when they think of courts, they think almost exclusively of upper courts and of their written opinions. For, in these opinions, the facts are largely "given" to the upper courts —given to those courts by the trial courts.

It should now be obvious that the conventional description of the decisional process needs alteration. For that description implies that the *F,* in the $R \times F = D$ equation, is an objective fact—what might be called an *OF*—so that, seemingly, $R \times OF = D$. But, as the *F* is subjective—what might therefore be called an *SF*—the formula should read: $R \times SF = D$.

5

I can feel that at this moment some lawyer-critic, reading this book, is itching to reply: "Doubtless, decisions in 'contested' cases turn on the judge's or jury's belief, and that belief may be mistaken. Court-orders may depend upon such beliefs of the trial judges or the juries who happen to try the cases. But a man's legal rights are what they are, even if a trial court, through an erroneous belief about the facts, decides against him."

That I deny. At any rate, I deny that the words "legal rights" have any practical meaning, if used as my critic uses them. If a court decides that Smart has, in fact, done no legal wrong to Sensible, then Sensible has no meaningful legal right against Smart. Not on this earth, not in this life. If a court, after listening to conflicting oral testimony, mistakes the facts and decides for Smart, and Sensible appeals, losing his appeal, that's all there is to Sensible's legal rights—there isn't any more. His legal rights, so far as the courts are concerned, consist precisely of what he can persuade a court to make Smart do. If Sensible wins the court-fight, then he'll have a legal right; if he loses, he won't. There is no middle ground, no judicial Purgatory. If Sensible loses in court, I think it plain nonsense to say that nevertheless he still has a legal right against Smart, or that Smart owes him a legal duty. Please note that I say nothing of moral rights. Moral considerations should, and unquestionably do, play a part in many court decisions. But when a court, once and for all, holds that a man is without a legal right, his remaining moral rights are usually of no interest to the courts, for usually the courts will do nothing more for him.

See, then, the lawyers' difficulties: (1) Contested law-suits turn on *F*'s. (2) No one knows whether law-suits will arise or which of them will be contested. (3) The *F*'s of future contested law-suits are not now knowable. (4) Legal rights and duties mean law-suits lost or won. (5) Accordingly, legal rights and duties depend on the outcome of future law-suits which turn on presently unknowable *F*'s. (6) Wherefore, no matter how well-settled are the pertinent legal rules, a lawyer, before suit is begun, frequently cannot tell a man his legal rights. For the lawyer faces a multitude of variable factors which he cannot definitely ascertain.

A lawyer friend of mine once objected when he heard me express such views. He said that it is not difficult for a lawyer of experience to answer unequivocally most of the legal questions that confront him in his daily practice. If my friend meant that a lawyer can unequivocally answer a generalized question, such as whether a gift by a man who was insolvent when he made it can be set aside by the man's creditors, then, of course, my friend was correct. But the client usually is not interested in getting answers to merely general questions of that character. He doesn't want his lawyer to copy rules for him out of law-books. The client wants to know, for example, whether he can induce a court to set aside a gift of $50,000 made by a definite person, John Jones, so that the client can collect the $10,000 Jones owes him.[15]

The ability to answer unequivocally many so-called legal questions does not, then, signify, by any manner of means, that a lawyer, however experienced, can unequivocally tell his client that which the client wants to know. Only a soothsayer, a prophet, or a person gifted with clairvoyance, can tell a man what are his enforceable rights arising out of any particular transaction, or against any other person, before a law-suit with respect to that transaction or that person has arisen. For only a clairvoyant can foretell what evidence will be introduced and will be believed, and can foresee what will be the reaction of the trial judge or the jurors to such testimony as he or they may believe.

[15] This brings up a matter which, although most important, I can but mention here: Ordinarily, a client does not want merely a decision. He wants a decision which will be enforced or with which the loser will voluntarily comply. A court's judgment against Jones for $10,000 will usually be of no value unless Jones is able to pay that judgment. Many a judgment is not paid because the losing party is insolvent or has successfully secreted his property. Legal rights should therefore be viewed from the angle of their actual enforcibility. In my teaching, I call this the "enforcement approach" or the "credit man's approach." It calls for a study of bankruptcy and many other subjects relative to the collection of judgments. See Chapter XVI and Frank, "Are Judges Human?," 80 *Un. of Pa. Rev.* (1931) at 49 note 74.

I think the reader will now see that a lawyer's ability successfully to predict a decision varies with the stage at which he is asked for his opinions:

(1) When a client, having just signed a contract, asks what are his rights thereunder, at that time neither the client nor the other party to the contract has as yet taken any steps under the contract. The lawyer's prediction at this stage must include a hazardous guess as to what each of the parties will do or not do in the future. Frequently the prediction must be so full of if's as to be of little practical value.

(2) After events have occurred which give rise to threatened litigation, the client may inquire concerning the outcome of the suit, if one should be brought.

a. Before the lawyer has interviewed prospective witnesses, his guess is on a shaky foundation.

b. After interviewing them, his guess is somewhat less shaky. But, unless the facts are certain to be agreed upon, the guess is still dubious. For, if, as is usual, the witnesses are to testify orally and will disagree about what they saw and heard, seldom can anyone guess how the trial judge or jury will react to the testimony. Especially is the guessing wobbly if the lawyer does not know who the judge will be, should the trial be jury-less; it is still more so, if there may be a jury trial, since the lawyer cannot know what persons will compose the jury.

(3) After the trial, but before decision, the lawyer's prophecy may be better. For he is now estimating the reaction to the testimony of a known trial judge or a known jury, observed in action in the particular case. Yet, if the testimony was oral, that guessing is frequently not too easy.

(4) After trial and a decision by the trial court, the guess relates to the outcome of an appeal, should one be taken. It therefore usually relates solely to the rules the upper court will apply to the facts as already "found" by the trial judge or jury. At this stage, a competent, trained lawyer can often (not always) predict with accuracy.

6

Let me summarize: Law-suits are fights. They are legal battles fought in a court-room. They are historically (and contemporaneously) substitutes for private gun-fights and knife-fights. Instead of using your knife or gun to make Robinson do what you want him to do, you fight in a court-house with non-lethal weapons, with implements of persuasion, to induce a court to enter an order directing Robinson to do what you want—fight to produce a court-order which will direct the sheriff, if necessary, to use his gun to make Robinson do what you want. And law-suits alone—nothing else—ultimately fix tested legal rights. If Robinson, voluntarily—or because he is ashamed not to, or afraid not to—does what you want, you haven't tested out your legal rights against him, or his legal obligations to you. It is only if he doesn't do what you want, and if you try to get a court to order him to do so, that you really learn what those legal rights and duties are. Jones's tested legal rights against Smith on a mortgage, a lease, an employment contract, or because of an automobile accident, are unknown until Jones sues Smith and a court decides that suit.

We are all Smiths and Joneses. You can't really know your legal rights (your court-enforceable rights) against any other person, about anything, until you obtain an enforceable decision in a specific law-suit brought against that other person. No law-suits, no tested legal rights. Until there has been an enforceable court-order in a specific law-suit, there can be only guesses about any legal rights or duties. And those guesses—even if they are lawyers' guesses—are not always too good, especially before a law-suit arises. For court-decisions in law-suits depend on at least two things (Rules and Facts) and one of those is peculiarly unguessable—namely what the trial court (judge or jury) will believe were the facts. Guessing legal rights, before litigation occurs, is, then, guessing what judges or juries will guess were the facts, and that is by no means easy. Legal rights and duties are, then, often guessy, if-y.

See what this means: Most legal rights turn on the facts as "proved" in a future lawsuit, and proof of those facts, in "contested" cases, is at the mercy of such matters as mistaken witnesses, perjured witnesses, missing or dead witnesses, mistaken judges, inattentive judges, biased judges, inattentive juries, and biased juries. In short, a legal right is usually a bet, a wager, on the chancy outcome of a possible future lawsuit.[16]

[16] When I so state, and when I also state that potential force lies behind court decisions, of course I am not expressing a worship of force, or taking a neutral attitude toward morality and moral rights. I am describing the actualities of court-house government—doing so indeed because I think that such a description will help to promote an understanding of both the avoidable and unavoidable imperfections of our legal system. See Frank, *If Men Were Angels* (1942) 297-300, 307-309.

7

I must now modify somewhat the disturbing picture I have painted. I turn to lawyers as preventers of litigation.

Lawyers do not confine themselves to trying law-suits. Many of them spend all or most of their time in their offices advising clients. Many clients go to them to obtain assurance, confidence. For life is hazardous, and among the hazards are the dangers of being sucked into litigation and being defeated in court. The lawyer thus often serves as a tranquillizer, as an allayer of the doubts of perplexed men. In that sense, one might say he acts as a psychiatrist, subduing his clients' fears, enabling them to act without undue apprehensions.

Some lawyers sometimes raise unnecessary doubts in the minds of their clients. To that extent, they are bad psychiatrists. However, the lawyer who too glibly gives assurances may be an equally bad psychiatrist. The competent psychiatrist, as I understand it, does not create illusions in his patients, but seeks to enable them, in adult fashion, to recognize and bravely cope with reality. He does not act as his patients' emotional wet-nurse. No more should the lawyer with respect to his patients, his clients. He should deal with them as grown-up persons. He should not illusion them about their legal rights. He should, for his own sake and theirs, tell them the facts of life. And included in those facts is the inherent uncertainty of litigation—and therefore of legal rights.

The wise lawyer often tries to prevent litigation. For just as there is preventive medicine, so there is preventive legal practice. The lawyer often can and does keep people from litigating. Here we come to lawyers' paper work—the legal documents they prepare. In theory, that paper work is generally efficacious in preventing law-suits, by so equipping one side with legal weapons that its easily foreseeable victory deters the other side from commencing court-warfare. Let us examine into that theory.

A client has his lawyer draw his contract, or his mortgage, his lease, his deed. Then the client feels secure, for his lawyer presumably has safeguarded him against successful attack. And we lawyers, generally, seeing how little of our paper work is ever assailed, how few of our contracts or deeds are ever called into question, take pride in the efficacy of our handiwork as litigation-preventives. But is that pride always justified? When no litigation occurs, is it usually our draftsmanship that kept the parties from disputing? To what extent does the explanation of non-litigation lie in the fact that most people are usually not litigious? Perhaps lawyers resemble Chanticleer who thought the sun could not rise without his crowing. Perhaps this lawyer-pride rests largely on the false principle of *post hoc ergo propter hoc,* nicely illustrated by the case of the savage rainmaker: He performs a ceremony. Two days later it rains. His reputation with his group is assured. They assume that, if *A* follows *B* in time, then *B* is caused by *A.* They imagine a causal relation where none exists.

Consider this fact: Any lawyer who examines many abstracts of title to real estate finds hundreds of instances of defective papers prepared by lawyers—defective deeds or wills or corporate resolutions, and the like—which were potential provocatives of litigation. Most of these defects are cured by mere lapse of time ("adverse possession"). In other words, such abstracts reveal lawyers' written contrivances which did not prevent litigation but which, on the contrary, created potential law-suits that did not occur—thanks to other factors, including ignorance of the errors, or inertia.

One of my favorite lawyer stories is relevant. A lawyer friend of mine—call him Mr. Inquisitive—represented a corporation which was about to borrow a million dollars on mortgage-bonds. One of the leading New York law firms—call them Messrs. Big, Keen & Snappy—represented the bankers. They sent Mr. Inquisitive a sixty-page printed draft of the mortgage trust deed for his client to sign. My friend, it happens, hadn't had much experience in such matters. So he read through the proposed document with exceeding care. Then he phoned Messrs. Big, Keen & Snappy.

"I can't," he said, "understand the meaning of pages 42 to 51. What is it all about?"

"Oh," they replied, patronizingly, "that is our usual form. We have used it just that way for the last four years. At least a billion dollars of bonds are issued and outstanding under similar instruments."

"All right," said Mr. Inquisitive, "I'll admit I am stupid. But, for my peace of mind, just write me a few lines telling me the meaning of those pages."

A day later, on the phone, he received this surprising answer from Big, Keen & Snappy: Two years before, in getting out a trust deed in a hurry, the printer had dropped three pages and spoiled the sense of some dozen other pages. The error, undetected, had been perpetuated ever since.

Well, there they were—about a billion dollars of bonds issued by divers corporations and sold to the public under defective instruments. Now how many law-suits did that mistake occasion? Probably none. For most people don't go around looking for law-suits. The absence of such litigation cannot be said to be due to what was done by the lawyers who drafted those mortgages. It was in spite of their work that court-fights did not occur.

How far the instruments drafted by lawyers act prophylactically we simply do not know. To have such knowledge we would need, at the least, to learn (1) the instances in which lawyers' mistakes were never found out, and (2) the instances in which threatened litigation, growing out of such mistakes, was settled out of court. We would need also to take into account the fact that, in some areas of business, there would seem to be a peculiarly strong social tabu against litigation. It would be interesting to know whether, in a period of sharp business decline, law-suits do not become more frequent even in those business areas in which, in normal times, this litigation tabu governs.

A paper carefully drafted by a lawyer does, undoubtedly, sometimes prevent law suits. For the courts have evolved what is known as the "parol evidence" rule. Roughly speaking, that rule says that a court will not listen to evidence which is at variance with, contradicts, a writing. Seemingly, that means that most oral evidence will be shut out, and that therefore the dangers of mistaken testimony will be absent. That rule, however, is subject to so many exceptions that it resembles a swiss-cheese with more holes than cheese. That rule permits a man who wants to contest such a paper to nullify it by introducing oral testimony which, if believed, will show, for instance,

that his signature is a forgery; or
that he was induced by fraud to sign it; or
that both parties who signed it intended it to be a joke or a sham; or
that by mutual mistake it omitted important matter which gives it a different meaning; or
that it was orally agreed that the paper was not to have any effect until something happened which has never happened; or
that, after it was signed, the other party and he orally agreed to cancel it.[17]

If the court believes the witnesses who testify in support of any of those alleged facts, it does not matter one iota whether such facts are

[17] This last exception is not recognized by all courts.

true. What solely matters is the trial court's belief in their truth. The written paper will be effective or not according to that belief. Oral testimony may create fatal chinks in the paper armor. For instance, in many a will contest, the will itself, carefully prepared, contains no legal flaws, but the court sets it aside because the court believes from some of the oral testimony that the making of the will was the result of "undue influence."

But I must not exaggerate. In all probability, because of the parol evidence rule, carefully prepared, lawyer-made documents not infrequently forestall litigation. My good friend Professor Karl Llewellyn, in recent discussion with me, estimated that, in certain sorts of business situations, skillful documents mean that the chances of victory in a law suit become 3 out of 4, or 4 out of 5. Whether that figure is correct, no one knows. Doubtless, as to some kinds of transactions, skilled legal paper-work often does the trick. Yet that belief cannot be verified statistically.

This, too, should be kept in mind. Many documents of the kind to which Llewellyn refers are used by economically powerful corporations. Suppose it could be proved that, in suits relating to such documents, their batting-average was very high, and that, consequently, few persons venture to "go to law" with them concerning those documents. Even so, we would not have a "controlled experiment." For these giant institutions employ exceptionally competent trial lawyers, better on the average than those employed by their adversaries. And allowance must be made for the fact that many a man is unable to finance litigation with those giants, or, when able, is reluctant to do so, either because of the giants' prestige, or out of fear—often more imaginary than real—of indirect harm to himself, by way of retaliation, through loss of credit or supplies needed in his business.

We shall never, I think, obtain reliable information on these subjects. No one will ever know just how much more or less men would litigate if lawyers were to abandon their paper-work. But this much one may say: The fact that, in general, there is a relatively small amount of litigation should almost surely not be ascribed principally to the preventive paper-work of lawyers. The legal profession cannot reasonably claim most of the credit for whatever it is that makes folks more peaceable, less litigious, than they conceivably might be. Let lawyers, then, be modest in asserting the extent to which the words they dictate to their stenographers serve to prevent quarrels, in the court-room or elsewhere. Above all, remember that only a small part of the human activities which become or might become law-suits could be fully covered by lawyer-made instruments or be otherwise lawyer-guided. At most, the activities open to prophylaxis must be few.

8

Many non-lawyers and some lawyers, when they talk of "facts" in litigation, refer not to the kind of facts I have been considering (i.e., whether Jones ran over young Tommy Smith), but to what might be called "background" or "social and economic" facts, often of a statistical character—the sort of facts presented to the courts in the famous "Brandeis briefs." Facts of that sort do not involve witnesses' credibility.[18] But the great majority of actual law-suits do involve some crucial fact issues which turn on determinations by the trial courts of orally-testifying witnesses' credibility. There the trial court usually has the final say about the facts. There we have what Tourtoulon calls the "sovereignty of the trial court." With that in mind, Judge Olson recently suggested that law-suits are misnamed: They should be called "fact suits."[19]

Chief Justice Hughes—who distrusted administrative agencies, considering them far less entitled to respect than orthodox courts—once remarked: "An unscrupulous administrator might be tempted to say, 'Let me find the facts . . . , and I care little who lays down the general principles.'" The Chief Justice failed to note that his observation related also to fact-finding by trial courts—and not merely to fact-finding caused by unscrupulousness but, as well, to erroneous fact-finding caused by honest mistakes of trial judges and juries.

[18] That such facts are not, however, immune from subjectivity, see Chapter XIV.

[19] *Warning:* Only where a trial court sees and hears witnesses, and thus is in a more advantageous position than the upper court to ascertain witness' credibility, are its fact-findings usually accorded finality by the upper court. Where, then, no oral testimony is involved, no such finality necessarily exists. And it may not exist, at least in the case of a trial judge, where the oral testimony is "in conflict with contemporaneous documents" of such character that it would be unreasonable to believe what the witnesses said. See United States v. U.S. Gypsum Co., 333 U.S. 364.

Nor does it exist with respect to a finding which does not turn directly on credibility. To illustrate: Suppose that, after hearing witnesses, a trial judge finds that Shadrach and Abednego had a certain conversation on a certain day. While an upper court usually will not question that finding, it will not feel similarly obliged to acquiesce in the trial judge's further conclusion as to the meaning of the words of those two men or as to the intention manifested by those words; for the significance of the conversation is a question apart from the reliability of the testimony concerning the fact that it occurred. See discussion in Chapter XXIII of the "interpretation" of "facts."

Hughes's remark serves to bring out the importance of trial-court fact-finding. For suppose that a trial court, in deciding a case, makes a mistake about the facts, and applies to those facts, mistakenly found, the correct legal rule, i.e., the rule which it ought to have applied if those were the actual facts. Then injustice results fully as much as if the court had applied an incorrect rule to the actual facts. In other words, it is as unjust to apply the "right" rule to the wrong facts as to apply the "wrong" rule. Or, rather, no rule can be the "right" rule, the just rule, in any specific law suit, if applied to facts that did not occur, to unreal, spurious facts. Can it be said, for instance, that the court enforced a just rule when Mr. Campbell was sent to jail for a crime he had not committed? It is as if a surgeon, flawlessly following approved rules of surgery, mistakenly removed the gall-bladder of a healthy man.

Indeed, in a case where a correct rule is misapplied by a court because applied to unreal facts, it is not really enforced, its enforcement becomes illusory. And that misapplication, that illusory application of a rule, means a frustration of the community ideal or policy embodied in that rule; for the misapplication of such an ideal or policy is at least the equivalent of its non-application. Mistaken findings of the facts render impotent such ideals or policies. You may perhaps think that, because I have stressed trial-court fact-finding, I consider the legal rules of little importance. Not at all. As I sit on an upper court which spends most of its time on legal rules, it should be obvious that I do not regard them lightly. Indeed, it is precisely because I think that the rules are of great importance that I am distressed when, due to unnecessarily defective fact-finding, they are frustrated by being applied to the wrong facts. Since, however, the specific applications of the rules depend on fact-finding, the upper courts, which function primarily as guardians of the rules, have far less importance in our legal system than the trial courts. In the first place, the overwhelming majority of cases are not appealed; probably 95% of all cases end in the trial courts. In the second place, since, in most of the few cases that are appealed, the upper courts accept the trial court's fact-findings, the trial courts decide the fate of, say, 98% of all cases.

9

Throughout this book, I shall continue to be critical of some courthouse ways. I must therefore take notice of a recently developed argument opposed to such criticism: American democracy, it is said, competes today in world affairs with Russian totalitarianism. Consequently, it is urged, we should observe a "hush" policy concerning any faults, eradicable or not, in the American economy or government, even if by so doing we diminish the possibility of removing some of those faults. For otherwise, so the argument goes, Soviet critics, taking advantage of the disclosures, will win away America's friends or potential friends.

Surely that cannot be sound policy. It tries to preserve democracy by negating it. It proposes that we should employ the very mode of undemocratic suppression of the truth for the use of which we often criticize totalitarianism. It asserts that democracy, in order to survive, must cease to be democratic. Such an argument, applied to proposed reforms, economic or governmental, is a cowardly counsel of despair. Only a robust, developing democracy, true to its own fundamental principles, can successfully compete with Sovietism for world influence.

That our judicial system is not as good as it could and should be does not mean, however, that, as it stands, it does not have many features deserving of high praise. I therefore agree with Bar Associations when, recurrently, they deplore reckless, uninformed, blanket denigrations of our courts. But, in part, those denigrations are invited by almost equally deplorable excessive praise of our courts sometimes uttered by some prominent members of Bar Associations. Significantly, in such utterances they often quote Cicero. That fascinating Roman, as a legal philosopher, eloquently maintained that any civilized legal system must be based on reason, grounded on universal, eternal, principles of justice, and on the ideal we today phrase as "equality before the law." Yet Cicero, as a practicing court lawyer, felt free to use a lawyer's wiles to pervert reason, and to render ineffective the doctrines which he, as legal philosopher, purported to worship. In his non-philosophic moments, he boasted of his prowess as a lawyer in winning law-suits for clients which they should have lost, and would have lost but for his clever stratagems. Now if, à la the philosophic Cicero, a legal system approximates rationality and "equality before the law," then cases which are substantially the same should, at any given time, be identically decided. In so far as such like cases are decided differently, solely because of inequalities in the skills in wiliness of lawyers, then just to that extent the legal ideals proclaimed by Cicero are traduced. Cicero did nothing to close the gap between those ideals and the judicial realities. He kept his noble principles in one pocket and his actual lawyer's practices in another. Since he never sought to actualize the high principles he mouthed, he could not have entertained them seriously.[20] I suggest that you examine critically the mouthings of our modern Ciceros.

Recently I read a book written for laymen by a lawyer. The author says that, should you lose a law suit, because the court misapprehended the facts, and should you leave the court-room complaining of injustice, you would be an unreasonable, small-minded critic. For, he explains, in every suit there must be a loser, and you must learn to appreciate that no legal system can be perfect.

That not uncommon patronizing lawyer's way of brushing off laymen leaves me indignant. Of course, no legal system can be perfect. But think of this: A man is accused of killing another man and is tried for murder. If the accused is convicted, the government will kill him. The government's killing is lawful and therefore not murder. But if the government's killing follows a conviction brought about by the trial court's mistaken belief about the facts, so that the government, although acting according to legal forms, kills an innocent man—what then? Then a shocking act of judicial injustice has occurred. Yet our author writes, "Such a contingency does not justify condemnation of a system which is necessarily subject to human judgment; and if this complacent view exasperates a victim who has been found guilty of a crime which he has never committed, it is an incontrovertible fact," it is inevitable, like an "Act of God," as when a stroke of lightning kills a man.

That defense of grave miscarriages of justice is legitimate only if they are inevitable—that is, only if everything practical has been done to avoid such injustices. But, often, everything practical has not been done. Thanks to avoidable court-room errors, innocent men are convicted of crimes; and every week, for similar reasons, someone loses his life's savings, his livelihood, his job. Most of such injustices stem not from lack of justice in the legal rules but from mistakes in fact-finding. And a high percentage of those mistakes derive from needless defects in the court-house methods of getting at the facts.

It is up to the non-lawyers to demand a reform of those methods. They should not, I repeat, demand perfection. Perfect justice lies be-

[20] See Chapter XXVI for further discussion of Cicero.

yond human reach. But the unattainability of the ideal is no excuse for shirking the effort to obtain the best available. As the poet MacNeice puts it:

"And to the good who know how wide the gulf, how deep,
Between Ideal and Real, who being good have felt
 The final temptation to withdraw, sit down and weep,
We pray the power to take upon themselves the guilt
 Of human action, though still ready to confess
The imperfection of what can and must be built. . . ."

10

The legal profession, as a whole, however, should not be singularly blamed for the remediable faults of our legal system. Most of those who comprise any profession or trade tend to venerate almost all its traditions, to overlook its defects, and are unable to inspect with much detachment its customary ways. And many noted lawyers, including some leading members of that conservative lawyers' organization, the American Bar Association, have been conspicuous as constructive critics of legal and judicial practices, just as they have been foremost in other phases of American life.[21] Nevertheless, I believe that, to achieve substantial reforms of our trial court methods, it is necessary to enlist the assistance of the non-lawyers.

[21] I think this statement of such importance that I have included it in the Preface also.

IV. MODERN LEGAL MAGIC

I HAVE discussed the invention of courts as a means of preserving the peace, and the substitution of court-room fights, called lawsuits, for private peace-disturbing wars. In a later chapter I shall say more of that subject; I shall there try to show that the fighting method of judicially administering justice has been carried too far, and needs very substantial modification, if justice is to be well administered by the courts. But, as a preface to that discussion, I want to show in this and the next chapter how and why many lawyers have obscured, to themselves and to the public, the fighting character of present-day trials, and some of the resultant uncertainties and injustices of court-house government.

2

Since the actual facts of a case do not walk into court, but happened outside the court-room, and always in the past, the task of the trial court is to reconstruct the past from what are at best second-hand reports of the facts. Thus the trial court acts as an historian, its job being much the same as the historian's.[1] The historian, too, tries to reconstruct the past, but usually he relies on second-hand or third-or-fourth-hand reports of dead witnesses. Indeed, the historian has been called a judge of the dead.

Increasingly, competent historians—at least in books written for other historians—confess that theirs is not a science but a guessy art.[2] They admit that, on many issues, their knowledge of the past is far from sure to be accurate, because of a variety of circumstances which include (1) the unavailability of important data, (2) disagreements among the witnesses on whom the historians must depend for information as to what happened, and (3) the errors, prejudices or mendacity of those witnesses. "The historian," wrote Pirenne, himself a noted Belgian history-writer, "only rarely finds himself face-to-face with an authentic fragment of the past . . . Even if we had observed all that

[1] See my opinions in U.S. v. Rubenstein, 151 F. (2d) 915, 920 note 4, and in In re Fried, 161 F. (2d) 453, 462 note 21. See also Frank, "Say It With Music," 61 *Harv. L. Rev.* (1948) 923, 943-947.

[2] For an extended discussion of this subject, see Frank, *Fate and Freedom* (1945) 11-63, 76-84, 334-336.

had been written about an event, we could not pretend to have complete information. No account, detailed as it may be, ever exhausts its subject. . . . In spite of all his efforts, therefore, the historian cannot gain an adequate knowledge of what has been." Two famous French historians have said, "Facts which we do not see, described in language which does not permit us to represent them in our minds with exactness, form the data of history."

The historian's job, we are told, is to study "events not accessible to . . . observation, and to study those events inferentially, arguing to them from something else which is accessible . . . to observation. . . ." i.e., the evidence. For he "is not an eye witness of the facts he desires to know. . . ." His "only possible knowledge is mediate or inferential or indirect, never empirical." He must endeavor to "re-enact the past in his own mind."[3] In this endeavor, he performs two tasks: (1) He first critically examines the evidence, attempting to determine which (if any) of his witnesses made reliable reports. To discover the real meanings which lie behind a witness' words, the historian must try to identify himself with the witness, to relive the witness' life. The witness' "personality intervenes between" the historian and "the facts."[4] This task leaves "a very large role to the tact, finesse, and intuition" of the historian, involves an evaluation of credibility which is largely "subjective."[5] For the historian does not passively accept testimony but interprets it, and the criterion in his critical interpretation "is the historian himself."[6] (2) Having evaluated the credibility of the testimony, the historian must construct a narrative of the past events. This narrative "is at once a synthesis and a hypothesis. It is a synthesis inasmuch as it combines the mass of known facts in an account of the whole; it is a hypothesis inasmuch as the relations that it establishes between the facts are neither evidence nor verifiable by themselves. . . . Everything then depends . . . upon the degree of the creative imagination of the historian and upon his general conception of human affairs."[7] The historian "imagines the past." His picture of the past is a "web of imaginative construction stretched between certain fixed points" provided by his critical judgment of his witnesses' testimony.[8]

[3] Collingwood, *The Idea of History* (1946) 251-52, 282.

[4] Pirenne, "What are Historians Trying To Do?" in Rice, *Methods in Social Science* (1931) 435, 437-39.

[5] *ibid.* 439.

[6] See Collingwood, 138.

[7] Pirenne, 435, 441.

[8] Collingwood, 242.

Here, obviously, subjectivity enters. "The human actions which [historians] study cannot appear the same to different historians. It needs only a moment of reflection to understand that two historians using the same material will not treat it in an identical fashion, primarily because the creative imagination which permits them to single the factors of movements out of chaos varies, but also because they do not have the same ideas as to the relative importance of the motives which determine men's conduct. They [divers historians] will inevitably write accounts which will contrast as do their personalities. . . . Thus, historical syntheses depend to a very large degree not only upon the personality of their authors but upon all the social, religious, or natural, environments which surround them. It follows, therefore, that each historian will establish . . . relationships determined by the convictions, the movements, and the prejudices, that have molded his point of view." These elements shape his peculiar "conjectural reconstruction of the past." [9]

The franker historians, then, admit that learning the "facts" about the past involves "interpretations" of the available data; that those "interpretations" depend on selection of, and emphasis on, some of the data as "significant"; and that, unavoidably, historians differ in their choice of the "significant," with the result that we have sharply discrepant accounts in divers history-books concerning, say, Nero, Cromwell, Napoleon, the American Revolution, or our Civil War. Since every history book is a "conjectural reconstruction of the past," Pirenne concludes that, due to the differences among historians, "history is a conjectural science, or in other words, a subjective science." "How," asked the English historian Froude, "can we talk of a science in things long past which come to us only in books?"

Froude's comment suggests that the historian, in one important way, is at a disadvantage as compared with the trial court: Usually, as all or most of the historian's witnesses are dead, he cannot examine and cross-examine them. But he has some marked advantages as compared

[9] Pirenne, 433-34. Collingwood, by ingenious semantics, tries to show that the historian's subjectivity can translate itself into a kind of objectivity. See Collingwood, 292 et seq. But see the comments of his editor, Knox, in the Preface, *ibid.* xiv.

Of course, the historian, like the trial judge, may have before him evidence the authenticity of which is indubitably clear. Thus he may have no possible doubt of the words of a particular treaty or that Lincoln issued his emancipation proclamation on a certain day. But, when it comes to a determination of the causal relations of any such facts to other facts, each historian must often draw on his "constructive imagination." Wherefore historians often disagree about such matters—just as two trial judges often disagree about the facts of a case.

with a court: He can take as much time as he wants to gather his evidence, and to reflect on it, while a trial in court cannot go on endlessly. Moreover, the historian is free to consider any kind of evidence; but, in court, some kinds of evidence, for wise or unsound reasons, are excluded.

If the honest historian confesses to the conjectural and subjective character of his products, surely lawyers should similarly confess the conjectural nature of the products of the judicial process. But the lawyers' resistance to so confessing is astonishingly persistent. There are many possible explanations of that resistance. I shall not here attempt to discuss, or even mention, all of them. But one explanation ought to be obvious: Many men fear the chanciness of life. The uncertainty of legal rights, due to their dependence on imperfect human fact-finding, therefore provokes terror. In the 16th century, Montaigne advised, "We must shun lawsuits," even at the cost of suffering "very manifest injustice." "No judge has yet, thank God," he exclaimed, "spoken to me as a judge in any cause whatsoever, whether my own or another's, whether criminal or civil. . . . I . . . will never, if I can help it, place myself in the power of a man who can dispose of my head, when my honor and life depend on the skill of a lawyer more than on my innocence. . . . How many innocent people we have known to be punished, I mean without the fault of the judges; and how many there are that we have not known of!"

That fear of litigation was uttered some three centuries ago in France. In this country, in the 20th century, eagerness to escape that terror induces self-deluding denials that the source of that terror exists, to denials that litigation is extraordinarily chancy in its outcome. To be sure, Judge Learned Hand, after much experience as a trial judge, not long ago remarked, "I must say that, as a litigant, I should dread a lawsuit beyond almost anything else short of sickness and of death." But only occasionally does a modern American lawyer forthrightly make such a comment.

3

To support my suggestion that fear accounts for much of the unwillingness of many lawyers today to acknowledge the immense hazards of litigation and the guessiness of legal rights, I shall make an historical detour. I shall go back to the early day of the European legal systems from which our own system derived. In those days, men had recourse to a device designed, they thought, to avoid mistakes or lies in testimony, and to preclude human errors of judgment grounded upon such testimony. I refer to the ordeals. They were methods of fact-finding which have been used, not universally, but in many parts of the globe, in what we moderns are pleased to call "primitive" or "archaic" societies.

The ordeals have taken many forms. There was, for instance, the "trial by battle," a "judicial duel" fought under court supervision. This fight, although socially regulated, was still overt warfare, conducted with physical weapons, between the parties to the dispute or their agents. There was also the ordeal by fire, or hot water, or cold water, or the balanced axe, or the suspended sacred object, or by poison, or the morsel, or the scales. For example, a person accused was required to plunge his hand into boiling water; then the hand was bandaged for three nights; if, when the bandage was removed, the hand was uninjured, he was deemed innocent. In the ordeal of the morsel, the accused was compelled to try to swallow a piece of bread, or cheese, of a prescribed size. If he succeeded without difficulty, he was innocent. If he choked and grew black in the face, he was guilty. In the ordeal of the scales, the accused was weighed in the scales and then removed. The judge then adjured the scales, and the accused was again placed in the balance. If he increased in weight, he was guilty; if his weight was the same or less, his innocence was established. (In passing, recall the modern symbols of justice, the sword and the scales—the fight and the ordeal, shall we say?)

The pertinent rule, the *R,* was announced by the court, in advance of the trial. That pronouncement was not too difficult. The serious difficulty was with the facts, the *F.* The function of the ordeal was to ascertain that *F.* When it was once ascertained, the final decision followed.

Always, you see, in the ordeals, the *F,* and therefore the decision, turned on one or the other party to the dispute passing a perilous test. The court set him a task. If he performed it, he won the judicial fight. If he failed in his performance, he lost. "He whom the blazing fire burns not," runs the ancient Hindu code of Manu (about 300 B.C.), "whom the water forces not to come quickly up, who meets with no speedy misfortune, must be held innocent." The trial, as Radin suggests, was more literally a "trial"—a test—than is a trial as we conduct it.

Here we get a clue to the inner meaning of all ordeals. They were supernatural, apparently non-human, means for determining whether a man spoke the truth. He was put in peril. If he came through safely, that was a sign that he spoke truly. If he succumbed to the peril, it was a sign that he lied. Whence came this sign? It is usually said that it was deemed to come from heaven—from deity (the Gods or God) —that heaven decided the issue of fact. The ordeal is therefore often called *judicuum dei,* God's decision. But in some "primitive" communities, we find that the appeal was not to heaven but to a power residing in things—in fire, in water, in poison, and so on. Some anthropologists use the word *mana* to describe this latent power. *Mana* is supernatural, impersonal, non-human power.[10] Belief in such a power and in the possibility of its use in human affairs was a belief in magic. The ordeals, then, represent one aspect of a magico-religious attitude.

I want here, for the moment, to stress the more strictly magical aspects of the ordeals. Let us, then, inquire how and why "primitive" or "archaic" societies utilize magic. In this necessarily brief discussion, I shall rely largely on the writings of Malinowski.[11] His views need qualifications. For such qualifications, I refer you to Ruth Benedict's brilliant article.[12] I shall say a little something of her views later. But for my immediate purpose, Malinowski's portrayal of magic, slightly modified, will suffice. On that basis, I may summarize as follows:

Primitive man has a considerable amount of correct technical knowledge. He learns a deal, from observation, about his environment and how, by rationally-conceived techniques, to control it. Of the ways of domesticating plants and animals, of agriculture and husbandry, fishing, house-building, boat-making, he knows much. These techniques, for direct control of the environment, based upon observation, we might call "primitive science."

But there are forces at large that the so-called savage cannot thus control, evils that stalk him, perils which strike at his food supply, that capsize his boats, destroy his houses, take his life. There is "magic power" in things. That power, that *mana*, man feels he must learn to control. Not by the ordinary techniques; they fail him. And so, alongside "primitive science," we find the "savage" using magic. Where ignorance is thickest about the ways of things, where dangers

[10] See, e.g., Marett, *The Threshold of Religion* (1909).

[11] See especially, Malinowski, "Magic, Science and Religion," in the volume *Science, Religion and Reality* (Needham ed. 1925) 21; Malinowski, *A Scientific Theory of Culture* (1944). Malinowski revises the theory put forward by Frazer in his *Golden Bough*. Malinowski is somewhat critical of the *mana* theory.

[12] "Magic," 10 *Encyc. of Soc. Sciences* (1933) 39.

are the greatest, where luck plays the largest part—there magic is employed.

Magic, then, appears to be primitive man's ways of dealing with specific practical problems when he is in peril or in need, and his strong desires are thwarted because his rational techniques, based upon observation, prove ineffective. "We do not," says Malinowski, "find magic wherever the pursuit is certain, reliable and under the control of rational methods and technological processes . . . We do not find it wherever absolute safety eliminates any elements of foreboding." So, he continues, "in lagoon fishing, where man can rely completely upon his knowledge and skill, magic does not exist, while in the open-sea fishing, full of danger and uncertainty, there is extensive magical ritual to secure safety and good results."

When "primitive" man loses his way, when he reaches an impasse, when he is terrified by uncertainty, or baffled or trapped, he turns to magic. We can understand his mental and emotional processes if we observe similar conduct in some of those about us in our own society who seek to climb out of oppressing difficulties (such as economic problems, for instance) by the wish-route, or on what James called the faith-ladder, the rungs of which are: What I want *might* conceivably be true. It *may* be true. It *must* be true. It *is* true.

With "primitive" man, the wish-route to desired ends was overt, openly acknowledged, definitely crystallized and routinized. The words and gestures employed to evoke magical power were worked out in conventional patterns, prescribed by tradition. There was a fixation of beliefs in standardized spells, in elaborated rituals. To a considerable degree, magic came to be based on precedents, became a professional task, esoteric and unpracticed by the group at large.

Magic, then, was one of the ways of coping with practical problems. If we designate as "primitive science" the primitive arts of fishing, hunting, agriculture, and the like, so far as they are based on direct observation, then magic might be called "primitive pseudo-science." For magic, like science, is technological in a sense. It is, says Benedict, "essentially mechanistic," involving "a manipulation of the external world by techniques and formulae" that are assumed to "operate automatically." But, in its reliance on wishes, it departs from science. Primitive science, we are advised, "is founded on the conviction that experience, effort and reason are valid; magic on the belief that hope cannot fail, nor desire deceive."

Magic is stereotyped, wishful thinking applied to the overcoming of obstacles. It is the non-empirical, illusory, way of achieving practical aims. It is born of panic fear, of dread, of the felt need to believe that what is helpful can be and has been discovered, of driving, insistent, longings. "The integral cultural function of magic consists," it has been said, "in the bridging-over of gaps and inadequacies in highly important activities not yet completely mastered by man."

Thence the ordeal. What human contrivances are there, in litigation, for learning the truth about past events? How to ascertain whether men honestly tell what they know? What lie-detectors are available? What man can look into the mind of his neighbor? Lives and possessions, wives and honor, hang on the determination of whether a claimant in the judicial contest and his witnesses are telling the truth. Since a trial's just outcome depends on truth-telling, and since the outcome may deprive a man of his life, or his dearest possessions, successful perjury is as grave a danger as drought, disease, lightning or the fierce claws of wild beast. Leave to the inadequate judgments of mere human judges the testing of the truth-telling of witnesses, when life or property are at stake? By no means. There the human techniques fail. Then call in magic, the mystic power of fire, water, poison, the scales —summon that invisible force, by appropriate spells, to find out the truth mechanically. Magic, and nothing else, is needed in the difficult and dangerous task of discovering the guilty, of getting at the truth.

"Oh Fire," runs the ritual, "thou seest, even as a witness, into each human being's heart. Thou alone knowest that which mortals alone cannot know." This, you observe, is an expression of confidence in a power inherent in the object employed. The supernatural supplies a perfect, infallible, decision. The magical power is charged with revealing the truth. It is clairvoyant, as man is not. It penetrates into the secret places of the heart. What is private and hidden is revealed by the super-natural, the super-human.

Whenever religion absorbs much of "white" or "good" magic, when magic is, so to speak, deified, embodied in the gods or God, then deity takes the place of or supplements magic in the ordeals. The ordeals survive, but now it is largely with divine aid that they function. See the Germanic tribes emerging from quasi-primitive thoughtways under the influence of Christianity. Hear their priest's prayer when the ordeal of the morsel is used: "Holy Father, Omnipotent, eternal God, maker of all things visible and of all things spiritual; who dost look into secret places, and dost know all things; who dost search the hearts of men and dost rule as God, I pray thee: that whoever has committed or carried out or consented to that theft—that bread and cheese may not be able to pass through his throat."

The oath may be considered a late form of the ordeal. What is an oath? It is an imprecation, a curse. If I curse you, I call down evil upon you. But an oath, used in "primitive" dispute-deciding, is a self-curse, conditionally made. The oath-taker says, in effect, "If I do not tell the truth, may destruction or torments be visited upon me." The oath is an ordeal in words, instead of acts. Supernatural power vouches or refuses to vouch for the oath-taker. If he tells his story and goes unharmed, he has told the truth. If he lies, he will be stricken by the supernatural.

So the early trials by oath of the party, or of the party and his oath-helpers, were not at all the kind of trial conducted today. The oath was ipso facto (mechanically) efficacious. No more than in the ordeal by water did the judge weigh the evidence, consider the testimony and determine the credibility of the witnesses. If a party's witnesses swore according to the formula, making no slips of the tongue, that party won. For it was presumed that no man, having taken an oath, would dare swear falsely and thus risk supernatural vengeance. Supernatural power was, in effect, the judge of the facts.

However, skepticism arises. Men begin to doubt the efficacy of the ordeals. It becomes obvious that these performances can be humanly manipulated, that there can be fraud and favoritism involved in their use. There grow up what lawyers call the "rational" mode of trial. The stories told by witnesses are heard by human beings who, on the basis of these stories, are to ascertain the past facts. The acceptance of this method was a gradual process. For a long time the magical and the "rational" modes of trial both continue to be used—the ordeals for those cases where someone is charged with an act committed in a solitary forest, or at night, or in the interior of a house. In such cases, God, the all-seeing, all-knowing, ever-present, is still called to judge the truth.

In England, the jury trial finally put the ordeals to rout. The early days of the English jury are of interest here. It was imported into England by the Norman dukes, and more or less forced by them on the people of England as a desirable method of trial. At first, it was vastly unpopular.[13] Let Maitland tell the story: "Doubtless there was a very strong feeling that to try a man by a jury, when he had not submitted to be so tried, was thoroughly unjust," a feeling that the "mere oaths

[13] See Chapter VIII.

of . . . witnesses are not enough to fix a man with guilt, unless indeed he has voluntarily submitted his fate to this test; he ought to be allowed to demonstrate his innocence by supernatural means, by some such process as the ordeal . . . God may be for him, though his neighbors be against him. . . ."

Putting the matter in our modern terminology, our ancestors were unwilling to rely in all cases on the subjective reactions of any human being, on the unknowable vagaries of the "personal" element in fact-finding. Only with reluctance did they wholly give up their dependence on the supernatural in deciding the *F* in disputes. But in England, as on the Continent, trials before men, who determine the past facts, finally superseded the ordeals. The use of Magic and the appeals to Heaven appear to have been abandoned. They lent themselves to trickery and chicane. They seem absurd, irrational, to us today.

Let us, however, note one last obvious vestige of these primitive ideas. The witness in court today raises his right hand, or puts his hand on the good book and says, "I swear to tell the truth, the whole truth and nothing but the truth, so help me God." Is that a mere form? Must the witness believe in God? The answer in this country was clear until recently. In the early nineteenth century the courts said that the testimony of a witness could not be received unless he not only took an oath but believed that his oath was a solemn invocation upon him of the vengeance of omniscient deity if he did not tell the truth. Accordingly, atheists were disqualified as witnesses. For, as the courts often said, on the belief in an avenging deity "rests all our institutions and especially the distribution of justice between man and man." But that attitude is virtually obsolete today. Generally, the oath now merely signifies a knowledge of the solemnity of testimony and of the liability to indictment and conviction for perjury if the witness deliberately lies.

It would be pleasant to end here, to say, "We are now thoroughly rational. The sword and the scales do not today signify the substitution of magical settlement of quarrels for private wars. Our attitude towards our legal system is thoroughly non-magical." But I think that would be inaccurate reporting. Current views of the judicial process are, to a considerable extent, expressed in what appear to be highly sophisticated terms. But, as I shall try to show you, those views are still permeated with magic.

4

If you translate into our current speech-forms the "primitive" attitude operative when men used the ordeals, you will see that what bothered them was the imperfection of the art of psychology. They would not thus have phrased the matter. We have progressed at least this far beyond our early predecessors: We have a label, "psychology," for a mass of difficult problems. But the inadequacy of the art of psychology, with respect to that problem which bothered "primitive" and "archaic" societies, is today almost as great as it was then. We are still usually unable to look into the minds of others, still frequently stumped when it comes to learning whether witnesses are lying or innocently mistaken. The road to the subjective remains obstructed.

Our ancestors faced this problem squarely. They tried to meet it—with magic. Most of us today do not face it squarely. Most of us look at it obliquely, meet it with evasions, and, I think, with a sort of sophisticated verbalized magic—which we refuse to recognize as such.

In our modern method of trial, as I told you, there are two factors which make subjectivity unavoidable. The first relates to the witnesses. They do not reproduce mechanically the events which they saw and heard. Their sight and hearing are often faulty, and so are their memories. More than that, they often err in telling their stories in court. So here is one element of subjectivity. There is another, which, as I said, is less frequently recognized and acknowledged: The trial judges or juries are fallible witnesses of the fallible witnesses.

Consider, first, cases in which the second factor is absent: Even in upper courts, where all the testimony is in writing, the ablest judges often differ with one another about the facts of a case. Said Mr. Justice Miller, "In my experience in the conference room of the Supreme Court of the United States, which consists of nine judges, I have been surprised to find how readily those judges came to an agreement upon questions of law, and how often they disagree in regard to questions of fact." That point is neatly illustrated in a case which arose in 1908, United States v. Shipp.[14] Johnson, a Negro, was indicted in the Tennessee state court and convicted of rape. The United States Circuit Court denied his petition for habeas corpus. An appeal from this decision was allowed by the United States Supreme Court, which ordered the state sheriff to retain custody of Johnson, until the determination of the appeal. While the prisoner was in the custody of the sheriff, a

[14] 214 U.S. 386.

mob seized the prisoner and lynched him. An original proceeding was begun in the Supreme Court, charging the sheriff with contempt, in that he had aided, abetted and conspired with the mob which lynched the prisoner. The Supreme Court appointed a commissioner merely to take and report the testimony; (i.e., he was directed not to make any findings of fact of his own or to state any legal conclusions). Accordingly, he transmitted to the court a written record of the testimony. Briefs were filed, and the case was argued orally. The court split, five to three. Chief Justice Fuller wrote an opinion, concurred in by four other judges, holding the sheriff liable for contempt. One judge took no part. Mr. Justice Peckham filed a dissenting opinion which was concurred in by two other judges.

There was no disagreement as to any legal question (any *R*). The court divided solely on a question of fact. The majority opinion devoted seventeen pages to the discussion of the facts; the minority opinion, eight pages. The majority opinion stated: "Only one conclusion can be drawn from these facts, all of which are clearly established by the evidence—Shipp not only made the work of the mob easy, but in effect aided and abetted it." The minority opinion stated: "A careful consideration of the case leaves us with the conviction that there is not one particle of evidence that any conspiracy had ever been entered into or existed on the part of the sheriff, as charged against him."

This case illustrates how difficult it is to criticize a judge's statement of the facts, even when the testimony is entirely in writing. When a trial judge must find the facts from conflicting oral testimony of witnesses he heard, then criticism is far more difficult for anyone who has before him merely a printed or typewritten transcript. How, in such a case, is anyone to say that the trial judge's finding of facts is right or wrong? How can there be any objective means of testing the correctness of that finding? In a suit by Johnson, a switchman, against a railroad, Trial Judge White, after listening to the discrepant stories of witnesses for Johnson and the railroad, believes Johnson's witnesses; he therefore thinks, and finds as a fact, that Johnson lost his leg because the railroad had carelessly failed to repair a defective brake on a freight car. If another trial judge, Judge Black, had heard the same witnesses, he might reasonably have believed the railroad's witnesses; and he would then have thought, and found as a fact, that the railroad had repaired the brake. Certainly no one reading the printed record of the conflicting testimony would be in a position to challenge either judge's finding of facts.

Let us approach the problem from a somewhat different angle. Is there any standard of belief a trial court can employ when trying to determine the facts? We talk of the "weight" of the evidence, of "weighing" evidence, of the "preponderance" of the evidence. But can conflicting evidence be weighed? [15] Is there any accurate device for measuring which witnesses are worthy of belief? The courts and the great masters of evidence have said "No" to all these questions. "The reasons for believing particular witnesses or particular testimony in preference to others cannot be defined," said one court. "There is no standard for the sufficiency of evidence to induce belief," declared another court. The only standard, it has been said, is a "feeling of probability." But that feeling is subjective; it varies from man to man.

Wigmore has written a book—now in its third revised edition—on the Principles of Judicial Proof. That book, of over 1,000 pages, demonstrates that there are no principles of that kind, and probably never will be. For Wigmore confesses that the difficulty is that "belief is purely mental" (that is, subjective). Wigmore hoped to find scientific or logical "laws" for determining rationally "the net persuasive effect of a mixed mass of evidence." But, he tells us, there are no such "laws." There is, to use his phraseology, no scientific or logical "method of solving a complex mass of evidence in contentious litigation." He adds that such laws "will perhaps some day be discovered." He is not too sanguine in that hope. For "the data available from judicial annals . . . are almost always defective, in that the objective truth, necessary to test the correctness of any belief, can seldom be indubitably ascertained, as it often can be in the physical sciences. E.g., if we were to study one hundred murder trials, so as to ascertain some law of thought lurking in certain combinations of evidence, the very basis of that study, viz., the actual guilt or innocence of the accused, cannot usually be known to us, and our study is useless without that fact."

No means, then, have as yet been discovered, or are likely to be discovered, for ascertaining whether or to what extent the belief of the trial judge about the facts of a case corresponds to the objective

[15] For centuries on the European continent, and for a period in England, there prevailed a theory of the quantification of evidence; weight, measured in numerical terms, was assigned to the testimony of each type of witness. See Millar, in Engelmann, *History of Continental Civil Procedure* (1927) 41-49; Wigmore, *Evidence* (1940) VII, 241ff; Frank, *If Men Were Angels* (1942) 90-91.

Kenny, *Criminal Law* (1936) 456, says that at one time, under Canon Law, no Cardinal could be convicted of adultery except on the evidence of seven eye-witnesses.

Aquinas, in the *Summa Theologica*, says: "A bishop shall not be condemned save on the evidence of seventy-two witnesses. . . ."

facts as they actually occurred, when the witnesses disagree, and when some of the oral testimony, taken as true, will support the judge's conclusion. In other words, in such a case there is no objective measure of the accuracy of a judge's finding of the facts. There exists no yardstick for that purpose.

In a "contested" law-suit, therefore, with the witnesses in disagreement, usually no one can adequately criticize the trial judge's fact-finding. If, at the end of the trial, the trial judge says that Jones hit Smith, or that Mrs. Moriarity called Mrs. Flannagan a liar, or that old widow Robinson was insane when she made her will, or that Wriggle used fraud in inducing Simple to sign a contract—the judge's word goes. And the same would be true if, in most of those instances, the trial judge had found exactly the opposite to be the facts.

Do you see where we have arrived? We are at last honestly confronting the problem which drove our ancestors to the ordeals—to magic or to God. The development of our legal system can indeed be described in terms of an increasing tolerance of the human element in judicial dispute-deciding. That human element is unavoidable. It was present but unrecognized even in the ordeals; after all, a human being had to decide whether the perilous test had been successfully passed. It enters more obviously, once the so-called "rational" mode of trial is introduced. For legal rights are then dependent on human guesses about the facts of cases. And usually, in such circumstances, no one can tell what another human being will guess. Primitive man could say that legal rights were on the knees of the gods. We must say that they are on the knees of men—of the trial judges or the juries.

5

Many lawyers, I repeat, are reluctant to admit that state of affairs and its concomitant chanciness. Like "primitive" men, they consider that chanciness terrifying. "Primitive" man, to overcome his terror, used magic, openly and unashamed. Many modern lawyers use magic —without being aware of it. I mean that, in order to avoid facing up to disagreeable situations and difficulties in court-house government, they have contrived a description, and a theory, of its workings which do not jibe with its observable realities.

This modern legal magic will be found in books, written by profound legal thinkers, books sometimes labeled with the high-sounding names "legal philosophy" or "jurisprudence." The legal theory of the pundits carries over to the less reflective lawyers. They, in turn, invoke that theory when explaining our courts' operations to non-lawyers. So that, if at the core of the pundits' legal theory we find magical notions, those magical notions will be likely to affect public attitudes towards, and beliefs about, our judicial system.

What, then, is the generally accepted legal theory? As I have said, it runs something like this: The basic component of court decisions consists of the legal rules. In so far as those rules are crisp and definite, declares the theory, future court decisions usually are nicely forseeable. Some few of the rules, the *R*'s, are indefinite, not finally fixed and settled. To that limited extent, prediction of future decisions is difficult. This lack of precision of some few of the *R*'s is, the pundits declare, virtually the only impediment to precise predictions. So that, whatever little uncertainty there may be about how courts will deal with one's legal rights, it is, for the most part, a function of the uncertainty in a relatively few legal rules. So runs the theory.

Here, for instance, is a considered statement by Dickinson, a highly respected legal thinker who has written much concerning the judicial process:[16] "It is submitted," he declares, "that the sound way to anticipate a future decision is to attempt to put oneself in the place of the judge . . . who will actually make the decision." If, so doing, one knows "the rule . . . which exists for a case of the kind in question, . . . a fairly safe prediction may often be hazarded as to the judge's decisional behavior without knowledge at all of the more esoteric factors" such as "the social, economic, political, psychological, physiological and other pressures operating unconsciously" on him.

Dickinson's statement would be correct, on the whole, if the *F* factor could always be taken for granted. Since, however, in many cases the *F* cannot be taken for granted, but is in sharp dispute, Dickinson's thesis is anything but correct. It is hopelessly defective because it erroneously assumes that most decisions derive directly from the *R*'s without the intervening necessity of ascertaining the *F*.

That thesis would be tenable only as a "fiction." That is, it would at most be proper to make use of the experimental device of saying: "Let us, for the time being, talk as if established rules were always the controlling influences affecting trial-court decisions, although we know perfectly well that what we are saying is untrue. For the purpose of bringing out one aspect of the decisional process, we will temporarily exaggerate that aspect. Let's pretend that all other factors are

16 Dickinson, "Legal Rules," 79 *Un. of Pa. L. Rev.* (1931) 833.

always subordinate and unimportant. But we will never forget that, at best, we are telling a 'convenient lie.'" In other words, in thus describing how trial courts decide cases, we would be knowingly falsifying, treating a single factor as if it were the sole factor. But we would do so only in so far and as long as such a conscious fabrication increased our knowledge of or means of improving the decisional process. If and whenever our fiction turned out to be of little use, or harmful, we would abandon it. But Dickinson and those who agree with him have not so stated their thesis.

Nor have they advanced it as an hypothesis, i.e., they have not said: "Perhaps the legal rules are always the dominant influences which induce decisions. Let us test out this hypothesis, by checking it against court-room happenings." They have announced their thesis either as a dogma or as a verified, tested, statement of what does actually happen. One may doubt whether it can legitimately function as a sufficiently useful fiction to warrant its use. As an hypothesis, a dogma, or a piece of verified knowledge, it cannot pass muster. It is, then, a myth —a statement of purported fact contrary to the truth, which deceives the person making the statement, an elaborated bit of self-deception which also deceives others who believe it.[17] In short, it is a magical device.

Again, Dickinson asserts that any precise legal rule operates "with the deadly inevitability of a guillotine"; that the application of such a rule is "practically automatic"; that, consequently, the outcome of a suit involving such a rule is easily predictable; and that, therefore, the existence of such exact rules "is one of the greatest preventives of litigation." That assertion is unfounded. Nothing could be more precise than the rule which requires driving on the right side of the street. Yet, as anyone who visits our trial courts can see, there is a huge volume of litigation which turns entirely on the question whether that rule (or some similar simple traffic rule) has, in fact, been violated. In such law-suits, the crucial factor is not the legal rule, but solely the "facts." The definiteness of such *R*'s does not prevent law-suits, nor render easy the prediction of trial-court decisions. Indeed, the very precision of a rule may be a guide for the unscrupulous lawyer: It tells him just how

[17] For more extended discussions of fictions, dogmas and myths, see, e.g., Vaihinger, *The Philosophy of 'As If'* (1925); Tourtoulon, *Philosophy in the Development of Law* (1922) 385ff, 644-53; Frank, *Law and the Modern Mind* (1930) 37-40, 167, 288, 312-22, 327; Frank, *Fate and Freedom* (1945) 184-85; Fuller, "Legal Fictions," 25 *Ill. L. Rev.* (1930-1931) 363, 513, 877.

to coach witnesses. It furnishes a perjury chart. It helps to canalize lying testimony. The courts, for that reason, have refused to make a crisp rule as to what does or does not constitute fraud. One court has said that "were courts to cramp themselves by defining [fraud] with a hard-and-fast definition, their jurisdiction would be cunningly circumvented by new schemes beyond the definition. Messieurs, the fraud-doers, would like nothing half so well as for courts to say they would go thus far and no further in its pursuit." In sum, Dickinson's thesis, because of its complete divergence from court-room realities, I call a beautiful specimen of sheer legal magic (or legal rule-magic). Yet it has been unquestioningly accepted by many lawyers, forgetful of the vagaries of trials and trial-court fact-finding.

Roscoe Pound, another highly respected legal thinker, writing of court decisions, states that, from the public judicial records, always "one may find exactly . . . how the questions of fact were determined . . . in the form of special findings of fact" by the jury or trial judge; that always the judge's findings are accompanied by a report published by the judge of the legal rules applied by him; and that, consequently, "the materials for criticism . . . of judicial decisions are always available and readily accessible." [18] That statement, widely quoted, is singularly inaccurate. For trial judges often render decisions without reporting their views of the facts or publishing any explanation whatever; [19] and most decisions in jury cases are similarly unexplained.[20] Pound has also written that rigid legal rules "secure us against the well-meant ignorance of the weak judge and are our mainstay against improper motives on the part of those who administer justice." [21] Patently, that statement does not click with observable court-house realities. It would be true if, and only if, there were no *F* in the decisional process. But since there is such an *F,* and that *F* is often a subjective matter, since trial judges often do not report the subjective *F,* and since, when they do, usually one cannot effectively criticize that *F,* it is not at all true, it is pure magic, to say that rigid legal rules can effectively safeguard us against judicial ignorance or weakness or improper judicial motives.

Even more strikingly does legal rule-magic show up when Pound purports to describe how legal rules operate in two different kinds of

[18] "For the Minority Report," see 27 *Amer. Bar Ass'n. J.* (1941) 664.

[19] See further, Chapter XII.

[20] See further, Chapter VIII.

[21] "Justice According to Law," 13 *Col. L. Rev.* (1913) 696. To the same effect, see Llewellyn, *The Bramble Bush* (1930) 62.

cases:[22] (1) The first kind relates to such matters as fraud, good faith, negligence, and the duties of trustees. There, says Pound, the courts can and should consider the uniqueness of each particular suit; for instance, "no two cases of negligence have been alike or ever will be." (2) But, he says, vastly different are suits dealing with "property" or "commercial transactions." There, according to Pound, the legal rules are, as they must be, precise, "authoritatively prescribed in advance and mechanically applied." The "commercial world" demands such precise rules because "no one . . . engages in complex commercial undertakings trusting to" decisions which may vary according to unique features of particular cases. There "is nothing unique" about promissory notes. "All such cases are alike," Pound asserts; they "admit of no individualization."

That description of the effect of strict rules on decisions in this second kind of case is magical, i.e., wholly at odds with what anyone can see daily in the trial courts. As I put it, when criticizing Pound in 1931:[23] "In cases involving . . . promissory notes . . . , it is always possible to introduce some question of fact relating to fraud, negligence, mistake, alteration, or estoppel. In most 'contested' cases, one side or the other usually injects such a question. Suppose such a case is tried before a jury and, on the question of fact, 'goes to the jury.' Is it not absurd to say that the rules will then be mechanically applied? Anyone who has ever watched a jury trial knows that the rules often become a mere subsidiary detail, part of a meaningless but dignified liturgy recited by the judge in the physical presence of the jury and to which the jury pays scant heed.[24] To say that fixed rules invariably govern property and commercial cases when the jury sits and decides is to deny the plain truth. The pulchritude of the plaintiff or his religion or his economic status or the manners of the respective attorneys, or the like, may well be the determining factor inducing the decision. And if a judge sits and decides without a jury, and similar questions of fact are raised, will the crystallized unalterable rules, about identical . . . promissory notes, mechanically produce the decision? Surely not. Of course, if the judge writes an opinion, the stereotyped rules will appear in the opinion. But the judge will decide one way or the other on the 'facts,'

[22] Pound, *Interpretations of Legal History* (1923) 121ff, 154-55; Pound, *An Introduction to the Philosophy of Law* (1922) 142ff; Pound, "The Theory of Judicial Decision," 36 *Harv. L. Rev.* (1922) at 851ff, 915ff, 951ff, 957ff.

See Frank, *Law and the Modern Mind* (1930) 208-13, 216; Frank, *If Men Were Angels* (1942) 64-65, 341-345.

[23] Frank, "Are Judges Human," 80 *Un. of Pa. L. Rev.* (1931) at 235-36.

[24] See further Chapter VIII.

and those 'facts' vary with the particular case and with the judge's impressions of those 'facts'—although the instrument in suit is a promissory note precisely like every other promissory note. The truth is that the talk about mechanical operation of rules in property, or commercial, or other cases is not at all a description of what really happens in courts in 'contested' cases. It is a dogma based upon inadequate observation. For it fails to take into account the important circumstance that any future law suit about a piece of property or a commercial contract can be 'contested,' and that, if it is contested, questions of fact can be raised involving the introduction of conflicting testimony. . . . The 'facts,' as we have seen, may be crucial when, as is often the case, a question of 'fact' is injected into litigation. . . . And those facts are, inter alia, a function of the attention of the judge. Certain kinds of witnesses may arouse his attention more than others. Or may arouse his antipathies or win his sympathy. The 'facts,' it must never be overlooked, are not objective. They are what the judge thinks they are. And what he thinks they are depends on what he hears and sees as the witnesses testify—which may not be, and often is not, what another judge would hear and see. Assume ('fictionally') the most complete rigidity of the rules relating to commercial transactions. . . . Still, since the 'facts' are only what the judge thinks they are, the decision will vary with the judge's apprehension of the facts. The rules, that is, do not produce uniformity of decisions in . . . 'contested' cases, but only in that portion of opinions containing the rules. Judge Alpha may try a 'contested' case relating to a promissory note and decide for the holder. If Judge Beta tried the same case he might decide for the maker. The opinions of Judges Alpha and Beta would contain identical rules. That, and little more, is what truth there is in the dogma about the non-uniqueness of promissory notes in 'contested' cases."

The notion of rules "mechanically applied"—of rules that operate "automatically"—here we hark back to the "mechanical" magic of the ordeals. Perhaps with something of the sort in mind, Bentham in 1826 referred to "Decision without Thought, or Mechanical Judicature." In 1871, Jhering ridiculed the conception of a "judging machine" into the front of which a case is inserted and which then ejects a judgment.[25]

[25] See Jhering, Law As Means to an End (translated 1924) 295. In a later writing, on The Heaven of Juristic Concepts, he delightfully satirized "legal mathematics"; see Seagle, 13 Un. of Chicago L. Rev. (1945) 70, 89.

As to vestiges in Jhering of the sort of legal thinking he criticized, see Frank, Law and The Modern Mind (1930) 218-221; Nussbaum, Fact Research in Law, 40 Col. L. Rev. (1940) 189, 190-191.

In 1906, Kantorowicz derided the idea of a court as a legal slot-machine. In 1908, Pound (citing Kantorowicz) wrote critically of "mechanical jurisprudence." But Pound, for all that, is unwilling wholly to forego the dream of such a magical process.

Cardozo is properly esteemed as one of our most distinguished legal thinkers as well as one of the very ablest of upper-court judges. I can bear witness to the incalculable value of his writings to at least one upper-court judge. Yet he gave much aid and comfort to the devotees of legal magic. In his off-the-bench legal writings, his major interest was in the development of legal rules and doctrines at the hands of judges. Alarmed by the apprehension that his writings would create the impression of an extensive legal uncertainty, he took pains to say that, while there was some difficulty in predicting court decisions, it was restricted largely to what he termed "exceptional" cases, cases in which, because of social change or the emergence of novel problems, the courts altered the legal rules. But the great body of the legal rules, he maintained, "have such an element of certainty that in a vast majority of instances, prediction ceases to be hazardous for the trained and expert judgment."[26] Which is to say that a competent lawyer can predict the outcome of most lawsuits. Indeed, Cardozo declared: "Nine-tenths, perhaps more, of the cases that come before a court are predetermined—predetermined in the sense that they are predestined. . . ."[27]

The key to this surprising conclusion is to be found in another statement Cardozo made: "In countless litigations," he wrote, "the law is so clear that judges have no discretion."[28] To clarify that statement, I must explain what he meant by "discretion": Some legal rules are purposely vague, wide, loose. Illustrative are rules which contain elastic words like "good faith," "fair," "reasonable."[29] When a trial judge

[26] Cardozo, "Jurisprudence," an address delivered in 1932, reprinted in *Selected Writings of Cardozo* (1947) 7, 22. In the sentence from which the quoted statement is taken, Cardozo included rules which involve "discretion." So much the more, then, should he be understood as saying that prediction is easy when a court applies a rule so worded as to exclude "discretion."

[27] Cardozo, *The Growth of the Law* (1924) 60.

[28] Cardozo, *The Nature of the Judicial Process* (1921) 160.

[29] The legal generalizations are sometimes subdivided. Pound, for instance, calling them legal "precepts," divides them as follow: (1) "Detailed rules . . . , precisely determining what shall take place upon a precisely detailed state of fact." (2) Legal principles; they are "general premises for . . . . judicial . . . reasoning, . . . made use of to supply new rules, to interpret old ones, to meet new situations, to measure the scope and application of rules and standards and to reconcile them when they conflict or overlap." (3) Legal conceptions which "are more or less exactly defined

applies such a rule, he has considerable choice or leeway to decide one way or another. That leeway is labelled "discretion." If the trial judge does not go beyond the bounds of that leeway, an upper court, on appeal, will not disturb his decision. Most of the legal rules, however, are so precisely worded that apparently the judge has no choice, no "discretion." Such rules tell him that, if the facts are thus-and-so, one and only one decision is open to him. Cardozo had in mind those precise rules when he said that "in countless litigations, the law [the rule] is so clear that the judges have no discretion."

The trouble with that statement is that trial judges have another kind of "discretion" which I have already described but which Cardozo ignored: When the oral testimony is in conflict as to a pivotal fact-issue, the trial judge is at liberty to choose to believe one witness rather than another. In other words, in most cases the trial judges have an amazingly wide "discretion" in finding the facts, a discretion with which upper courts, on appeals, seldom interfere, so that, in most instances this "fact discretion" is almost boundless. And this is true regardless of the precision of the applicable legal rule (as, for example, the rule about driving on the right side of the road). As one court put it, "the word 'discretion' is properly enough used to express the judicial judgment in discriminating as to weight and cogency between different witnesses . . . which must be exercised in reaching any conclusion of fact from evidence." [30]

Cardozo was thinking solely of "rule discretion." He overlooked the immense area of "fact discretion." He was, then, exploiting legal magic (rule-magic) when he said that most legal rules "have such an element of certainty" that well trained lawyers can predict most decisions.

Cardozo's leaning to legal rule-magic was due to the fact that, having

---

types, to which we refer cases or by which we classify them, so that when a state of facts is classified we may attribute thereto the legal consequences attaching to the type." (4) Legal standards of conduct (such as "due care" or "good faith"). See Pound, *An Introduction to the Philosophy of Law* (1922) 115ff; Pound, "The Administrative Application of Legal Standards," 15 *Amer. Bar Ass'n. Rep.* (1919) 445.

As in this book I am writing non-technically, I shall employ no such subdivisions, but shall generally refer to all the legal generalizations as "legal rules."

[30] Nash v. Fries, 129 Wis. 120, 108 N.W. 210, 211.

In Weiler v. U.S., 323 U.S. 606, 608, the Court said: "Triers of fact in our tribunals are, with rare exceptions, free in the exercise of their honest judgment to prefer the testimony of a single witness to that of many." In Woey Ho v. U.S., 109 F. 888, 890 (C.C.A. 9), the court said: "The question whether a witness is credible must ordinarily be determined by the tribunal before whom the witness appears, and in the decision of which that tribunal must necessarily be vested with a very wide discretion."

See also, Frank, *If Men Were Angels* (1942) 91-92; Frank, "Words and Music," 47 *Col. L. Rev.* (1947) 1259, 1273-74; Wigmore, *Evidence* (3d ed. 1940) Vol. VII, 244-45.

spent most of his professional life, as lawyer and judge, in upper courts, when he spoke of prediction he meant the prediction of upper-court decisions.[31] Indeed, he narrowed the meaning of the phrase "judicial process"—which had theretofore been defined to include "all the steps in a case from its commencement to its conclusion"[32]—so that it included virtually nothing but what occurs in upper courts. He excluded, as if non-existent, the events occurring in the trial stage of thousands of cases, events which occur in trial courts but never in upper courts: the witnesses testifying, the lawyers examining and cross-examining the witnesses, the jurors listening to the witnesses and to the arguments of the lawyers, the trial judge (when sitting without a jury) passing on the credibility of the witnesses' oral testimony. The omission of all these phenomena—familiar to every trial judge, trial lawyer, and newspaper reporter who "covers the courts"—renders Cardozo's exposition, as a description of how courts work, seriously misleading. Eminently satisfactory as an account of appellate-court ways, it is bizarre as an account of trial-court ways—as bizarre as would be an account of manners at Buckingham Palace if taken as also applicable to rush-hour behavior in the New York subways.[33]

In 1928, Dean Leon Green, an enemy of legal magic, wrote that "the control of judges is not to be found in rules. . . ."[34] Green was saying, in effect, that the rules are but one component of decisions, and that, in another component—fact-finding—there often inheres an externally uncontrollable factor which involves immense "discretion." In 1931,

[31] In *The Nature of the Judicial Process* (1921) 163, he disclosed how little he was interested in the findings of fact in trial courts: "In what I have said, I have thrown, perhaps too much into the background and the shadow the cases where the controversy turns not upon the rule of law but upon its application to the facts. Those cases, after all, make up the bulk of the business of the courts. They are important for the litigants concerned in them. They call for intelligence and patience and reasonable discernment on the part of the judges who must decide them. But they leave jurisprudence where it stood before." So he does not further discuss such cases which "make up the bulk of the business of the courts" and are vitally important "for litigants," because he is preoccupied with "jurisprudence." And "jurisprudence," as he restricts it, is confined to the construction and revision of legal rules and principles.

[32] See U.S. v. Murphy, 82 F. 893, 899; State v. Guilbert, 56 Ohio St. 575, 47 N.E. 551, 557; Blair v. Maxbass Security Bank, 44 N.D. 12, 176 N.W. 98, 100; cf. Wayman v. Southard, 10 Wheat. 1, 27.

[33] For more elaborate discussions of Cardozo, see Frank, "Cardozo and The Upper-Court Myth," 13 *Law and Contemporary Problems* (1948) 369; Frank, *If Men Were Angels* (1942) 285-293; Frank, *Law and the Modern Mind* (6th Printing, 1949) Preface, xxv-xxvi.

[34] Whenever in this book I cite or quote Green, I am referring to Green, *Judge and Jury* (1930).

Morris Cohen (a brilliant philosopher who has written much on legal topics) severely criticized Green's statement. Cohen asserted, as if that clinched the matter, "Uncontrolled discretion of judges would make modern complex life unbearable."[35] Isn't that a curious position? Apparently, according to Cohen, the rules always do control judges, since it would be "unbearable" if they didn't. But as, in fact-finding, such discretion is a part of modern life, what shall we do? Shall we say it "would be unbearable" if it existed, and then deny its existence? To do so is to practice magic, to make one's wish the father of one's thought. Apparently Cohen would have it that what one considers desirable, what one thinks ought to be, one must take as true. In other words, "unbearable" actualities must be refused recognition. What Sir Frederick Pollock observed in another context is apposite here: When "a man cries aloud that something is 'unthinkable,' his real meaning is apt to be that he is afraid of it." Cohen's position reminds one of Bernard Shaw's picture of a false ideal as a mask for disguising a terrifying reality, "a fancy picture invented" as a "mask for the reality which in its nakedness is intolerable" to the mask-maker. Shaw differentiates false and true ideals: The first are existing realities with their masks on. The second are "the future possibilities which the masks depict." Those future possibilities, says Shaw, can be realized only "by tearing the mask and the thing masked asunder." Cohen, clinging to the mask, a magical device, grew wrathy at efforts to sever it from the masked reality. His attitude recalls Holmes's comment: "We fear to grant power and are unwilling to recognize it when it exists."[36]

Once, in a brief passage written in 1931,[37] Cohen did grant that a judge may decide a case erroneously because of his mistaken "subjective impressions" of the facts. But Cohen added that "we can see" when a decision has been influenced by "facts which . . . should not have been decisive." He did not stop to inform us how "we can see" the operation of the hidden "subjective impressions" which the trial judge does not disclose. Cohen, that is, ignored the difficulties arising

[35] Cohen, *Law and the Social Order* (1933) 362.

[36] Tyson & Brother v. Banton, 273 U.S. 418, 445.

[37] Cohen, "Mr. Justice Holmes and the Nature of Law," reprinted in Cohen, *Law and The Social Order* (1933) 198, 217-218; "It is not at all certain that a similar state of facts in two cases will always produce a similar decision. When the judge is mistaken, . . . it is clearly not the objective facts but the judge's subjective impressions and reflections that operate. . . . But obviously a court may have been unwise precisely because, like a jury, it allowed itself to be influenced by the impact of present but irrelevant facts which on subsequent reflection we can see should not have been decisive."

from the subjectivity of fact-finding when the oral testimony is in conflict. This appears in a remark he made in 1932 that, "The actual decision . . . may be judged by norms applicable to it, such as logical consistency, and fidelity to established rules or principles of communal welfare." And surely legal rule-magic is manifest in his statement that "to the scientific student of law, the significance of any decision is the rule that it embodies." [38]

Hexner, like Cohen, recently declared prediction of decisions easily possible because "there is an adequate perceivableness of the legal rules . . . ," and because "experience shows that, in the prevailing majority of cases, the human mind recognizes whether the individual decision corresponds [approximately] to the legal rules." But Hexner, like Cohen, neglecting the nature of the *F* factor when orally-testifying witnesses disagree, fails to inform us how this "recognition" of correspondence between rule and decision can be tested. Another writer, Timasheff, is similarly silent about the *F*'s when he says that those who, like Green and me, stress the "variable factors" affecting decisions, overlook the "constant factor" which, he maintains, is ultimately "decisive" in "routine cases"—namely the "tendency of [divers] judges to apply the same . . . rules." [39]

In 1946, Patterson published a second edition of his book, *An Introduction to Jurisprudence.* In its two hundred and twenty-three pages, all the passages, scattered here and there, which treat of trials, total up to about three pages. One such passage reads: "In the 1920's, one sometimes heard the sophisticated question, was X convicted of murdering Y because he did the deed, or because certain witnesses swore that they saw X run out with a smoking revolver from a room in which Y was found shot to death by such a revolver?" Now why does Patterson speak of such doubts as "cynical?" Pretty plainly be-

[38] Cohen, *Law and the Social Order* (1933) 356. In 1937, Cohen seemed to have come somewhat closer to judicial realities. Writing of Pound, he said: "He denounces the law without rules as Cadi justice (which ignores the fact that in a simple community, governed by custom and the Koran, the rules are well known). Yet, in insisting on the element of judicial discretion and on the presence in the law of standards [i.e., broad, flexible legal precepts], he admits other elements than rules or principles. It is therefore hard to see the difference between Cadi justice and a judge or jury exercising . . . discretion." Cohen, in 2 *Law: A Century of Progress* (1937) at 298-299.

Perhaps Cohen there recognized the breadth of "fact discretion"; if so, these remarks fight with those in his earlier writings. Perhaps, however, he meant merely "rule discretion." That this is true is indicated by his exposition of "discretion" in his article, "Rule versus Discretion," reprinted in Cohen, *Law and the Social Order* (1933) 258.

See further discussion of Cohen in Chapter XIV.

[39] As to "routine cases," see discussion of Cook, Chapter XXIII.

cause he finds such doubts unpleasant—and therefore wants to give the doubters a bad name. The truth is that a conviction of murder does signify, at best, no more than that the trial judge or jury believed the testimony of some witnesses rather than that of others; but the believed witnesses may have lied or been honestly mistaken. Patterson's characterization of the resultant doubts as "cynical" discloses his unwillingness to face courageously the occurrence of such tragedies, an unwillingness, I suggest, traceable to an addiction to legal magic. His will to believe that subjectivity has relatively little importance in the decisional process has induced him to look away from the realities of trial-court fact-finding, to dwell on legal rules.

I could quote dozens of similar remarks by eminent, legal scholars and lawyers. Back of all such statements is the magical notion that uniformity in the use of precise legal rules must yield approximate uniformity in the decisions of specific cases, if only the judges conduct themselves properly. These legal thinkers say or imply that the only real leeway for the judges is in the rules: If the legal rules are tight and neat, then, if a judge is intelligent and behaves himself, his decision can be predicted; and, if he doesn't so behave himself, his misconduct will be glaringly obvious to third persons.

I hope that by now you perceive the fallacy of these notions. Remember the many cases, reported by Borchard, where innocent men were convicted of crimes. Here is Jones, charged with a theft, but innocent. He is acquitted. Here is Campbell, charged with the same crime, to which the very same legal rule applied. Although also guiltless, he was convicted. Why? Solely because the trial court mistook the facts. Such fact-mistakes are not confined to criminal cases. They can occur in any kind of law-suit. And no legal rules can prevent them.

Legal rules, therefore, will not suffice to control the trial courts, even if those rules are applied conscientiously. You cannot control such courts unless you can also control their fact-finding. But that you usually can't do. For the process of fact-finding is altogether too subjective and, consequently, too elusive. It is "un-ruly." The refusal to recognize such unruliness constitutes modern legal magic. It stems from a "desire to be deceived." [40]

[40] Said Bishop Butler long ago: "Things and actions are what they are, and the consequences of them will be what they will be; why, then, should we desire to be deceived?"

V. WIZARDS AND LAWYERS

I TRUST the reader will understand what I mean by designating as "magical" the statements of the legal thinkers I have been quoting. The statements are not based upon actual observation. And yet they are not deliberate falsifications. These assertions concerning the efficacy of the legal rules are reached by the wish-route; they derive not from experience but from wishes. They are magical verbal devices for concealing what I have stressed—that one's rights to life, liberty or property are subject to the effect of such variable factors as crooked lawyers, crooked witnesses, mistaken witnesses, absence or death of witnesses, loss of documents, competence of lawyers, mistaken judges, biased judges, inattentive judges, stupid judges, crooked judges, inattentive juries, biased juries.

The essential function of such verbal legal magic is exactly the function of magic in primitive communities—namely, "to end the uneasiness which a man would experience in the presence of disconcerting phenomena," to supply him with grounds for expecting victories over the causes of his fright. These practitioners of modern legal magic desire a legal system in which there is relatively little of chance, contingency. They are afraid to admit to themselves that such is not the essential nature of our legal system. They want to believe that their desires are realized. Instead of saying, "This is what I *wish would happen* in court," they say, "This is what usually *does happen* in court." They run away from a close inspection of the actual legal world, because such inspection would compel them to confess to themselves that that world does not meet their desires.

They are frightened by the unavoidable reliance, in attempting to ascertain the facts of law-suits, on the reactions of fallible humans. They fear the risk involved; and that fear drives them to conceal the inescapable realities of trials. Where "primitive" man used fire or water, or the scales, they invoke the legal rules or some uniformities they discern behind the rules.[1]

[1] "The only value of the Pound-Dickinson axioms [discussed in the previous chapter] is the doubtful one that they mesh with ancient fears and antiquated hopes." Frank, Mr. Justice Holmes and Non-Euclidean Legal Thinking, 17 Cornell L.Q. (1932) at 582.

If you point out to them that, in many particular instances, their theory does not work out in experience, their response is much like that of "primitive" man, of whom it has been said, "Should his fetishes fail him, he will not rail against the belief that has played him false. He will regard his failure rather as a confirmation of his faith and it is himself he will accuse for not having been able to utilize what magic had placed at his disposal." In other word, they say that the theory is sound, and that the trouble is solely in those who apply it.

Consider Goodhart, acclaimed in England and this country as a safe-and-sound legal thinker. In a long essay ardently defending what I describe as legal magic, he characteristically disposes of a grave doubt about its reliability. He says that, often, "we are bound by the facts as seen by the judge," with the result, Goodhart concedes, that the judge, even if he sticks to the legal rules, may be able "deliberately or by inadvertence" to decide a case erroneously "by basing his decision upon facts stated by him as real . . . but actually non-existent." That admission, one would think, would fatally impair the theory that settled rules usually render it easy to predict decisions. But Goodhart brushes off that doubt. In all seriousness, he writes that, according to the "theory" of our legal system, "judges do not make mistakes . . . of fact." In other words, you must disregard any evidence that rule-magic does not work as advertised. If the realities are out of line with the theory, that is just too bad for the realities. At all costs, retain the theory, applying impeccable logic to assumptions which fly in the face of the actual.

Buckland reasons similarly.[2] He says that the existence of a legal right does not depend on whether a court will or will not enforce it. He insists that anyone who asserts that a man has no legal right—say, to a house—until a court has passed on that right, resembles a child who thinks that an electric switch is "all there is" to electric light, because the child, seeing that the existence of the light depends on turning on the switch, ignores the fact that the switch is merely a device by which the organization behind the light is controlled. "The judge too is merely a device," says Buckland, "to control the working of the institution we call law. . . . The judge is a concession to the human intellect." A "judge . . . has to turn out the legal result much as a calculating machine turns out the result of complex numerical data. No doubt he is not nearly so infallible as the machine, but he is the best we can do. . . . The fact that the judge may go wrong is a

[2] Buckland, Some Reflections on Jurisprudence (1945) 97-106.

defect in the device; it is not his essential function." Buckland's position, in short, is this: Because "to go wrong" is not a court's "essential function," a court's denial forever of a man's legal right to a house, due to the court's "going wrong," does not extinguish that legal right, since that right exists in legal theory, although for all practical purposes it is dead. It is as if one said that, when a physician, by administering a certain drug, which in theory should cure his patients, killed them, those disasters had little significance, because the physician's "essential function" is to cure not kill, and that in theory the patients still lived.

Belief in the continued aliveness of legal rights which are dead in fact has no place except in a world of magic. If we live in such a world—a world of phantasms or make-believes treated as the actual world—"we no longer have to master the outer world and to overcome the resistance of its objects," says Schuetz.[3] "What occurs in the outer world no longer . . . puts a limit on our possible accomplishments." True, the fantast, living in his world of phantasms, is confronted at times with the realities of the actual world. But he regards them as phantasms, not as realities. To Don Quixote, the windmills against which he tilts are not windmills but giants. There are, writes Schuetz, no imagined giants in his world, only real giants. When his giants act like windmills, Don Quixote does not submit to the "explosion of experience." He "does not acknowledge his delusion, and does not admit that the attacked objects have always been windmills and never giants." He gives the fact of windmills an interpretation according to the theory of his fantast's world. "He explains it by the theory that, in order to vex him, his arch-enemy . . . must have transmogrified . . . the real giants into windmills." By reaching this conclusion, he has "definitely withdrawn the accent of reality" from the actual world and "has bestowed such an accent upon the world of his imageries;" converting the realities of the actual world into unrealities, illusions, he gets rid of them, shoves them under the rug.

Ruth Benedict, who notes that those who utilize magical techniques "rely upon wish fulfilments rather than upon mundane labor in order to attain their ends," says that magic has a striking "analogy with neurotic behavior." The "usual course" of magic in any culture "has been to erect in a neurotic manner an . . . edifice of ceremonial by means of which . . . the object of dread [is] pushed off the scene or brought back in some more acceptable guise. Even in regions where magic as an

[3] "On Multiple Realities," 5 *Phil. and Phenom. Research* (1945) 533, 535ff.

objectification of panic is balanced by its use as a control over the external world, the social control it exercises is characteristically through the institutionalizing of a fear neurosis."

Let us follow that lead. The neurotic and the insane are, says Gardner Murphy, like the rest of us—simply "more so." Each one of us "normal" folks has tendencies which, were they to become more pronounced, would be diagnosed as symptoms of a serious abnormality. So any of us may be described as a mild case of paranoia, or melancholia, etc. In that sense, a magic-addict betrays schizophrenic attributes. The legal-magic mongers might then be described by a wag as mildly schizoid, since they insist on portraying as existent a legal system which plainly does not exist. For the real schizophrenic, the psychiatrists say, "lives in a world of words, which he so completely identifies with—or mistakes for—reality, that reality, as others know it, hardly exists for him. The question as to whether his statements are true . . . simply doesn't arise, so far as he is concerned, because he takes it for granted that his statements are absolutely true. . . . The maladjustive significance of words gone wild, as seen in the language of schizophrenia," writes Johnson, "lies mainly in the fact that assumptions and beliefs go unchecked. They are not tested against non-verbal observation and experience, because they are identified, in value, with observation and experience."[4] Perhaps the modern magical legal thinkers resemble —remotely, to be sure—the case, reported by a psychiatrist, of a man who wrote the word "beefsteak" on a piece of paper and then ate the paper.

Analogous, too, is this tendency, common to all of us but often peculiarly pronounced in the "abnormal mind": A particular group of ideas, greatly over-valued, takes on, as it were, an independent life of its own; there develops a sort of amnesia of facts not associated with the favored group of ideas.

I submit that our early predecessors, when they had recourse to the ordeals, were, in one respect, wiser than these brilliant moderns. Those early predecessors were aware that, no matter how clean-cut the legal rules might be, judicial decisions were bound to be uncertain—just to the extent that the actual facts were not certain to be proved in litigation. They understood, too, that, if a human being, even if you called him a judge, found the facts, then the facts would often be at large, and that therefore the decisions would often be unpredictable. They

[4] *People in Quandaries* (1946) 274-275.

correctly recognized that, no matter how much the rules, the *R*'s, were nailed down, the *D*'s were on the loose unless you nailed down the *F*'s. They erred only in their belief that by magic, or God's aid, they could nail down the *F*'s.

Much of our contemporary legal theory has gone astray through neglecting the critical significance of the *F*'s. Surely we can learn something here from so-called primitive man: Had you asked him what would happen if magic or Deity failed him, and if consequently the *F*'s were dubious, he would have answered, in his way, that then many law-suits would be gambles, that the outcome of many court-room fights, and therefore many legal rights, would be even more risky than the unregulated physical combats for which litigation was a substitute.

2

One great aid to modern legal magic has been the word "law." That word drips with ambiguity. But it has a traditionally emotive quality which makes it highly serviceable to the legal magicians. There are dozens of discrepant definitions of that word.[5] However, almost all of them, in one way or another, are so phrased that "Law" is displayed as fairly reliable, definite and uniform, although court decisions are not. By excluding from the definition everything that is markedly uncertain and un-uniform, the law-definers have been able to make it appear, to themselves and to many others, that the peculiarly uncertain and wayward elements of litigation—since these elements are not part of Law, as defined by the definers—are without significance. In that way, the legal magicians manage to take comfort in a Law which is, or can be, rather stable, and to refuse to contemplate the chancy results of everyday law-suits.[6]

Some nineteen years ago, I published a book [7] in which I was foolish enough to attempt my own definition of "law," one which, as it stressed trial-court decisions, did highlight the uncertain elements of litigation. I found myself at once in the middle of a fierce terminological quarrel

[5] See, e.g., Pound, *Outline of Jurisprudence* (5th ed. 1943) 70-73 for numerous definitions.

Compare Blakey's comment on logic: "The use of the word logic is almost the only thing which logicians have in common: If we venture a step beyond this, and ask for definition of what is implied in it, we are instantly stunned with a thousand discordant voices from all parts of the world."

[6] See Frank, *If Men Were Angels* (1942) 279-84; Frank, *Law and the Modern Mind* (1930) 48-54.

[7] See Frank, *Law and the Modern Mind* (1930).

with other law-definers—who, incidentally, did not agree with one another. I promptly backed out of that silly word-battle. Since then, I have, whenever possible, avoided the use of the word "Law." [8] I have instead (as in this book) stated directly—without any intervening definition of that vague and troublesome word—just what I was talking about, namely, what courts and lawyers do, and should do, or the entire province of the "administration of justice." For I think that one may say of "Law" what Croce said of the word "sublime": It is "everything that it is or will be called by those who have employed or will employ that name."

3

Those who have read the books and essays of the modern purveyors of legal magic may feel that I have overlooked the occasional passages in which some of them refer to factors not consistent with their magical thesis. I grant that here and there in their writings they do mention such factors—and, too, that these legal magicians do sometimes intimate an underlying disquietude about the complete validity of their dogmas. You will find, for instance, many such intimations in Pound's works; [9] and Dickinson comments that what he calls "law" does "not always work out in fact." [10] But such intimations of disquietude are peripheral.[11] The skepticism is occasional, and generally suppressed. I must acknowledge, then, that there are degrees of devoutness in the belief in rule-magic. Some of these thinkers are more skeptical than others. There is a spectrum of doubt, ranging from full belief to quarter-belief.

But these same manifestations have been found in "primitive" com-

[8] See Preface to sixth printing (1949) of *Law and the Modern Mind* (1930).

[9] See discussion of Pound in Frank, *If Men Were Angels* (1942) 63-64, 332, 341-45.

[10] Morris Cohen, as already noted, occasionally side-glances at the difficulties of trial-court fact-finding. See further as to Cohen, Chapter XIV.

Patterson, in 1942, briefly called attention to the effects of the "peculiar drives and preferences" of individual judges on their selections of facts. See *Logic in the Law*, 90 *Un. of Pa. L. Rev.* (1942) 875, 893-894. But he backed away from that attitude in the 1946 edition of his book on Jurisprudence; see 222-23 where he restricts his discussion to the "judge's views on economic, moral and social questions," and minimizes their effects. In 1947, he briefly adverted to the over-emphasis in "juristic theory" on the "judicial process of appellate courts." See Patterson, "Pound's Theories of Social Interests," in the volume, *Interpretations of Modern Legal Philosophies* (1947) 558, 567-568.

[11] Carl Becker, referring to the idea of evolution, says: "The idea was present in the eighteenth century. But no one made it welcome; it wandered forlornly in the fringes of consciousness, it timidly approached the threshold, but it never really got across." cf. Lovejoy, *The Great Chain of Being* (1936) 7-8, 294-96.

munities which practice magic. Observers report that, while some wizards are "strongly persuaded of the genuineness of their art," others have only a "limited confidence" in the predicted outcome of their magic, and still others approach a thorough disbelief. Yet even those wizards who, at moments, incline to skepticism about the efficacy of their rites, usually become, nevertheless, the "dupes of their own jugglery." A primitive wizard's inner doubts are generally overcome by the reaction of his public: "The faith of society and his own faith act and react upon one another." The primitive wizard, says Carveth Read, "has done what he learnt from his father, what respectable neighbors approve of; there is always some (good) crop to justify his wizardry."

We find in "primitive" societies three classes of wizards or professional practitioners of magic: (1) The first class devoutly believe in the efficacy of their rites. (2) The second are occasionally skeptical but, in varying degrees, manage to fool themselves. (3) The third class are outright skeptics, who deliberately gull their public. It is not too difficult to explain the first class, the thoroughly self-deluded. Nor the third: That a thoroughly disbelieving wizard should continue to practice magic is comprehensible, for, writes Read, "a cheat needs no explanation."

The second class—the occasionally skeptical—are less understandable. "What chiefly needs to be accounted for," says Read, "is the persuasion of those who—in spite of so many circumstances that seem to make disillusion inevitable—are in some manner true believers—in the manner, that is to say, of imaginative belief, founded on tradition and desire, unlike the perceptual belief of common sense." Read explains this phenomenon thus: "After failures, . . . there may come many chilling reflections, only, however, to be dispersed by an invincible desire to believe . . . in the profession to which he is committed. . . . For a wizard's belief in his art is supported by the testimony of other wizards, in whom he also believes, and by the belief of the tribe generally in the power of the profession. . . ." Do we not have here an explanation of the preachment of our modern legal magicians? Do they not resemble the semi-skeptical wizards?

Consider the manner by which the modern believers in the magical effect of legal rules verbally dispose of instances in which predictions of decisions by way of the legal rules do not succeed. Dickinson and Cardozo, for instance, say that such instances are exceptional; others say they are due to unusual ("illegitimate") influences. Similarly the "primitive" wizard with respect to his failures: "There had been a mistake in the rites . . . or another wizard had counteracted his efforts." Or compare a modern legal wizard like Timasheff (who asserts the controlling effects of "constant" factors in court decisions) with ancient believers in omens as described by Read: "Though in their nature infallible, omens are not always fulfilled—at least, their fulfilment is not always ascertainable. But this is easily explained. . . . For . . . any kind of a magical force is only infallible as a tendency; it may be counteracted. . . . So an omen indicates a course of events which may, perhaps, be turned aside. . . . Hence, however well observed and interpreted, the tendency of an Omen . . . may be diverted or reversed by an unknown cause."

Can it not be said, however, that modern legal magic—by granting emotional relief from anxiety about the major uncertainties of the judicial process—has a value? Such is the position of some anthropologists concerning "primitive" magic. They deem it beneficent, on the ground that it brings mental ease to distracted primitive man, lends him confidence in the face of trouble. So Malinowski regards primitive magic as virtually a psychiatric remedy; he says that it "standardizes the emotional tone and establishes a line of conduct which carries man over the dangerous moment . . . ," that, "as the type of activity which satisfies [the] need of standardized optimism, it is essential to the efficiency of human behavior."[12] Read talks in a similar vein: Because, he insists, of the wizard's ministrations, "the hunter's hand has been steadier; the sower and reaper work more cheerfully; and the warrior fights more courageously. . . ."

But that most sagacious anthropologist, Ruth Benedict, says that, "For the most part, . . . it is difficult to regard" magic "as a satisfactory compensatory emotional release," and that "the contention that magic has had a salutary role in human history must be balanced by facts which present it in a different light. Far from being an asset it has often been a heavy liability. . . . Its procedures . . . tend in both primitive and modern societies to substitute unreal achievements for real."

[12] Says Malinowski: "Let us realise . . . the type of situation in which we find magic. Man, engaged in a series of practical activities, comes to a gap; the hunter is disappointed by his quarry, the sailor misses propitious winds, the canoe-builder has to deal with some materal of which he is never certain that it will stand the strain, or the healthy person suddenly feels his strength failing. What does man do naturally under such conditions? . . . Forsaken by his knowledge, baffled by his past experience and by his technical skill, he realises his impotence. Yet his desire grips him only the more strongly; his anxiety, his fears and hopes, induce a tension in his organism which drives him to some sort of activity. Whether he be savage or civilised, whether

To "substitute unreal achievements for real"—is that not the unfortunate result of modern legal magic? It would seem that, with a few changes, we could apply to our contemporary legal thinkers who use magical ideas the following description of the adverse effects of magic on "primitive" man: "Having . . . discovered in magic a solace for his troubled mind, he no longer thinks of seeking elsewhere. Reassured amid disquieting circumstances, he becomes incapable of normal curiosity, inaccessible to experience. . . . He grows more and more powerless to form reasonable conceptions of facts, or to regard them through any other medium than his own . . . dreams."

Because their legal magic renders its practitioners relatively "inaccessible to experience" in the trial courts, it is surely harmful. It diverts attention from that immense area of legal practice which relates to trial court fact-finding. The result is indeed unfortunate. Judicial fact-finding constitutes the most difficult part of court-house government. It should be improved. It can be improved. But such improvement requires the concentrated attention of our best minds. Largely ignored by legal theory, pushed off to the edge in most descriptions of our legal system, it does not receive the study which must be given to it, if the administration of justice is to be made as adequate as is humanly possible.[13]

4

I might express myself in terms more familiar to students of philosophy by quoting Francis Bacon's 17th century discussion of what he calls the "Idols of the Theater," false notions which "have immigrated

---

in possession of magic or entirely ignorant of its existence, passive inaction, the only thing dictated by reason, is the last thing in which he can acquiesce. His nervous system and his whole organism drive him to substitute activity. . . . The substitute action in which the passion finds its vent, and which is due to impotence, has subjectively all the value of a real action, to which emotion would, if not impeded, naturally have led."

[13] Myres writes of "the disastrous consequences when Pride, in the person of the seer who believes that he knows, in virtue of his double portion of discernment, reinforces prestige by unholy alliance with panic Fear; tabu sustaining mana and perverting aristocracy, which is the rule of the seer, into oligarchy, the despotism of an 'inner ring,' with its watchwords 'hush-hush' and 'verboten.' Nobody likes amateur intervention in matters of which he at least knows the perilous delicacy; and it is only too easy for the niceties of magical manipulation . . . to be restricted to the gifted or cunning few. Not that specialism is not liable to occur in far later stages of rational scientific research, with the same ominous consequence of the formation of an 'inner ring.' For the seer, ancient or modern, remains human, after all; and the key of knowledge has been used at times to double-lock the door: 'this people that knoweth not the law are cursed.'" Myres, "The Beginning of Science," in the volume *Science and Civilization* (1923) 24-25.

into men's minds from the various dogmas of philosophies." He dubbed them Idols of the Theater because, he said, they were "so many stage-plays, representing worlds of their own creation after an unreal and scenic fashion." For, he remarked, "in the plays of this philosophical theater you may observe the same thing which is found in the theater of the poets, that stories invented for the stage are more compact and elegant, and more as one would wish them to be, than true stories. . . ." The "human understanding," he noted, "is no dry light, but receives an infusion from . . . the emotions; whence proceed sciences which may be called 'sciences as one would.' For what a man had rather were true he more readily believes. Therefore he rejects difficult things from impatience of research; sober things, because they narrow hope. Numberless, in short, are the ways, and sometimes imperceptible, in which the affections color and infect the understanding."

It encourages me that Bacon was a lawyer. It suggests that lawyers are not, necessarily, altogether hopelessly infected with magic. Bacon's insight serves to offset the attitude of the legal magicians, an attitude the cause of which was recently revealed by one of them, Bodenheimer. He criticized the writings of certain persons who, he declared, pay too much attention to trial-courts and who look at "law" from "the point of view of the trial lawyer. . . ." For, he went on, to depict realistically the happenings in trial courts is to make manifest the presence of irrational factors in the judicial process, and the undesirable result will be to shake public confidence in the "rationality" of "law." It is as if a physician were to decry disclosures of the existence of infantile paralysis or cancer, for fear that those disclosures would create a belief that all men do not enjoy perfect health.

Indeed, that sort of dogmatical thinking once pervaded medical learning. Galen, relying largely on the Bible, taught that man has one more rib than woman. For hundreds of years, physicians accepted that dogma. Then Vesalius had the temerity to dissect the dead bodies of men and women. He reported that Galen's non-observational dogma was incorrect. For a considerable time, Vesalius was denounced as a liar, and an impious detractor of his famous precursor. Fortunately for human welfare, among physicians the spirit of Vesalius finally won out. It has not yet penetrated the thinking of many lawyers.

The magical approach of altogether too many lawyers brings to mind a letter written, several centuries ago, by Galileo to Kepler: "Here at Padua," he wrote, "is the principal professor of philosophy whom I have repeatedly and urgently requested to look at the moon and planets through my glass, which he pertinaciously refuses to do. Why are you not here? What shouts of laughter we should have at this glorious folly? And to hear the professor of philosophy at Pisa, laboring before the Grand Duke with logical arguments, as if with magical incantations, to charm the new planets out of the sky."

Philosophers today do look through telescopes at the moon and planets. Most of our eminent legal philosophers and teachers, however, still use logical arguments as magical incantations to exorcise unpleasant legal realities, instead of using their eyes to see what happens in trial courts.

They recall Marlowe's lines:

> "Nothing so sweet as magic is to him,
> Which he prefers before his chiefest bliss:
> And this the man that in his study sits."

5

The persistence of magical thinking in our day has numerous causes. One of them I explored in an earlier book [14]—the magical attitudes of the young child which many otherwise intelligent men, because of emotional immaturity, carry over into adult years. I shall not here expand that theme, but merely note a few thoughtways of children in our civilization which (as reported by Piaget)[15] resemble the thoughtways of our modern legal magicians: The young child uses words to bring about what action itself is powerless to do. He creates his own "reality" by "magical language," by "working on things" by "means of words alone, apart from any contact with them or with persons." Sometimes he "forgets his activity and does nothing but talk. The word then becomes a command to the external world." His "vision is distorted by his ideas." He "conceives the world as more logical than it is. This makes him believe it possible to connect everything and to foresee everything." His notion of causality is "full of considerations that are foreign to . . . observation." The idea of the accidental eludes him; he "refuses to admit that experience contains fortuitous concurrences" beyond explanation. He "connects the most heterogeneous ex-

[14] *Law and the Modern Mind* (1930) Part One, Chapters VIII, IX and X.

[15] See especially these books by Piaget: *The Language and Thought of the Child* (1926); *Judgment and Reasoning in the Child* (1928); *The Child's Conception of Causality* (1930.) The "child," as described by Piaget, is not a constant. Nor are all children identical; there are developmental periods in the growth of children; for convenience, I have not here differentiated the periods.

planations and always contrives to justify any sort of connection." He is a wishful thinker who creates for himself an artificial reality to match his wishes.

6

Some twenty years ago there emerged a group of American lawyers, unfortunately called "legal realists." This group is by no means homogeneous. Its "members" disagree sharply with one another on many points. Their sole common bond consists of their skepticism concerning the traditional lawyer's description of what courts do. This group may be roughly divided into two sub-groups.

The first sub-group, of whom Karl Llewellyn of Columbia is perhaps the outstanding representative, I would call "rule-skeptics." They aim at greater legal certainty. That is, they consider it socially desirable that lawyers should be able to predict to their clients the decisions in most law-suits not yet commenced. They feel that, in too many instances, the layman cannot act with assurance as to how, if his acts become involved in a suit, the court will decide. As these rule skeptics see it, the trouble is that the formal legal rules enunciated in courts' opinions—sometimes called "paper rules" [16]—too often prove unreliable as guides in the prediction of decisions. The rule skeptics believe that they can discover, behind the "paper rules," some "real rules" descriptive of uniformities or regularities in actual judicial behavior, and that those "real rules" will serve as more reliable prediction-instruments, yielding a large measure of workable predictability of the outcome of future suits.[17] In this undertaking, the rule skeptics concentrate almost exclusively on upper-court opinions. They do not ask themselves whether their own, or any other, prediction-device, will render it possible for a lawyer or layman to prophesy, before an ordinary suit is instituted or comes to trial in a trial court, how it will be decided. In other words, these rule skeptics seek means for making accurate guesses, not about decisions of trial courts, but about decisions of up-

[16] There are also references to "pseudo rules," or "accepted rules," or "verbally formulated rules."

[17] Alternative locutions for "real rules" are "latent rules," or "rules akin to but deeper than" the "paper rules." Reference is also made to a "working approximation" of uniformity or regularity" in "judicial behavior" or in the "practices of the courts," such uniformity to be learned by "cutting below" the superficial level." See, e.g., Llewellyn, "A Realistic Jurisprudence—The Next Step," 30 *Col. L. Rev.* (1930) 431; Llewellyn, "The Rule of Law in Our Case Law," 47 *Yale L.J.* (1938) 1243; Llwellyn, "On Reading and Using the Newer Jurisprudence," 26 *Am. Bar Ass'n. Journal* (1940) 418.

Medway High Schoo.
Library

per courts when trial-court decisions are appealed. These skeptics cold-shoulder the trial courts. Yet, in most instances, these skeptics do not inform their readers that they are writing chiefly of upper courts.

The second sub-group I would call "fact-skeptics." They, too, engaging in "rule skepticism," peer behind the "paper rules." Together with the rule skeptics, they have stimulated interest in factors, influencing upper-court decisions, of which, often, the opinions of those courts give no hint. But the fact-skeptics go much further. Their primary interest is in the trial courts. No matter how precise or definite may be the formal legal rules, say these fact-skeptics, no matter what the discoverable uniformities behind these formal rules, nevertheless, it is impossible, and will always be impossible, because of the elusiveness of the facts on which decisions turn, to predict future decisions in most (not all) law-suits not yet begun or not yet tried. The fact skeptics, thinking that therefore the pursuit of greatly increased legal certainty is, for the most part, futile—and that its pursuit, indeed may well work injustice—aim rather at increased judicial justice. This group of fact skeptics includes, among others, Dean Leon Green, Max Radin, Thurman Arnold, William O. Douglas (now Mr. Justice Douglas), and perhaps Professor E. M. Morgan.

Within each of these sub-groups there is diversity of opinion as to many ideas. But I think it can be said that, generally, most of the rule-skeptics, restricting themselves to the upper-court level, live in an artificial two-dimensional legal world, while the legal world of the fact-skeptics is three-dimensional. Obviously, most events occurring in the fact-skeptics' three-dimensional cosmos are out of sight, and therefore out of mind, in the rule-skeptics' cosmos. The rule-skeptics are but the left-wing adherents of the old magical tradition. It is from the tradition itself that the fact-skeptics have revolted. Their position is that consideration of trial-court processes calls for legal thinking in three dimensions.[18]

I was one of the original fact-skeptics. My experiences as a "quasi-judicial" fact-finder on the SEC and my service on the bench have not changed my fundamental belief that trial-court fact-finding is the soft spot in the administration of justice.

Now, as distinguished from the fact-skeptics, who abandon legal magic, the rule-skeptics, should, I think, be included in the second class of legal wizards, the semi-skeptical believers in such magic. For,

[18] See Chapter XII for a suggestion that four-dimensional thinking may be needed.

in spite of side-glances at the trial courts, they go on trying, as I have said, to ferret out judicial uniformities in terms, principally, of upper-court behavior and of upper-courts' written opinions. Inevitably, the efforts of the rule-skeptics, as they are confined to the upper-court level and to the rule-ingredient of decisions, can have relatively little value with respect to the great mass of law suits.

The rule-skeptics would escape my criticism if, in all their writings, they announced that they were not attempting to deal with trial courts, or with the effects on upper-court decisions of fact-determinations in the trial courts. But, as I have said, these writers seldom announce this.

Llewellyn is perhaps the most brilliant of the rule-skeptics. In early writings, published in 1929-1931, he warned his readers that his discussion of courts was defective, because, he said, as he knew little about trial courts, he could not informedly discuss their activities, although he admitted that those activities had far more significance than those of upper courts. He said that, like most legal scholars, he had succumbed to the "threat of the available," had limited his studies to the easily accessible books, including the published reports of upper-court opinions, which could be studied in the library without visits to trial courts. He confessed, indeed, that, without participation in trials, one was likely to be imperceptive about what went on in those courts. "The man," he said, "who sees line-play in the foot-ball game is the man who once tried playing in the line himself." [19]

Nevertheless, he then indicated, here and there, the difficulties of fact-finding. In 1930, he asked how a trial court was to determine which of the "divergent stories" of witnesses was to be believed.[20] He pointed to the emptiness of a legal right which a man cannot enforce because his "only witness dies." [21] In the same year, speaking of the "supposed right" to have a contract performed, he said that it could "accurately be phrased as follows: If the other party does not perform as agreed, you can sue, and *if* you have a fair lawyer, *and* nothing goes wrong with the witnesses or the jury, . . . you will probably get a judgment. . . ." [22] Yet he balked at facing the consequences of this insight. The "record of the facts" of a case when it reaches the upper court,

[19] See Llewellyn, *The Bramble Bush* (1930) 89-91, 143; Llewellyn, "Legal Tradition and Social Science Method," in the volume, *Essays in Research in the Social Sciences* (1931) 89, 95-96.

[20] *The Bramble Bush* (1930) 20.

[21] *Ibid.* 82.

[22] "Realistic Jurisprudence—The Next Step," 30 Col. L. Rev. (1930) 430, 437-38.

he wrote in 1929,[23] "is thrice distorted. The story people tell in court may or may not reflect the actual transaction. The rules of evidence, the procedural set-up of the case, the presentation of the case in terms of lawyers' theories, again twist the reflection of the true transaction. Again the statement of facts by appellate judges involves their picking over, their reorganization, this time in terms of so grouping, so phrasing them, as to make plausible the decision which the court has reached. For all this, the facts break through in the record." That last statement amazes. On Llewellyn's own previously stated assumptions, it cannot be true: If, as he admitted, the witnesses' stories in the courtroom often do not "reflect the actual transaction," how can that actual transaction "break through in the record"? It would be (as he recognized in 1930) a "miracle" if it did. But Llewellyn wanted to believe in such a miracle because it relieved him of the need to bother about trial courts, and made it possible for him to assume that, by merely reading upper-court records, he could know the actual past facts of cases.

Llewellyn has given no warning that he was not discussing trial courts in his more recent writings, so that a reader would naturally suppose they were intended to cover "lower," as well as "upper," courts. In one such article, in 1940 (which, so far as appears, relates to both kinds of courts), he waxed enthusiastic about the search "for the similarities in [the] attitudes and behavior" of divers judges. This, he said, involved, not "a delving into vagaries of individuals," but a "search for predictabilities . . . which transcend individuality." [24] In another article, in 1941,[25] which again did not differentiate between trial and upper courts, Llewellyn says that, whenever "a rule is clear, and plainly wise, and plainly applicable," it "can be predicted" that a judge will "follow it." Llewellyn concedes that there are, "besides the rules," non-rule factors which seem "at first blush to lead into all the vagaries of individual psychology and so into hopeless additional complications." But, he continues, those "vagaries" and other "complications" can be ignored, and "a great realm of workable predictability" can be discovered, in cases where a rule "is clear both in application and reason, and when the reason also makes sense" to judges, "as men, as Americans, as lawyers, and as judges." Then, Llewellyn concludes, individual differences between judges will not prevent prediction of decisions.

[23] Llewellyn, "The Conditions For and The Aims and Methods For Legal Research," *Handbook of Ass'n. of American Law Schools* (1929) 35.

[24] "On Reading and Using the New Jurisprudence," 26 *Am. Bar Ass'n. Journal* (1940) 418.

[25] See his article in the volume, *My Philosophy of Law* (1941) 183, 191, 196-97.

Why did Llewellyn in these 1940 and 1941 articles omit any mention of the problem arising from the "vagaries of individual psychology" in the process of trial-court fact-finding? Because, I surmise, it would have ruffled up his prediction thesis. Perhaps that explains why, in the decade 1931-1941, instead of studying the trial courts, he found ample time (in 1935-1936) to take a long journey to Montana, accompanied by an anthropologist, to study the legal system of the Cheyenne Indians, about which he and the anthropologist wrote a brilliant book (published in 1941).[26] By spending a few nickels on subway-fares for short trips from Columbia Law School, where he teaches, to lower New York City, Llewellyn could have studied in detail the trial courts of that metropolis. He could then have written a book on the anthropology of Tammany-Hall Indians, many of whom are first-rate trial judges.

As it is, his description of our judicial process is, concerning the bulk of it, seriously deficient anthropology, for he has obtained his information about our trial courts derivately. The anthropologist, said Malinowski, "working through an interpreter by the question and answer method, can . . . collect only opinions, generalizations and bald statements. He gives us no reality, for he has never seen it." Malinowski urged "anthropological field-work" through "study by direct observation," since "hearsay anthropology is constantly exposed to the danger of ignoring the seamy side" of affairs and results in "futile simplifications of a very complicated state of things." [27]

Llewellyn has an exceptionally alert, constructively skeptical mind. But his flashes of intuitive perception can be no adequate substitute for personally seeing and participating in trials. Without such experience, his vision is defective. He is like a color-blind artist attempting to paint the vivid colors of a sun-drenched autumn landscape. His shying away from lower-court fact-finding indicates, I think, the sort of reluctance to observe disturbing court-room realities which justifies classifying him as a second-class wizard. And, I repeat, he is perhaps the most brilliant of the rule-skeptics. It may fairly be said, then, that the rule-skeptics are magic addicts.[28]

[26] Llewellyn and Hoebel, *The Cheyenne Way*.

[27] *Crime and Custom in Savage Society* (1926) 125, 127.

[28] I shall again discuss the legal magic of the rule-skeptics in connection with the jury, with "behaviorism," with "legal reasoning," and with the "anthropological approach."

7

But what of the seasoned trial lawyer? Doesn't he know, from his daily experiences, the inadequacies of legal rule-magic? The answer is curious: His actual conduct is out of line with the magic theory—else he would lose most of his cases. Yet usually he intones the theory at Bar Association meetings and in speeches to non-lawyers. He is not, however, himself a theory-maker. He borrows his theories from the professional theorists.

We find much the same in "primitive" societies. Paul Radin writes that the practical man in such societies repeats mechanically what the medicine-man has formulated in intellectual or symbolical terms. "The thinker's formula stands on its own, and the [practical] facts stand on [their own]. Neither can possibly contradict the other, for they lie in different planes." So, "in the main, the practical man unhesitatingly accepts the form which the thinker has given to ideas." Read says: "The primitive hunter uses all the [practical] resources of his art in hunting; he also practices rites and spells. . . . Suggest to him that he try the hunting without the rites? He is afraid to. . . . Well then, let him try the rites without the hunting. He is not such a fool." He "trusts in magic—and keeps his bowstring dry." So old Joseph Choate, a famous trial lawyer, said in 1878, "The longer I practice law, and the more success I have, the more it seems to me to depend upon luck. . . ." But so he did *not* speak in public addresses.

To round out the story, I must add that there are some legal thinkers who, although they know full well the falsity of legal magic, urge that its falsity should not be publicized. You may think that all these men are hypocrites. Elsewhere I have ventured a different suggestion as to some of them: Despite their awareness of the sham nature of this magic, it still emotionally enthralls these thinkers. Because of its emotional fascination for them, they are not entirely ready to relinquish it. Accordingly, they justify their failure publicly to expose the sham by saying that the public can't stand the exposure. What they really mean is that they, themselves, cannot bear to have the sham revealed. They find a lingering comfort in a public still under the magical spell. Such an attitude, I have suggested, is a symptom of emotional immaturity. These men, having attained only a partial emotional adulthood, cannot fearlessly witness the coming-of-age of their fellow-men.[29]

[29] See Frank, *Law and the Modern Mind* (1930) 235.

8

To sum up: Almost always behind the use of magic lurks wishful thinking, the powerful desire to believe that what one urgently wants is real. Such wishful thinking characterizes our present-day legal magic. Most of those who exploit it yearn for a kind of legal system which does not now exist. They reject adequate observation of the existent. They substitute their wishes for their eye-sight.

It is fashionable to jeer, indiscriminately, at all kinds of wishful thinking, to deride it as neurotic day-dreaming, "escapism." But there is one kind of wishful thinking which deserves not derision but hearty approbation. A wish that a present evil will cease to exist can be a powerful instrument of human progress—if the wisher does not content himself with supposing that his wish *is* true but, instead, takes his wish as a goal to be won by hard thought and effort. That method of "escaping" evil merits warm praise. The best in our civilization is a product of such wishes—wishes expressive of aims which men set out to, and did, achieve. It used to be said that, if wishes were horses, beggars could ride. Inventors went to work on that wish, experimentally, with the result that men who once were beggars now do ride in horse-less carriages. The wish to fly, once the dream of a wishing-rug, became, through experimentation, the art of aviation. Experimentation with the wish for political freedom gave us democratic government.

Some wishes, of course, no matter how hard we work on them, never come true. But it is always open to us to substitute for neurotic "wishful thinking" what Neurath happily called "thinkful wishing." Let us thus use the wish that the administration of justice may be improved. If we do, we will not refuse to observe what our trial courts now actually do. We will admit that their fact-finding frequently results in grave injustices. We will then seek to discover in what ways that job can be done better. I surmise that, although such efforts will fall far short of perfection, they will, by no means, go wholly unrewarded.[30]

[30] See further, on the subject of wishing, Chapter XXXI.

VI. THE "FIGHT" THEORY versus THE "TRUTH" THEORY

When we say that present-day trial methods are "rational," presumably we mean this: The men who compose our trial courts, judges and juries, in each law-suit conduct an intelligent inquiry into all the practically available evidence, in order to ascertain, as near as may be, the truth about the facts of that suit. That might be called the "investigatory" or "truth" method of trying cases. Such a method can yield no more than a guess, nevertheless an educated guess.

The success of such a method is conditioned by at least these two factors: (1) The judicial inquirers, trial judges or juries, may not obtain all the important evidence. (2) The judicial inquirers may not be competent to conduct such an inquiry. Let us, for the time being, assume that the second condition is met—i.e., that we have competent inquirers—and ask whether we so conduct trials as to satisfy the first condition, i.e., the procuring of all the practically available important evidence.

The answer to that question casts doubt on whether our trial courts do use the "investigatory" or "truth" method. Our mode of trials is commonly known as "contentious" or "adversary." It is based on what I would call the "fight" theory, a theory which derives from the origin of trials as substitutes for private out-of-court brawls.

Many lawyers maintain that the "fight" theory and the "truth" theory coincide. They think that the best way for a court to discover the facts in a suit is to have each side strive as hard as it can, in a keenly partisan spirit, to bring to the court's attention the evidence favorable to that side. Macaulay said that we obtain the fairest decision "when two men argue, as unfairly as possible, on opposite sides," for then "it is certain that no important consideration will altogether escape notice."

Unquestionably that view contains a core of good sense. The zealously partisan lawyers sometimes do bring into court evidence which, in a dispassionate inquiry, might be overlooked. Apart from the fact element of the case, the opposed lawyers also illuminate for the court niceties of the legal rules which the judge might otherwise not perceive. The "fight" theory, therefore, has invaluable qualities with which we cannot afford to dispense.

But frequently the partisanship of the opposing lawyers blocks the uncovering of vital evidence or leads to a presentation of vital testimony in a way that distorts it. I shall attempt to show you that we have allowed the fighting spirit to become dangerously excessive.

2

This is perhaps most obvious in the handling of witnesses. Suppose a trial were fundamentally a truth-inquiry. Then, recognizing the inherent fallibilities of witnesses, we would do all we could to remove the causes of their errors when testifying. Recognizing also the importance of witnesses' demeanor as clues to their reliability, we would do our best to make sure that they testify in circumstances most conducive to a revealing observation of that demeanor by the trial judge or jury. In our contentious trial practice, we do almost the exact opposite.

No businessman, before deciding to build a new plant, no general before launching an attack, would think of obtaining information on which to base his judgment by putting his informants through the bewildering experience of witnesses at a trial. "The novelty of the situation," wrote a judge, "the agitation and hurry which accompanies it, the cajolery or intimidation to which the witness may be subjected, the want of questions calculated to excite those recollections which might clear up every difficulty, and the confusion of cross-examination . . . may give rise to important errors and omissions." "In the court they stand as strangers," wrote another judge of witnesses, "surrounded with unfamiliar circumstances giving rise to an embarrassment known only to themselves."

In a book by Henry Taft (brother of Chief Justice Taft, and himself a distinguished lawyer) we are told: "Counsel and court find it necessary through examination and instruction to induce a witness to abandon for an hour or two his habitual method of thought and expression, and conform to the rigid ceremonialism of court procedure. It is not strange that frequently truthful witnesses are . . . misunderstood, that they nervously react in such a way as to create the impression that they are either evading or intentionally falsifying. It is interesting to account for some of the things that witnesses do under such circumstances. An honest witness testifies on direct examination. He answers questions promptly and candidly and makes a good impression. On cross-examination, his attitude changes. He suspects that traps are being laid for him. He hesitates; he ponders the answer to a simple question; he seems to 'spar' for time by asking that questions be repeated; perhaps he protests that counsel is not fair; he may even appeal to the court for protection. Altogether the contrast with his attitude on direct examination is obvious; and he creates the impression that he is evading or withholding." Yet on testimony thus elicited courts every day reach decisions affecting the lives and fortunes of citizens.

What is the role of the lawyers in bringing the evidence before the trial court? As you may learn by reading any one of a dozen or more handbooks on how to try a law-suit, an experienced lawyer uses all sorts of stratagems to minimize the effect on the judge or jury of testimony disadvantageous to his client, even when the lawyer has no doubt of the accuracy and honesty of that testimony. The lawyer considers it his duty to create a false impression, if he can, of any witness who gives such testimony. If such a witness happens to be timid, frightened by the unfamiliarity of court-room ways, the lawyer, in his cross-examination, plays on that weakness, in order to confuse the witness and make it appear that he is concealing significant facts. Longenecker, in his book *Hints On The Trial of a Law Suit* (a book endorsed by the great Wigmore), in writing of the "truthful, honest, over-cautious" witness, tells how "a skilful advocate by a rapid cross-examination may ruin the testimony of such a witness." The author does not even hint any disapproval of that accomplishment. Longenecker's and other similar books recommend that a lawyer try to prod an irritable but honest "adverse" witness into displaying his undesirable characteristics in their most unpleasant form, in order to discredit him with the judge or jury. "You may," writes Harris, "sometimes destroy the effect of an adverse witness by making him appear more hostile than he really is. You may make him exaggerate or unsay something and say it again." Taft says that a clever cross-examiner, dealing with an honest but egotistic witness, will "deftly tempt the witness to indulge in his propensity for exaggeration, so as to make him 'hang himself.' And thus," adds Taft, "it may happen that not only is the value of his testimony lost, but the side which produces him suffers for seeking aid from such a source"—although, I would add, that may be the only source of evidence of a fact on which the decision will turn.

"An intimidating manner in putting questions," writes Wigmore, "may so coerce or disconcert the witness that his answers do not represent his actual knowledge on the subject. So also, questions which in form or subject cause embarrassment, shame or anger in the witness may unfairly lead him to such demeanor or utterances that the impression produced by his statements does not do justice to its real testimonial value." Anthony Trollope, in one of his novels, indignantly reacted to these methods. "One would naturally imagine," he said, "that an undisturbed thread of clear evidence would be best obtained from a man whose position was made easy and whose mind was not harrassed; but this is not the fact; to turn a witness to good account, he must be badgered this way and that till he is nearly mad; he must be made a laughing-stock for the court; his very truths must be turned into falsehoods, so that he may be falsely shamed; he must be accused of all manner of villainy, threatened with all manner of punishment; he must be made to feel that he has no friend near him, that the world is all against him; he must be confounded till he forget his right hand from his left, till his mind be turned into chaos, and his heart into water; and then let him give his evidence. What will fall from his lips when in this wretched collapse must be of special value, for the best talents of practiced forensic heroes are daily used to bring it about; and no member of the Humane Society interferes to protect the wretch. Some sorts of torture are as it were tacitly allowed even among humane people. Eels are skinned alive, and witnesses are sacrificed, and no one's blood curdles at the sight, no soft heart is sickened at the cruelty." This may be a somewhat overdrawn picture. Yet, referring to this manner of handling witnesses, Sir Frederic Eggleston recently said that it prevents lawyers from inducing persons who know important facts from disclosing them to lawyers for litigants. He notes, too, that "the terrors of cross-examination are such that a party can often force a settlement by letting it be known that a certain . . . counsel has been retained."

The lawyer not only seeks to descredit adverse witnesses but also to hide the defects of witnesses who testify favorably to his client. If, when interviewing such a witness before trial, the lawyer notes that the witness has mannerisms, demeanor-traits, which might discredit him, the lawyer teaches him how to cover up those traits when testifying: He educates the irritable witness to conceal his irritability, the cocksure witness to subdue his cocksureness. In that way, the trial court is denied the benefit of observing the witness's actual normal demeanor, and thus prevented from sizing up the witness accurately.

Lawyers freely boast of their success with these tactics. They boast also of such devices as these: If an "adverse," honest witness, on cross-examination, makes seemingly inconsistent statements, the cross-examiner tries to keep the witness from explaining away the apparent inconsistencies. "When," writes Tracy, counseling trial lawyers, in a much-praised book, "by your cross-examination, you have caught the witness in an inconsistency, the next question that will immediately come to your lips is, 'Now, let's hear you explain.' Don't ask it, for he may explain and, if he does, your point will have been lost. If you have conducted your cross-examination properly (which includes interestingly), the jury will have seen the inconsistency and it will have made the proper impression on their minds. If, on re-direct examination the witness does explain, the explanation will have come later in the case and at the request of the counsel who originally called the witness and the jury will be much more likely to look askance at the explanation than if it were made during your cross-examination." Tracy adds, "Be careful in your questions on cross-examination not to open a door that you have every reason to wish kept closed." That is, don't let in any reliable evidence, hurtful to your side, which would help the trial court to arrive at the truth.

"In cross-examination," writes Eggleston, "the main preoccupation of counsel is to avoid introducing evidence, or giving an opening to it, which will harm his case. The most painful thing for an experienced practitioner . . . is to hear a junior counsel laboriously bring out in cross-examination of a witness all the truth which the counsel who called him could not" bring out "and which it was the junior's duty as an advocate to conceal." A lawyer, if possible, will not ask a witness to testify who, on cross-examination, might testify to true facts helpful to his opponent.

Nor, usually, will a lawyer concede the existence of any facts if they are inimical to his client and he thinks they cannot be proved by his adversary. If, to the lawyer's knowledge, a witness has testified inaccurately but favorably to the lawyer's client, the lawyer will attempt to hinder cross-examination that would expose the inaccuracy. He puts in testimony which surprises his adversary who, caught unawares, has not time to seek out, interview, and summon witnesses who would rebut the surprise testimony. "Of course," said a trial lawyer in a bar association lecture in 1946, "surprise elements should be hoarded. Your opponent should not be educated as to matters concerning which you believe he is still in the dark. Obviously, the traps should not be uncovered. Indeed, you may cast a few more leaves over them so that your adversary will step more boldly on the low ground believing it is solid."

These, and other like techniques, you will find unashamedly described in the many manuals on trial tactics written by and for eminently reputable trial lawyers. The purpose of these tactics—often effective—is to prevent the trial judge or jury from correctly evaluating the trustworthiness of witnesses and to shut out evidence the trial court ought to receive in order to approximate the truth.

In short, the lawyer aims at victory, at winning in the fight, not at aiding the court to discover the facts. He does not want the trial court to reach a sound educated guess, if it is likely to be contrary to his client's interests. Our present trial method is thus the equivalent of throwing pepper in the eyes of a surgeon when he is performing an operation.

3

However unpleasant all this may appear, do not blame trial lawyers for using the techniques I have described. If there is to be criticism, it should be directed at the system that virtually compels their use, a system which treats a law-suit as a battle of wits and wiles. As a distinguished lawyer has said, these stratagems are "part of the maneuvering . . . to which [lawyers] are obliged to resort to win their cases. Some of them may appear to be tricky; they may seem to be taking undue advantage; but under the present system it is part of a lawyer's duty to employ them because his opponent is doing the same thing, and if he refrains from doing so, he is violating his duty to his client and giving his opponent an unquestionable advantage. . . ." These tricks of the trade are today the legitimate and accepted corollary of our fight theory.

However, some tactics, unfortunately too often used, are regarded as improper by decent members of the legal profession. We know, alas, that an immense amount of testimony is deliberately and knowingly false. Experienced lawyers say that, in large cities, scarcely a trial occurs, in which some witness does not lie. Perjured testimony often goes undetected by trial courts and therefore often wins cases. Judge Dawson of the Kansas Supreme Court found one of the "real and crying hindrances to a correct and efficient administration of justice . . . the widespread prevalence of perjury practiced with impunity by litigants and witnesses. . . ." A wag has it that courts decide cases according to the "preponderance of the perjury." Some

—not all—of that lying testimony results from coaching of witnesses by dishonest lawyers.[1]

But much inaccurate testimony, not to be classified as perjurious, results from a practice that is not dishonest: Every sensible lawyer, before a trial, interviews most of the witnesses. No matter how scrupulous the lawyer, a witness, when thus interviewed, often detects what the lawyer hopes to prove at the trial. If the witness desires to have the lawyer's client win the case, he will often, unconsciously, mold his story accordingly. Telling and re-telling it to the lawyer, he will honestly believe that his story, as he narrates it in court, is true, although it importantly deviates from what he originally believed. So we have inadvertent but innocent witness-coaching. The line, however, between intentional and inadvertent grooming of witnesses cannot easily be drawn. Now, according to many lawyers of wide experience, the contentious method of trying cases augments the tendency of witnesses to mold their memories to assist one of the litigants, because the partisan nature of trials tends to make partisans of the witnesses. They come to regard themselves, not as aids in an investigation bent on discovering the truth, not as aids to the court, but as the "plaintiff's witnesses" or the "defendant's witnesses." They become soldiers in a war, cease to be neutrals.

"I do not think I am exaggerating," wrote Eggleston in 1947, after a resume of the ways of trial lawyers and trial courts, "when I say that the evidence contains only kaleidoscopic fragments of the facts. It is as if a checker of light and dark patches were held over reality. All that gets down in the record is that seen through the light patches. It is quite clear," he continues, "that reality does not survive in the process of analysis to which" the contending lawyers "submit it from opposite poles. Cases are won by the exercise of the last degree of ingenuity, and this marginal utility makes the contest highly artificial."

In 1906, the French lawyer, De la Grasserie, said that, in a modern (civil) trial, "deceit" has "succeeded to . . . force, bringing with it almost the same disasters. It is . . . a conflict . . . which has been substituted for the primitive conflict of force. . . . Its wounds are often as deep, its risks as serious. . . . The battle of craft is enacted by the parties under the eyes of the judge. . . . Each [party] strives to conceal what is contrary to his interests and to take advantage of everything that helps his cause. . . . No doubt craft is preferable to violence from

[1] See Rovere, Howe and Hummel (1947)

the point of view of the social order, but the risk that judgment is wrong is at times as great." An English lawyer, at about the same time, said that, in litigation, "one party or the other is always supremely interested in misrepresenting, exaggerating, or suppressing the truth"; and he spoke "of the characteristic dangers of deception . . . to which judicial tribunals are exposed. . . ." As applied to all contemporary American trials, these statements are excessive, misdescriptive. Yet one who visits many of our trial courts, or who reads the books and articles on practical trial techniques to which I have referred, will perhaps incline to believe that, in many cases, matters are not altogether different in this country today. The views of so competent a student of trials as Judge Learned Hand (whom I shall quote in a moment) tend to support such a depressing belief.

4

The effects of the contemporary American fighting or adversary method must sorely puzzle many a litigating citizen. The parties to a suit, remarks Eggleston, "know exactly what they are fighting about when the writ is issued, but find themselves fighting a very different case when the trial is actually launched. It is a wise litigant who knows his own quarrel when he sees it in court." "If," said Judge Learned Hand to the lawyer, "you lead your client into the courtroom with you . . . , you will, if you have the nerve to watch him, see in his face a baffled sense that there is going on some kind of game which, while its outcome may be tragic to him in its development, is incomprehensible." The legal profession should not take much pride in a system which evokes from Judge Hand the remark, "About trials hang a suspicion of trickery and a sense of result depending upon cajolery or worse." To Judge Hand's comments I would add that, were it impossible to contrive a better system, we lawyers could legitimately defend ourselves, saying, "We do the best we can." But I think such a defense not legitimate because I think we do not do the best we can, since an improved system can be contrived.

Mr. Justice Frankfurter recently observed that a criminal statute is not unconstitutional merely because in one trial under that statute a man goes scot-free while in another trial under the same statute another man is sent to jail for "similar conduct." Such "diversity in result . . . in different trials," said the Justice, is "unavoidable," because, in each trial, the ascertainment of the facts must be left to "fallible judges and juries." He concluded that "so long as the diversities are not designed consequences, they do not deprive persons of due process of law." This statement by Justice Frankfurter—which I think correctly states the judicial attitude towards trials—has such significance that I want the reader thoroughly to understand it. When, in that context, the Justice spoke of "due process of law," he meant a "fair trial," that is, one which meets the minimum test of fairness required by the Constitution. The Supreme Court holds that a trial is constitutionally "fair," if only it does not depart from the methods usually employed in our trial courts. I am not criticising the Supreme Court when I suggest that one imbued with a lively sense of justice will not be satisfied with that minimal constitutional test. A particular trial may be thus minimally "fair" when measured by the standard of our present usual trial practices. But the question remains whether those usual practices can be regarded as actually fair when, due to practically *avoidable* human errors, they deprive men of life or liberty in criminal proceedings, or of property or money in civil suits. I would answer, No. Our mode of trials is often most unfair. It will, I think, continue to be, until everything feasible has been done to prevent avoidable mistakes. Only avoidless mistakes should we accept among life's necessary dangers.

After careful scrutiny of the record of the famous Sacco-Vanzetti case, lawyers of experience have concluded that those men received an egregiously unfair trial, because obviously the trial judge was poisonously biased against the accused, and the prosecutors hit below the belt, resorting to measures which violated the Marquis of Queensbury rules governing court-room bouts. However, in the case of Campbell, and many others like it, innocent men have been convicted after trials from which such glaring defects were absent. Were those trials fair? Yes, in a constitutional sense. They would be pronounced technically fair by the lawyers who criticize the Sacco-Vanzetti decision. But forget the lawyer's perspective. In terms of common sense, how can we say that those trials were fair since, almost surely, in their course, the government lawyers utilized some of the legitimized lawyer-tactics which were likely to mislead the trial courts? Intelligent laymen should insist that it is not enough that a trial seem fair to many lawyers, who, indurated to the techniques of their trade, have become so calloused that they acquiesce in needless judicial injustices.

Take, for instance, a speech made last year, before a Bar Association, by a highly respected judge. He began by saying, "We start with the fundamental conception that a trial, under our procedure, is not a game or battle of wits but a painstaking, orderly inquiry for the discovery of the truth." Now that judge, I have no doubt, believed that statement—or, rather, believed that he believed it. Yet a few minutes later in his speech, he cautioned the lawyer never on cross-examination "thoughtlessly [to] ask the one question which will supply an omission in your opponent's case." He quoted, with approval, the remark of an expert cross-examiner that, if you put such a question, "you may find the witness has had time to think, and you will get an answer" that hurts your client. So here you have a judge who, after seriously depicting a trial as "an inquiry for the discovery of truth," goes on to encourage lawyers to avoid bringing out the truth. That bewildered judge—and alas there are too many like him—will make no serious effort to change a system which permits a lawyer to act as did Mr. Chaffanbrass in another of Trollope's novels: "Nothing would flurry this [witness he was cross-examining], force her to utter a word of which she herself did not know the meaning. The more he might persevere in such an attempt, the more dogged and steady she would become. He therefore soon gave that up . . . and resolved that, as he could not shake her, he would shake the confidence the jury might place in her. He could not make a fool of her, and therefore he would make her out a rogue. . . . As for himself, he knew well enough that she had spoken nothing but the truth. But he . . . so managed that the truth might be made to look like falsehood,—or at any rate to have a doubtful air."

I repeat that we ought not to blame the trial lawyers for employing such tactics. Yet the legal profession is somewhat responsible for the fact that non-lawyers do sometimes assess such blame. For lawyers and judges declare solemnly that every lawyer is an "officer of the court." So to designate the lawyer, said one court, "is by no means a figure of speech," since "it is his duty to help save the court from error and imposition, and to aid the court to a proper determination of the law and the facts. Theoretically, at least, it is counsel's first duty to see that the issue is justly decided, however his client is affected." His "office" is "indispensable to the administration of justice. . . ." But these words mean only that a lawyer must not affirmatively mislead a court, must not introduce in evidence, at a trial, documents which he knows to be false, testimony which he knows to be perjured. Most courts do not effectively disapprove of the lawyers' wiles I have described. Little wonder, then, if laymen sometimes smile cynically when they hear lawyers called court "officers," think it a strange sort of judicial officer who is authorized ingeniously to obscure the facts from trial judges and juries.

The layman's bafflement at the workings of the judicial system has been remarkably described by Kafka, in his book, *The Trial.* There, too, he gives a layman's attitude towards the apathy of many lawyers concerning reforms of the system. Although "the pettiest Advocate," he writes, "might be to some extent capable of analysing the state of things in the Court, it never occurred to the Advocates that they should suggest or insist on any improvements in the system, while—and this was very characteristic—almost every accused man, even quite ordinary people among them, discovered from the earliest stages a passion for suggesting reforms which often wasted time and energy that [the Advocates thought] could have been better employed in other directions. The only sensible thing [for an Advocate] was to adapt oneself to existing conditions. . . . One must lie low, no matter how much it went against the grain. Must try to understand that this great organization remained, so to speak, in a state of delicate balance, and that if someone took it upon himself to alter the disposition of things around him, . . . the organization would simply right itself by some compensating reaction in another part of its machinery—since everything interlocked—and remain unchanged, unless, indeed, which was very probable, it became still more rigid, more vigilant, more severe, and more ruthless."

Kafka's reaction is one of mild bitterness. Jonathan Swift was more vitriolic. He referred to lawyers as "a society of men . . . bred up from their youth in the art of proving by words, multiplied for the purpose"—and in "a jargon of their own that no other mortal can understand"—that "white is black, and black is white, according as they are paid." Kipling talks of "the tribe who describe with a jibe the perversions of justice"; and Soddy calls lawyers "charlatans" who aim to "mystify the public."[2] Those strictures are altogether too severe; their analyses of lawyers' motivations are inaccurate. And such writers, being uninformed laymen, cannot be constructively critical. What we need today is the kind of vigorous, patient, reformist zeal of a knowing critic like Jeremy Bentham, whose untiring attacks (in the late 18th and early 19th centuries) on lawyers' complacency in the

[2] For other similar strictures, see Frank, *Law and the Modern Mind* (1930) 1-2, 325.

face of judicial injustice, led to the elimination of some of the worst features of judicial procedure.[3]

5

Our contentious trial method, I have said, has its roots in the origin of court trials as substitutes for private brawls. But that does not altogether explain its survival. Wigmore (following up a suggestion made by Bentham) suggested that "the common law, originating in a community of sports and games, was permeated by the instinct of sportsmanship" which led to a "sporting theory of justice," a theory of "legalized gambling." This theory, although it had some desirable effects, "has contributed," said Wigmore, "to lower the system of administering justice and in particular of ascertaining truth in litigation, to the level of a mere game of skill or chance . . .", in which lawyers use evidence "as one plays a trump card, or draws to three aces, or holds back a good horse till the home-stretch. . . ."

Damon Runyon had much the same idea. "A big murder trial," he wrote, "possesses some of the elements of a sporting event. I find the same popular interest in a murder trial that I find . . . on the eve of a big football game, or a pugilistic encounter, or a baseball series. There is the same conversational speculation on the probable result, only more of it. . . . The trial is a sort of game, the players on the one side the attorneys for the defense, and on the other side the attorneys for the State. The defendant figures in it merely as the prize. . . . And the players must be men well-schooled in their play. They must be crafty men. . . . The game of murder trial is played according to very strict rules, with stern umpires, called judges, to prevent any deviations from these rules. . . ." The players "are supposed to be engaged in a sort of common cause, which is to determine the guilt or innocence of the defendant. . . . A player . . . for the State represents the people. His function, as I understand it," Runyon continued, "is to endeavor to convict any person who has transgressed the law. . . . It is inconceivable that he would wish to convict an innocent person. But it has been my observation that the player or attorney for the State is quick to take any advantage of the rules

[3] That Bentham, however, seemed to have believed it possible to eliminate subjectivities in fact finding, see Maine, *Early History of Institutions* (1875) 48-50; Frank, *If Men Were Angels* (1942) 116-118; cf. Kessler, "Theoretic Bases of Law," 9 *Un. of Chicago L. Rev.* (1941) 98, 107.

. . . that puts his side in front, and equally quick to forestall any moves by the other side."

This Wigmore-Runyon explanation may be partially sound, but it seems to me to over-emphasize sportsmanship. I suggest, as an additional partial explanation of the perpetuation of the excessive fighting method of trials, both civil and criminal, the belief in uncontrolled competition, of unbridled individualism. I suggest that the fighting theory of justice is not unrelated to, and not uninfluenced by, extreme laissez-faire in the economic field.

"Classical" laissez-faire economic theory assumed that, when each individual, as an "economic man," strives rationally, in the competitive economic struggle or "fight," to promote his own self-interest, we attain public welfare through the wisest use of resources and the most socially desirable distribution of economic goods. The "fight" theory of justice is a sort of legal laissez-faire. It assumes a "litigious man." It assumes that, in a law suit, each litigious man, in the court-room competitive strife, will, through his lawyer, intelligently and energetically try to use the evidential resources to bring out the evidence favorable to him and unfavorable to his court-room competitor; that thereby the trial court will obtain all the available relevant evidence; and that thus, in a socially beneficial way, the court will apply the social policies embodied in the legal rules to the actual facts, avoiding the application of those rules to a mistaken version of the facts. Legal laissez-faire theory therefore assumes that the government can safely rely on the "individual enterprise" of individual litigants to ensure that court-orders will be grounded on all the practically attainable relevant facts.

Most of us have come to distrust, in the economic field, ultra let-alone-ism, the ultra laissez-faire theory with its anti-social concept of an "economic man." For observation of social realities has shown that the basic postulates of that theory, although in part correct, are inadequate as exclusive postulates. I think that, in like fashion, observation of court-room realities shows that the postulates of legal laissez-faire are insufficient as exclusive postulates. We should retain what there is of value in the fighting theory of justice, eliminating what is socially harmful. We should retain, I repeat, so much of "individual initiative" in the trial of cases as serves to bring out evidence that might be overlooked and the niceties of legal rules a court might otherwise ignore.[4]

[4] However, there may be aspects of the rules to which neither litigant will call the court's attention. As Demogue suggests, the "duellistic" nature of litigation may create

But the fight should not so dominate a law-suit that it leads to the non-discovery of important evidence and the distortion of testimony.

6

The fighting theory has, in part, broken down. Time was when a litigant could refuse to disclose evidence in his possession to the adversary party before trial. But so-called "discovery" procedure has been developed which requires such disclosure in non-criminal cases. The federal courts are particularly energetic in compelling such "discovery." Thus far, at least, have we advanced towards effectuating the "truth" theory.

There have been other advances, such as increased insistence on the power and right of the trial judge to take a hand in examining witnesses, and even to summon witnesses of whom he is aware and whom neither litigant has called. I must add, however, that regrettably (as I see it) few judges avail themselves of that power. Judge Shientag, a learned and respected judge, recently said that "a litigant has the right to expect . . . that the judge will not interfere in the examination of witnesses, even though he believes he can do a better job than counsel, except to correct patent errors, misconceptions or misrepresentations. . . ." Some bolder trial judges disagree.[5]

But even if the judge does "interfere," and even if "discovery" procedure is open, the trial court may fail to learn of crucial evidence. Partly this may be due to the incompetence of the lawyer for one side. For lack of means to retain an able lawyer, the impecunious litigant may here be singularly disadvantaged. To some extent we are overcoming that handicap, through Legal Aid Services, although much remains to be done before the legal procession catches up with the medical profession in assisting the indigent and the "white-collar" men.[6]

Apart from failure to bring out the evidence, the mistakes of a man's lawyer may cause him to lose his case—a proper result under strict legal laissez-faire theory. But is it fair that a litigant should be

---

a false "dualistic" attitude towards the pertinent legal rules. See Aero Spark Plug Co. v. B. G. Corporation, 130 F. (2d) 290 at 299 and notes 27 to 31.

In *Fate and Freedom,* I have discussed "economic" ultra-laissez-faire.

[5] Judge Pecora, for instance.

[6] Through "lawyer reference" programs and "low-cost service bureaus" the legal profession is making a start in assisting the white-collar man. In England, a statute will soon be enacted by which legal services of that kind will be provided. See Smith, "The English Legal Assistance Plan," 35 *Am. Bar Ass'n J* (1949) 453.

punished because he retained an incompetent lawyer?[7] When an error of a trial court, resulting from a lawyer's blunder, is egregious, the upper courts sometimes relieve the litigant. But there persists a reluctance to grant such relief. Maybe that reluctance is justified. I am not sure.

7

There is one most serious handicap in litigation that has received little attention:[8] With the ablest lawyer in the world, a man may lose a suit he ought to win, if he has not the funds to pay for an investigation, before trial, of evidence necessary to sustain his case. I refer to evidence not in the files of the other party and therefore not obtainable by "discovery" procedure. What I mean is this: In order to prove his claim, or to defend against one, a man may need to hire detectives to scour the country—even sometimes foreign countries—in order to locate witnesses who alone may know of events that occurred years ago, or to unearth letters or other papers which may be in distant places. Or, again, he may need the services of an engineer, or a chemist, or an expert accountant, to make an extensive—and therefore expensive—investigation. Without the evidence which such an investigation would reveal, a man is often bound to be defeated. His winning or losing may therefore depend on his pocketbook. He is out of luck if his pocketbook is not well-lined with money. For neither his lawyer nor any legal-aid institution will supply the needed sums. For want of money, expendable for such purposes, many a suit has been lost, many a meritorious claim or defense has never even been asserted.

Let me illustrate. Fisher, in his recent excellent book, *The Art of Investigation,* writes: "The percentage of witnesses who cannot be found if enough effort is exerted is infinitesimal. A famous investigator once said that the man who could not be found is the man at the bottom of the sea, and even then he must be at the bottom at its points of greatest depth. Anyone alive can be found if enough effort is put forth." That statement may be exaggerated. But you get the point: Suppose there is one man, John Brown, who alone could testify to a crucial event—such as that Sam Jones was in New York City on June 12, 1948. Brown is missing. He may be in China, India or Peru.

[7] See Cleary, Book Review, 62 *Harv. L. Rev.* (1949) 902; In re Barnett, 124 F. (2d) 1005, 1011.

[8] I have discussed this handicap more in detail in "White Collar Justice," *Saturday Evening Post,* July 17, 1943, p. 7. See also In re Fried, 161 F. (2d) 453, 464; Frank, Book Review, 56 *Yale L.J.* (1947) 594.

If he can be found, and if he testifies, the plaintiff will win his suit; otherwise he will lose it. If the plaintiff can afford to pay enough to investigators to scour the world for the missing witness, he may be located. If the plaintiff is a man of means, he will hire such investigators. But if he has little money, he can't do so—and will lose his case which may involve all his worldly goods.

That is not true justice, democratic justice. This defect in our judicial system makes a mockery of "equality before the law," which should be one of the first principles of a democracy. That equality, in such instances, depends on a person's financial condition. The tragedy of such a situation is etched in irony when a man's impoverished condition has resulted from a wrong done him by another whom he cannot successfully sue to redress the wrong. Many of our state constitutions contain a provision that "every person ought to obtain justice freely and without being obliged to purchase it." But, as things stand, this is too often a provision in words only. For the advantage in litigation is necessarily on the side of the party that can "purchase justice" by hiring private assistance in obtaining evidence when his adversary cannot. Unless we contrive some method to solve the problem I have posed, we must acknowledge that, in a very real sense, frequently we are "selling justice," denying it to many under-incomed persons. It should shock us that judicial justice is thus often an upper-bracket privilege. Here we have legal laissez-faire at its worst.

That brings me to a point which the fighting theory obscures. A court's decision is not a mere private affair. It culminates in a court order which is one of the most solemn of governmental acts. Not only is a court an agency of government, but remember that its order, if not voluntarily obeyed, will bring into action the police, the sheriff, even the army. What a court orders, then, is no light matter. The court represents the government, organized society, in action.

Such an order a court is not supposed to make unless there exist some facts which bring into operation a legal rule. Now any government officer, other than a judge, if authorized to do an act for the government only if certain facts exist, will be considered irresponsible if he so acts without a governmental investigation. For instance, if an official is empowered to pay money to a veteran suffering from some specified ailment, the official, if he does his duty, will not rely solely on the applicant's statement that he has such an ailment. The government officer insists on a governmental check-up of the evidence. Do courts so conduct themselves?

In criminal cases they seem to, after a fashion. In such cases, there is some recognition that so important a governmental act as a court decision against a defendant should not occur without someone, on behalf of the government itself, seeing to it that the decision is justified by the actual facts so far as they can be discovered with reasonable diligence. For, in theory at least, usually before a criminal action is begun, an official investigation has been conducted which reveals data sufficient to warrant bringing the defendant to trial. In some jurisdictions, indigent defendants charged with crime are represented by a publicly-paid official, a Public Defender—a highly important reform which should everywhere be adopted. And the responsibility of government for mistakes of fact in criminal cases, resulting in erroneous court judgments, is recognized in those jurisdictions in which the government compensates an innocent convicted person if it is subsequently shown that he was convicted through such a mistake.

In civil cases (non-criminal cases), on the whole a strikingly different attitude prevails. Although, no less than in a criminal suit, a court's order is a grave governmental act, yet, in civil cases, the government usually accepts no similar responsibilities, even in theory. Such a suit is still in the ancient tradition of "self help." The court usually relies almost entirely on such evidence as one or the other of the private parties to the suit is (a) able to, and (b) chooses to, offer. Lack of skill or diligence of the lawyer for one of those parties, or that party's want of enough funds to finance a pre-trial investigation necessary to obtain evidence, may have the result, as I explained, that crucial available evidence is not offered in court. No government official has the duty to discover, and bring to court, evidence, no matter how important, not offered by the parties.

In short, the theory is that, in most civil suits, the government, through its courts, should make orders which the government will enforce, although those court-orders may not be justified by the actual facts, and although, by reasonable diligence, the government, had it investigated, might have discovered evidence—at variance with the evidence presented—coming closer to the actual facts.

Yet the consequence of a court decision in a civil suit, based upon the court's mistaken view of the actual facts, may be as grave as a criminal judgment which convicts an innocent person. If, because of such an erroneous decision, a man loses his job or his savings and becomes utterly impoverished, he may be in almost as serious a plight as if he had been jailed. His poverty may make him a public charge.

It may lead to the delinquency of his children, who may thus become criminals and go to jail. Yet in no jurisdiction is a man compensated by the government for serious injury to him caused by a judgment against him in a non-criminal case, even if later it is shown that the judgment was founded upon perjured or mistaken testimony.

I suggest that there is something fundamentally wrong in our legal system in this respect. If a man's pocket is picked, the government brings a criminal suit, and accepts responsibility for its prosecution. If a man loses his life's savings through a breach of a contract, the government accepts no such responsibility. Shouldn't the government perhaps assume some of the burden of enforcing what we call "private rights"?

Some few moves have been made in the right direction. In an English divorce court, an official, the King's Proctor, brings forward evidence, bearing on possible collusion, not offered by either contestant; some American states provide that the public prosecutor shall do likewise in divorce actions. In our own Domestic Relations Courts, government officers procure and present most of the evidence. Lawyers for any of the parties may cross-examine any witness, may offer additional evidence, and may argue about the applicable legal rules. The advantages of the adversary method are fully preserved, but the fighting spirit is much diminished. Under the Chandler Act, enacted in 1938, in certain types of cases relating to corporate reorganization, the SEC, at large public expense, uses its expert staff to obtain and present to the court evidence which usually no private party could afford to procure; the judge and the private parties may treat this evidence like any other evidence, and the parties may introduce further supplementary or conflicting evidence.

Many of our administrative agencies have large and efficient staffs to conduct investigations in order to ferret out evidence put before those agencies in their own administrative proceedings. I know, from personal experience, that not much evidence escapes an agency like the SEC.[9] Mr. Justice Jackson has said: "Such a tribunal is not as dependent as the ordinary court upon the arguments of skilled counsel to get at the truth. Skilled advocacy is neither so necessary to keep such a body informed nor is stupid or clever advocacy so apt to blur the merits of a controversy."

I do not suggest that courts, like such administrative bodies, conduct their own investigations through their own employees. I do suggest

[9] See Frank, *If Men Were Angels* (1942) 124-28.

that we should consider whether it is not feasible to provide impartial government officials—who are not court employees, and who act on their own initiative—to dig up, and present to the courts, significant evidence which one or the other of the parties may overlook or be unable to procure. No court would be bound to accept that evidence as true. Nor would any of the parties be precluded from trying to show the unreliability of such evidence (by cross-examination or otherwise) or from introducing additional evidence. Trials would still remain adversary. As I concede that to use that device in all civil cases would lead to many complications, I do not urge that it be at once generally adopted. But I think experiments along those lines should now be made.

This proposal resembles somewhat the procedures long used in criminal cases on the European continent. Critics may oppose it on that ground, saying that we should not take over ideas from countries which have been less democratic than ours. To any such argument, Woodrow Wilson gave the answer: "But why should we not use such parts of foreign contrivances as we want if they may be in any way serviceable? We are in no danger of using them in a foreign way. We borrowed rice, but we do not eat it with chopsticks."

It will also be said that any such proposal is absurdly radical. Yet something of the sort was endorsed by President Taft, by no means a radical. More than thirty years ago he said: "Of all the questions . . . before the American people I regard no one as more important than this, the improvement of the administration of justice. We must make it so that the poor man will have as nearly as possible an opportunity in litigating as the rich man, and under present conditions, ashamed as we may be of it, this is not the fact."[10] Moreover, we now have public-utility commissions which, on behalf of private persons, bring rate-suits against utility companies. With that in mind, Willoughby wrote a book, published in 1927 by the conservative Brookings Institution, in which he proposed the appointment of a "public prosecutor of civil actions." If a complaint were made to the prosecutor, he would first try to settle the matter or to have the parties agree to submit the dispute to arbitration. Only if these efforts failed would he bring suit. No one would be obliged to retain prosecutor; his em-

[10] Chief Justice Hughes, urging the need of "legal aid," said in 1920: "There is no more serious menace than the discontent which is fostered by a belief that one cannot enforce his legal rights because of poverty. To spread that notion is to open a broad road to Bolshevism."

ployment would be optional; and, if any action were brought on a person's behalf by the prosecutor, that person would be at liberty to retain a private lawyer to assist in the preparation for, and conduct of, the trial. That idea, I think, merits public discussion and consideration. Were it adopted, it should perhaps be supplemented to include a practice now adopted, in some states, by the Public Defender in criminal actions: That official is authorized to expend public funds to seek out and procure what he regards as essential evidence.

Statutes in some jurisdictions authorize the trial judge to call as a witness an expert selected by the judge. Judges might sometimes avail themselves of that power to help indigent or under-incomed litigants. But I believe that none of those statutes, as they now read, provides for payment by the government to judge-called experts in non-criminal suits. Moreover, those statutes will not meet the difficulties of a prospective litigant when making up his mind whether to bring or defend a suit. Nor do they permit expenditures for detectives and other investigators not regarded as "experts." Nevertheless, this expedient might be expanded so as partially to solve the problem I have presented.

None of these proposals, if adopted, would usher in the millenium. Official evidence gatherers, or public prosecutors of civil actions, will make mistakes, or become excessively partisan. The trial process is, and always will be, human, therefore fallible. It can never be a completely scientific investigation for the discovery of the true facts.

8

I said that, in theory, in criminal suits the government seems to take greater responsibility than in civil suits, that theoretically, in each criminal trial, the public prosecutor has made a pre-trial investigation and that he brings out, at the trial, the evidence he has uncovered. Actually, many prosecutors, infected badly by the fighting spirit, in partisan manner produce only the evidence they think will cause convictions. In most jurisdictions, "discovery" in criminal cases is denied; even where permitted it is narrowly limited. We should, I think, follow the practice now well settled in England where, before trial, the prosecutor must disclose to the accused all evidence the prosecutor intends to offer.

The "third degree" is widely employed by our police, too often with the tacit approval of prosecutors, to extort confessions which, obtained by physical or mental torture, are not infrequently untrue.[11] To our shame be it said that the English, who do not tolerate the "third degree," call it the "American method." Competent American police—such as the FBI force—do not resort to that outrageous device. To rid ourselves of it, we must have a public demand for properly trained police forces. And to rid ourselves of unfair prosecutors, we should not permit any man to hold that office who has not been specially educated for that job and passed stiff written and oral examinations demonstrating his moral and intellectual fitness.

9

It has been suggested that trained psychologists, called by trial judges as the court's experts, be permitted to testify as "testimonial experts" concerning the witnesses. Such an expert, it is proposed, having interviewed and examined a witness out of court, would testify at the trial about the witness's capacity for hearing, seeing, touching, tasting, his capacity for attention and memory, and any "abnormal" tendencies (such as "pathological lying," for instance).[12] The expert would be subject to cross-examination, and his testimony about a witness would not be binding on the trial judge or jury.

Applied to every witness at every trial, this proposal (of which Wigmore approves)[13] is open to the objection that it would make trials endless. Yet I think we ought to experiment with the idea. Aware that judges and juries lack competence in medicine, physics, chemistry, and a host of other subjects, we now use expert witnesses to guide our trial courts. Sizing up a witness from his statements and demeanor when on the witness-stand is a difficult task at best, and one at which juries and most judges are amateurs. Expert aid in the discharge of that task might do much to minimize mistakes in fact-finding.

10

Suppose that, in a crude "primitive" society, A claims that B took A's pig. If that is true, B violated a well-settled tribal rule. But B

[11] See, e.g., Frank, *If Men Were Angels* (1942) 317-24.

[12] In some cities, applicants for drivers' licenses are examined by experts to determine whether they are neurotic or psychotic, for such persons will be menaces if they drive cars. Yet we now allow men's lives and fortunes to be menaced by witnesses of that sort whose defects are undisclosed.

[13] Wigmore, "Evidence in the Next Century," in the volume *Law: A Century of Progress*, II, 346, 360.

denies that he took the pig. A attacks B and kills him. Does A's killing of B prove that B was wrong about the facts? Does that killing constitute the enforcement of the tribal rule? Now suppose somewhat the same sort of dispute in the U.S.A. A sues B, claiming that, by fraud and deceit, B got A's pig. A legal rule says that if B did those acts, then A has a legal right to get back the pig or its money value. If A wins that suit, does the decision in his favor constitute the enforcement of that legal rule, even if A won through perjured testimony or because the trial court erroneously believed an honest but mistaken witness?

A lawyer friend of mine, to whom I put this question, replied, "Yes, in theory. In theory, the facts as found must be assumed to be true." His answer does not satisfy me. That we must accept the facts found by a trial court does not mean that a rule against fraud is really enforced when a court holds a man liable for a fraud he did not commit. My friend is saying, in effect, that, even were it true that the courts misfound the facts in 90% of all cases, still the courts would be enforcing the rules.

That conclusion does not bother the hardened cynic. "In the long run," one may imagine him saying, "what is the difference whether courts make many mistakes in fact-finding, and, as a result, render erroneous decisions—as long as the public generally doesn't learn of those mistakes? Take, for instance, all this to-do about 'convicting the innocent.' One of the important purposes of punishing a man for a crime is to deter others from becoming criminals. Conviction and punishment of the innocent serve just as effectively as if they were guilty to deter others from crime—provided only the errors are not, too frequently, later discovered and publicized. It's tough on the innocent; but we can afford to sacrifice them for the public good. In the same way, if a non-criminal legal rule is of a desirable kind—for instance, a rule concerning the duty of a trustee to the beneficiaries of a trust—why bother whether, in particular law-suits, the courts, through failure to discover the actual facts, apply it to persons who haven't violated it? Public respect for that rule, and its infiltration into community habits, will come just as well from its misapplications as from its correct applications—if only the public doesn't learn of its misapplications. If you call it injustice to punish the innocent or mistakenly to enter money judgments against men who have done no legal wrongs, then I answer that effectively concealed instances of injustice are not only harmless but socially beneficial. They serve as useful examples. Don't get squeamish about such mistakes." I doubt whether any reader will agree with the cynic.

11

No one can doubt that the invention of courts, which preserve the peace by settling disputes, marked a great step forward in human progress. But are we to be so satisfied with this forward step that we will rest content with it? Should not a modern civilized society ask more of its courts than that they stop peace-disrupting brawls? The basic aim of the courts in our society should, I think, be the just settlement of particular disputes, the just decision of specific law-suits.

The just settlement of disputes demands a legal system in which the courts can and do strive tirelessly to get as close as is humanly possible to the actual facts of specific court-room controversies. Court-house justice is, I repeat, done at retail, not at wholesale. The trial court's job of fact-finding in each particular case therefore looms up as one of the most important jobs in modern court-house government. With no lack of deep admiration and respect for our many able trial judges, I must say that that job is not as well done as it could and should be. No wonder it is not, when a leading law-teacher, Professor Morgan of Harvard, a close student of trials, can write that a law-suit, as most law-suits are now required to be conducted, is not "a proceeding for the discovery of truth," but "a game in which the contestants are not the litigants but the lawyers." Reviewing a book on trial techniques by an experienced trial lawyer, which revealed in detail the tactics of court-room fighting—tactics considered entirely legitimate, but which patently impede the discovery of the true facts, so far as they are practically discoverable—Morgan commented sadly, "If only a reviewer could assert that this book is a guide not to the palaces of justice but to the red-light districts of the law. But a decent respect for the truth compels the admission that [the author] has told his story truly."

A distinguished legal historian, Vinagradoff, has said that an "ancient trial" was little more than a "formally regulated struggle between the parties in which the judge acted more as an umpire or warden of order and fair play than as an investigator of truth." To continue that ancient tradition, unmodified, to treat a law-suit as, above all, a fight, surely cannot be the best way to discover the facts. Improvement in fact-finding will necessitate some considerable diminution of the martial spirit in litigation.

VII. THE PROCEDURAL REFORMERS

IN MY discussion of the legal rules—the *R*'s in the $R \times F = D$ formula—I have dwelt on what lawyers call "substantive" rules. Those rules, it is said, state what a man may or may not lawfully do out of court, before any litigation occurs. The orthodox theory holds that, from those rules, grow "substantive legal rights," such as the right not to have others trespass on one's land or the right to have a contract performed.

Many legal writers declare that those "substantive" legal rights—which they also call "primary" or "independent" rights—exist quite apart from the courts. "If," says Pomeroy, "mankind were so constituted that disobedience to legal rules was impossible, the law would be entirely made up of the rules which create these primary . . . rights"; and Buckland says that "if all men were law-abiding and well-informed . . . , law courts could go out of business." In other words, only because all men are not angels do we need courts and law-suits. A law-suit, so the theory runs, is brought only because, un-angel-like, some man has violated (or threatened to violate), a "substantive" rule, has invaded (or threatened to invade) a "primary" or "substantive" right conferred by such a rule.

But if one of a man's "substantive" rights has been invaded, or threatened with invasion, and he does bring a law-suit, the suit is supposed to be governed by another kind of rules, rules of "procedure," which relate to what must be done in court. Those conduct-in-court rules cover such subjects as the way a suit must be commenced, the way in which a party must state ("plead") his claim or defense, the sort of evidence the courts will receive or reject. These "procedural" rules are customarily designated as "adjective," or "remedial," or "dependent," or "subordinate." Those labels indicate that these rules are really subordinate,[1] are mere means or "machinery," used in vindicating the rights given by the "substantive" rules, rights which supposedly pre-exist and are independent of what any court may do about them.

That notion of the "subordinate" character of "procedure" may easily mislead. For the failure of a lawyer to comply with a procedural rule (for instance, by filing a badly worded "pleading") may spell a

[1] See, e.g., Michael, *The Elements of Legal Controversy* (1948) 8.

litigant's defeat in a law-suit, completely frustrating his "substantive" right. Such a defeat, for "procedural" errors, is fully as disastrous to him as if the court held that he had no such right.

Instead, then, of saying, "If certain facts occur, a court will attach to them certain legal consequences," we might say, "If certain facts occur, and if the procedural rules are complied with, a court will attach these consequences." A more accurate way of stating the matter is this: "If certain facts are 'proved,' in accordance with the requirements and within the limits allowed by the procedural rules, then a favorable decision should result." Which is to say that, practically, "procedure" shows up as fully as important as the "substantive" rules. Indeed, the differentiation between the "substantive" and "procedural" rules, although useful for some purposes, is artificial from at least one viewpoint: All the rules, including the "substantive," may be looked at as "procedural" in the sense that they are all merely weapons in the courtroom fight.

Aware that the "substantive" rules, no matter how excellent, won't work, and become futile, if the procedural rules are too rigid or otherwise seriously defective, some wise lawyers, the "procedural reformers," have insisted that the procedural rules must be so revised as to provide efficient "machinery" for the vindication of "substantive" rights. These reformers, who at first glance seem to have escaped the thralldom of legal magic, have, in recent years, successfully achieved many of their reforms.

Yet, judged by their aims, these reformers have failed. For all their admirable efforts, they have not succeeded in bringing about what they promised—the easy, simple, unimpeded operation, in court, of the substantive rules in such a way as to prevent litigants from losing suits which, under those rules, they should win. Why? Because, having correctly concluded that improved procedure is necessary for the effective operation of the substantive rules, these reformers mistakenly thought that improved procedural rules, without more, would do the trick. They forgot the troublesome nature of the *F's*. They confused a "necessary" with a "sufficient" condition—a fallacy which William James illustrated when he said that the breaking of eggs is a necessary condition of an omelet but that an omelet does not appear whenever eggs are broken.

Note that the word "machinery" is often used by these reformers to describe procedure. But well-working judicial machinery, while essential, is not alone enough to enable the courts to give full effect to substantive rights. These reformers, by creating the erroneous belief that well-contrived substantive rules plus well-contrived procedural-rule "machinery" will suffice to produce competent judicial administration of justice, have raised false hopes. They have themselves largely disregarded, and thereby unfortunately deflected attention from, the non-machinery elements of the decisional process. Even if we have the best judicial machinery, those non-machinery elements will often lead to decisions which balk the operation of the substantive rules.

For the products of a machine depend (1) on the material which goes into the machine and (2) on the persons who operate it. As to the first (the materials on which the machine works), think of such items as the failure of a litigant to obtain crucial evidence because he lacks funds to make a pre-trial investigation, or the mistakes (deliberate or inadvertent) of witnesses. The second (the "machine operators," trial judges and juries), I shall discuss in succeeding chapters.

2

The procedural reformers are fond of saying that wherever there is a substantive legal "right," there should be a "remedy." But they narrow the meaning of "remedy" so that it means only that the rules afford the "holder" of the "right" ample opportunity to bring before the trial court all the evidence he can procure in order to "prove" the facts on which his right is based. That opportunity, however, will not be enough to give the litigant the one thing in which he is most interested—a decision in his favor.

As such a decision is not a resultant merely of substantive plus procedural rules, those rules, no matter how excellent, will frequently fall far short of ensuring that a man who ought to win, on the basis of the actual objective facts, will do so. In any practical sense, if he loses such a suit, he has no remedy—and therefore no right. A right that cannot be enforced or vindicated is like a hole in a doughnut.

It has been correctly said that, if a right can be proved in only one way, the right does not exist unless that proof is available. If, then, a procedural rule is too strict in its requirement as to the kind of evidence necessary to prove a right—if it rules out the only evidence a litigant can lay his hands on—a change in that rule may avert injustice. But, when expensive investigation is needed, but not obtainable,[2] to render available the proof required under the most flexible procedure,

[2] See Chapter VI.

no procedural rule will suffice. Nor will any such rule suffice to guide the trial judge or jury in determining which of the witnesses are reliable.

Let me enlarge on that idea by taking as illustrative some substantive rules about agreements. Those rules seem to provide that if, for instance, Black and White exchange certain kinds of promises, they create a contract, and that, if White breaks his promise contained in the contract, then a court should give Black a judgment against White for the damages Black sustained. These substantive rules, at first glance, seem to provide that if those facts—the making and breaking of the promise—occurred, Black will be entitled to such a decision in his favor. But if we examine those substantive rules more carefully, we see that what they really provide is this: Black, to win his suit against White, must "prove" that those facts happened. We may therefore restate these substantive rules this way: If Black "proves" that he and White exchanged promises and that White broke his promise, then Black will be entitled to a decision against White.

But what does "prove" mean? It usually means that Black, by the oral testimony of witnesses, persuades a trial judge or jury that those facts occurred. "Persuades," in turn, means that the judge or jury so believes. For purposes of obtaining a court-decision, it does not make the least difference whether those facts ever actually happened.[3] As I have explained, all that counts is the trial court's belief. So that, for court purposes, a substantive legal right does not depend on (1) substantive legal rules plus (2) the procedural rules plus (3) the actual facts. It depends on (a) those rules, and (b) the court's guess about the facts.[4] And that guess usually depends, among other things, upon the personalities of the trial judge or jury in reacting to the conflicting oral testimony.

Since about such matters the procedural rules are silent, the procedural reformers err in over-emphasizing the importance of the rule-aspects of procedure. For, as we have seen, often the "unruly" elements in the trial process—the factors that inherently cannot be formulated in rules—play a dominant part in producing decisions. Thus these reformers turn out to be, not "fact-skeptics," but merely one species of "rule-skeptics." They, too, live in a one-dimensional legal world, an artificial world in which rules control decisions. Insufficiently bitten by "fact-skepticism," these reformers have under-estimated the effects

[3] See In re Fried, 161 F. (2d) 453, 462-463.

[4] For further complications, see Chapter XII.

of trial-court "discretion" concerning credibility. The procedural reformers are, then, in part, devotees of legal magic. (From this criticism there must be excepted some of these reformers, among them my colleague, Judge Charles E. Clark, and Professor Morgan.)

I suggested that the success of a trial, if regarded as an inquiry to ascertain the true facts, is limited by at least two factors: The first—the procuring of the evidence—I have now discussed. In the next chapters I shall turn to the second, the competence of those conducting the inquiry.

VIII. THE JURY SYSTEM

As you know, sometimes a case is tried before a trial judge, sometimes before a judge and jury. I shall for the time being treat principally of jury trials.[1]

Blackstone called the jury "the glory of the English law." Jefferson, who detested Blackstone as a Tory, agreed with him at least on that one subject. Judge Knox, chief federal district judge in the Southern District of New York, said a few years ago, "In my opinion, the jury system is one of the really great achievements of English and American jurisprudence."

As you'll see, I dissent from those views. When I hear the jury praised as the "palladium of our liberties," I keep thinking that, while a palladium (a word derived from the ancient use of the image of Pallas Athena) means something on which the safety of a nation or an institution depends, it also is the name of a chemical element which, in the spongy state "has the remarkable quality of absorbing, up to nearly 1,000 times its own volume in hydrogen gas."

To comprehend the jury's laudation, we need to take a quick (even if superficial) look at its history: The Greeks had a jury system, but ours did not derive from it. Although all historians today are not in accord on this topic, many of them say that the germ of the modern English jury is to be found in 9th century France, where it began as a royal administrative device, perhaps borrowed from 5th centry Roman procedure. When, in the 9th century, certain of the king's rights were in question, twelve men of the neighborhood were called in to state the facts on their oath. The jury then consisted, in effect, of witnesses. And so it remained, as a king's implement, when it was imported into England, via Normandy, by William the Conqueror. (Parenthetically, if this be correct history, it has its amusing aspects: The jury, prized today by many who dislike the administrative agencies, began its life as such an agency.)

[1] See, in connection with this chapter, my opinion in Skidmore v. Baltimore and Ohio Railroad Co., 167 F. (2d) 54 which includes some matter omitted here. See also Frank, *Law and The Modern Mind* (1930) 170-185, 302-309; Frank, *If Men Were Angels* (1942) 80-90, 95-96.

At any rate, in England, it spread as a mode of trial, competing with the ordeals. According to Maitland, as we saw, the jury was not by any means immediately popular; he says that at first the ordeals were generally considered more desirable, more safe. But the jury later superseded the ordeals. By the end of the 15th century, in England the jury had grown into substantially what it is today—no longer a body of witnesses but a body which hears witnesses. In the 17th century contests with the Stuart kings, it came to be highly regarded, popularly, as a check on royal judges doing the Crown's bidding.

In the American colonies, in the 18th century, juries often stood up to judges controlled by a hostile British government. Little wonder that our federal constitution and our state constitutions adopted after the American Revolution began, embodied provisions guaranteeing trial by jury. Later, in the period when the Jeffersonians were pitted against Federalist judges, juries often were anti-judge. So, on our soil, too, the jury was considered a champion of the popular cause, cherished as a bulwark against oppressive government, acclaimed as essential to individual liberty and democracy. It is not improper, then, to regard the modern jury as essentially an Anglo-American institution.

Trial by jury was exported to other countries. The victorious revolutionaries in France successfully espoused the jury in criminal cases. And, as a result of the 19th century revolutions, on the European continent the jury in criminal (but not in civil) cases was adopted as a symbol of liberty.

In the United States, the jury still retains much of its glamour. True, there has been something of an increase in the number of civil (i.e., non-criminal) suits in which jury trials have been waived. But in criminal cases the jury still largely keeps its hold. Except in this country, however, trial by jury fell into disfavor in the 20th century. In some Swiss cantons it was abolished. In pre-Hitler Germany and France, its use was more and more limited. This unpopularity cannot be explained as a symptom of decreased interest in liberty and democracy. For Scotland, surely a land of liberty-loving individuals, having virtually rejected the non-criminal jury in the 16th century, readopted it in 1815, and subsequently all but gave it up. In England, even before World War II, it was seldom employed in civil suits, was abandoned in criminal prosecutions except for major crimes, and even there was, and is, used decreasingly. Surely that attitude in England, the birthplace of the modern jury, should give us pause. Especially should it do so, when it is recalled that American defenders of the jury have often asserted that the major ills of our jury system would vanish if only we adopted the English way of using it. If, as Judge Knox says, the jury system "is one of the really great achievements of English and American jurisprudence," why has it all but gone into the discard in England, except in a decreasing percentage of major criminal prosecutions? And why has Congress never granted the privilege of trial by jury in a suit against the United States?

It will not do then to make Fourth-of-July speeches about the glorious jury system, to conceal its grave defects, or merely to palliate them with superficial, cosmetic-like, remedies. We need to have our public comprehend what the jury actually is like in order to arouse public interest to the point where steps will be taken to eradicate its most glaring deficiencies.

2

I have said that, supposedly, the task of our courts is this: To make reasoned applications of legal rules to the carefully ascertained facts of particular law-suits. You will recall my crude schematization of the alleged nature of the process—$R \times F = D$—i.e., the Rules times the Facts equals the Decision. Where, in that scheme, does the jury fit in?

In most jury trials, the jury renders what is called a "general verdict." Suppose that Williams sues Allen claiming (1) that Allen falsely told him there was oil on some land Williams bought from Allen, but (2) that in fact there was no oil there, so that Williams was defrauded. The jury listens to the witnesses. Then the judge tells the jurors, "If you find Allen lied, and Williams relied on that lie, a legal rule requires that you hold for the plaintiff Williams, and you must compute the damages according to another rule," which the judge explains. "But if you find that Allen did not lie, then the legal rule requires you to hold for the defendant Allen." The jury deliberately deliberates in the jury-room and reports either, "We find for the plaintiff in the sum of $5,000," or "We find for the defendant." In other words, the jury does not report what facts it found. Such an undetailed, unexplained, jury report is called a "general verdict."

There are three theories of the jury's function:

(1) The naive theory is that the jury merely finds the facts; that it must not, and does not, concern itself with the legal rules, but faithfully accepts the rules as stated to them by the trial judge.

(2) A more sophisticated theory has it that the jury not only finds the facts but, in its deliberation in the jury-room, uses legal reasoning

to apply to those facts the legal rules it learned from the judge. A much respected judge said in 1944 that a jury's verdict should be regarded as "the reasoned and logical result of the concrete application of the law [i.e., the rules] to the facts."

On the basis of this sophisticated theory, the jury system has been criticized. It is said that juries often do not find the facts in accordance with the evidence, but distort—or "fudge"—the facts, and find them in such a manner that (by applying the legal rules laid down by the judge to the facts thus deliberately misfound) the jury is able to produce the result which it desires, in favor of one party or the other. "The facts," we are told, "are found in order to reach the result."

This theory ascribes to jurors a serpentine wisdom. It assumes that they thoroughly understand what the judge tells them about the rules, and that they circumvent the rules by falsely contriving—with consummate skill and cunning—the exact findings of fact which, correlated with those rules, will logically compel the result they desire.

(3) We come now to a third theory which may be called the "realistic" theory. It is based on what anyone can discover by questioning the average person who has served as a juror—namely that often the jury are neither able to, nor do they attempt to, apply the instructions of the court. The jury are more brutally direct. They determine that they want Jones to collect $5,000 from the railroad company, or that they don't want pretty Nellie Brown to go to jail for killing her husband; and they bring in their general verdict accordingly. Often, to all practical intents and purposes, the judge's statement of the legal rules might just as well never have been expressed. "Nor can we," writes Clementson, "cut away the mantle of mystery in which the general verdict is enveloped, to see how the principal facts were determined, and whether the law was applied under the judge's instructions. . . . It is a matter of common knowledge that the general verdict may be the result of anything but the calm deliberation, exchange of impressions and opinions, resolution of doubts, and final intelligent concurrence which, theoretically, produced it. It comes into court unexplained and impenetrable."

The "realistic" theory, then, is that, in many cases, the jury, often without heeding the legal rules, determine, not the "facts", but the respective legal rights and duties of the parties to the suit. For the judgment of the court usually follows the general verdict of the jury, so that the verdict results in a decision which determines those rights and duties.

3

Some lawyers indignantly repudiate this "realistic" theory. They deny that juries can disregard the judicial instructions concerning the legal rules. The history of that denial is enlightening. In this country, during the latter part of the 18th century and the early part of the 19th, judges told juries, especially in criminal cases, that it was for the jury to decide not only the facts but also the "law"—i.e., what legal rules were applicable—and that the jury was not bound to accept the judge's instructions concerning the rules. In the federal courts and in most states, that practice was later repudiated. The judges and lawyers who then denounced that earlier practice declared that, if juries had the right to ignore the judge's charge as to the applicable rules, horrible consequences would ensue.

Here are some sample statements of what those consequences would be: The "law" would "become as variable as the prejudices, the inclinations, and the passions of men." "The parties would suffer from an arbitrary decision." "Decisions would depend entirely on juries uncontrolled by any settled, fixed legal principle," and would be "according to what the jury in their own opinion suppose the law is or ought to be." "Jurymen, untrained in the law, would determine questions affecting life, liberty or property, according to such legal principles as in their judgment were applicable in the particular case." Our government "would cease to be a government of laws and become a government of men." "Jurors would become not only judges but legislators as well." The "law" would "be as fluctuating and uncertain as the diverse opinions of different juries in regard to it." Jurors would be "superior to the national legislature, and its laws . . . subject to their control," so that "a law of Congress" would "be in operation in one state and not in another."

Now the truth is, as every lawyer knows, that, in many criminal cases, the jury does have an "uncontrollable power" to disregard rules laid down in the judge's instructions. For if, in a criminal case, the jury brings in a verdict for the defendant, the judge (because of constitutional provisions) must follow that verdict, even if he is convinced that the jury ignored his legal instructions. In other words, such a verdict is final and conclusive.[2]

At first blush, the situation may seem very different in non-criminal suits. In such a suit, if the evidence is insufficient to justify a verdict

[2] In some few states, the prosecutor may appeal from a judgment of acquittal.

for one side, the judge may and should "direct a verdict" for the other side; that is, in effect, he dispenses with the jury and himself decides the case for that side. But when conflicting oral testimony is such that it would justify a verdict for either side, then, if the judge behaves correctly, he lets the jury return a verdict. Unless he knows—as he seldom does—that the jury ignored the *R*'s of which he told them, he should let that verdict stand. True, the judge can grant a new trial. But he is not supposed to do so, in such a case, if it was properly tried. And, if nevertheless, he does order another trial, he is merely exercising a veto which may be over-ruled. For another jury will then decide the case; and it may again, unknown to the judge, ignore the *R*'s. Moreover, if two juries, in successive trials of that case, bring in the same verdict, then, in many states (with exceptions that need not here concern us) that concludes the matter. So you see, even in non-criminal cases, many juries do have the power to make decisions regardless of the legal rules.

Those who point to what, they say, would be the dire results of allowing the jury to disregard the rules, have deluded themselves with words. "It is true," said Judge Thompson, typically, "the jury may disregard the instructions of the court, and in some cases there may be no remedy; but it is still the right of the court to instruct the jury on the law and the duty of the jury to obey the instructions." Sometimes there is a verbal play on the distinction between the jury's "power" and the jury's "right": The jury, it is said, has the power but cannot "rightfully exercise it." Chamberlayne states that most American courts in this connection "very properly distinguish between a *right* and an incorrectible *abuse* of power."

I think the reader will agree, however, that, to the litigant interested in a jury's verdict, it makes no practical difference, when the jury uses its "incorrectible power," whether their exercise of that power is called a "right," a defiance of its "duty," or an "abuse." The important fact is that juries have that incorrectible power and frequently use it.

Practically, then, we do have the very conditions which we were warned would exist if juries had the right to ignore the judge's instructions as to the correct rules: Cases *are* often decided "according to what the jury supposes the law is or ought to be"; the "law" *is* "as fluctuating and uncertain as the diverse opinions in regard to it"; often juries *are* "not only judges but legislators as well"; jurors do become "superior to the national legislature," and its laws *are* "subject to their control" so that "a law of Congress" *is* "in operation in one state and not in another."

This truth the general verdict conceals. "Whether," says Sunderland, "the jurors deliberately threw the law into the discard, and rendered a verdict out of their own heads, or whether they applied the law correctly as instructed by the court, or whether they tried to apply it properly but failed for lack of understanding—these are questions respecting which the verdict discloses nothing. . . . The general verdict serves as the great procedural opiate, . . . draws the curtain upon human errors, and soothes us with the assurance that we have attained the unattainable."

4

Now what does bring about verdicts? Longenecker, in a book written by a practical trial lawyer for practical trial lawyers, says: "In talking to a man who had recently served for two weeks on juries, he stated that in one case after they had retired to consider the verdict, the foreman made a speech to them somewhat like this: 'Now boys, you know there was lying on both sides. Which one did the most lying? The plaintiff is a poor man and the defendant is rich and can afford to pay the plaintiff something. Of course the dog did not hurt the plaintiff much, but I think we ought to give him something, don't you?' There were several 'sures'; we thought the plaintiff might have to split with his lawyers, so we gave him a big verdict." A case is reported in which the jurors explained their verdict thus: "We couldn't make head or tail of the case, or follow all the messing around the lawyers did. None of us believed the witnesses on either side, anyway, so we made up our minds to disregard the evidence on both sides and decide the case on its merits." "Competent observers," says Judge Rossman, "who have interviewed the jurors in scores of jury trials, declare that in many cases . . . principal issues received no consideration from the jury." Bear that in mind, when considering these remarks by Ram: "And to what a fearful extent may a verdict affect a person! It may pronounce a man sane or insane; it may establish character, or take it away; it may give liberty to the captive, or turn liberty into slavery: it may continue life to a prisoner, or consign him to death."

Again and again, it has been disclosed that juries have arrived at their verdicts by one of the following methods: (1) Each juror, in a civil case, writes down the amount he wants to award; the total is added and the average taken as the verdict. (2) The jurors, by agreement decide for one side or the other according to the flip of a coin.[3] (3) A related method, reported in a case where a man was convicted of manslaughter and sentenced to life imprisonment, is as follows: The "jury at first stood six for assault and battery, and, as a compromise, the six agreed to vote for manslaughter, and the vote then stood six for manslaughter, and six for murder in the second degree; it was then agreed to prepare 24 ballots—12 for manslaughter and 12 for murder in the second degree—place all of them in a hat, and each juror draw one ballot therefrom, and render a verdict either for manslaughter or murder in the second degree, as the majority should appear; the first drawing was a tie, but the second one resulted in eight ballots for murder in the second degree and four for manslaughter, and thereupon, according to the agreement, a verdict was rendered for murder in the second degree."

How do the courts react to such a disclosure? When it is made known before the jury is discharged, a court will usually reject the verdict. But, frequently, the revelation occurs after the jury's discharge. In most states, and in the federal system, the courts then refuse to disturb the verdict.[4] They say that any other result would mean that jurors would be subjected to pressures, after a case is over, to induce them to falsify what had occurred in the jury-room, so that all verdicts would be imperilled.

One may doubt whether there is much danger of such falsifications. I surmise that the underlying reason for that judicial attitude is this: The judges feel that, were they obliged to learn the methods used by jurors, the actual workings of the jury-system would be shown up, devastatingly. From my point of view, such a consequence would be desirable: The public would soon discover this skeleton in the judicial closet.

My surmise as to the basic reason for judicial unwillingness to examine jury operations closely is perhaps borne out by the following:

[3] Recall Rabelais' account of Judge Bridlegoose who decided cases by shaking dice.

[4] Consider Johnson v. Hunter, 144 F. (2d) 565, 567, where the convicted defendant unsuccessfully sought release by a habeas corpus. The court said: "There remains for consideration the charge that one negro juror was intimidated by eleven white jurors and by reason of such intimidation agreed to a verdict of guilty. This fact if true, would invalidate the verdict. The difficulty that is presented is that it probably is a fact incapable of being proved. It is evident that proof of the fact, if true, would be impossible by anyone other than the negro juror whom the petitioner seeks to have called as a witness in his behalf, and unless this negro juror is a competent witness to testify in support of the allegations contained in the sixth paragraph of the petition for the writ, no hearing was required. The general rule is that evidence of jurors is not admissible to impeach their verdict. Mattox v. U.S., 146 U.S. 140."

In 1947, two enterprising, able, and earnest law-school students sought to study at first-hand how jurors decide cases. They wanted to have a trial judge, after a jury trial had concluded, present to the jurors a carefully worded questionnaire, with the suggestion that they answer it in writing if they wished, and with the further suggestion that, if they cared to, they should allow themselves to be interviewed by these students. This proposal was made without success to nine judges of several different jurisdictions. One federal judge said he did not approve "a holier-than-thou attitude toward juries," and that the project could serve "no worthy end," but would only increase differences among federal judges concerning the value of the jury system. Another federal judge, in refusing his cooperation, remarked that he had never made such a study when he was in law-school. Still another federal judge, unwilling to have jurors interrogated, said, "How they decide is their business." Two state-court judges deemed the undertaking "improper." One highly intelligent state-court judge, enthusiastic about the study, submitted the questionnaire to the jurors in one case and gave the written answers to the students. He also granted them permission to conduct informal interviews, but withdrew that permission because he had received adverse criticism from some of his colleagues.

5

Are jurors to blame when they decide cases in the ways I've described? I think not. In the first place, often they cannot understand what the judge tells them about the legal rules. To comprehend the meaning of many a legal rule requires special training. It is inconceivable that a body of twelve ordinary men, casually gathered together for a few days, could, merely from listening to the instructions of the judge, gain the knowledge necessary to grasp the true import of the judge's words. For these words have often acquired their meaning as the result of hundreds of years of professional disputation in the courts. The jurors usually are as unlikely to get the meaning of those words as if they were spoken in Chinese, Sanskrit, or Choctaw. "Can anything be more fatuous," queries Sunderland, "than the expectation that the law which the judge so carefully, learnedly and laboriously expounds to the laymen in the jury box becomes operative in their minds in true form?" Judge Rossman pointedly asks whether it "is right to demand that a juror swear that he will obey the instructions (which the lawyers frequently say they are not sure of until they have been transcribed) and return a general verdict in obedience thereto."[5] Judge Bok says that "juries have the disadvantage . . . of being treated like children while the testimony is going on, but then being doused with a kettleful of law, during the charge, that would make a third-year law student blanch."

Under our system, however, the courts are obligated to make the unrealistic assumption that the often incomprehensible words, uttered in the physical presence of the jurors, have some real effect on their thought processes. As a logical deduction from that unfounded assumption, the trial judge is required to state the applicable rule to the jury with such nicety that some lawyers do not thoroughly comprehend it. If the judge omits any of those niceties, the upper court will reverse a judgment based on the jury's verdict. For, theoretically, the jury actually worked in accordance with the $R \times F = D$ formula, applying the *R* they received from the judge, so that, if he gave them the wrong *R,* then, in theory, the *D*—their verdict—must logically be wrong. Lawyers thus set traps for trial judges. Decisions, in cases which have taken weeks to try, are reversed on appeal because a phrase, or a sentence, meaningless to the jury, has been included in or omitted from the charge.[6]

When a decision is reversed on such a ground, there results, at best, a new trial at which the trial judge will intone a more meticulously worded *R* to another uncomprehending jury. This leads to an enormous waste of time and money. And note that the prospect of a prolonged expensive new trial often induces a litigant who won in the first trial, and who has only modest means, to accept an unfair settlement.

Many of the precise legal rules on which, according to the conventional theory, men in their daily affairs have a right to and supposedly do rely, are found solely in upper-court opinions admonishing trial

[5] In People v. Sherwood, 271 N.Y. 427, 434, the court slyly expressed a doubt as to the efficacy of the jury, saying: "In the practical administration of justice in civil cases, courts necessarily assume that jurors live up to their oath and that they are capable of, and do perform, extraordinary intellectual feats."

[6] Dean Green says that some upper courts, when they dislike jury verdicts, are astute to discover errors in the instructions, as a means of requiring new trials. It is a curious fact that many upper courts, which refuse to reverse decisions for "procedural" errors those courts call "harmless," nevertheless will be prompt to reverse for an error in a trial judge's charge about the "substantive" legal rules—although the first kind of error (e.g. an improper, highly inflammatory, remark to the jury by the winning lawyer) may be the very sort of thing which is within the comprehension of the jurors and may have influenced their verdict, while the second kind frequently are beyond the jurors' understanding and could not have affected the verdict.

judges to use, in charges to juries, words and phrases stating those rules. But if jurors do not understand those words and phrases, and consequently do not apply those rules, then reliance on the rules is unreliable: Men who act in reliance on that purported right to rely are deceived. I cannot, therefore, agree with Dickinson when he says that, although no precedents emerge from the verdicts of successive juries "so long as the application of a rule is left to the jury under no other guidance than the statement of the rule as such by the court," yet "the moment of elaboration of a rule is definitely isolated and registered as that at which a court for the first time instructs a jury that a rule does or does not apply to a particular state of facts, and this instruction is tested and approved on appeal," and that "this is an important and powerful aid in minting new law into stable and recognizable form, and offers one of the cogent arguments for the preservation of the jury system."[7]

6

Suppose, however, that the jurors always did understand the *R*'s. Nevertheless, often they would face amazing obstacles to ascertaining the *F*'s. For the evidence is not presented all at once or in an orderly fashion. The very mode of its presentation is confusing. The jurors are supposed to keep their minds in suspense until all of the evidence is in.

Can a jury perform such a task? Has it the means and capacity? Are the conditions of a jury trial such as to make for the required calm deliberation by the jurors? Wigmore, who defends the jury system, himself tells us that the court-room is "a place of surging emotions, distracting episodes, and sensational surprises. The parties are keyed up to the contest; and the topics are often calculated to stir up the sympathy, or prejudice, or ridicule of the tribunal." Dean Green remarks: "The longer the trial lasts, the larger the scanning crowds, the more intensely counsel draw the lines of conflict, the more solemn the judge, the harder it becomes for the jury to restrain their reason from somersault."

We may, therefore, seriously question the statement of Professors Michael and Adler that, unlike the witnesses, the jury "observes the

[7] Dickinson, Legal Rules, 81 *Un. of Pa. L. Rev.* (1931) 1052, 1053. Dickinson quotes with approval this excerpt from a House of Commons speech: "One of the chief advantages of civil trial by jury with a view to fixing the rules of law with greater certainty is that more than any other contrivance it facilitates the analysis of complex issues into matter of fact and matter of law."

things and events exhibited to its senses under conditions designed to make the observation reliable and accurate. In the case of what (the jury) observes directly the factor of memory is negligible." As shown by Wigmore, Green, and Burrill, the first of those comments surely does not square with observable courtroom realities. As to the second—that the factor of the jurors' memory is negligible—consider the following: Theoretically, as we saw, the jury, in its process of fact-finding, applies to the evidence the legal rules it learns from the judge. If the jury actually did conduct itself according to this theory, it would be unable to comprehend the evidence intelligently until it received those instructions about the rules. But those instructions are given, not before the jury hears the evidence, but only after all the witnesses have left the stand. Then, for the first time, are the jurors asked to consider the testimony in the light of the rules. In other words, if jurors are to do their duty, they must now recollect and assemble the separate fragments of the evidence (including the demeanor of the several witnesses) and fit them into the rules. If the trial has lasted for many days or weeks, the required feat of memory is prodigious. As Burrill says: "The theory of judicial investigation requires that the juror keep his mind wholly free from impressions until all facts are before him in evidence, and that he should then frame his conclusion. The difficulty attending this mode of dealing with the elements of evidence (especially in important cases requiring protracted investigation) is that the facts thus surveyed in a mass, and at one view, are apt to confuse, distract, and oppress the mind by their very number and variety. . . . They are, moreover, necessarily mixed up with remembrance of the mere machinery of their introduction, and the contests (often close and obstinate) attending their proof; in the course of which attempts are sometimes made to suppress or distort the truth, in the very act of presentation."

In a discussion I recently had with Professor Michael, he maintained that, since jurymen, in their daily out-of-court living, conduct most of their affairs on the basis of conclusions reached after listening to other men, they are adequately equipped as fact-finders in the court-room. One answer to this argument is that often the issues in trials are of a complicated kind with which most jurymen are unfamiliar. But let us ignore that answer. A more telling criticism of Michael's assertion is this: The surroundings of inquiry during a jury trial differ extraordinarily from those in which the juryman conducts his ordinary affairs. At a trial, the jurors hear the evidence in a public place, under conditions of a kind to which they are unaccustomed: No juror is able to withdraw to his own room, or office, for private individual reflection. And, at the close of the trial, the jurors are pressed for time in reaching their joint decision. Even twelve experienced judges, deliberating together, would probably not function well under the conditions we impose on the twelve inexperienced laymen.

7

In 1930, I pointed out that what might be called "jury-made law," as compared with "judge-made law," is peculiar in form. It does not, I said, issue in general pronouncements. You will not find it set forth in the law reports or in text-books. It does not become embodied in a series of precedents. It is nowhere codified. For each jury makes its own "law" in each case with little or no knowledge of, or reference to, what has been done before, or regard to what will be done thereafter, in similar cases.[8]

Three years later, in 1933, Judge Ulman, with long experience in a trial court, confirmed my statement. He told in his book how, in case after case relating to traffic accidents, "the jury has made the law . . . in . . . direct conflict with the law as laid down by the highest law-making authority of the state" and told to them by the trial judge. "The jury has substituted its own notion of law for that which the law-books say is the law." Noting that, in his court, generally, juries refuse to accept the law-book doctrine of contributory negligence, he said, "The strange part of it is that in the classical law-books you will not find a single word even hinting that the law of contributory negligence is what it has become by this habitual action of juries. This is because the men who write the law-books have not troubled to look at the law as . . . it actually works in the courtroom. They, like other members of the legal profession, have riveted their eyes . . . upon the printed page . . . The jury gets in the way of their neat formulae, and messes up their rules and doctrines."

Judge Ulman, however, implied that all juries uniformly reject the legal rule about contributory negligence. This involves an untenable belief that the verdict in any specific jury case would be the same, regardless of the particular men or women who composed the jury. Were such a belief well-founded, practicing lawyers would be fools for spending much time in selecting jurors.

[8] Frank, *Law and the Modern Mind,* 174 note.

But they do indeed spend time on that project. Typically, in his book for practicing trial lawyers, Longenecker writes: "No more important matter presents itself in the trial of a case than that of selecting a jury . . . Do not take a chance (in this matter) because you have no right to gamble with your client's interests."

Do the lawyers strive to pick impartial jurors? Do they want jurymen whose training will best enable them to understand the facts of the case? Of course not. If you think they usually do, watch the trial lawyers at work in a court-room. Or read the books written for trial lawyers by seasoned trial lawyers.

Here are a few excerpts from such a book, Goldstein's *Trial Techniques,* a book commended for its accuracy by Professor Morgan of Harvard. Always demand a jury, says Goldstein, if you represent a plaintiff who is a "woman, child, an old man or an old woman, or an ignorant, illiterate or foreign-born person unable to read or write or speak English who would naturally excite the jury's sympathies," especially if the defendant is a large corporation, a prominent or wealthy person, an insurance company, railroad or bank.[9] Then, he advises, seek the type of juror who "will most naturally respond to an emotional appeal." Make every effort, this author counsels, to exclude from the jury anyone "who is particularly experienced in the field of endeavor which is the basis of the law suit." As such a person is likely, says Goldstein, to have too much influence with the other jurors, it is always better to submit the issues "to a jury who have no knowledge of the particular subject."

In that book much is made of the fact that "the jury tries the lawyers rather than the clients," that, "without realizing it, the jurors allow their opinions of the evidence to be swayed in favor of the side represented by the lawyer they like." That notion is repeated in some of the pamphlets, written by eminent trial lawyers, published in 1946 under the auspices of the American Bar Association. They advise the lawyer to "ingratiate himself" with the jury. One of these pamphlets says

[9] Compare that advice, the counterpart of which will be found in dozens of similar books by trial lawyers, with the following typical charge of a judge to a jury: "You cannot take into consideration for any purpose grief, the sorrow of the parents or relatives, nor of course may you go outside of the evidence and indulge in speculation and conjecture as to damages. Nor should your verdict be influenced in any way by sympathy for the deceased or his parents, or by a prejudice against the railroad; you must base your verdict on evidence that has been produced here before you and the fair and reasonable inferences from the proven facts, by a fair preponderance of the evidence. It is almost unnecessary for me to suggest that you can't let your verdict be based on the fact that the defendant is a railroad company, a large corporation."

that the jurors' reaction to the trial lawyer "may be more important than the reaction to the client, for the client appears on the stand only during a relatively brief period, while the lawyer is before the jury all the time." Harris, in his well-known book on "advocacy," says, "It may be that judgment is more easily deceived when the passions are aroused, but if so, you [the lawyers] are not responsible. Human nature was, I presume, intended to be what it is, and when it gets into the jury-box, it is the duty of the advocate to make the best use of it he fairly can in the interests of his client." The Supreme Court of Tennessee has solemnly decided that "tears have always been considered legitimate arguments before a jury," that such use of tears is "one of the natural rights of counsel which no court or constitution could take away," and that "indeed, if counsel has them at command, it may be seriously questioned whether it is not his professional duty to shed them whenever proper occasion arises. . . ."

This is no laughing matter. For prejudice has been called the thirteenth juror, and it has been said that "Mr. Prejudice and Miss Sympathy are the names of witnesses whose testimony is never recorded, but must nevertheless be reckoned with in trials by jury." The foregoing tends to justify Balzac's definition of a jury as "twelve men chosen to decide who has the better lawyer."

In any law-suit, success or defeat for one of the parties may turn on his lawyer's abilities. But, in the light of the fact that juries "try the lawyers," it is peculiarly true, in many a jury trial, that a man's life, livelihood or property often depends on his lawyer's skill or lack of it in ingratiating himself with the jury rather than on the evidence. Not that lawyers, trying to protect their clients, should be censured for exploiting jurors' weaknesses—as long as we retain the general-verdict jury system.

Since, as every handbook on trial practice discloses, and as visits to a few jury trials will teach anyone, the lawyers are allowed—more, are expected—to appeal to the crudest emotions and predudices of the jurors, and jurors are known often to respond to such appeals, I confess that it disturbs me not a little that we require trial judges to perform the futile ritual of saying to each jury something like this: "The law will not permit jurors to be governed by mere sentiment, sympathy, passion or prejudice, and you will reach a verdict that will be just to both sides, regardless of what the consequences may be." [10] We

[10] Malinowski says of the "spells" used in primitive magic that "very conspicuous is the use of words to invoke . . . the desired aim."

tell jurors to do—have them take an oath to do—what we do not at all expect them to do.

8

As I said in a previous chapter, the search for the facts in a court-room must necessarily be limited by lack of time; also, for important reasons of public policy, some ways of obtaining evidence are precluded—by the rule against self-incrimination, for instance, or by the rule against any unreasonable search and seizure.

But there are other rules of exclusion which, no matter what their origin, have been perpetuated primarily because of the admitted incompetence of jurors. Notable is the rule excluding hearsay evidence. Hearsay may be roughly (and somewhat inaccurately) described as the report in court by a witness of a statement made by another person, out of court, who is not subject to cross-examination at the trial, when the report of that statement is offered as evidence to prove the truth of a fact asserted in that statement. It is, so to speak, second-hand evidence. Now doubtless hearsay should often be accepted with caution. But 90% of the evidence on which men act out of court, most of the data on which business and industry daily rely, consists of the equivalent of hearsay. Yet, because of distrust of juries—a belief that jurors lack the competence to make allowance for the second-hand character of hearsay—such evidence, although accepted by administrative agencies, juvenile courts and legislative committees, is (subject, to be sure, to numerous exceptions) barred in jury trials. As a consequence, frequently the jury cannot learn of matters which would lead an intelligent person to a more correct knowledge of the facts.

So, too, of many other exclusionary rules. They limit, absurdly, the court-room quest for the truth. The result, often, is a gravely false picture of the actual facts. Thus trial by jury seriously interferes with correct—and, therefore, just—decisions. Even if the juries could understand what the trial judges tell them of the *R*'s, the juries would often be unable to apply these rules to anything like the real *F*'s, because of the exclusion of relevant evidence.

But, even apart from that difficulty, since jurors frequently cannot understand the *R*'s, the general-verdict jury trial renders absurd the conventional description of the decisional process—the $R \times F = D$. To my mind a better instrument than the usual jury trial could scarcely be imagined for achieving uncertainty, capriciousness, lack of uniformity, disregard of the *R*'s, and unpredictability of decisions.

9

My attitude towards the jury is not unique. James Bradley Thayer, a great legal scholar and a profound student of jury trials, said in 1898 that, in civil cases, "I would restrict [jury trial] narrowly, for it appears to me . . . to be a potent cause of demoralization to the bar." Learned Hand remarked in 1921, "I am by no means enamored of jury trials, at least in civil cases. . . ." Mr. Justice Cardozo, in a Supreme Court opinion, wrote, "Few would be so narrow or provincial as to maintain that a fair and enlightened system of justice would be impossible without" jury trials. The noted historian, Carl Becker, one of the ablest students of American history and institutions, said in 1945: "Trial by jury, as a method of determining facts, is antiquated . . . and inherently absurd—so much so that no lawyer, judge, scholar, prescription-clerk, cook, or mechanic in a garage would ever think for a moment of employing that method for determining the facts in any situation that concerned him." Two very able and experienced trial judges, Judge Galston and Judge Shientag, have each recently indicated a belief that the use of the jury in civil suits should be severely restricted. Judge Shientag said: "The civil jury would seem to be unnecessary except in a few types of injury to the person, such as libel and slander, false arrest, and malicious prosecution."

Osborn, a keen observer of many jury trials, wrote in 1937: "When a group of twelve men, on seats a little higher than the spectators, but not quite so high as the judge, are casually observed it may appear from their attitude that they are thinking only about the case going on before them. The truth is that for much of the time there are twelve wandering minds in that silent group, bodily present but mentally far away. Some of them are thinking of sadly neglected business affairs, others of happy or unhappy family matters, and, after the second or third day and especially after the second or third week, there is the garden, the house-painting, the new automobile, the prospective vacation, the girl who is soon to be married and the hundred and one other things that come to the mind of one who is only partly interested in the tedious proceeding going on before him. There is probably more woolgathering in jury boxes than in any other place on earth. . . . Someone has said that the invention of this jury system is one of the 'splendid achievements of civilization,' but its splendor is now and then somewhat dimmed when some juryman frankly tells just what occurred in some jury-room. If for a term of court or two a complete transcript of all the comments, criticisms, and reasons of jurors in jury-rooms could be made and furnished to . . . the newspapers, it would no doubt furnish some suggestions looking toward improvement. If this exposure did not bring about the total abolition of the jury system, it would perhaps tend to bring about improvement in some of the methods of selecting jurors, or perhaps a selection of the kind of cases to be submitted to juries. . . . It is plainly said by those whose opinions command the utmost respect that the administration of the law in this land is on a lower plane than other phases of government and is unworthy of the civilization it poorly serves."[11]

[11] Perhaps even more enlightening is that excellent fictional narrative of how a jury reached its verdict, Postgate's *Verdict of Twelve*.

IX. DEFENSES OF THE JURY SYSTEM—PROPOSED REFORMS

LET US, now, consider the arguments of those who defend the jury system.

(1). *Juries said to be better at fact-finding than judges.* The first defense is that juries are better fact-finders than judges. Judge Cooley said: "The law has established this tribunal because it is believed that, from its numbers, the mode of their selection and the fact that the jurors come from all classes of society, they are better calculated to judge the motives," and "weigh the possibilities . . . than a single man, however . . . wise . . . he may be."

Is that a correct appraisal? Would any sensible business organization reach a decision, as to the competence and honesty of a prospective executive, by seeking, on that question of fact, the judgment of twelve men or women gathered together at random—and after first weeding out all those men or women who might have any special qualifications for answering the questions? Would an historian thus decide a question of fact? [1]

If juries are better than judges as fact-finders, then, were we sensible, we would allow no cases to be decided by a judge without a jury. But that is not our practice. Ordinarily if you sue a man for breach of a contract, you may have a jury trial; but not if you sue to have that same contract set aside for fraud, or if that man died or went into bankruptcy before you sued. If jurors were superior in fact-finding, such distinctions would be intolerable, as would also be the denial of trial by jury in thousands of admiralty and almost all "equity" cases, cases which affect legal rights fully as important as those involved in most jury trials. Yet I know of no one who proposes that all those cases shall be jury cases.

Professor George Braden makes this interesting observation: It is well settled that, when it is plain to the trial judge that the evidence is so clearly in favor of one of the parties to a suit that no reasonable man

[1] Says Green: "The data not infrequently assumes aspects as far above the understanding of the every-day citizen as modern science is beyond the science of the 14th century . . . The average jury in any case of difficulty is about as helpful as it would be in solving a problem in the higher mathematics . . . or in electrical engineering."

could decide against that party, the judge must not allow the jury to consider the evidence, but must direct them to bring in a verdict for that party. If the judge fails to "direct a verdict" in such circumstances, and if, as often happens in such cases, the jury returns a verdict for the other party, the judge must set that verdict aside as unreasonable; if he does not, the upper court, on appeal will reverse the decision. Such reversals frequently occur. Now, says Professor Braden, this "directed verdict" practice, which recognizes that juries may return verdicts which no reasonable man would consider justified by the evidence, demonstrates that the courts do not consider juries unusually competent as finders of facts.

(2). *Jurors as legislators.*

I now come to the argument for the jury system most frequently advanced. It is contended that the legal rules (made by the legislatures or formulated by the judges) often work injustice, and that juries, through their general verdicts, wisely nullify those rules. This argument, strangely enough, is put forward by many of the same lawyers who insist that substantial adherence by the judges to those rules constitutes an essential of a sound civilization, since, they say, without such adherence men could not know their legal rights or intelligently handle their affairs.

Hear, for instance, Dean Roscoe Pound. In an article, published in 1910, describing jury nullification of the legal rules as "jury lawlessness," he pronounces it "the great corrective of law in its actual administration." He says that the purpose of "jury lawlessness" is, "in largest part, to keep the letter of the law in the books, while allowing the jury free rein to apply different rules or extra-legal considerations in the actual decision of causes . . ." Because "popular thought and popular action are at variance with many of the doctrines and rules in the books," the function of the jury is to preserve the appearance that the rules are being applied while the popular attitudes, inconsistent with the rules, are actually followed. "If," said Pound, "the ritual of charging the jury on the law with exactness is preserved, the record will show that the case was decided according to law, and the fact that the jury dealt with it according to extra-legal notions of conformity to the views of the community, is covered up."

In 1929, Wigmore wrote: "Law and Justice are from time to time inevitably in conflict. That is because law is a general rule (even the stated exceptions to the rules are general exceptions); while justice is the fairness of this precise case under *all* its circumstances. And as a rule of law only takes account of broadly typical conditions, and is aimed at average results, law and justice every so often do not coincide. Everyone knows this, and can supply instances. But the trouble is that Law cannot concede it: Law—the rule—must be enforced—the exact terms of the rule, justice or no justice. 'All Persons Are Equal before the Law'; this solemn injunction, in large letters, is painted on the wall over the judge's bench in every Italian court. So that the judge must apply the law as he finds it alike for all. And not even the general exceptions that the law itself may concede will enable the judge to get down to the justice of the particular case, in extreme instances. The whole basis of our general confidence in the judge rests on our experience that we can rely on him for the law as it is. But, this being so, the repeated instances of hardship and injustice that are bound to occur in the judge's rulings will in the long run injure that same public confidence in justice, and bring odium on the law. We want justice, and we think we are going to get it through 'the law,' and when we do not, we blame 'the law.' Now this is where the jury comes in. The jury, in the privacy of its retirement, adjusts the general rule of law to the justice of the particular case. Thus the odium of inflexible rules of law is avoided, and popular satisfaction is preserved. . . . That is what jury trial does. It supplies that flexibility of legal rules which is essential to justice and popular contentment. And that flexibility could never be given by judge trial. The judge (as in a chancery case) must write out his opinion, declaring the law and the findings of fact. He cannot in this public record deviate one jot from those requirements. The jury, and the secrecy of the jury room, are the indispensable elements in popular justice."

Mr. Justice Chalmers, an English judge, stated this position thus: "Again there is an old saying that hard cases make bad law. So they do when there is no jury. The Judge is anxious to do justice to the particular parties before him. To meet a particular hard case he is tempted to qualify or engraft an exception upon a sound general principle. When a judge once leaves the straight and narrow path of law, and wanders into the wide fields of substantial justice, he is soon irretrievably lost. . . . But hard cases tried with a jury do not make bad law, for they make no law at all, as far as the findings of the jury are concerned. The principle is kept intact while the jury do justice in the particular case by not applying it."

By such use of the jury, you can eat your cake and have it, too. You can, in appearance, preserve your legal rules and principles unswerving and unyielding—in the form of the judge's instructions—and you can have a jury's decision (which determines the rights of the parties to the case) based upon scant respect for those rules as against emotional appeals. The *R*'s remain pure and unsullied—because, while clearly enunciated by the judge, they are not applied by the jury. "It cannot be doubted," says Chamberlayne, "that a principal claim of the jury to popular favor is its traditional ability to defy, in a general verdict, the law of the land as announced by the judge."

Does such a defense of the jury make sense? If it does, then we should reverse the theoretical roles of trial judge and jury: As obviously the judge is usually better trained at fact-finding, let him find the facts—and then let the jury decide what legal rules should be applied to those facts. Moreover, in that event, an upper court should never reverse a decision—as often such a court now does—on account of an erroneous statement, in the trial judge's instructions, concerning the proper legal rule.

The stock example cited by those who defend the jury as legal-rule defier is the refusal of many juries to apply the harsh fellow-servant rule, a legal rule which 19th century judges had made. Yet it is highly probable that the judges themselves, before long, would have abolished that judge-made rule had they not felt that the juries would not heed it in their verdicts. Subsequently, by enacted statutes, the legislatures wiped out that harsh rule. But meanwhile some juries, feeling obligated to do so, applied it with resultant injustice in those cases. It may well be, then, that judicial reliance on juries helped to perpetuate an unjust rule, to delay its eradication either by judges or legislatures. It should be noted that in the types of cases where juries do not sit—in equity suits, for instance—the judges have been less reluctant to contrive flexible rules and to revise undesirable ones. Moreover, legislatures are more prompt today in changing legal rules than they were in the days of the fellow-servant rule.[2]

The argument that juries make better rules than judges do has at least the virtue of honestly admitting the realities—of conceding that jurors often disregard what the trial judge tells the jurors about the *R*'s. But as a rational defense of the jury system, it is surely curious. It asserts that, desirably, each jury is a twelve-man ephemeral legislature, not elected by the voters, but empowered to destroy what the

[2] In 1789, Jefferson defended the power of juries to disregard the judge's instructions as follows: Juries "never exercise the power but when they suspect partiality in the judges." That position does not square with the actualities.

elected legislators have enacted or authorized. Each jury is thus a legislative assembly, legislating independently of all others. For even if a jury does no more than nullify a legal rule by refusing to apply it in a particular law-suit, yet it is legislating, since the power to destroy legal rules is legislative power. This argument for the jury should lead to a revised description of our legislative system to show that it consists, in the case of our federal government for instance, of (1) a Senate, (2) a House of Representatives, and (3) a multitude of juries.

I have one objection to such a description: I think it too sophisticated. It implies that the members of the ordinary jury say to themselves, "We don't like this legal rule of which the judge told us, and we won't apply it but will apply one of our own making." But when, as often happens, juries do not understand what the judge said to them about the applicable rule, it simply is not true that they refuse to follow it because they dislike it. Many juries in reaching their verdicts act on their emotional responses to the lawyers and witnesses; they like or dislike, not any legal rule, but they do like an artful lawyer for the plaintiff, the poor widow, the brunette with the soulful eyes, and they do dislike the big corporation, the Italian with a thick, foreign accent. We do not have uniform jury-nullification of harsh rules; we have juries avoiding—often in ignorance that they are so doing—excellent as well as bad rules, and in capricious fashion.[3]

Courts frequently say that juries are especially equipped to know the "average conscience" or the "social sense of what is right" at a particular time. But can we be sure that any basis in fact exists for the supposition that any single jury does reflect the "average" views of the community? One jury may have one view, and another, summoned the next week, may have another.[4]

Many of those who, like Pound, favor the general-verdict system precisely because of its opaqueness, also urge that most of the defects of that system would vanish if the trial judge were given ample power to express to the jury his view of the evidence. But federal trial judges have and use that power. Yet sponsors of that suggestion oppose the

[3] Said a lawyer who is now a United States Supreme Court Justice: "Juries return and courts sustain verdicts from almost nothing to almost anything for identical injuries." An "injury that will net one plaintiff five hundred dollars for 'pain and suffering,' will net another five thousand through the art of counsel, tact of witnesses, sex of the plaintiff, or financial condition of the defendant." Jackson, "Accident Litigation," 15 *Cornell L.Q.* (1929) 194, 200.

[4] Compare Judge Learned Hand's acceptance of a single jury's views as an index of current mores in United States v. Levine, 83 F.(2d) 156, 157, with his rejection of a jury verdict as such an index in Repouille v. United States, 165 F.(2d) 152, 153.

proposal that in the federal courts there should be full exposure by the jurors of the methods they used in reaching their verdict; and in the federal suits where there have been such exposures, the revelations have been most disquieting.

You will find lawyers, legal philosophers and statesmen often using such phrases as "The supremacy of law," "The reign (or rule) of law," "A government of laws, and not of men." Those phrases are related to one another. I cannot here explore them exhaustively;[5] but, for present purposes, stated briefly, they mean this: Liberty and democracy demand the elimination of arbitrariness, of caprice, and of wide unregulated discretion, in the activities of governmental officials.[6] Such officials must be disinterested and impartial, must not yield to their personal preferences for, or personal prejudices against, individual citizens. To all citizens they must apply standards uniformly. In the courts, this conception is embodied in the idea of "equality before the law"—the similar treatment, judicially, of substantially similar cases. According to this doctrine, "all agencies of government are bound to act upon principles and not according to arbitrary will." This doctrine, says one writer, "assumes as an accepted ideal that those who wield governmental powers and their agents are not free to follow their own wills, wherever mere will leads them, but are held to act upon principles and follow reason."

The basic principle, thus variously enunciated, is that of protecting the individual against official partiality. "One of the most fundamental social interests is that law should be uniform and impartial," Cardozo wrote. "There must be nothing in all its action that savors of prejudice or favor or even arbitrary whim or fitfulness." This principle links up with the ideal of known and knowable legal rules which will furnish reliable guidance for citizens concerning their future conduct. "Known general laws, however bad," wrote Maitland, "interfere less with freedom than decisions based on no previously known rule. When such decisions are frequent, a man can never know what liberty he has, and liberty is only valuable when we know that we have it." "Law as a guide to conduct," said Cardozo, "is reduced to the level of mere futility if it is unknown and unknowable."

[5] See Chapter XXX, as to a "government of laws."

[6] The "rule of law," said Dicey, means "the absolute supremacy or predominance of regular law as opposed to the influence of arbitrary power, and excludes the existence of arbitrariness . . . or even of wide discretionary power on the part of the government. . . . It means . . . equality before the law. . . ."

Now I submit that the jury is the worst possible enemy of this ideal of the "supremacy of law." For "jury-made law" is, par excellence, capricious and arbitrary, yielding the maximum in the way of lack of uniformity, of unknowability. It is acknowledged that jurors are governmental officials. Yet little, practically, is done to ensure that these officials, jurymen, "act upon principles and not according to arbitrary will," or to put effective restraints upon their worst prejudices. Indeed, through the general verdict, coupled with the refusal of the courts to inquire into the way the jurors have reached their decisions, everything is done to give the widest outlet to jurors' biases. If only a jury trial is properly conducted according to the procedural rules, the jurors' decision may be as arbitrary as they please; in such circumstances, their discretion becomes wholly unregulated and unreviewable.

The jury system, praised because, in its origins, it was apparently a bulwark against an arbitrary tyrannical executive, is today the quintessence of governmental arbitrariness. The jury system almost completely wipes out the principle of "equality before the law" which the "supremacy of law" and the "reign of law" symbolize—and does so, too, at the expense of justice, which requires fairness and competence in finding the facts in specific cases. If anywhere we have a "government of men," in the worst sense of that phrase, it is in the operations of the jury system.

I agree with Wigmore that some legal rules are excessively inflexible, and that there is need frequently to individualize cases. Legal rules, contrived by the courts in the decisions of past suits, may work serious injustice in later cases involving unique facts. For such reasons, "Law," if defined as the legal rules, does, as Wigmore has said, recurrently clash with notions of justice. Unique aspects of law-suits frequently do not fit into the more rigid legal-rule pigeon-holes. When a rule is too inflexible—when, if it were followed, harsh decisions would result, arousing a deep sense of unfairness, injustice—the urge becomes irrepressible to do justice by allowing for uniqueness. Much of such individualization there should be, and there is bound to be. Somehow, the stern over-rigid rules will often be made to bend. But individualization should be accomplished openly, not furtively by such a surreptitious technique as "jury lawlessness" which, as portrayed by Pound and others, smacks of something very close to hypocrisy and to deception of the public.[7]

If any legal rules are so inflexible that they work injustice, they should

[7] This theme will be developed in Chapters XXVIII-XXX.

avowedly be made more flexible. The disinclination to achieve "individualization" openly, through greater flexibility in most of the *R*'s, stems from the fatuous desire to have the results of the judicial process seem more certain, more knowable, than they actually are or can be. Two desires here conflict: (1) the desire to attain certainty and uniformity, and (2) the desire to make allowance for the unique aspects of cases. We satisfy the first, verbally, by so wording many of our *R*'s that they *seem* to exclude all discretion which would permit consideration of such uniquenesses; we then actually satisfy the second, circumventing those *R*'s through jury verdicts by means of which such discretion runs riot. Surely, it is socially undesirable, not only to create a false appearance of legal certainty—to hide from our citizens the actual workings of our legal system—but to do so by employing so capricious an agency as the jury.

Judge Hutcheson, after saying that, when the rules are too strict, "men do not get their just deserts," continues: "On the other hand, when each case stands alone, when there are no rules, no guides, no directing, restraining precedents and practices, there is not only no certainty of justice, but danger from caprice." Is that not a correct description of the "jury lawlessness" which Pound, Wigmore and others endorse?

If we want juries to act as legislators, we should tell them so. Instead, we have the judges tell them the exact opposite. We give them little handbooks advising them of their duties which state (I quote from a typical handbook of that kind): "Judges and jurors do not make the laws,—they only apply them, and must be careful not to usurp power which does not belong to them. People look at the law as it is written to know what their rights are and decide what they may or may not do with safety. Such people should not be expcted to guess whether a court or jury uphold the law. That is their sworn duty."

As I previously suggested, many of these lawyers who learnedly discuss our legal system are devotees of legal magic, men who let their wish for legal predictability close their eyes, most of the time, to observation of actual court-house government. Significantly, these legal pundits seldom, if ever, mention the jury. Their jurisprudence omits all reference to "juries'-prudence." One of these pundits, Morris Cohen, in a much-quoted statement, has said, "To be ruled by a judge is, to the extent he is not bound by law, tyranny or despotism."[8] If that be

[8] 27 *Col. L. Rev.* (1927) at 237.

true, then what of being ruled by juries? Is it not, in Cohen's words, "tyranny or despotism?"

Cohen seldom mentioned juries. But what of Roscoe Pound? How can one reconcile his praise of "jury lawlessness" in 1910 and his statement in an article published the year before (and to which I have already referred), that, in respect to commercial transactions "certainty and uniformity" in judicial decisions are demanded, and that our courts comply with this demand through definite legal rules, because "no one . . . makes large investments trusting . . . to free judicial search for the right."[9] One would think that juries never sit in cases relating to "property" or "commercial transactions"; but Pound, of course, knows they often do, and that, when they do, "jury lawlessness" frequently occurs.

Consider also Pound's criticism (published in 1941) of administrative agencies because, among other things, he said, they "give effect to policies" unauthorized by statute or the legal rules, and, by failing to differentiate "findings of fact and finding and application of law thereto," engage in "the method of personal justice?" I happen to think that most of such agencies do not have such characteristics. But assume that they do. Are those not the very characteristics for which Pound applauded juries? Pound deems administrators far inferior to courts because, he writes, in courts, the judges, by "professional habit and training," are "impelled to conform their action to certain known standards and to conform to settled ideals of judicial conduct," and also to "seek authoritative grounds of decision." But in court, as Pound himself had made clear, we also have juries with no "professional habit or training," and no experience with "settled ideals of judicial conduct," who often conform to no "known standards," and who often disregard—desirably, according to Pound's 1910 article—those "authoritative grounds of decision" which the trial judges, in their instructions, tell the juries to apply.

In an article published in 1948, Pound speaks of the need for "assurance of certainty, uniformity and predictability" in judicial administration, and says that such assurance "lies in scrupulous use of the authoritative process of legal reasoning" except in the "ordinary run of cases" in which the "experienced judge" relies on trained intuition. But, as he knows, the juries he lauded cannot scrupulously use "legal

[9] In 1922, he repeated that notion, saying that, as to "property" and "commercial transactions," the courts must and do reject "individualization."

reasoning," nor do they have the experience in trying cases necessary to give them "trained intuition."

If Pound, after he praised "jury lawlessness" in 1910, changed his mind, he should say so. But I think his inconsistency is not to be explained by any change of mind. The correct explanation probably is that Pound is one of those semi-believers in legal magic who occasionally lapse into skepticism but usually suppress it.

The same ambivalence, perhaps due to the same cause, appears in a 1946 report of the American Bar Association which declares that "the jury often stands as a bulwark between an individual and . . . an unreasonable law," but also says that "every juror" must "let the law prevail." The Canons of Judicial Ethics, adopted by the American Bar Association, says that, as "ours is a government of law and not of men," an American judge "violates his duty as a minister of justice if he seeks to do what he may personally consider substantial justice in a particular case and disregard the general law." But why bother to impose that obligation on judges and then call in juries who, if Wigmore and Pound report correctly, are expected to do the opposite—to "disregard the general law" and to accomplish what they "personally consider substantial justice in a particular case?"

(3). *The jury as an escape from corrupt or incompetent trial judges.* A third defense of the jury is seldom published: In a local community where some trial judges are corrupt, or subject to dictation by political bosses, or where some judges are rigid bigots or otherwise incompetent, lawyers prefer to take their chances with juries.

No one can deny that there is some force to that argument. It points to a fact I shall discuss later—that the electorate pays too little attention to the immense significance of trial courts. But unless honest, competent trial judges can be and are procured, the resort to juries is a feeble device. For, remember that, in many types of law-suits, the litigant cannot have a jury trial, must try his case before a judge without a jury.

(4). *The jury as alleged educator and creator of confidence in government.*

Another argument for the jury system is that it helps to educate citizens in government, gives them added confidence in democracy. Can that contention be proved? Do not many jurors become cynical about the court-house aspects of government? And should education in government be obtained at the expense of litigants?

(5). *Citizens said to demand this participation in government.*

Closely related to the previous argument is the contention that citizens demand participation in government through acting on juries. One wonders. If so, why do so many citizens seek to be excused from jury service?[10]

Nevertheless, the need for popular participation in the administration of justice is the argument most frequently advanced in defense of the jury system. If we take that argument seriously—as something more than a rationalization of an irrational adherence to tradition—then we face a clash of social policies: (1) the policy favoring such popular participation undermines (2) the policy of obtaining that adequate fact-finding which is indispensable to the doing of justice. Which policy should yield? Is it less important to do justice to litigants than to have citizens serve on juries?

(6). *Jury trials as popular entertainment.*

Doubtless, at one time, jury trials supplied cheap popular dramatic entertainment. This was true when the theater, the motion-picture and the automobile were not at hand. But now that these substitutes are available, now that we have Hollywood and television, surely the lives and fortunes of litigants need no longer be risked to provide such entertainment.

(7). *The jury in criminal litigation.*

Especially in criminal cases is the jury highly regarded as a means of necessary humane individualization. Not easily would our people relinquish to the judges the power to pass on the guilt or innocence of one accused of crime, if he prefers a jury trial. For the jury is assumed to be more merciful to the alleged criminal, more responsive to unique extenuating circumstances. Yet it may be doubted whether the popular estimate of the benevolent character of jurors in criminal cases is invariably correct. "Parties charged with crime," it has been wisely said, "need protection . . . against unjust convictions quite as often as the public needs it against groundless acquittals."

Recall Borchard's *Convicting the Innocent.* Did the juries in the cases reported by Borchard adequately protect the innocent defendants? Would not honest competent judges, sitting without juries, probably have done better?

(8). *"Passing the Buck" to juries.*

Juries, it is argued, provide buffers to judges against popular indig-

[10] Judge Sutliffe has said: "Jurors are a lot of men picked from poll-lists who have not enough political pull to get off, or who are out of a job and want to pick up a few dollars a day." Of course, that is an over-statement of a partial truth.

nation aroused by unpopular decisions. That is, the jury is an insulator for the judge, a buck-passing device. As a rational argument for the jury this seems indeed questionable. Men fit to be trial judges should be able and willing to accept public criticism. Moreover, they are obliged to do so in the many cases they must try without juries. Probably this argument is but an ingenious rationalization.

2

Some trial judges insist that jury verdicts are almost always correct. Perhaps they mean that the juries display marked skill in fact-finding.[11] If, so, how can those judges prove their contention? How many such trial judges listen as carefully to the witnesses in a jury trial, with a view to making up their own minds as to what they would decide, as they do when trying cases without juries? And, if juries possess such skill, why the mistaken verdicts in the cases reported by Borchard? Some of the judges in these cases were the sort who greatly esteem the jury. Perhaps those judges had complete confidence that those verdicts were correct. If so, then should we give much weight to their favorable appraisals of juries?

Moreover, the judges who thus applaud the jury nevertheless follow and usually endorse the practice of directing verdicts, a practice which, as we saw, recognizes that juries will often bring in verdicts which no reasonable man would accept as consistent with the evidence. Many such judges strenuously object to proposals to interrogate jurors carefully concerning the ways in which they arrived at their verdicts.

It may well be that the judges who assert the almost invariable correctness of jury verdicts do not mean to praise jury fact-finding. Probably they mean rather that juries wisely legislate out of existence legal rules they believe undesirable. But, as we saw, juries have often ignored rules, not because they disliked them, but because they misunderstood them, or for other reasons paid no attention to them, reaching verdicts, without reference to the rules or the evidence, by flipping coins or other aleatory devices.

I must add that from most (not all) of the trial judges for whose abilities I have especially high regard, I have heard denials of the notion that juries usually decide correctly. Judge Bok, in his recent de-

[11] This skill must be exercised on the evidence presented to the juries. But much important evidence, which might justify outstandingly different conclusions, is barred from the jury by exclusionary rules that are perpetuated because of belief in jurors' incompetence.

lightful book on the life of a trial judge, says: "He didn't always agree with the verdicts the juries brought in: he thought that he could see more clearly and sharply, because of his training." And I must also add that I know of no judge, no matter how much he exalts the jury, who urges that the many kinds of cases now required to be tried by jury-less courts should be tried by juries.

Trial lawyers, in public addresses, often extol the jury system. But many of those same lawyers, in private conversation, wax cynical about it. One such lawyer recently wrote a book in which he says that jury verdicts are usually correct. But he also says, "A fact is what a jury is flattered, deluded, or glamorized into believing as a fact by a skillful salesman, a trial lawyer. Good trial lawyers, every day in court, convince juries that black is white."

In part, the trial lawyers' public praise of the jury system stems from their vested interest in its existence. In part, too, they have come to enjoy the opportunity it affords them to engage in histrionics. Many a trial lawyer has much of the "ham" in him. Trial by jury is melodramatic. As Dean Green says, it is designed to make a stage for the trial lawyer, its chief actor. It is the trial lawyer's "artistic handiwork. The courthouse is his playhouse." Take the jury out of a trial, and most of the drama vanishes. Much of the tension disappears. The atmosphere becomes calm. This becomes apparent when, occasionally, the same case is tried first before a judge and jury, and later, with the same lawyers, before a judge alone.

3

I have told you of the excessive fighting spirit in trials which still unfortunately dominates too much of court-house government, and which prevents needed improvement in court-room fact-finding. The jury helps to keep alive this fight-theory. More than anything else in the judicial system, the jury blocks the road to better ways of finding the facts.

You will recall that the ordeals are today called an "irrational" mode of trial. Is trial by jury, then, "rational"? In 1890, Carter, a distinguished lawyer and scholar, said of the ordeals, "Let us not smile at the credulity of an age which could sanction such a device for the discovery of truth and the punishment of wrong. Our own boasted trial by jury, which affirms that all grades of capacity above drivelling idiocy are alike fitted for the exalted office of sifting truth from error, may excite the derision of future times."

Continental writers have referred to trial by jury as the "sentimental phase" of legal development. Tarde, discussing jury trials, speaks of the "superstition, the optimistic faith in the infallibility of individual reason, of common sense, of natural instinct"; he says that "proof by jury" rests on "an assumed revelation of the truth by a non-enlightened and unreasoning conscience." Maitland observed that superstitions seem odd to us when they are other people's superstitions. Allen, referring to "epidemic suggestions",—such as belief in the philosopher's stone and the "tulip craze"—paraphrases Tarde to the effect that "the extraordinary popularity of the jury . . . —a popularity maintained despite glaring defects and anomalies—is only another example of an epidemic suggestion."

It is extremely doubtful whether, if we did not now have the jury system, we could today be persuaded to adopt it. The chances are that most conservative lawyers would oppose such a "reform"; they would refer us to Scotland, an "Anglo-Saxon" country, where the jury has never played an important role. They would call attention to the marked decline of the jury's popularity in England. They would denounce trial by jury as an absurd New Dealish idea.

The point is that the jury, once popular thanks to its efficacy as a protection against oppression, has become embedded in our customs, our traditions. And matters traditional are likely to be regarded as inherently right. Men invoke all sorts of rationalizations to justify their accustomed ways. "No man," writes Ruth Benedict, "ever looks at the world with pristine eyes. He sees it edited by a definite set of customs and institutions and ways of thinking. . . . The observer will see the bizarre developments of behavior only in alien cultures, not in his own." The "importance of an institution in a culture gives no direct indication of its usefulness or its inevitability. . . . In a certain island in Oceana, fish-hooks are currency and to have large fish-hooks came gradually to be the outward sign of wealth. Fish-hooks are therefore very nearly as large as a man. They will no longer catch fish, of course. In proportion as they have lost their usefulness, they are supremely coveted."

It is not easy to get rid of deep-rooted customs. Aristotle wrote that "it is the customary that is intelligible." In the 17th century, Pascal said that "custom is our nature," or, rather "a second nature which destroys the former," so that "our natural principles are but principles of custom." Later, Tocqueville remarked, "What we call necessary institutions are often no more than institutions to which we have been accustomed"; Mill noted that most ideas which appear self-evident do so under "the magical influence of customs"; and Mr. Justice Holmes spoke of the "naivety with which social prejudices are taken for eternal principles."

Only thus, I think, can one explain why, in these United States, the jury still has its passionate defenders, its sincere admirers, and why, on the whole, the public finds no fault with it.

4

Boston, one of the leaders of the American bar, wrote in 1912: "I never pick up a book on advocacy, or the so-called art of the advocate, that I am not horrified at the frankly unethical attitude of the writers toward the jury. One would think that trickery, chicanery, and artful craftiness are the only elements that appeal to a jury. Courts are the institutions installed, presumably, to give correct judgments upon ascertained states of fact, in dispute, under the application of the established law. But when one takes up treatises on advocacy, he sees that he, a practitioner at law, must or must not resort to this petty trick, or fall into this or that trap, for fear of its effect on the jury. He must refrain from asking certain questions, or practice certain ways with witnesses, to capture or help the favor of the jury. The jury is the great bug-a-boo, whose childish impressionability must always be reckoned with in the administration of justice by its aid. One never hears such a suggestion in respect to a judge unless he is unfitted for his position." [12] Those are strong words; yet in the main I agree with them.

Nevertheless, we are saddled with the jury. For our federal and state constitutions require trial by jury in most criminal and many kinds of civil cases. In most jurisdictions, the defendant in a criminal action may waive a jury and go to trial by judge alone; both parties in a civil suit may give such waivers. The number of those jury-waived cases seems to be on the increase, but the number of jury cases still remains very considerable. As it will almost surely be impossible, in the reasonably near future, to repeal the constitutional provisions concerning the jury, we must, then, face the fact that, for many years to come, the jury will be with us. Accordingly, to meet the difficulties caused by the jury system, we can today look only to palliating reforms which aim at

[12] Boston, "Some Practical Remedies for Existing Deficiencies in the Administration of Justice," 61 *Un. of Pa. L. Rev.* (1912) 1.

making jurors somewhat better fact-finders. Let us now consider some proposed reforms.

1. Special (or Fact) Verdicts

As we saw, usually juries return general verdicts. There is, however, another type of verdict—a "special verdict" (or "fact verdict"): the trial judge tells the jury to report its beliefs, its findings, about specified issues of fact raised at the trial. The jury reports that Henry did or did not promise to deliver so many tons of coal to Williams on a particular day; or at what speed Jenkins was driving when he hit Olsen; or whether or not Adolf Brown and Helen Holt were present when John Gotrox signed his will. To those facts, thus "found" by the jury, the trial judge applies the appropriate legal rule.

A special verdict would seem to do away with some of the most objectionable features of trial by jury. The division of functions between jury and judge is apparently assured, the one attending to the facts alone, the other to the legal rules alone. The jury seems, by this device, to be shorn of its power to ignore the rules or to make rules to suit itself. As one court said, special verdicts "dispel . . . the darkness visible of general verdicts." The finding of facts, says Sunderland, "is much better done by means of the special verdict. Every advantage which the jury is popularly supposed to have over the [judge] as a trier of facts is retained, with the very great additional advantage that the analysis and separation of the facts in the case which the court and the attorney must necessarily effect in employing the special verdict, materially reduce the chance of error. It is easy to make mistakes in dealing at large with aggregates of facts. The special verdict compels detailed consideration. But above all it enables the public, the parties and the court to see what the jury has really done . . . The morale of the jury also is aided by throwing off the cloak of secrecy, for only through publicity is there developed the proper feeling of responsibility in public servants. So far, then, as the facts go, they can be much more effectively, conveniently, and usefully tried by abandoning the general verdict . . . The special verdict is devised for the express purpose of escaping the sham of false appearances." [13]

In some jurisdictions, the judge, when using a special verdict, need not—should not—give any charge about the substantive legal rules beyond what is reasonably necessary to enable the jury to answer intelligently the questions put to them. As, accordingly, the jury is less able

[13] Sunderland, "Verdicts General and Special," 29 *Yale L. J.* (1920) 253.

to know whether its findings will favor one side or the other, the appeal to the jurors' cruder prejudices will frequently be less effective. "A perverse verdict," it is said, "may still be returned, granted a jury clever enough to appreciate the effect of its answers, and to shape them to harmonize with its general conclusions. But it is much more difficult . . . , and by requiring the jury to return the naked facts only we may fairly expect to escape the results of sympathy, prejudice and passion."[14] That may be too sanguine a hope; but the fact verdict may often reduce the sway of the more undesirable emotions. It is suggested, too, that a special verdict "searches the conscience of the individual juror, as a general verdict does not," because "such are the contradictions in human nature that many a man who will unite in a general verdict for a large and unwarranted sum of money will shrink from a specific finding against his judgment of right and wrong."[15]

A related device is to retain the general verdict but to accompany it with written answers by the jury to special "interrogatories" concerning specific facts. This enables the trial judge to learn something about the jurors' reasons for their general verdict. "The submission of interrogatories . . . is," says Clementson, "a sort of 'exploratory opening into the abdominal cavity of the general verdict' . . . by which the court determines whether the organs are sound and in place, and the proper treatment to be pursued."[16]

The special verdict is nothing new. It was used in England centuries ago, and was early imported into this country. But it was used here in most states in so complicated a way that it fell into disrepute. However, in a few states, those complications seem to have been largely avoided.[17] A streamlined form of special verdict and of special interrogatories was authorized in the federal courts in 1938. In those courts, as in the courts of some states, it is optional with the trial judge in each civil jury case to employ either or neither of these methods, and the judges seldom use either of them. I think that one or the other should be made compulsory in most civil suits.[18]

Such a reform will not overcome all the objections to the jury system. Aside from the fact, already noted, that in a relatively simple case a jury will still be able to circumvent the rules by disingenuous answers to the questions, the special verdict does not eliminate the grave diffi-

[14] Clementson, *Special Verdicts and Special Findings by Juries* (1905) 12.
[15] Clementson, *loc. cit.*, 15.
[16] *loc. cit.*, 45-46.
[17] See Green, *Judge and Jury* (1930) 287.
[18] In several states, special verdicts are authorized in criminal trials.

culty that most jurors are not adequately equipped to find facts, are less competent to perform that task than a well-trained trial judge.[19]

2. *Special Juries*

At one time, in England, it was not unusual, when a case related to a particular trade, to have a jury consisting of men engaged in that trade. Such jurors could more informedly consider the matters in dispute.[20] Unfortunately, that practice was discontinued, and it has not been adopted in this country. It might be well to do so now,[21] although I will not guarantee the constitutionality of such a mode of jury selection. If juries of that sort had been in use, perhaps the remarkable recent growth of administrative agencies might not have occurred, and business arbitrations might not have become popular.[22]

In many kinds of cases, where jury trial is not required, a trial judge has the power to call in an "advisory jury" whose verdict does not bind him. If advisory juries were made up of "special" jurors of the kind I have just described, they could be of considerable value.[23]

3. *Intermediate Fact-Finders*

Where some of the facts of a civil jury suit are complex, the trial judge in some jurisdictions may refer those facts to an expert; the expert's report on those facts, together with the evidence on which he based it, are both presented to the jury, which, however, is not obligated to accept the report.[24] This helpful technique is too little employed.

4. *Revision of the Exclusionary Rules*

Judge Learned Hand, speaking of the exclusionary evidence rules, said that "it is entirely inconsistent to trust them [the jurors] as reverently as we do, and still surround them with restrictions which . . .

[19] See Chapter XVII as to the effect of a special verdict on what, in Chapter XII, I describe as the trial court's "gestalt."

[20] See Beuscher, "The Use of Experts by Courts," 54 *Harv. L. Rev.* (1941) 1105; Learned Hand, "Historical and Practical Considerations Regarding Expert Testimony," 15 *Harv. L. Rev.* (1901) 40, 45.

[21] I am not endorsing the so-called "blue-ribbon" jury or the usual special juries authorized in some states, which are not selected because of their peculiar acquaintance with trade usages or the like.

[22] See Chapter XXVII as to arbitration.

[23] As to laymen sitting with the trial judge as a substitute for the jury, see Chapter XVI.

[24] See Beuscher, *loc. cit.;* Ex Parte Peterson, 253 U.S. 300.

depend upon distrust." More emphatically, Boston remarked[25] that "our law requires that all matters for the consideration of the jury shall be, as it were, predigested food for mental invalids, and so it strains this food through the most highly developed rules of evidence . . . In short, we recognize in every imaginable way that the jury is the weakest element in our judicial system, and yet we ponder it as a sacred institution. We . . . regard it, in all ways in which our regard can be measured, as wholly incompetent for the purpose for which we establish it." In other words, if we have to have the jury, let us abolish, or modify, most (not all) of the exclusionary rules, since they often shut out important evidence without which the actual past facts cannot be approximated.

5. *Recording Jury-room Deliberations*

Judge Galston suggests[26] that a stenographic record be made of the jurors' discussions while they are deliberating in the jury-room; the trial judge, with such a record before him, could learn, to some extent, whether the verdict was reached by improper means; if so, he would set aside the verdict. That suggestion deserves consideration.

6. *Training For Jury Service*

The late Judge Merle Otis asserted that jurors should be men and women who have the "capacity quickly to comprehend the applicable law and intelligently to apply it." Judge Knox has said that, "to accomplish justice," we must have jurors "with intelligence" and "sound judgment" which will "enable them to decide intricate questions of fact." Each of those judges proposed to reach that highly desirable result by the quite simple means of providing, in very general terms, higher standards for jurors and of using more care (in part through better personnel) in the mode of selecting persons eligible to serve on juries. Such a reform seems to me incapable of doing the trick. It will not, I think, restrict jurors to those singularly few laymen who, without special training, can "quickly comprehend and intelligently apply" legal rules which lawyers must study to understand, or who are able "to decide intricate questions of fact" as they are presented in the course of a trial. Doubtless the impossibility of obtaining jurors of that caliber accounts for the virtual elimination of the civil jury in England and Scotland.

[25] *loc. cit.*
[26] Galston, "Civil Jury Trials and Tribulations," 29 *Am. Bar Ass'n. J.* (1943) 195.

Nor can we expect much from the practice of distributing to prospective jurors handbooks briefly describing the duties of jurors, or from short talks on that subject delivered by judges to jury panels. A practice established in Los Angeles has more merit: there a prospective juror must pass a written and oral test showing his aptitude for the job. But even that scheme, I think, falls far short of the bull's-eye.

A more helpful proposal is this: Let us, in the public schools and in adult education classes, give courses in which the students will be taught, in some detail, the function of the jury and the nature of trial-court fact-finding; require all citizens to attend such a course; bar from jury service any person who has not taken such a course and successfully passed an examination. Some such plan has been urged by Judge Galston and former Judge William Clark.[27] I heartily favor it. Again, I give no guaranty of constitutionality.

Were all those reforms adopted, trials by jury would be less dangerous to litigants than they now are; but I think they would still be far less desirable than jury-less trials before well trained honest trial judges.[28]

I must add that, despite my views about the undesirability of the jury (except perhaps in criminal trials), I have, as a judge, felt a strong obligation to see that, in cases which came before our court, trials by jury have been conducted in accordance with the rules supposed to govern such proceedings. As I said in an opinion:[29] "It has been suggested that a judge (like me) who shares the doubts about the wisdom of the jury system is inconsistent if he urges that the courts be vigilant in preserving the jury's function. I do not understand that criticism. It is the sworn duty of judges to enforce many statutes they may deem unwise. And so, when on the bench, our private views concerning the desirability of the jury system are as irrelevant as our attitudes towards bimetallism or the transmigration of souls. Consequently, as long as jury trials are guaranteed by constitutional or statutory provisions, it is the obligation of every judge, no matter what he thinks of such trials, to see that they are fairly conducted and that the jury's province is not invaded. That does not mean that a judge may not freely express his skepticism about the system, may not seek to bring about constitutional and statutory changes which will avoid or reduce what he considers its unfortunate results as it now operates."

[27] See Galston, *loc. cit.* [28] See Chapter XVII.

[29] United States v. Antonelli Fireworks Co., 155 F. (2d) (2d) 631, 642, 655 (dissenting opinion).

X. ARE JUDGES HUMAN?

For the time being, I shall largely ignore the jury: I shall treat law-suits as if they were always tried and decided solely by judges. Such a picture of court-house government is not wholly unjustified, for many trials are judge-trials, and perhaps some day—who knows—all will be.

That judges are human and share the virtues and weaknesses of mortals generally—that fact you may think so obvious as scarcely to deserve discussion. Why then do I discuss it? Because, among American lawyers, until fairly recently, that fact was largely tabu. To mention it, except in an aside and as a joke, even in gatherings of lawyers, was considered bad taste, to say the least. That tabu dominated most legal education during the 19th century and the early part of the 20th. Above all, it controlled what lawyers said to non-lawyers in publications and in public addresses. The Bar spoke to the laity as if the human characteristics of judges had little or no practical consequences. And when, not very long ago, some few of us ventured to violate that tabu, a considerable part of the legal profession called us subversive, enemies of good government, disturbers of "law and order."

No doubt, some of the lawyers who today support that tabu do so because, somehow, either they believe, more or less, that judges are super-human or that the human-ness of judges has virtually no effect on how courts decide cases. Such self-deceivers are not hypocrites but unquestionably sincere men. They come within my category of the second class of wizards. The same cannot be said, however, of some of those lawyers who deplore the public revelation that judges are not demi-gods or, at any rate, do not serve as almost flawless conduits of the divine. The deplorers, fully cognizant of the realities of court-house government, want to conceal them from the public. Their attitude is basically anti-democratic.

That sort of attitude received its best articulation in Plato's Republic. Plato, a totalitarian, who detested democracy, depicted the best state as a dictatorship by a handful of intellectuals. His guardians—or, more accurately, "guards"—were to be absolute rulers. They must, said Plato, have the privilege of employing "useful lies," "opportune falsehoods," for "the public good." Wrote Plato: "I mean . . . that our rulers will find a considerable dose of falsehood and deceit necessary for the good of their subjects." Paul Shorey defines such a Platonic "opportune falsehood" as "an ingenious device employed by a superior intelligence to circumvent necessity or to play providence to the vulgar." In Plato's ideal state, the few on top were to handle the multitude as if they were children, children to be duped—or rather, doped—with "magnificent lies."

That, I say, is the spirit of some of those who, themselves aware of the truth, wish to hide from the American public the human qualities of our court-house government. In one way or another, they seek to disseminate and perpetuate what they regard as an "opportune falsehood." Thanks to Hitler, we have come to recognize the utilization of such "ingenious devices" as the essence of fascism. If we cherish democracy, we must not tolerate that sort of deception of the public "for its own good." We must eliminate the myth or legend that judges are more—or less—than human.

2

Vigorous attacks on the myth about the non-human-ness of judges came in this country in the early twentieth century from some of the lawyers and legal thinkers who were interested primarily in the legal rules applied by the upper courts in important constitutional and labor cases. These thinkers demonstrated that the legal rules applicable to such cases were by no means as fixed and certain as they would be if the legend of the superhuman origin of decisions were true, that the formulation or interpretation of rules often varied with the particular judges who sat in particular cases. These students of the judicial process said that no judge was a mere judicial slot-machine, that the idea of a "mechanical jurisprudence" was an absurdity. Writers such as Pound, Frankfurter and Powell substituted so-called "sociological jurisprudence." They noted, for instance, that John Marshall's interpretation of the Constitution differed from Taney's, or Waite's from Field's; and that, on careful examination, the differences between judges often showed up as not merely differences in pure reasoning.

The key to the differences, most of these writers maintained, was to be found in the differing social, economic, and political backgrounds of the several judges. For the legal rules express social policies, and (said the "sociological" legal school) a judge's conception of such policies responds more or less to his social, economic and political outlook, which usually derives from his education, his social affiliations, his social environment.

The sociological school had its predecessors in the "historical school" of legal thinkers which had absurdly emphasized the Time Spirit,[1] and also in the Marxists and others who exploited the economic interpretation of the judiciary, with its deterministic explanations of all court decisions as inevitable derivatives of the class-biases of members of the bench.[2] Less radical, but no less vehement forerunners were such critics of high-court decisions as Teddy Roosevelt: T.R., having appointed men to the Supreme Court, knew from first-hand knowledge that judges were not fungible, like grains of sand or particles of wheat, that the pronounced economic and political views of the man within the judge sometimes influence the judge's decisions.

But the sociological jurisprudes, although they gave weight to the economic factors, were not economic determinists. They made a nicer, less crude, analysis than their predecessors of influences affecting judges. Among the influences they recognized were the judges' professional legal education and experience, and the power of judicial tradition. They observed that many a judge, as he develops, changes (or learns to keep in check) his personal social philosophy, often because of the judicial conventions, sometimes because he is persuaded by his fellow judges, sometimes because of the pressure of events. Far more keenly than their forerunners, the sociological jurisprudes perceived that they were talking about psychology, the psychology of judges.

Thus, in 1931, Professor (now Mr. Justice) Frankfurter, writing of the Supreme Court, explicitly mentioned the "psychological factor" and said that the judges' "unconscious" plays "an enormous role in the exercise of the judicial process, particularly where it closely touches contemporary economic and social problems." A brilliant younger member of this school, Felix Cohen, in 1935[3] asserted that, although "there is a large element of uncertainty in actual law," yet "actual experience" reveals "a significant body of predictable uniformity in the behavior of courts," that "reasonably certain predictions" of decisions are possible. He said that such prediction "is not a question of pure logic but of human psychology, economics and politics," and that "the

[1] For criticism of this notion of the Time Spirit, see Frank, *Fate and Freedom* (1945) Chapter 7; Frank, "A Sketch of An Influence," in the volume, *Interpretations of Modern Legal Philosophies* (1947) 189, 218-22.

[2] See Chapter XXV.

[3] F. S. Cohen, "Transcendental Nonsense and the Functional Approach," 35 *Col. L. Rev.* (1935) 809. Felix Cohen is one of our foremost "rule skeptics." His lack of "fact-skepticism" appears, for instance, in his failure to mention jury cases.

motivating forces which mold legal decisions" can be found in "the political, economic and professional background and activities of our various judges."

But note the rather severely limited scope of the psychological explorations of this school: (1) To the exclusion of virtually all else, they dwell on the rule-element in decisions or on the social policies behind the rules. (2) They therefore center their interest on decisions of upper courts. (3) They restrict the relevant judicial motivations almost entirely to those caused by the social, economic, political and professional influences affecting upper-court judges.

Frankfurter, for example, said that the "psychological factor is, of course, of infinitely greater significance where a court possesses the powers of our Supreme Court." Cohen, looking for "predictable uniformity in the behavior of courts," underscores the "social forces" [4] behind decisions, and discounts the effect of the "individual personality" of the judge; he dismisses attempted studies of individual judges' quirks, because (Cohen says) such studies had not produced any "significant results." I could quote similar views expressed by Pound, Powell, and other adherents of this school. Some of them have dwelt on the alleged uniformitarian effects of the similar education and professional experiences of the several judges.

The reader probably suspects what I regard as the flaws in this approach. Those who adopt it seek—and find—uniformities in the legal rules or in the social policies back of those rules. They ignore, however, that vast majority of decisions of cases in which social, economic, political and professional considerations are entirely, or almost entirely, absent, and where the rules are clear, the facts alone being in dispute. These thinkers, since their interest is in upper courts (where the facts are "given" by the trial courts), fail to take into account the numerous psychological factors in the non-rule element of the decisional process—that is, in trial-court fact-finding.[5] When they reject, as not "significant," any studies of the individual personalities of judges (especially of trial judges) which do not fall into the category of social-economic-political-professional influences, they do so, one suspects, because, most "significantly," the existence of those undiscoverable personal quirks knocks galley west the hope of discovering that "predictable uniformity in the behavior of courts" without which there can be no

[4] For criticism of the glib determinism which the words "social forces" often imply, see Frank, *Fate and Freedom* (1945) Chapter 1.

[5] Yet, like most "rule-skeptics," they disclose, here and there, some marginal disquietude about the "personal element" in such fact-finding.

"reasonably certain predictions" of decisions of most law-suits not yet commenced.[6]

The sociological school has made important contributions, has illuminated the methods of upper courts, and has valuably suggested improvements in those methods. But it has been too frock-coated, too preoccupied with "judicial statesmanship" in the so-called "higher" courts. The consequence of its aloofness from the trial courts has not been fortunate. For the chief impediments to adequate court-house government, to decent administration of justice, would remain even if there should disappear all the difficulties encountered in constitutional cases, in the interpretation of statutes, and in the contriving and revision of judge-made rules. "Sociological jurisprudence" has long been the fashion in the law schools, with the more sophisticated lawyers, and among writers of books on history, economics and political science. This fashion has led to a general disregard by educated nonlawyers of the impact of the idiosyncratic personalities of trial judges on the overwhelming majority of cases they decide, when they sit without juries, cases affecting the lives of citizens, cases which turn on questions of fact such as these: How fast was Smith driving? Did Robinson and Sullivan make an agreement for the purchase and sale of 1,000 tins of salmon? Was old lady Tompkins in her right mind when she deeded her house to Will Playboy? Into the answers to such questions the differing personalities of trial judges enter with a vengeance—and in ways about which sociological jurisprudence has been all but silent.

It is not difficult to expose the weakness of the "sociological approach": Assume that two trial judges have precisely the same social, economic and political background, that therefore (ex hypothesi) they have precisely the same social outlook, and that, accordingly, having the same attitude towards social policies, they would arrive at the same notion of the legal rule applicable to a given set of facts. It does not at all follow that, if they both heard the same witnesses, they would reach the same decision. Why? Because it is very, very far from certain that the two judges would believe and disbelieve the same witnesses, and, consequently, that they would "find" the "facts" identically.

[6] Patterson, referring to the notion that a "judge's digestion" may affect his decision, says: "Since judges suffering from indigestion do not have any uniform predilections, as far as I know, this theory never got very far." Patterson, *Introduction to Jurisprudence* (2d ed. 1946) 222-23. Earlier, Patterson seems to have considered a judge's "peculiar drives and preferences" important; see "Logic in the Law," 90 *Un. of Pa. L. Rev.* (1942) at 893-894.

You see what I'm driving at: The influences operating on a particular trial judge, when he is listening to, and observing, witnesses, cannot be neatly caged within the categories of his fairly obvious social, economic and political views. Even the older psychology would suggest that these pigeon-holes are insufficient. See, for instance, Spencer's *Study of Sociology* in which he considers at length the obstacles to dispassionate judgment; he includes impatience, irrational irritation in the presence of unpleasant truths which are disappointing cherished hopes, hates, antipathies, awe of power, loyalty to the group. Francis Bacon included in his "Idols" those of the "Den," that is, errors due to causes peculiar to a specific individual. The "new psychology," Freudian or otherwise, properly emphasizes these peculiarly individual factors.[7] These uniquely, highly individual, operative influences are far more subtle, far more difficult to get at. Many of them, without possible doubt, are unknown to anyone except the judge. Indeed, often the judge himself is unaware of them.

When it comes to "finding" the "facts" in law-suits where the oral testimony is in conflict, these obscure idiosyncracies in the trial judge are bafflingly at work. The judge's sympathies and antipathies are likely to be active with respect to the witnesses. His own past may have created plus or minus reactions to women, or blonde women, or men with beards, or Southerners, or Italians, or Englishmen, or plumbers, or ministers, or college-graduates or Democrats. A certain facial twitch or cough or gesture may start up memories, painful or pleasant. Those memories of the trial judge, while he is listening to a witness with such a facial twitch or cough or gesture, may affect the judge's initial hearing, or subsequent recollection, of what the witness said, or the weight or credibility which the judge will attach to the witness' testimony.

Ranyard West, a practicing psychiatrist and also a close student of matters legal, makes some comments pertinent here. He writes of the "formation of prejudice from fantasy, a process deeply hidden from all but the most penetrating introspection. . . ." The "mental processes involved" have two stages: In early life, each person has fantasies "compounded out of (a) genuine observations made by him as a young

[7] I am here lifting a passage from my book, *Law and the Modern Mind* (1930) 338-339. There I also said (p. 106): "In the first place, all other biases express themselves in connection with, and as modified by, these idiosyncratic biases. A man's political or economic prejudices are frequently cut across by his affection for or animosity to some particular individual or group, due to some unique experience he has had; or a racial antagonism which he entertains may be deflected in a particular case by a desire to be admired by someone who is devoid of such antagonism."

child, (b) perversions of truth introduced by misapprehended observations, and (c) pure inventions of the mind, imposed by the early emotional life of the child upon the real or semi-real figures around him" which "arouse his primitive and incoherent passions." In the adult period, "the unconscious mind" achieves an "identification . . . between personalities of . . . adult experiences and these . . . fantasy figures of infancy." The "realities of infancy . . . bias the tastes and judgments" of the adult, providing the "unconscious prejudices" of adult life. "We meet the persons, situations, and causes, X, Y, Z of our adult life; and to our conscious appraisement of them is contributed a factor from our unconscious memories, which judges them as if they were the A B C of some forgotten, far-off experiences of childhood." Many of us therefore often "do not see things and people as they are." In "the very act of labeling an experience we must needs go on and identify it with some fantasy or other, and docket it accordingly." Once "unfavorable unconscious identification occurs, we falsify . . . our judgments . . ." of others. It is, says West, by no means easy for a man to "realize and feel the scope of his own prejudicial judgments," to "appreciate fully the measure of . . . prejudice" in his own life.

Now the trial judge is a man, with a susceptibility to such unconscious prejudiced "identifications" originating in his infant experiences. Sitting at a trial, long before he has come to the point where he must decide what is right or wrong, just or unjust, with reference to the facts of the case as a whole, he has been engaged in making numerous judgments or inferences, as the testimony dribbles in. His impressions, colored by his unconscious biases with respect to the witnesses, as to what they said, and with what truthfulness and accuracy they said it, will determine what he believes to be the "facts of the case." His innumerable hidden traits and predispositions often get in their work in shaping his decision in the very process by which he becomes convinced what those facts are. The judge's belief about the facts results from the impact of numerous stimuli—including the words, gestures, postures and grimaces of the witnesses—on his distinctive "personality"; that personality, in turn, is a product of numerous factors, including his parents, his schooling, his teachers and companions, the persons he has met, the woman he married (or did not marry), his children, the books and articles he has read.

The following discussion, by West, of the unconscious factors which may affect the decision to hire an employee, applies as well to a judge's estimate of a witness: "A man may gain employment because of the tone of his voice, or lose it because of the color of his necktie, without his master being in the least aware at his point of relevant decision that these were factors in determining that decision. . . . How can we have one mind about the appointment of a stenographer of moderate qualifications, who looks like a now dearly loved sister of whom we were once envious? Intellect counsels, 'Look for a better'; conscious emotion says, 'I feel she'll suit me'; unconscious emotion says 'Beware!' Under such circumstances, decisions lie on the knees of the gods." [8]

Usually, then, it is all but impossible to predict how a particular trial judge will react to particular witnesses. In other words, a judge is not a mechanical comptometer. Prophecies of future trial-judge decisions cannot be worked out by the use of anything resembling a slide-rule. There is no standardization of trial judges, so that all of them will be sure to react in identical fashion to any particular body of conflicting oral testimony. Trial judges, being human, vary in their respective qualities of intelligence, perceptiveness, attentiveness—and other mental and emotional characteristics operative while they are listening to, and observing, witnesses.

Hans Gross says of witnesses: "The numberless errors in perceptions derived from the senses, the faults of culture, mood of the moment, health, . . . environment, all these things have so great an effect that we scarcely ever receive two quite similar accounts of one thing. . . ." Remember that the trial judge is a witness of the witnesses, and apply those comments to him. Consider the honest intelligent trial judge who is tired, and consequently inattentive, when an important witness is testifying. A well-known trial judge, now retired from the bench, told me that he found it necessary at intervals to withdraw to his chambers, there to pour cold water over his wrists, because his wits began to wander. One of my first jobs as a young lawyer was to drop books loudly on the court-room floor in order to keep awake a judge with a marked propensity to drowse when witnesses were testifying.

A half-century or more ago, Maine referred to the absence of any rules to guide a trial judge "in drawing inferences from the assertion of a witness to the existence of the facts asserted by him. . . . It is," said Maine, "in the passage from the statements of the witness to the inference that those statements are true, that judicial inquiries generally break down." It "is," continued Maine, "the rarest and highest

[8] "A Psychological Theory of Law," in the volume, *Interpretations of Modern Legal Philosophies* (1947) 766, 775.

personal accomplishments of a judge to make allowance for the ignorance and timidity of witnesses, and to see through the confident and plausible liar. Nor can any general rules be laid down for the acquisition of this power, which has methods of operation peculiar to itself, and almost undefinable." In plain English, skill in judicial fact-finding is by no means uniform.

In sum, we may (for the sake of argument) assume judicial uniformity in judicial use of all the legal rules. But when it comes to the fact-component of decisions, uniformity may easily be absent in law-suits in which the orally testifying witnesses disagree. If so, then—what? Then, in any one of the vast majority of juryless cases of that kind, the decision will depend on the peculiar personality of the particular trial judge who happens to be sitting.[9] "Art," said Zola, "is nature through the medium of a temperament." One may say the same of that segment of nature constituting the facts of a lawsuit.[10]

It is sometimes suggested that the hidden biases of divers judges will correct each other and largely cancel out. So said Cardozo.[11] That is partly true of judges sitting together in deciding a case. But that suggestion cannot be true of many trial judges sitting in separate court-rooms and separately making findings of fact in separate law-suits.

Studies of the restricted sort of background factors which interest the "sociological" school give some help, within limits, in prophesying how upper-court judges will decide some types of cases.[12] But they will give slight help in fore-knowing what trial judges will do in "contested" cases.[13] Even where the oral testimony is not conflicting, pre-

[9] Fromm, *Man For Himself* (1947) makes an important distinction between "temperament" and "character." But I have ignored that distinction in this book because it is not germane to my discussion.

[10] One should add that, in a law-suit, the facts are seen through many temperaments, i.e., those of the witnesses and the trial judge; in a jury trial, one must add the jurors' temperaments.

[11] "The eccentricities of judges balance one another." Cardozo, *The Nature of the Judicial Process* (1921) 112.

[12] For a pioneering study of that type, see Haines, "General Observations on the Effect of Personal, Political and Economic Influences in The Decision of Cases," 17 *Ill. L. Rev.* (1923) 98. See also the several detailed biographies of Justices of the United States Supreme Court. Compare Frank, Book Review, 54 *Harv. L. Rev.* (1941) 905-06.

[13] For an attempted study in that field, see Schroeder, "The Psychologic Study of Judicial Opinions," 6 *Calif. L. Rev.* 89. Schroeder was overly optimistic; he asserted that every opinion of a judge "amounts to a confession." For criticism of his article, see Frank, *Law and The Modern Mind* (1930) 113-14.

Even the most detailed studies of individual trial judges will be of little aid in prophesying how they will react to particular witnesses; consequently they will be of little value in predicting how those judges will find the facts on which they base their decisions. See the discussion, infra, of Lasswell and McDougal, Chapter XIV.

dictions of trial judges' decisions are not always easy, since such judges are not robots. Practicing lawyers, therefore, attempt to learn the idiosyncracies of particular trial judges: Judge Brown is known as a former railroad lawyer, who, fearful of showing favoritism, leans over backwards and is likely to be unduly hostile to railroads. Judge Green, who for years had served in the office of the city's Corporation Counsel, is partial to municipalities. Judge Blue is markedly puritanical. Armed with such information, lawyers try to have (or avoid having) some cases tried before certain judges. Knowledge of that character might be called "rules for decision" by Judge Brown, Green, Blue, Yellow, Purple, etc. It is perhaps conceivable that such data can be skillfully organized in great detail.[14] But even such data will seldom, if ever, be enough when the oral testimony is in conflict.

3

In defining "objectivity" in rules, Braden has supplied us with an invaluable test by which to tell when a legal rule obviates the need to consider the personalities of judges. "By objectivity," he says, "I mean that quality of a rule of law which enables it to be applied to similar situations without regard to the identity of the judges who apply it."[15] Doubtless, many rules possess that quality, when the facts of the "situation" are settled. But no rule has that quality with respect to any "situation" the facts of which are not settled; and such is the condition of "situations" in all cases where the facts can be ascertained only by determining the credibility of witnesses. By Braden's test, therefore, the personalities of trial judges (in jury-less cases) are almost always important. To bring out my point sharply, I challenge Felix Cohen (or anyone else he selects) to predict, by his method, the decisions in a hundred ordinary, mine-run, law-suits, chosen at random and now awaiting trial, where the controlling issues are solely disputed facts as to which there will be nothing but conflicting oral testimony.

4

I suggest that, in this connection, the reader consider once more what enlightened historians have said about the manner in which the personality of each historian affects his version of past facts.[16] Let me here

[14] See Frank, "What Courts Do in Fact," 26 *Ill. L. Rev.* (1932).
[15] 57 *Yale L. J.* (1948) 571, 572 note 5.
[16] See Chapter IV.

add, for convenience, the views of two distinguished historians, Berre and Febvre. No historian, they write, "however balanced he may be, however determined to maintain himself on the line of strict impartiality, can ever escape from the thousand biases created in him by the many particular acquired or inherited . . . traits of his personal nature. Against [such] causes of error what precaution is possible? To preach criticism and impartiality, that the historian should remain as unmoved before human facts of the past as the naturalist observing the wing of a mosquito under the microscope or the astronomer viewing a familiar comet through the telescope? But by his very definition the scholar exerts himself with all his being toward impartiality . . . It is not purposeful distortion by the partisan disguised as a scholar which is of supreme importance, but the unconscious involuntary distortion, the distortion which the bona fide historian does not even perceive, the error committed by him at the very moment when he feels himself the most rigorously impartial of all observers. . . ."[17] Substitute the words "trial judge" for "historian" and "scholar" and you have much of my point.

[17] 7 *Encyc. of the Soc. Sciences* (1932) 357, 367.

XI. PSYCHOLOGICAL APPROACHES

THE psychological aspects of trial-judging should long have been a lively subject. For judicial administration of justice is, in considerable part, a psychological process. As our legal vocabulary shows, courts constantly deal with "mental" problems. The courts must cope with such matters as, for instance, "intention," "motive," "malice," "mental cruelty," "insanity," "delusions," and "undue influence." As an English judge said in 1882, "the state of a man's mind is [for a court] as much a fact as his digestion." The trial judges, who daily try to probe the minds of witnesses, know that job is not easy, even if they do not wholly agree with the medieval judge who said that "the devil himself knoweth not the mind of man." Yet many judges and lawyers who think it important to recognize the practical effects of the lack of psychological uniformity among litigants or among witnesses, jeer at the suggestion that it is important to recognize that the same lack of uniformity among trial judges has important practical results.

A good example is Paton.[1] In a recent book he underscores the familiar fact that differences in witnesses' reactions gravely influence their discrepant stories told at trials. But he scoffs at the idea that the "personality of judges" is worthy of serious consideration by legal thinkers. "The bar," he says, "has always studied the personality of judges, but it has been too modest to dignify such research by the name of jurisprudence." His reason for that conclusion is revelatory: We "must be skeptical of discovering results that are of great value," because "if we wish to emphasize the influence of the individual characteristics of the judge, we are confined to a blind guess as to what really affected his decision. . . ." But is not the very blindness of that guess a fact of "great value," since it discloses the guessiness of many decisions?

2

Perhaps the most curious suggestion for overcoming the "personal element" in the judiciary is that made by Rohrlich.[2] He admits that

[1] Paton, Jurisprudence (1946) 21-22, 147, 158.

[2] "Judicial Technique," 17 *Amer. Bar Ass'n. J.* (1931) 480.

judges seldom disclose the "real motives and reasons" which induce their decisions. He says, however, that it is "salutary" that the judges should (by omissions) misinform the public. He concedes that such misreporting does not prevent the intrusion of the judge's personality into the determination of the facts, nor "change the impelling reasons which produce a decision" and which remain unpublished. Nevertheless, Rohrlich argues that such judicial misdescription is "salubrious" because it "does tend to reduce the influence" on the judge "of those factors which dare not be written down."

As best I can understand it, that argument comes to this: A judge, by deceiving the public, will be the better able to deceive himself; and the judge's self-deception, his concealment from himself of some powerful factor which brought about his decision (such as dislike of a witness because he has red hair), will reduce the effect of that influence on the judge. This goes Plato one better: When a Platonic ruler told the citizens a falsehood, he was to know what he was about; he could, therefore, being concerned for the public good, critically evaluate the bearings of his fabrication on the public weal. But when a judge not only omits from his published report the "real motives and reasons" for his decision but also hides them from himself, he cannot critically examine them, in order to consider reflectively whether his decision, founded on such motives, is or is not in the public interest.

Moreover, unless ancient learning and modern psychology are utterly mistaken, concealment of one's motives from oneself tends not to reduce but to increase their influence. "Know thyself" is a maxim which today is more than ever valued as the foundation of intelligent moral conduct. The self-deluded we regard as likely to be dangerously anti-social. The judicial self-delusion Rohrlich inculcates can but serve to give the judge a sense of freedom from responsibility for permitting the intrusion of his most undesirable prejudices. It thus fosters judicial irresponsibility. I cannot believe that a judge who, when publishing opinions worded in terms of apparently imperturbable dispassionateness, camouflages his biases, thereby nullifies them. It would seem that a judge should seek to avoid being influenced by "factors which dare not be written down"; and that, if he is under the sway of factors so undesirable that they should not be published, he will be the better able to loosen their grip on him if at least he is fully conscious of them. Moreover, as Montaigne, many years ago, sagely remarked, "they who conceal" their faults from others, "usually conceal them from themselves." "I dislike . . . ," he said, "unpublishable thoughts"; and he admonished, "Let us not be ashamed to say what we are not ashamed to think."

3

The "rule-skeptics," whom I previously mentioned, were dissatisfied with the orthodox theory's reliance on the legal rules as precision instruments. On the look-out for more dependable sources of judicial uniformity lurking behind the formal legal rules, they were not content with the vagueness of sociological jurisprudence. Some of these "rule-skeptics" turned directly, and with enthusiasm, to psychology, but to a psychology of a very special kind. They sought a new road to legal predictability and legal certainty by recourse to a then popular brand of psychology, Behaviorism, popularized by Watson.

Outstanding was Oliphant of Columbia Law School. In 1928, explaining that "each case is a record of judicial behavior," he asserted that one could prophesy judicial decisions by disregarding what the judges said in their opinions, their "vocal behavior," and by concentrating on their "non-vocal behavior." The thing to do, Oliphant declared, was to look at the printed records of cases, at what he called the "facts." Thereby, he maintained, one could foresee the decisions—which, he insisted, were nothing but the judge's responses "to the stimuli of the facts." By studying how judges so responded in past cases, lawyers could know just how judges would act in future cases. That was sophisticated but glib nonsense, as anything more than a casual look at behaviorism was bound to reveal. Let us take a good look at it.

The founder of Behaviorism, Watson, had devoted several years to watching monkeys and white rats. Since those creatures were speechless, he could learn nothing about their psychology except by observing their behavior. This restricted technique, which perforce governed the study of those non-speaking animals, Watson applied, without qualification, to human beings. He treated men like monkeys and rats—as if men's own reports in speech of their conscious reactions were useless and could throw no light on their conduct. Speech, he said, is produced by certain muscles in the larynx, and is therefore to be considered merely muscular activity, "laryngeal behavior." There resulted the "wind-pipe" theory of human thought.

Behaviorism, as Watson named it, was a sort of "veterinary's psychology." I call it that, having in mind a story about Prince Bismarck. Being ill, he summoned a physician who asked the Prince about his symptoms. Bismark resented the questioning. "Very well, Highness," said the doctor, "but if you want to be cured without being questioned, you had better send for a veterinary." "Descartes," remarks Bertrand Russell, "said, 'I think, therefore I am.' Watson says, 'There are white rats, therefore I don't think.'" Over-simplifying as he did, Watson became dogmatic. He confidently proclaimed that, using proper controls, he "could build any infant along specified lines—rich man, poor man, beggar-man, thief." [3] He encouraged the idea that, with easily acquired knowledge of external stimuli, human responses could be foreseen.

Watson's veterinary psychology was founded on Pavlov's work with dogs, and stimulated Lashley's with rats. This popularized the concept of the "conditional reflex," which illuminated the behavior not only of dumb animals but also, to some extent, that of men. However, as to men, its value was limited. For dumb animals, aside from lacking the power of speech, have a brain-equipment far simpler than man's. In 1926, Herrick, in his book, *Brains of Rats and Men,*[4] said that the human brain contains about 12,000 million nerve cells or neurons, of which more than half are in the cerebral cortex, so that potentially the number of patterns of inter-neuronic connections, in the cortex alone, is so great as to be almost beyond computation. Monkeys and rats have brains of far less complexity. Concluding that "rats are not men," Herrick rejected the glibness of the behaviorists. Most physiologists and psychologists agreed. As one writer put it, "at the level of self-consciousness and rational activities, it is well-nigh impossible to put one's finger on the specific causes of human behavior."

Matching the optimism of the behaviorists was that of some bio-chemists. They indicated that variations in human personalities correlated with "bio-chemical individualities." One bio-chemist surmised that each person exudes odorless molecules which set up hormonic responses in other persons. That seemed to open up this fascinating possibility: A lawyer could learn just how a particular judge would respond hormonically to the exudations of the witnesses and lawyers, and thereby anticipate the judge's decision. But, alas, the more cautious bio-chemists warned of the infinite varieties of "bio-chemical individ-

[3] Behaviorism's "primary contention," he wrote, "is that . . . if organized society decreed that the individual or group should act in a definite, specific way, the behaviorist could arrange the situation or stimulus which would bring about such action. . . ."

I am not here considering the more modest and restrained "behaviorism" of George Mead. See Mead, *Mind, Self and Society* (1934).

[4] A wag suggested a companion volume on the brains of cats and women.

ualities" and the consequent unpredictability of most individual reactions.

Accordingly, even if one were a devout determinist or mechanist,[5] he would be dubious as to the likelihood that—via Watsonionism, conditioned reflexes, or bio-chemistry—the conduct of any man, except in any but the simplest circumstances, could be accurately foretold. And, as trial judges, in hearing testimony and deciding cases, are not in simple circumstances, this road to legal prediction appears hopelessly dark.

Indeed, it does not require any profound criticism of behaviorism to see that Oliphant's thesis is founded on quicksand. For suppose that, before a judge makes his decision in a law-suit, you read the printed or typewritten record of the testimony. It will reveal what the witnesses said—but not what witnesses the trial judge will believe, and, therefore, not what he will regard as the "facts" of the case. Usually, so many and such diverse factors in the evidence combine in impelling the particular trial judge's mind to his finding of facts that prediction of his decision can be but a shaky, doubtful, guess.

However, it will not do to reason that, because the pseudo-scientific legal behaviorists were wrong in what they affirmed, they were therefore also wrong in what they denied, i.e., the possibility of predicting a judicial decision through a knowledge of the legal rules which the trial judge will probably employ in deciding any particular law-suit.

Nor does rejection of behaviorism as a legal prediction-technique justify the scorn sometimes heaped on those who point to the numerous non-rational factors in the decisional process. Many legal scholars, instead of giving serious consideration to that subject, resort to derision. Absurdly lumping together all the non-rational, non-logical, elements, and describing them as the "state of the judge's digestion," these scholars often jeeringly speak of "gastronomical jurisprudence."[6] Under the heading of gastronomical ailments, one cannot subsume all the irrationalities of judges. For instance, we learn from a judicial opinion[7] that important occupants of the bench have suffered delusions, some of them severely: "Lord Brougham,[8] upon more than one occasion, was

[5] For extensive criticism of determinism, see Frank, *Fate and Freedom* (1945). See also Kallen's discussion of Thorndike's views, in Kallen, *The Liberal Spirit* (1948) 46-47.

[6] See e.g., Patterson, *An Introduction to Jurisprudence* (2d ed. 1946) 210, 222-23. In 1942, he had intimated that such factors deserved attention; see "Logic in the Law," 90 *Un. of Pa. L. Rev.* (1942) 893-94.

[7] Wilcox v State, 94. Tenn. 106, 28 S.W. 312, 315.

[8] An English judge.

placed in seclusion, his mind being clearly off balance. . . . A distinguished New England judge imagined that a dropsical affection under which he labored was a sort of pregnancy." Can we be sure that those afflictions had no effect on their decisions? And how can we know that many another judge, in deciding cases, has not been affected by mental aberrations, although less abnormal and entirely imperceptible?

Of course, no one, except jocularly, has ever proposed explaining all or most decisions in terms of the judges' digestive disturbances. Yet, at times, a judge's physical or emotional condition has marked effect. No one denies that a witness may have made a serious mistake about what he saw or heard because of acute indigestion or a sleepless night. Why refuse to admit the same as to a trial judge when functioning as a witness of the witnesses? In the 18th century, La Mettrie referred to "a gentleman who was, when fasting, the most upright and merciful judge, but woe to the wretch who came before him when he had made a hearty dinner; he was then disposed to hang everybody, the innocent as well as the guilty." A contemporary criticized La Mettrie thus: "Champaign will never change a peasant into a doctor; nor brown bread a philosopher into a fool." Needham, a 20th century biologist, comments: "And yet La Mettrie might answer out of his grave, the vitamin in rice husks, more potent than brown bread, may turn the fool into a philosopher, ..." Out of my own experience as a trial lawyer, I can testify that a trial judge, because of overeating at lunch, may be so somnolent in the afternoon court-session that he fails to hear an important item of testimony and so disregards it when deciding the case. "The hungry judges soon the sentence sign, And wretches hang that juryman may dine," wrote Pope. Dickens' lovers well remember Perker's advice to Pickwick: "A good, contented, well-breakfasted juryman, is a capital thing to get hold of. Discontented or hungry jurymen, my dear sir, always find for the plaintiff."

Perhaps, at the present time, the subject of the effects of the contents of the judicial alimentary canal cannot be discussed other than in a semi-facetious manner. In that vein, Lord Campbell in the early 19th century, discussed the related subject of the behavior of Parliamentary orators: "There might be," he wrote, "a cautious chapter, in a treatise De Claribus Oratoribus, on the mode of their preparing themselves physically. Sheridan could not speak without a pint of brandy; and a celebrated speech in the House of Lords is said to have been inspired by mulled port. One of the greatest orators of the House of Commons is most powerful and imaginative after eating a pound of cold roast-beef and drinking a quart of small beer; while it is a well-known fact that the finest speech of the younger Pitt was delivered after a violent fit of vomiting. Some recommend tea; some camphor julep; and one orator, that he might electrify his audience, as often as he is going to speak, repairs to the Polytechnic and receives several shocks from a Leyden jar."

Said Montaigne, writing in the 16th century: "The lawyers . . . have a customary saying, referring to a criminal who happens to have a judge in good humor and an indulgent mood: . . . 'Let him rejoice in his good fortune!' For it is certain that we meet with judges who are at times harsher, more captious, more prone to convict, and at another more easy-going, complaisant and more inclined to pardon. When Justice So-and-So leaves his house suffering from the Gout, from jealousy or from resentment against his valet who has been robbing him, his whole soul dyed and steeped in anger, we cannot doubt that his judgment will be warped accordingly. . . . Not only do fevers, potions, and serious happenings upset our judgment; the least thing in the world will turn it like a weather-cock. And there is no doubt, though we are not conscious of it, that if a continuous fever can prostrate our soul, the tertian fever will impair it to a certain extent, in proportion to its severity. . . . And consequently, hardly for a single hour in life will our judgment chance to be in its proper trim, our body being subject to so many continual changes and stuffed with so many different springs of action that . . . it will be strange if there is not always one that shoots wide of the mark. Moreover, this infirmity is not so easily detected, unless it be extreme and quite past remedy; inasmuch as reason always walks crooked, lame and broken-hipped, and in the company of falsehood as well as of the truth. Hence it is always difficult to discover her miscalculations and irregularities. I always call by the name of reason that semblance of it which every man imagines himself to possess. This kind of reason, which may have a hundred counterparts around one and the same object, all opposed to one another, is an implement of lead and wax that may be bent and stretched and adapted to any bias and any measure; it needs but the skill to mould it. However well-meaning a judge may be, if he does not closely hearken to his conscience, his leaning toward friendship, kinship, . . . and revenge, and not only things so weighty, but that fortuitous instinct which inclines us to favor one thing more than another, and which, without the permission of reason, gives us the choice between two like objects, or some equally empty shadow, may imperceptibly creep into his judgment, and prompt him to allow or disallow a cause, and give a tip to the scales." Are matters distinctly different in the 20th century?

XII. CRITICISM OF TRIAL-COURT DECISIONS—THE GESTALT

I MUST now make a confession. Up to now I have been writing as if the principal obstacle to predicting a decision were the subjectivity of the trial court's finding of facts. I have been over-simplifying. The situation is far more complex. This will become clear if we consider in some detail a trial judge's decision, not before but after it has been made, and if we then attempt to appraise it as correct or incorrect.

Sometimes in connection with a decision, a trial judge publishes a statement, called an "opinion," in which he purports to explain why he decided as he did. In his "opinion," he reports the facts as he finds them (the *F*) and the legal rule (the *R*) he applied. Theoretically, one can then see whether his decision (his *D*) was correct, can favorably or unfavorably criticize his decision on the basis of his explanation.

To illustrate: There is a legal rule (an *R*) that an oral (unwritten) agreement for the sale of goods, if not to be performed within a year, is not binding unless in part confirmed in writing. Mr. Small sues Mr. Big for breach of contract. At the trial, Small testifies that Big orally offered to sell Small a thousand tons of coal, at $10 a ton to be delivered, on Small's orders, during the next two years; that Small promptly accepted that offer; but that Big refused to deliver any coal; and that Small, as a consequence, suffered a loss of $5,000. Small also testifies that he received a letter from Big, a few days after the oral agreement, confirming it. Big, however, testifies that he never made such an offer, that the signature to the letter is not his, and that he had not authorized anyone to write such a letter. The trial judge gives a $5,000 judgment for Small. In his published opinion, the judge states that there was such an oral agreement, that Big signed the letter, that he refused to deliver the coal, that Small's loss was $5,000, and that, applying the legal rule, Small is entitled to the decision. That decision seems unquestionably correct—just as it would seem unquestionably erroneous if the trial judge had said that Big neither signed nor authorized the letter. A moment's reflection shows that that criticism, favorable or unfavorable, of his decision has little meaning. For the judge's *F* (his "finding" of the facts) is at best but an *SF;* at best, it is only what the judge thinks were the facts, and that thought depends on his belief in the story of one witness rather than that of another. No one, reading the judge's opinion can effectively criticize his belief, can tell whether it was right or wrong. So that, if his reported *F* has a foundation in some of the conflicting testimony, one must accept his *F;* it is then beyond criticism. True, one can still partially criticize his decision, his *D:* One can say that he did or did not use the proper legal rule, or that if the *R* he used is proper, nevertheless his decision is or is not erroneous, in that he did or did not reach it by logically applying that *R* to the *F* he found. Such criticism is obviously limited in scope, and therefore not very satisfactory.

But even such partial criticism is often impossible. For, in many states at least in some kinds of cases, a trial judge is not required to report anything but a laconic *D* ("Judgment for defendant," or "Judgment for plaintiff for $5,000"). He need not state what facts he found (his *F*) or the *R* he used. If he does not so state—and many a trial judge in such jurisdictions does not—usually, his decision is wholly beyond intelligent criticism by anyone but himself. It may be that, if he had reported his *F,* it would have appeared that (on the basis of that *F*) his decision was wrong, i.e., that he used an improper *R* or illogically deduced his *D* from his *F* and the *R* he used. Thus, in the Small-Big case, if the judge had publicly reported that Big did not sign or authorize the letter, it would have been clear that his decision for Small was wrong, because he had used an incorrect *R.* But, without such a report, no one knows what witnesses he believed or disbelieved. Since no one knows even his *SF,* it follows that the *R* he applied is also undiscoverable. His decision, his *D,* is even more obscure than a jury's general verdict.

Yet, if any such decision is appealed, the upper court is asked to criticize it. What does the upper court do? Generally, it tries to sustain the decision. If the upper court can, it works out for itself some combination of a correct *R* and an assumed *F* which will logically justify the trial judge's *D.* It will assume that the judge found that *F,* if there is some oral testimony which will support it.[1] In the Small-Big case,

[1] See United States Clay Products Co. v. Linder, 119 F. (2d) 456: "The [trial] court made a 'Trial Finding For Defendant' [the appellee], without more, and entered judgment accordingly. We must assume that the court found all the disputed facts . . . in appellee's favor." National Surety Co. v. Lincoln County, 238 F. 705: "We must assume from the general finding that the court found. . . ." See also Frayne v. Bahto, 57

the judge may actually have believed Big's testimony; if so, according to the accepted legal rule, the decision should have been for Big and should be reversed. But, as the judge decided for Small, the upper court will assume he believed Small's testimony, i.e., believed that Big and Small made the oral agreement and that the letter was signed or authorized by Big. Yet the upper court cannot possibly know whether the trial judge did so believe, and whether he grounded his decision on that belief. The real reasons for his decision are a mystery.

Such unexplained, inscrutable, general-verdict-like, trial-judge decisions have been deemed undesirable, because they put a burden on the upper courts, and for other reasons. Consequently, in some jurisdictions, published explanations by the trial judge have been made mandatory. For instance, in the federal courts, the Rules of Civil Procedure require the trial judges in most non-criminal cases to publish special findings of fact, and, separately, statements of the *R*'s they used.

Significantly, many federal trial judges resent this requirement. The reason for that resentment was given in a recent comment by former Federal District Judge McLellan. He was discussing a new federal rule which provides that, if a defendant so requests, the trial judge must make special findings of fact in a criminal case tried without jury. Of that rule, Judge McLellan said: "We all know, don't we, that when we hear a criminal case tried, we get convinced of the guilt of the defendant or we don't; and isn't it enough if we say guilty or not guilty, without going through the form of making special findings of fact designed by the judge—unconsciously, of course—to support the conclusions at which he has arrived?" Judge McLellan there pithily expressed the conviction that a trial judge's published explanation does not disclose the actual basis of his decision so as to expose it to effective criticism.

Let us spell out Judge McLellan's position in terms of what I have been saying. The argument would then be as follows: The facts of a case are not the actual past facts as they happened in the past. At first glance they seem to be what the trial judge thinks happened. But that is a superficial analysis: When the judge publishes his findings, we can never be sure that they report what he thinks were the facts. Those findings report merely what he *says* he thinks the facts were. And seldom, if ever, can we learn whether what he says on the subject of what he thinks matches what, in truth, he does think. To discover what he

---

Atl. (2d) 520 (N.J.); United States v. Standard Accident Insurance Co., 106 F. (2d) 200, 203.

thinks, it would be necessary to learn what "went on in his mind." But it is difficult to explore the mind of any man. In the case of a witness, cross-examination and other devices are available which may sometimes show, in part at least, what he is thinking while on the witness-stand and what he had previously thought. But no one is permitted to cross-examine a judge or to use other methods applicable to witnesses. How, then, can one "investigate his secret thought. . . ? He is the master of them, and what he says must be conclusive, as there is nothing to contradict or explain it." [2]

The trial judge is therefore in this position: He can begin with the decision he considers desirable, and then, working backwards, figure out and publish an *F* and an *R* which will make his decision appear to be logically sound, if only there is some oral testimony which is in accord with his reported *F,* and if he applied the proper *R* to that reported *F.* If so, it does not matter whether actually he believed that testimony, i.e., whether the facts he reports are the facts as he believes them to be. In other words, he can, without fear of challenge, "fudge" the facts he finds, and thus "force the balance." No one will ever be able to learn whether, in the interest of what he thought just, or for any other cause,[3] he did thus misstate his belief.

I will never forget one of my experiences as a young lawyer. I participated in a law-suit, lasting a week, tried by an able trial judge without a jury. During the course of the trial, on every doubtful question concerning the admission or exclusion of evidence, the judge, to my great indignation, ruled in favor of the other side. To my surprise, a few weeks after the trial ended, the judge decided the case in my client's favor, with strong findings of fact. A year later I met the judge who referred to the case, saying: "You see, on the first day of the trial, I made up my mind that the defendant, your client, was a fine, hard-working woman who oughtn't to lose all her property to the plaintiff, who had plenty of money. The plaintiff was urging a legal rule which you thought was wrong. I thought it was legally right, but very unjust, and I didn't want to apply it. So I made up my mind to lick the plaintiff on the facts. And by giving him every break on procedural points during the trial, and by using in my opinion the legal rule he urged, I made it impossible for him to reverse me on appeal, because, as the testimony was oral and in conflict, I knew the upper court would never upset my findings of fact." That judicial conduct was not commend-

[2] Duke of Buccleuch v. Metropolitan Board, L.R. 5 H.L. 418, 434 (1872).

[3] Such as corruption or political influence.

able. But the judge's story did open my eyes to the way in which the power of a trial judge to find the facts can make his decision final, even if, had he correctly stated his honest notion of the facts, his decision would have been reversed for error in applying the wrong legal rule.

I recently said in an opinion that since, when a trial judge's decision turns on his view of the credibility of witnesses, "his 'finding' of 'facts,' responsive to [some of the] testimony, is inherently subjective (i.e., what he believes to be the facts is hidden from scrutiny by others), his concealed disregard of evidence is always a possibility. An upper court must accept that possibility, and must recognize, too, that such hidden misconduct by a trial judge lies beyond its control." I doubt whether many trial judges thus deliberately "fudge" or "force the balance"; when this practice is employed, I think it is usually unconscious or only semi-conscious. As, however, such findings are possible, and are certainly sometimes made, we can never be sure whether, when a trial judge publishes his findings, he is accurately reporting even his true *SF*. The upshot is this: In most law-suits, the issues are solely issues of fact and the testimony oral; in those suits, the decisions, even if erroneous, are often exempt from criticism and from reversal by the upper courts.

There is a delightful World War I tale of General Pershing's first visit to the front. After he and his party had advanced some distance, he asked his aide how far they were from their goal. Down the line went the question and up the line came the answer, in a whisper, "Five miles." After a further advance, Pershing whispered the same question and received, in a whisper, the reply "Four miles." "Why in the devil," queried the General, "are we whispering?" This question went down the line to a buck private who responded, "Because I have a sore throat." In our judicial system, most of the time, the trial judge plays the role of the private in the Pershing tale. If he has a sore throat, the upper court whispers.

"The . . . trial judge," says Tourtoulon, ". . . may ignore competent witnesses; . . . nevertheless his decision rests supreme. . . . If he should make a rule that he would never decide between contending parties except according to the length of their noses, it would always be easy for him to render judgments whose reasonings were perfectly correct according to law and absolutely unassailable, and no one could ever suspect him of the true motive which caused his decision. It is said," Tourtoulon continues, "that the judgment is often reached . . . before it has assumed its final form, and that the flood of arguments and authorities which uphold it if attacked, were accordingly not known by the judge at the time of his decision. . . . The judge may . . . by inexact appraisement of the facts, always extricate himself from the restraint of the law." Tourtoulon was writing of the French judicial system. But his remarks apply as well to ours.

2

I have probably amplified Judge McLellan's remarks to include more than he intended. Let me now adhere more literally to what he said. He voiced a sentiment often expressed by trial judges, but usually, in private conversations only. However, Judge Hutcheson, after years of service on the trial bench, published an article in which he stated that a trial judge "really decides by feeling, by hunching, and not by ratiocination," that the ratiocination appears only when he writes an opinion, which is but an apologia to "justify his decision to himself" and to "make it pass muster with his critics." This published justification (in the form of a reasoned $R \times F = D$) is *ex post facto*.[4]

Is Judge Hutcheson's description wholly mistaken? And is Judge McLellan's use of it wholly without warrant? I believe not. Pertinent here is gestalt psychology, the main thesis of which is, roughly, this: All thinking is done in forms, pattern, configurations. A human response to a situation is "whole." It is not made up of little bricks of sight, sound, taste, and touch. It is an organized entity which is greater than, and different from, the sum of what, on analysis, appear to be its parts.[5] The gestaltist's favorite illustration is a melody: A melody does not result from the summation of its parts; thus to analyze a melody is to destroy it. It is a basic, primary, unit. The

[4] Hutcheson, "The Judgment Intuitive: The Function of the 'Hunch' in Judicial Decisions," 14 *Cornell L.Q.* (1929) 274.

[5] See, e.g., Koffka, "Gestalt," 6 *Encyc. of Soc. Sciences* (1931) 642 for discussion and citations. See also my opinion in Skidmore v. Baltimore & Ohio R.R. Co., 167 F. (2d) 54, 68-69 and notes 35-37. As to ancient roots of the idea, see McKeon, "Aristotle's Conception of Scientific Methods," 8 *J. of History of Ideas* (1947) 3, 14.

Akin to the gestalt thesis are those of the "functional" anthropologists, of the "institutional" economists, and of those legal thinkers who espouse the "functional approach." See, e.g., Benedict, *Patterns of Culture* (Penguin ed., 1946); Rice, *Methods in Social Science* (1931) 55, 113-117, 549, 553-554; Lynd, *Knowledge for What?* (1945), ch. 8; Gambs, *Beyond Supply and Demand* (1946) 25, 74-75, 81; Cohen, "Transcendental Nonsense and the Functional Approach," 35 Col. L. Rev. (1935) 809.

I think the gestalt idea has been carried to excess, for instance, in the idea of the completely "integrated" personality and in that of "patterns of culture."

melody, a pattern, determines the functions of the notes, its parts; the notes, the parts, do not determine the melody. Just so, say the gestaltists, no analysis of a pattern of thought, of a human response to a situation, can account for the pattern. Thus George, a natural scientist, asserts the need of "contrapuntal thinking," a type of mental activity like that of the artist who can "pay infinite attention to detail without losing sight of the whole." [6]

I do not suggest that anyone swallow whole this notion of the "whole." But it does illuminate, does tell us something of importance about, men's reactions to experience. In particular, it sheds light on a trial judge's "hunching." The trial judge, we may say, experiences a gestalt. That is why he has difficulty in reporting his experience analytically. That is why, too, when he has heard oral testimony, his decision, even though accompanied by an "opinion," may defy intelligent criticism. One recalls Kipling's lines: "There are nine-and-sixty ways of constructing tribal lays, And every single one of them is right."

Some nineteen years ago, I wrote: "The decision of a judge after trying a case is the product of a unique experience." To justify that remark, I shall now approach the subject of judicial fact-finding from a slightly different angle. This approach involves a more probing consideration of logic as applied to trial-court decisions, of the assumption that, when a trial judge files a written opinion, or otherwise publishes his *R* and his *F,* he reveals the logic, or illogic, of his decision for observation by critics.

Relatively recent studies of logic have emphasized its inseparable connection with language. Perhaps the most perfect products of logic are the physical sciences, aided by mathematics—which is, itself, a highly developed language, and which, in its "pure" form, is today generally regarded as another name for logic. Stressing language as the source of logic, certain thinkers, sometimes called "logical positivists" or "scientific positivists," maintain that, in effect, "What can I know?" means, "What can I intelligently ask?" They assert that the answer is this: I can intelligently *ask* whatever questions language clearly expresses; I can *know* (at least potentially, or in theory) what

[6] George, *The Scientist in Action* (1938). He describes "pattern properties." The "term 'pattern property' is here used," he says, "to mean any property of a whole which is characteristic only of the whole and not of parts into which the whole may be divided. Pattern properties seem to depend upon the totality of parts, rather than upon simple addition." They are "selected properties of objects or events which cannot be recognized as inherent in the properties of separate parts, even when separate parts are discernible in the object or event under examination."

experiment—verification—will reply to such queries. Whatever under no circumstances could be thus stated and be thus verified or refuted, is a "pseudo-proposition." It is not true or false. It is unthinkable, "meaningless." Of course, say these "positivists," men do utter unthinkables; but those utterances are not "rational." They express "mere" emotions, feelings, like tears, laughter, or profanity. Feelings, therefore, have only subordinate importance, are but the irrational reactions of that pitiable creature, man.

Susanne Langer, in her stimulating book, *Philosophy in a New Key,* criticizes the logical positivists. She points to an important defect of language: Words "have a linear, discrete, successive form; they are strung together like beads on a rosary; beyond the very limited meanings of inflections . . . we cannot talk in simultaneous bunches of names." This fact gives a peculiar character to logic, i.e., "discursive" reasoning. "Language has a form which requires us to string out our ideas, even though the objects rest one within the other" as "pieces of clothing that are actually worn over one another have to be strung side by side on the clothesline." Only thoughts which can be arranged in this peculiar order can be spoken at all; any idea which does not lend itself to this "projection" is ineffable. This "restriction on discourse sets bounds to the complexity of speakable ideas. An idea that contains too many minute yet closely related parts, too many relations within relations, cannot be 'projected' into discursive form; it is too subtle for speech. A language-bound theory of mind, therefore, rules it out of the domain of understanding and the sphere of knowledge."

Professor Langer maintains that the logical positivists go astray because they disregard this inherent weakness of language. On that account they mistakenly depict human rationality as a "tiny grammar-bound island in the middle of feeling expressed by sheer babble," and deny reality to feelings. "Everybody knows that language is a very poor medium for expressing our emotional nature. It merely names certain vaguely and crudely conceived states, but fails miserably in any attempt to convey the ever-moving patterns, the ambivalences and intricacies of inner experience, the interplay of feelings with thoughts and impression, memories and echoes of memories . . . all turned into emotional stuff." Much that we call "intuitive knowledge" is "itself perfectly rational, but not to be conceived through language."[7]

[7] Kristol refers to the "logical positivists with their mincing distaste for 'unanswerable questions' who incline to see the life of man as a kind of grammatical misadventure."

Professor Langer (to sketch her views rapidly and skimpily) asserts that language, which inadequately communicates feelings, is not our only medium of articulation, not our sole means of symbolizing our responses to experience. Notable for this invention of non-logical forms to symbolize feelings are the fine arts.[8] They use "Wordless symbolism, which is non-discursive and untranslatable, . . . and cannot directly convey generalities." Their "symbolic elements . . . are understood only through the meaning of the whole, through their relations within the total structure." Such symbolizing is as rational as that of language. Our feelings, which dwell "on the deeper level of insight," can be known through "wordless knowledge" expressed in "non-discursive forms"—as, for instance, in music. As Victor Hugo said: "Music expresses that which cannot be said, and on which it is impossible to remain silent."

Sullivan, a distinguished mathematician and philosopher, in his life of Beethoven, says much the same. "Language," he writes, "is . . . particularly poor in names for subjective states. . . . Language, in poetry, expresses states for which language has no names except, perhaps, vague portmanteau names, like triumph, joy. . . . The meaning is to be found in the subjective state . . . that the poem expresses. The number of subjective states that a man may experience is infinite. . . . Those elements of our experience that science [i.e., logic] ignores are not thereby shown to have no bearing upon the nature of reality." One cannot, I have elsewhere suggested,[9] write, in the form of an equation, his response to the kiss of his beloved or to the cry of his sick child.

Return now to the trial judge who has heard conflicting oral testimony on a pivotal issue, and you will perhaps the better understand his difficulty when he tries to articulate the bases of his "hunch," to state logically in words—i.e., by "discursive" reasoning—why he decided as he did: His decisional process, like the artistic process, involves feelings that words cannot ensnare.[10] A large component of a

[8] "We are," says Sullivan, "conscious of so much in us that cannot be stated in the form of propositions; we desire illumination on so many things that the language of logic is incompetent to deal with. And the miracle of art is that it can convey just those messages, satisfy just these needs. . . ."

"Poetry," writes the poet Robinson, "is language that tells us, through a more or less emotional reaction, something that cannot be said." Poetry, says Wicher "gives an inclusive understanding of situations. . . . Its ultimate pattern is a paradox." It requires "synthetic imagination" as distinguished from "analytic reason."

[9] Frank, *Fate and Freedom* (1945) 325.

[10] The judge, we say, pronounces a "sentence"; the word "sentence" comes from the Latin "sentire" which means "to feel."

trial judge's reaction is "emotion." That is why we hear often of the judge's "intuition." Holmes, referring to the decision of an administrative agency, said it expressed "an intuition of experience which outruns analyses and sums up many unnamed and tangled impressions; impressions which may lie beneath consciousness without losing their worth." That comment applies as well to the decisions of a trial judge. He cannot, with entire adequacy, formulate in logical, lingual, form, his reaction to the conflicting testimony at a trial. His response to that testimony is, in part, "wordless knowledge." To be completely articulate, to communicate that response satisfactorily, he would be obliged—as a once popular song put it—to "say it with music." For his emotion-toned experience is contrapuntal.

Since the trial judge is not, then, engaged in a wholly logical enterprise, the effort to squeeze his "hunch," his wordless rationality, into a logical verbal form must distort it, deform it. His ineffable intuition cannot be wholly set down in an *R* and an *F*. There are overtones inexpressible in words.[11] He has come upon non-logical truth. One may doubt whether, even if he resorted to music or poetry, he could make himself thoroughly understood by others, when one considers the many discrepant interpretations of artistic compositions and performances.[12] When the trial judge tries really to express his com-

[11] "Just as grammarians concerned only with their syntax and sentences," says Dixon, "pass by the inspirations of the poets, so the logicians and rationalists can make nothing of human motives. . . ."

[12] "It is unquestionable that the actual experiences, which even good critics undergo when reading, as we say, *the same poem,* differ very widely. In spite of certain conventions, which endeavour to conceal these inevitable discrepancies for social purposes, there can be no doubt that the experiences of readers in connection with particular poems are rarely similar. This is unavoidable. . . . But no one in a position to judge, who has, for example, some experience of the teaching of English, will maintain that Shakespeare's appeal, to take the chief instance, is homogeneous. Different people read and go to see the same play for utterly different reasons. Where two people applaud we tend to assume, in spite of our better knowledge, that their experiences have been the same: the experience of the first would often be nauseous to the second, if by accident they were exchanged, and the first would be left helpless, lost and bewildered." Richards, *Principles of Literary Criticism* 115, 212 (4th ed. 1930).

See Lasswell, *Psychology and Politics* (1930) 31-39: "Because of our faulty methods of education, we turn people loose on the world armed with a faith in logic, and incapable of making their minds safe for logic . . . Logical thinking is but one of the special methods of using the mind." It cannot "achieve self-knowledge without the aid of other forms of thinking . . . The ultimate paradox of logical thinking is that it is self-destroyed when it is too sedulously cultivated. It asserts its own prerogatives by clamping down certain restrictive frames of reference upon the activity of the mind which it purports to guide into creative channels. It becomes intolerant of the immediate, unanalyzed, primitive abundance of the mind, and by so doing destroys its source."

See also Frank, *Law and the Modern Mind* (1930) 71, and 167-69; Ortega, *Concord and Liberty* (1946) 61-75.

posite response by a finding of fact (an *F*) and a legal rule (an *R*), he may well feel that the result is a misrepresentation of his actual experience in the decisional process. Accordingly, he may, not unreasonably, resent criticism of his decision, when that criticism rests on that misrepresentative analysis.

"It is not a good thing," said an English judge, Lord Macmillan, "to consider arguments from the point of view of how they can be stated rather than from the point of view of whether they are sound or not. There is a danger even in logic in human affairs. The practical problems of humanity are not solved . . . by neatly framed codes. I think there is a proneness in the legal mind to prefer formulas to facts and to place too much reliance on the power of words." [13]

Frequently (although without resort to the word "gestalt") something like the gestalt aspect of an artist's efforts has been stressed by those who declare the futility of criticism of artistic products. For instance, recently the novelist, E. M. Forster, writing "especially of music," asserted the existence of "a gulf between artist . . . and critic." When a critic approaches a work of art, "two universes have not even collided, they have [merely] been juxtaposed." For the critic to claim that he "actually entered into [the artist's] state" is "presumptuous." If a "critic comes along and tells [the artist] what is right and wrong" about "his product, [the artist] has a feeling of irrelevance." For there is "a basic difference between the critical and creative states of mind." Why? Because the artist "lets down as it were a bucket into his subconscious. . . . When the process is over, . . . looking back on it, he will wonder how on earth he did it. . . . There is . . . [a] connection between the subconscious and the conscious, which has to be effected before the work of art can be born, and there is the surprise of the creator at his own creation." It follows that "the critical state is grotesquely remote from the state responsible for the work it affects to expound. It does not let buckets down into the subconscious."

A trial judge's composite response to conflicting oral testimony has something of this opaque quality.[14] For he, too, has "let down a bucket into his subconscious." Bok, one of our most gifted trial judges, re-

[13] Macmillan, *Law and Other Things* 255 (1937).

[14] There are, of course, differences between the fine-artist and the judge-artist. The former is free to deal with his material as he pleases. No matter how much he deliberately or inadvertently distorts it, no one can complain. Whether or not his published expression deviates from what he meant to express is no one's business but his own. Seldom can the critic discover any such deviation. It is in this last respect that the trial judge's decision closely resembles the fine-artist's product.

cently said: "Each case [was] a work of art, so far as possible, and not an act of grace or a scientific demonstration. . . . It is here, at the point of the greatest judging, that the law can cease to be a matter of rule and compensation and reach the realm of the intangibles: gentleness of heart, with clarity of mind and the quiet salt of faith. . . . The Law suffers from being thought of as an intellectual profession. It is intellectual, of course. . . . But it is not scientific in the sense of a science whose rules are impersonal and beyond the reach of human emotions or behavior. Emotion and behavior are the raw materials from which the law is distilled in one way or another. . . . There is no plea to be made except to keep the law personal."

3

I revert to my statement that it oversimplifies to ascribe the difficulty met in predicting a trial judge's decision to the subjectivity of his fact-finding: The subjectivity is more complex; it inheres in his total reaction to the trial. If the judge's own effort logically to explain his decision, after he reaches it, is so baffling because it results from an experience to which he cannot give complete expression in logical terms, it must also be true that any person other than the judge will seldom be able to know at all accurately, in advance, what the decision will be. For the judge's reaction is unique.

Probably, many of the experiences of every man are unique; even when an experience appears to recur, often it is with some slightly novel difference. "We do not fall in love twice in the same way," says Sullivan. "Even boredom has its shades."[15] To criticize effectively a trial judge's decision, after he renders it, we should, then, in many cases have to re-live his unique experience. To predict his decision we should have had to live it, as he did. That we cannot do. Nor will empathy carry us more than a part of the way into the emotional reactions of another person. As I suggested in 1930, the ultimately important influences in the decisions of a trial judge "are the most obscure, and are the least easily discoverable—by anyone but the judge himself. They are tied up with the intimate experiences which no biographer, however sedulous, is likely to ferret out, and the emotional significance of which no one but the judge, or a psychologist in the

[15] "Situations," writes Bridgman, "do not exactly recur, experience is lived through only once, and the matrix in which any situation is embedded and which constitutes an inseparable part of the situation itself is always changing and never recurs."

closest contact with him, could comprehend. What we may hope someday to get from our judges are detailed autobiographies containing the sort of material that is recounted in the autobiographical novel; or opinions annotated, by the judge who writes them, with elaborate explorations of the background factors in his personal experience which swayed him in reaching his conclusions. For in the last push, a judge's decisions are the outcome of his entire life-history." [16] And, of course, this life history can never be duplicated by the critic.

It is reassuring to have my thesis confirmed by Judge Bok, himself an outstandingly able trial judge. In his recent semi-autobiographical novel he says of the "average" trial judge: "His friends, his family life, his vacations, his religion—a little of these must be known in order to feel the integrity of experience of which his work is the outward expression. But there still remains the mystery of each man's personality, and it defies analysis."

In part, it defies analysis because no man's personality is unified. Even Hume, eager to found a "science of human nature" through discovering human uniformities, said that in human nature "nothing is pure and entirely of a piece. . . . The most sprightly wit borders on madness; the highest effusions of joy produce the deepest melancholy; the most ravishing pleasures are attended with the most cruel lassitude and disgust." Sir Thomas Browne said much the same: "Notable virtues are sometimes dashed with notorious vices, and in some vicious tempers have been found illustrious acts of virtue. . . . There is dross, alloy, and embasement in all human temper, and he flieth without wings, who thinks to find ophyr or pure metal in any." Diderot, in the same vein, wrote that "everything, even among the greatest sons of man, is incomplete, mixed, relative; everything is possible in the way of contradiction and limits; every virtue neighbors elements of incongenial alloy; all heroism may hide points of littleness; all genius has its days of shortened vision." Then, too, a man's personality is not static but varies as he grows older. "Men," noted Browne, "are not the same through all divisions of their lives. Time, experience, self-reflections . . . make men to differ from themselves as well as from other persons." All this has a bearing on the ability to prophesy how a trial judge w ll decide a particular "contested" law suit. It bears also, I repeat, on the ability to criticize the decision after he has rendered it.

It is no answer that, in certain kinds of thinking, the predilections

[16] Frank, *Law and the Modern Mind* (1930) 114-5.

of a thinker lack significance to anyone interested in the validity of his conclusion. Perhaps one may properly assert that the "personal history of Gauss is entirely irrelevant to the question of the adequacy of his proof that every equation has a root; and the inadequacy of Galileo's theory of the tides is independent of the personal motives which led Galileo to hold it."[17] But that cannot be said of the trial judge's decision after a trial, when the oral testimony was in conflict. For one premise of his reasoning—the fact premise[18]—may be the product of his biases, biases of a kind usually immune from scrutiny. He is, so to speak, like one of Leibniz's windowless monads: his experience is not fully penetrable by any human being.

When I speak of the obscure influences—reflecting the trial judge's life-history and personality—which affect his decisions, I do not (à la the "sociological school") refer primarily to his biases and predilections relative to the rules (the *R*'s). I refer, rather, to his reactions to the witnesses. Such biases, remember, are usually deeply buried, unknown to others, often unknown to the judge himself.

With the exception of Austin, most legal thinkers, until recently, brushed aside such obscure influences; and even those who did not do so failed to observe the effects of such factors on trial-court decisions. Austin, in discussing the "motives" which induce the making of legal rules, whether by a legislature or a judge, included such matters as the blandishments of an emperor's wife. Gray rejected consideration of such "motives," calling them "illegitimate." He wrote: "Of course, the motives of a judge's opinion may be almost anything—a bribe, a woman's blandishments, the desire to favor the administration or his political party, or to gain popular favor or influence; but those are not sources which jurisprudence can recognize as legitimate." Holmes, earlier, had admitted the existence of "singular" (unique) motives for a judge's decision, such as a doctrine of political economy, a woman's blandishments, political aspirations, or the gout. But he said that such motives should not be considered because they cannot "be relied upon as likely in the generality of cases to prevail" and therefore do not "afford a ground for prediction" of decisions.[19] Goitein, defining "law" as the "sum of the influences that determine decisions

[17] Cohen and Nagel, *An Introduction to Logic and Scientific Method,* 380 (1934).

[18] More accurately, perhaps, his gestalt.

[19] Holmes, Book Notice, 6 *Am. L. Rev.* 723 (1872), reprinted in 44 *Harv. L. Rev.* 788, 790 (1931). Holmes did not elsewhere repeat these ideas. His later writings indicate that he may have abandoned them. cf. Holmes, *The Common Law* 1, 5, 35-36 (1881).

in courts of justice," seems to exclude all but "legitimate" influences.

Even with respect to upper courts, it is hard to understand why unique and "illegitimate" influences should be ignored, since they often do operate and often do block predictions of decisions. To ignore the effects of such influences on trial judges is still less understandable—unless you want to believe that such predictions are far easier than they actually are.

The "sociological school," as we saw, wisely noted the effects of the social, economic, and political views of judges. But because that school primarily studied the legal rules, and, therefore, the published opinions of upper courts, it disregarded, for the most part, the less obvious components of judges' attitudes. Cardozo was less restricted. He wrote: "Deep below consciousness are other forces, the likes and dislikes, the predilections and the prejudices, the complex of instincts and emotions and habits and convictions, which make the man, whether he be litigant or judge." However, as Cardozo had little interest in trial-court fact-finding, because he believed it did not affect "jurisprudence," he never discussed the impact of such influences on trial judges' findings of fact. Yet the way those influences affect trial judges has far more significance for most litigants than the way they affect upper-court judges, because, for reasons previously canvassed, trial-court decisions usually have finality.

4

Spingarn regards as the sole function of the critic of poetry a critical understanding of the poet's aim; the critic should "re-dream the poet's dream," should ask, "What has the poet tried to express and how has he expressed it?" Assuming it to be possible to answer that question with respect to poetry, often it is not possible to answer a similar question with respect to the trial judge who decides a case involving a credibility issue: because of the inaccessibility of what the trial judge has tried to express, his critic cannot "re-dream" the judge's "dream." Although some persons contend that no objective aesthetic standards exist, that contention is too sweeping. There are minimal uniformities in human nature, and, in any given culture at any given time, minimal cultural uniformities; these uniformities yield an irreducible minimum of artistic norms. For similar reasons, there is an irreducible minimum of moral norms. These moral norms (group ideals and values) express themselves, to some extent, in the substantive legal rules. In that sense, we can attain objectivity in criticism of the *R*'s which the courts employ, and therefore of upper-court opinions, which concern themselves chiefly with the *R*'s. But similar objectivity is not possible in criticism of most trial-court decisions.

For most of those decisions, resulting from idiosyncratic reactions to orally-testifying witnesses, express unique and hidden norms—individual, personal, norms—which, varying from judge to judge, lack uniformity and are therefore peculiarly subjective.[20] It is this kind of subjectivity which has been ignored by the legal thinkers who minimize the difficulties of criticism and prediction of decisions. Such thinkers overlook the distinction between the more or less "objective" character of the norms embodied in the legal rules and the "subjective" character of the trial judge's response to oral testimony. They are thinking of upper-court opinions in cases in which those courts accept as their *F* the explicit findings of the trial courts. In any such upper-court decision, the *F* is given, and the critic therefore need ask merely whether the appellate court in its opinion (1) used a proper *R* and (2) logically applied it to the given *F*. Subjectivity and the gestalt factor often have relatively little effect on the opinion accompanying such a decision.

In assuming that upper-court and trial-court decisions are equally suspectible of prediction and criticism, conventional legal thinking blunders egregiously. It forgets that a trial judge, faced with oral testimony, does not wholly differ from a jury. Lord Bramwell once observed: "One third of a judge is a common-law juror if you get beneath his ermine"; and Mr. Justice Ridell added that "the other two-thirds may not be far different." The New Hampshire Supreme Court has said: "Judges are men, and their decisions upon complex facts must vary as those of jurors on the same facts. Calling one determination an opinion and the other a verdict does not . . . make that uniform and certain which from its nature must remain variable and uncertain."

5

It is true that a conscientious trial judge will pay more attention to the legal rules than a jury usually can or does. That means that, in a jury-less case, there may occur, in the trial judge's mental processes, interactions of the *R*'s and the *F* which may be exquisitely complicated in many obscure ways. I shall here note but one of those ways.

[20] See Chapter XXVI for further implications of these diversities.

As I previously stated, it is a wise and accepted principle that a trial judge's finding of the facts should be affected not merely by the words of the witnesses but by their manner of testifying. Suppose, then, that when listening to the testimony the judge thinks a particular formulation of a particular rule will govern the case. That rule will serve as his attention-guide, i.e., it will focus his attention sharply on the testimony and demeanor of those witnesses who testify with respect to matters specifically germane to his version of that rule. But suppose that, when the trial is over, and the judge comes to his decision, he concludes that his earlier formulation of that rule was wrong. He cannot now vividly recall the demeanor of those witnesses whose testimony is relevant to what he now considers the correct formulation of the proper rule.[21] As a result, he may well find the facts erroneously. Yet neither he nor any critic is able to know whether or not he did thus err.[22]

6

The presence of what, by way of shorthand, I have labeled the gestalt factor is alone enough to expose the misleading over-simplification of the conventional theory that a trial judge's decision results from his "application" of a legal rule (or rules) to the "facts" of the case. For note the word "application," and consider the following: Suppose that a trial judge has a strong unconscious animus against, or liking for, Catholics or Negroes, and that such a predilection influences his attitude towards important witnesses who testify at a trial—

[21] Consider here the situation when, after all the testimony is in, the plaintiff amends his complaint to conform to the proof, thus introducing new *R*'s or new aspects of the *R*'s.

Michael ignores this problem. Michael, *The Elements of Legal Controversy* (1948) 8.

[22] The interaction of rules and "'facts" may have some paradoxical results, baffling to both the trial judge and his critics: A trial judge may want to decide in favor of one of the parties, say the plaintiff. However, it may happen that, if the judge applies to the facts—as he believes them to be—what he considers the correct, well-settled, legal rule, he cannot logically justify such a decision. Sometimes, thus circumstanced, a trial judge, as we saw, will "force the balance," i.e., he will deform his real view of the facts and so "fudge" them in his findings that, applying what he considers the correct rule, he thinks he can make his decision seem justifiable. If he has heard and seen the witnesses, his reported finding of the facts will usually be accepted on appeal by the appellate court. But if that court concludes that he applied an incorrect legal rule, it will itself apply what it considers the correct rule to the facts reported in his "fudged" findings, and, reversing his decision, it will decide the case for the defendant. Now it may well be that, had the trial judge found the facts in accordance with his view of them, and, accordingly, decided for the defendant, the upper court, would have reversed him; it would thus have rendered the decision for the plaintiff which the trial judge had thought desirable but which, due to his incorrect notion of the applicable legal rule, he had felt unable to render on the basis of his real view of the facts.

and thus influences his decision. Would it be helpful to say that his decision resulted from his "application" of that bias? A more dispassionate description would be this: That bias was one among many stimuli which helped to bring about the decision. Similarly, one should say that the legal rule is but one of a multitude of such stimuli.

Answering those who asserted that such an attitude means a denial of the existence of legal rules, I once replied:[23] "To deny that a cow consists of grass is not to deny the reality of grass or that the cow eats it. So that while rules are not the only factor in the making of . . . decisions, that is not to say there are no rules. Water is not hydrogen; an ear of corn is not a plow; a song recital does not consist of vocal cords; a journey is not a railroad train. Yet hydrogen is an ingredient of water, a plow aids in the development of corn, vocal cords are necessary to a song recital, a railroad train may be a means of taking a journey, and hydrogen, plows, vocal cords and railroad trains are real. No less are legal rules."

The traditional formulation ($R \times F = D$) being inadequate, especially with reference to trial-courts, one might, then, for the benefit of those who like mathematical-looking formulas, suggest, as a substitute, $S \times P = D$, when P represents the trial judge's "personality," and S represents the stimuli that affect him (those which influence his belief as to the facts, and all other stimuli). But such a formula has little value for predictive and critical purposes. The "personality" of the judge denotes an exquisitely complicated mass of phenomena. Break down P, and you will find a mass of subjective, unascertainable factors. Break down S, and you will find a horde of conflicting stimuli, some of them being the so-called "social forces," some of them being the legal rules (the R's), some of them being undiscoverable.[24]

7

I suggested earlier that most legal thinking is two-dimensional, that consideration of trial-court processes in "finding" the "facts" demands three-dimensional legal thinking. Perhaps that suggestion should be amended: The physicists now deem it artificial to separate space and time. Using the idea of space-time, they add space as a fourth dimension. In the same way, if we take into account the trial court's gestalt,

[23] Frank, *Law and the Modern Mind* (1930) 132.

[24] See Frank, "What Courts Do in Fact," 26 *Ill. L. Rev.* (1932) 762, 775-76, where I suggested and criticized that formula.

we should perhaps regard it as adding a fourth dimension, and see the need of fourth-dimensional legal thinking, which requires not mere intellectual but also artistic insights.

8

Despite the futility of the attempt to use the written opinion as a basis for complete evaluation of trial-court fact-finding, I think it highly desirable to require trial judges to make special findings of fact. The usual argument for such a requirement—that it aids the appellate courts[25]—seems to me to be far less cogent than the argument that the breaking down of his decisional process into two parts, the rule and the "facts," compels the trial judge carefully to examine his decision. For, as every judge knows, to set down in precise words the facts as he finds them is the best way to avoid carelessness in the discharge of that duty. Often a strong impression that, on the basis of the evidence, the facts are thus-and-so gives way when it comes to expressing that impression on paper. A trial judge, every now and then, thus discovering that his initially contemplated decision will not jell, is obliged to decide otherwise.

It is no sufficient rejoinder that the judge's decision has its roots in a non-logical hunch. Logic need not be the enemy of hunching. Most of the conclusions men reach in their daily lives are similarly hunch-products, originally arrived at in non-logical ways; yet we do not deny that frequently the correctness of many of these conclusions can profitably be tested by logical analysis. That a conclusion is prior in time to the reasoning which logically justifies it may make that reasoning seem artificial, but does not necessarily make that reasoning fallacious or useless. Even physicists and mathematicians frequently use logically-tested hunches.[26] Of course, the mere fact that the reason given for an

[25] In 61 *Harv. L. Rev.* (1948) 1434, 1437-1438, seven reasons are given for requiring special findings: (1) To help the upper court evaluate the trial judge's reasons. (2) To help the upper court study a voluminous trial record. (3) To help it narrow the issues on appeal. (4) To determine the scope of the decision for purposes of res judicata. (5) To define its scope, in the case of an injunction, for later purposes of determining whether the injunction has been violated. (6) To guide the community with respect to the legal rules. (7) To maintain public confidence in the courts.

One might add another: to satisfy the litigants that their case has been carefully considered by the trial judge.

[26] As to the "hunch" element in all sorts of thinking, including that of mathematicians and scientists, se, e.g., Wallas, *The Art of Thought* (1926) 80ff.; Wallas, *The Great Society* (1914) 180-182; Lewis, *The Anatomy of Science* (1926) 90ff.; Leuba, *The Psychology of Religious Mysticism* (1925) 245ff.; Porterfield, *Creative Factors in Scientific Research* (1941) 97ff.; Cairns, *Theory of Legal Science* (1941) 57-60; Poincaré,

act or a judgment is *ex post facto* does not invalidate that reason. Jones may hit Smith, or make love to a girl, or explore the Arctic without reflecting on his conduct. When asked to justify his acts, he may give excellent reasons which are entirely satisfactory. That is, in spite of the fact that he did not act on the basis of logically-tested reasoning, his conduct may, on subsequent analysis, show up as having been logically justifiable. When any man tries to determine whether his appraisal of persons or events is sound, he tests it by seeing whether it is a legitimate inference from his data and from some generally accepted principle or assumption.

So it may be with a trial judge's decision: He may first arrive at it intuitively and, then only, work backward to a major "rule" premise and a minor "fact" premise to see whether or not that decision is logically defective. In so working, the judge is doing nothing improper or unusual. (There is the story of the old lady, accused of being illogical, who, when told what "logic" was supposed to be, exclaimed: "Logic! What nonsense! How can I know what I think until I know what I say?") The chronological priority of the judge's hunch does not mean that his subsequent logical analysis is valueless. That analysis may have an artificial appearance. But such an appearance does not detract from the worth of such *ex post facto* analyses in other fields. If one chooses, loosely, to call that hunch-testing process "rationalization," then, in that sense, most logical rationality involves some "rationalization." [27]

Logic, said Balfour, "never aids the work of thought; it only acts as its auditor and accountant general." That is too limited a statement of the role of logic.[28] But even if logic's role were solely that of "auditing," it would be immensely valuable. As F. C. S. Schiller said, "to put an argument in syllogistic form is to strip it bare for logical in-

---

Science and Method (1914) 75; Cannon, *The Way of an Investigator* (1945) Ch. 5; Montmassari, *Invention and Discovery* (1942); Benjamin, *Introduction to the Philosophy of Science* (1937) 176ff.; Bell, *Men of Mathematics* (1937) 547-552; Frank, *Law and The Modern Mind* (1930) 169; Heim. v. Universal Pictures Co., 154 F. (2d) 480, 488.

[27] The great chemist, Kekulé, talking of the "inspirational" source of some of his scientific discoveries, remarked: "Let us learn to dream, gentlemen. Then perhaps we shall find the truth . . ., but let us beware of publishing our dreams before they have been put to the proof by our waking understanding."

See Reichenbach, *Experience and Prediction* (1938) 4-7, 381-382, as to the distinction between the "context of discovery" and the "context of justification."

[28] See, e.g., Frank, "Mr. Justice Holmes and Non-Euclidean Legal Thinking," 17 *Cornell L.Q.* (1932) 568. For an important discussion of legal logic, see Patterson, "Logic in the Law," 90 *Un. of Pa. L. Rev.* (1942) 875.

spection. We can then see where its weak point must lie, if it has any, and consider whether there is reason to believe that it is actually . . . weak at these points. We thereby learn where and for what the argument should be tested further." That a trial judge should make special findings of fact is therefore of importance, since his doing so is essential to his own logical assaying of his decision. In sum, because of the inescapable and un-get-at-able subjectivity of his reactions, and because of the gestalt factor, his published report will leave an unbridged gap between him and his critics; yet findings of fact will act as a partial check on that subjectivity.

Nevertheless, to require the trial judge to make and publish his findings of fact will yield no panacea where, because of a conflict in the oral testimony, the credibility of witnesses becomes crucial. Frustration of the purpose of the requirement occurs where, as too often happens, the judge uncritically adopts the findings drafted by the lawyer for the winning side. For then the judge may ostensibly make a finding of some facts of which—although they are based on some testimony—the judge never thought, and which, had he done his own job, he would not have included; in that event, his finding does not represent any real inference he drew from the evidence—does not reflect his own actual views concerning the witnesses' credibility. With conscientious trial judges, however, that difficulty is not insurmountable.

But a graver difficulty remains: the facts, as "found," can never be known to be the same as the actual past facts—as what (adapting Kant's phrase) may be termed the "facts in themselves."[29] How closely the judge's "findings" approximate those actual facts he can never be sure—nor can anyone else.

[29] See Miss Silving's brilliant article, "Law and Fact in the Light of the Pure Theory of Law," in the volume, *Interpretations of Modern Legal Philosophies* (1947) 642.

XIII. A TRIAL AS A COMMUNICATIVE PROCESS

WHAT I have been saying with reference to the gestalt suggests that a trial may be considered as a communicative process. That suggestion tends to confirm my views. Wendell Johnson [1] points out the difficulties of a simple effort at communication when Mr. A talks to Mr. B: An event occurs which stimulates A's sense organs, resulting in nervous impulses which travel to A's brain and thence to his muscles and glands. This produces pre-verbal "feelings" or "tensions," which A then begins to translate into words, according to his accustomed "verbal patterns"; out of all the words he "thinks of," he selects certain ones which he arranges in some fashion. Then, by means of sound and light waves—his spoken words, gestures, facial expression, bodily attitude—Mr. A speaks to Mr. B. The same course of events, in reverse, now goes on in B. At every stage in the process, in both A and B, selections (abstractions) and "evaluative reactions" occur. And, at every stage, there may be "disorders" in the selections: There may be defects affecting the sense organs or the nerve tracts. There may be psychological factors causing inattentiveness, stupor, aversion to certain colors or sounds. There may be defects of "translation" into words of the "pre-verbal feelings," such as deficiencies in vocabulary, aphasias, or defects in education, or in knowledge. So, also, as to verbal expressions, gestures, tone of voice, manner of utterance, appearance. The defects in the speaker, A, may affect the listener, B. Any one of these defects may seriously interfere with the communication, which is "the attempt of one person to convey some of the products of his own abstracting to another person" who, in turn, abstracts. Since much may be omitted, the communication is likely never to be complete. We usually entertain "an uncritical assumption of mutual understanding" in even as simple a situation as that of A talking to B. How much more unjustified is the equivalent assumption about a trial. For, usually, there are many speakers (witnesses) each of whom may suffer some defects; and the listener

[1] *People in Quandary* (1946) 471-981. I think that Johnson's account inclines too much to behaviorism.

(the trial judge) may have some of those defects affecting his reception [2] and his subsequent communication—his "findings." [3]

Apply to a trial the following remarks of Schlauch: [4] "Two human beings who talk together are accomplishing an act of 'communication,' . . . Since the effort succeeds so well in most cases, we are apt to forget that the act is and must always be an approximation. To each of his friends, even to his closest alter ego, a man talks out of a private world of his own: the sum total of his memories and experiences. Persons strongly attracted to each other by the emotions are prone to attempt a more intimate approaching of the two worlds, so that by some kind of magic extension of personality each one may reach back into the early days of the other and build the same structure of experience. But despite the torrents of eloquence with which the miracle is sometimes attempted, the isolation remains a dreary fact. The reason is simple. It is impossible for any two persons ever to have learned the same word under precisely the same circumstances; occupying, as it were, the same space in time, and apprehending the new term with precisely the same background. Therefore each will take it into his consciousness ringed about with a special context of associations, differing from the associations of everyone else hearing it. This is what Hermann Paul means when he says that each linguistic creation—and re-creation—is and remains the work of an individual. Yet procedures repeat themselves and approximations of understanding do occur. Our speech is a compromise between the ultimate incommunicability of one person with another and the conventional communication values attached to certain symbols."

2

I have made much use of the word "subjectivity." Disputations about "subjectivity" and "objectivity" are never-ending. I cannot here discuss that subject at length, but I make these tentative and elliptical suggestions. Man encounters at least five kinds of "subjectivities": (1) those which stem from the divers social heritages of divers social groups, (2) those due to the grammatical structures of particular languages; [5] (3) those arising from physical location (Russell calls them

[2] Compare the inattention of the trial judge with a break in a telephone line.

[3] Consider the increased complications when there are many listeners—jurors.

[4] Schlauch, *The Gift of Tongues* (1948) 113.

[5] Whorf, "Science and Linguistics" in Hayakawa, *Language in Action* (1940) 302; Whorf, "Relation of Habitual Thought and Behavior" in the volume *Language, Culture and Personality* (1941) 75; Frank, *Fate and Freedom* (1945) 313-14.

"physical" subjectivities); (4) those which derive from the unique ("private") attitudes of particular persons; (5) those which inhere in the finite, limited, capacities of all human beings. The first and second (which are related) can be eliminated to some considerable extent, perhaps some day completely. The third has been successfully eliminated in part by modern physicists (Einstein & Co.). The fourth would seem to be largely unconquerable. The fifth, of course, will never be eradicated;[6] one recalls Bacon's statement that men are uniformly "mad," and Santayana's that all of us are victims of "normal madness."

Neglecting the other sources of subjectivity, some persons look to the improved use of language as a means of attaining complete objectivity. For many years, I have been an enthusiastic sponsor of semantic reform, but, as I have said elsewhere, I think the word-doctors are over-optimistic.[7] As a consequence of this over-optimism, recent years have witnessed the revival of a presumptuous thesis considered as far back at least as Plato. It runs something like this: Whatever can be communicated between human beings without any possibility of misunderstanding is "public."[8] All else is "private." The "public" is the equivalent of "objective," the "private" of "subjective." It is argued that the "public" alone possesses "reality." Since mathematics (or the like) is the only medium which completely eliminates the "private," it is said that only those subjects which can be communicated in mathematical terms (or the like) are "real," since they alone are in a "pub-

[6] See Frank, "The Place of the Expert in a Democratic Society," 16 *Phil. of Science* (1949): "I am (merely!) asserting that man cannot ever be aware of all its aspects. But we humans are reluctant so to admit. Men, confronted with a puzzling universe, about which they can obtain but a limited amount (and kind) of information, have always invented 'just-so stories,' some of which are more plausible or useful than others. But no such man-made interpretations will ever accurately describe, or cope with, all that goes on in the universe (or multiverse). Inescapably, we are confined in our 'private' human world, our sub-universe. Conceivably, we might be able to merge the 'private' worlds of individual men, or groups of men, into a 'public' human world. Perhaps some day we can thus achieve such a 'public' world to this extent: that men everywhere on this planet will confront experience with the combined understanding of our ablest scientists and our wisest philosophers and poets. But it is not conceivable that we can ever rid ourselves of all our human limitations. A thoroughly 'public' world, in that sense, lies beyond our power. The ultimate perfection of our capacities would still leave us provincials." See also Frank, *Fate and Freedom* (1945) 312-14.

[7] For comments on the value of semantics with criticism of the excessive hopes of many semanticists, see Frank, *Law and The Modern Mind* (1930) 84-92; Frank, *If Men Were Angels* (1942) 313-14; United Shipyards v. Hoey, 131 F. (2d) 525, 527 note 5.

[8] Note that "public" means "common"; that "communication" has "common" as its root; and that "publication" and "communication" are related. Consider also some theories about "common sense."

lic world."[9] This presumptuous idea (related to that of the logical positivists already discussed) denies "reality" to all human feelings, all human values and ideals.[10] In its extreme form, it would shove off into the "unreal" virtually everything outside the realm of the natural sciences,[11] a preposterous idea the fallacy of which Professor Langer's analysis exposed.

That idea, in somewhat milder form, has bitten those who equate "objectivity" with "inter-subjectivity." Hexner has applied that terminology to the judicial process in defending his position that knowledge of the legal rules will generally make it possible to predict decisions. He writes that "a legal rule is essentially an *inter*-subjective (social) act contrasting with both the *intra*-subjective acts (not yet expressed *in* the external world) and pure monologues (not yet expressed *to* the external world), which are expressed but not knowable to other persons."[12] But Hexner has not considered how thoroughly "intra-subjective" are a trial judge's reaction to oral testimony, and how, gestalt-like, the rules and the "facts" intertwine in such a judge's thinking.

One suspects a neurotic basis of the notion that the "private" lacks reality: "Private" suggests "alone-ness"; the ascription of "reality" solely to the "public" seems to express an undue yearning for a "shared experience," a "belonging," a hoped-for escape from the "separation anxiety" intolerable to the young child and to the emotionally immature adult. The excessive yearning to "scientificize" everything[13] may therefore be looked upon with some suspicion. With that in mind, let us consider efforts to create a "legal science."

[9] See, e.g., Hogben, *The Nature of Living Matter* (1931) 30, 221, 246, 248, 260-61, 270.

[10] This notion is related to the old "scientific" division of "qualities" into those which are "primary" and "secondary." As to the history and fallacy of that division, see, e.g., Frank, Fate and Freedom (1945) 92-93, 101-04.

[11] For criticism, see Frank, "Are Judges Human," 80 *Un. of Pa. L. Rev.* (1931) 233, 249-256; Wallas, "The Idol of the Laboratory," in Calverton, *The Making of Society* (1937) 764, 767-74; Zell v. American Seating Co., 138 F. (2d) 641, 647 note 20b.

[12] Hexner, *Studies in Legal Terminology* (1941) 44-45.

[13] Not all modern scientists and scientific thinkers have such a yearning. Bridgman, for example, says: "I do not find the clear-cut separation of the emotional from the rational that the assumption of universal communicability would imply."

XIV. "LEGAL SCIENCE" AND "LEGAL ENGINEERING"

MR. JUSTICE HOLMES once said: "You can give any conclusion a logical form," but the "logical method and form" may result in a certainty which is "illusory." That is, you can present any conclusion in the guise of a mathematical formula, but that formula will not yield certainty in practical results if it contains many variables, each of which is so vague and ineradicably unknowable that no correlations between them can be worked out with any approximate degree of exactness. More to the point, since most persons consider that a true science makes predictions possible,[1] we ought to put an end to notions of a "legal science" or a "science of law," unless we so define "legal" or "law" as to exclude much of what must be included in the judicial administration of justice, because no formula for predicting most trial-court decisions can be devised which does not contain hopelessly numerous variables that cannot be pinned down or correlated.

True, by restricting "law" or "legal" to the legal rules, or to other discernible constants or uniformities in the decisional process, one might conceivably work out some sort of crude "science," although it would lack much precision. But that science would go to pot as a means of controlling or predicting the outcome of most law-suits, except, at best, on the upper-court level, after the facts had been "cooked" in the trial courts.

The chief impediment to the creation of a comprehensive legal science is that trial courts must deal with a multitude of situations that are unique—unique both (1) objectively, i.e., as to the actual past facts, and (2) in the subjective responses of the trial courts. To be sure, those situations have some aspects which can be generalized. But often the individualized facets of those situations defy nice categorization.[2] As we saw, the urge to individualize cases is frequently irre-

[1] Generally speaking, scientific prediction means that, if stated operations are performed, stated phenomena (a) will occur or (b) will be observed.

[2] "Everything ultimate, unique, exceptional—and nothing is more so than the individual soul—is anathema to scientific rationalism," says Dixon, "and in consequence unmentionable. Every soul is a living idiosyncrasy . . .; and for a scientific age . . . beyond measure exasperating." That statement is unfair to the wiser scientists.

pressible; in our own judicial system, much of that individualization is surreptitiously achieved through juries' general verdicts or trial judges' fact-finding;[3] when the rules apparently preclude all discretion, it creeps in via discretion in trial courts' choice of facts, due to their determinations of credibility. A legal science would therefore have to be a "science of the unique"—which is self-contradictory, like a red-hot piece of ice or a live dead man.

Approaching the problem from another angle, we reach the same conclusion: Most of the so-called "laws" of physics are now recognized as "crowd laws," i.e., statements of the average behavior of a huge multitude, or "crowd," of minute individual particles; the minute individual particles each behaves at random, and in a manner not predictable or statable in the form of a law.[4] For most purposes, the physicist can and does ignore the unpredictable behavior of the individual particles, and concerns himself with the regularities of the "crowd" or macroscopic phenomena. But the trial courts must deal with individual law-suits which resemble the physicist's particles rather than his "crowds." The trial courts, that is, cannot ignore the unique conduct involved in each suit, cannot rest content with the merely macroscopic aspects of human behavior. Similarly, the lawyer cannot predict the outcome of many a particular future law-suit not yet begun; for it, also, is not a "macroscopic" phenomenon, and therefore the "charted configuration" of averages of a large number of decisions in previous cases will not help as a prediction-guide.[5] Wherefore, the attempt to build a "legal science" on the analogy of physical science breaks down.

Some of those intent on having a "legal science," recognizing that there cannot be a science of the unique, go to great lengths to get

[3] I shall come back to that theme in Chapter XXIX.

[4] See, e.g., discussion in Frank, *Fate and Freedom* (1945) 149-158, 333-334; Frank, Book Review, 15 *Un. of Chi. L. Rev.* (1948) 462.

See Kallen, *The Liberal Spirit* (1948): "Not only do electrons within the atom have their separate and arbitrary motions, the atom as a whole has a motion without direction, without order. This . . . is . . . anarchic. . . . Thus, the closer we get to the intimate stuffs of existence, the less repetitive, the less predictable . . . its behavior becomes. *To achieve prediction . . , we must move from the depths to the surface of existence.* We must envisage the atoms and their energies in immense numbers, transfinite numbers, and measure them . . . statistically." See also, Wiener, *Cybernetics* (1948) 34.

[5] Compare Goble's suggestion that, because "accurate predictions are made possible by the so-called classical laws of the physical sciences," perhaps "there is a range in the legal field within which prediction of results can be made with the probabilities weighing most heavily in favor of its accuracy." Goble, 9 *Ind. L. Rev.* (1934) 294.

See Chapter XXV for further discussion of "averages" in the prediction of decisions.

rid of this problem of uniqueness. One method is that used by Cowan, an able legal thinker. He says that "reflection" turns a "unique" law-suit into its opposite, converts it into a "universal." Why? Because, Cowan argues, "uniqueness is the most universal of all qualities" since "everything possesses it."[6] Surely that is a specimen of verbal magic. For to say that differences between law-suits constitute an attribute common to all of them does not eliminate the differences.[7] To say that it does, is the equivalent of assigning the name "unclassifiable" to what one cannot classify, and then asserting that the name solves the problem of classification; it is like labelling "unknowable" what lies beyond human ken, believing that the label removes human ignorance.

2

Because I underscore the need of keeping one's eye on the practical activities of courts, I am not to be understood as under-valuing theories about court-house government. No one, no matter how intent on being practical, can get along without theories. For theories induce much practice, good or bad; and any practice usually, sooner or later, gives rise to some theory, explicit or implicit. "Practical lawyers," who deride legal theorizing as a frivolous subject unworthy of their attention are theorists nonetheless. But their theories, being inarticulate and unconscious, are more likely to do harm than those of the lawyers who more consciously theorize. The self-delusion of the unconscious theorists "makes it psychologically easier for them to mold [their practices] in accordance with their beliefs and prejudices without feeling the weight of responsibility that burdens lawyers with greater consciousness of the issues at stake."[8] Theory, as Holmes said, is "not to be feared as unpractical, for, to the competent, it simply means getting to the bottom of the subject. . . . To an imagination of any scope, the most far-reaching power . . . is the command of ideas."

But just as practical activities are based on theories, so intelligent theories must rest on an understanding of practice. Consequently, it may be that one of the most important of theories is the theory of the relation of theory to practice. Of that theory, and with particular refer-

[6] Cowan, "Legal Pragmatism and Beyond," in the volume *Interpretations of Modern Legal Philosophies* (1947) 137-38.

Demos more wisely says: "The individual is not a universal . . . The concept of individuality, of course, is a universal."

[7] Of course, I do not suggest that every law-suit does have sufficiently unique elements to justify treating it as unique. I say only that many suits do.

[8] Friedmann, *Legal Theory* (1944) 250-251.

ence to theories and practice of government, including court-house government, Aristotle had much to say which is still meaningful. For he had closely observed the actual practices and carefully studied the theories.[9]

One cannot, he said, have a science of "politics" (i.e., government), only an art, since science (as he defined it) is knowledge of what always or usually "happens in the same way." Knowledge of government is "practical"; it deals "with what is relative" and, within limits, a matter of human choice. The "end of practical knowledge is action." In the art of government, then, one must employ "practical wisdom," which is based on experience. Those "who aim at knowledge of the art of politics need experience as well" as theory. Both are desirable, since "practical wisdom" is "concerned with particulars," with the ultimate particular fact," yet "details can best be looked after" by a man "who has the general knowledge" (theories). As Aristotle likened the art of government to the art of medicine, in discussing government he said, by way of analogy, that, in order that each patient will "get what suits his case," the physician must have "general knowledge of what is good for everyone or for people of a certain kind," such knowledge as may be obtained from books. But experience with patients is also necessary, as "medical men do not seem to be made by a study of textbooks," because information about "how particular classes of men can be cured and should be treated . . . seems useful to experienced people, to the inexperienced it is valueless." So if one "has a theory without experience, he will often fail to cure." Repeatedly Aristotle urged that "credit must be . . . given to theories only if they accord with observed facts." "The truth in practical matters is judged from operations and life, for the decisive factor is to be found in them," and theory in such matters should be brought "to the test of operations and life, and if it . . . disagrees with them, we must suppose it to be mere theory." He said that "political writers, although they have excellent ideas, are often impractical." Government, in that respect, differs from mathematics: "While young men become geometricians and mathematicians and are wise in matters like these, it is thought that a young

[9] John Dewey and his disciples have written much about the theory of the relation of theory to practice. These pragmatists—and some of Dewey's disciples far more than Dewey—have rather scornfully described Aristotle as if he had walled off theory from practice, as if he had regarded practice as something rather sordid and unworthy of a cultivated man. Actually, with reference to government, Aristotle was a wiser pragmatist than are many Dewey-ites. For his theories of government rested on far more intensive observation of governmental practice. It is therefore worth while briefly to consider his approach to such theories.

man of practical wisdom cannot be found. The cause is that such wisdom is concerned not only with universals [generalizations] but with particulars, which become familiar from experience, but a young man has no experience, for it is produced only by length of time."[10] Aristotle always objected to theories of government—including notably what I call court-house government—if the theorizer did not fully recognize that, as practical experience shows, human frailties affect the operation of all rules, and that nice exactitude in such theories is therefore unattainable.[11] Modern advocates of a "legal science" would do well to adopt Aristotle's practice in legal theorizing, and to recall these famous Aristotelian lines: "We must not look for the same degree of accuracy in all subjects; we must be content in each class of subjects with accuracy of such a kind as the subject matter allows. . . ." And I suggest that these "legal scientists" never forget Aristotle's admonition that "those whom devotion to abstract discussions has rendered unobservant are too ready to dogmatize on the basis of a few observations." Of course, Aristotle did not mean (nor do I) that any theory, in any field, can exactly match all the observed facts, for a theory (like a word) is an abstraction—a "drawing away"—from some of the facts.[12] But, as Aristotle advised, theories must not stray too far from ultimate check-ups by the facts.

3

The up-in-the-air character of the notion of any proposed "legal science" is in marked contrast with that of physical science. "Legal science," which resembles sociology, reminds one of Poincaré's remark that physicists have a subject matter but sociologists have only

10 "Practical wisdom" is not necessarily accompanied, he said, by "strict reasoning," and therefore "we ought to attend to the undemonstrated sayings of experienced older people not less than to demonstration; for, because experience has given them an eye, they see aright." In other words, the "hunches" of the experienced men may be more valuable in "practical wisdom" than articulate theories.

11 See Chapter XXVI for further discussion of Aristotle on the workings of the courts.

12 The quotations in this paragraph are from the following writings of Aristotle: Nicomachean Ethics; Politics; Metaphysics; On the Generation of Animals; On Generation and Corruption.

"But, of course, a theory even if true may be inadequate. Indeed, generally speaking, no theory can exhaust all that is involved in the existence of any subject however limited. If *per impossible* any theory were as complicated as the actual facts, it would have no real value. All theory is a simplification and therefore incomplete. However, to despise theory is the essence of unwisdom, and those who quote Goethe as the authority for the statement, 'gray is theory,' forget that this is the advice of Mephistopheles to corrupt the callow student." Cohen, *A Preface to Logic* (1944) 181-82.

a method. That remark evokes the question, Whence came the physicists' subject matter? The answer carries a moral for would-be "legal scientists": The physicists' subject matter came from the combination of theory and technology, from the interactions of theories and instruments, such as, for example, the balance, the microscope, the telescope, the thermometer. Galileo inaugurated the systematic employment of skilled mechanics in the making of new instruments; the existence of a class of professional instrument-makers, writes Singer, was a main condition of the rapid progress of sciences in the succeeding centuries. Galileo, it is said, "worked out the theory of the telescope"; in that sense, much of physics consists of ingenious instrument-theories.[13] Now the crude implements from which the more refined scientific implements derived were initially devices employed in practical pursuits, i.e., technology. Often, too, though not always, the great physicists have been stimulated, in part, by the requests of non-scientists for improvement of practical technological methods.[14] Here is a parable: Legal theorizing should be interacting with legal technology, with the actual doings of the courts.

I am not suggesting that the quest of a "legal science" must necessarily be justified by results which are utilitarian (at any rate immediately). The natural sciences owe their practical advance, in part, to much thinking that had no empirical aim, to theories contrived by men whose mood resembled that of the creative fine-artist,[15] men who had in mind nothing "useful" but who were merely playing with ideas, just for fun.[16] Moreover, the current practitioners of those sciences successfully utilize ideas which refer to "ideal" or non-existent entities, such as "frictionless engines" or "free bodies"; these entities, expressing relations between existing particulars, do, however, derive from, and are helpful in understanding and controlling empirical reality. As Cairns says, "Traditionally science abstracts from the circumstances of the world, and concerns itself only with those distilled realities which yield to its manipulation. Its view of the world is necessarily incomplete, but it nevertheless achieves an insight into the nature of things

[13] A physicist uses an instrument to test out a tentative theory (hypothesis); he revises his theory in the light of the consequent observations; often he then makes (or has made) a new instrument to test his revised theory; with the new instrument, he tests this theory, etc. etc.

[14] For criticism of the notion that all great advances in science have come in response to practical needs, see Frank, *Fate and Freedom* (1945) 59-51, 76-77, 183-84.

[15] See Frank, *Fate and Freedom* (1942) 200-01. See Chapter XII above as to the "hunches" of scientists.

[16] See Frank, *Fate and Freedom* (1945) 49-51.

which, for its purposes it accepts as satisfactory."[17] The suggestion has therefore often been made that there can and should be a "legal science" which deals similarly with the legal world: Let men theorize about it playfully, just for fun; not only is such play worth while as an end in itself,[18] but some of the resultant theories, originally constructed for purely non-utilitarian purposes, may later turn out to be practically valuable—as did Pascal's originally "useless" theory about gambling (which contributed to subsequent practical work in statistics and physics) or the non-Euclidean geometries (which originated in a spirit of play but which later greatly aided modern science). Through such legal theorizing, we may attain fundamental assumptions ("axioms") of a "utopian" character, from which we may logically arrive at startling new practical notions of matters legal, and invaluable new devices for coping with them. We may develop the legal equivalents of concepts like "frictionless engines" that will serve us in good stead.

We should not laugh off that suggestion. As I have elsewhere said, there can and should be non-Euclidean legal thinking.[19] But that suggestion should be handled with care. Cairns is fascinated by it.[20] He thinks that "legal theory may eventually be reduced to something approaching the status of geometry so that we will have sets of entities from which we can account for all the important propositions of the legal order."[21] Nevertheless he warns that advances in the natural sciences "are seldom made unless the ideas which control the investigation are constantly brought into relationship with the available factual data," that there "must be a constant reciprocal checking of data by ideas and of ideas by data," and that in the legal realm, we must "attempt to ascertain whether or not there are contradictions between the operations of the legal order and the conceptual foundation which endeavors to account for these operations."[22]

Prominent among those "operations of the legal order" in any society which has existed, now exists, or conceivably will ever exist, is the "operation" of judicial fact-finding. A "legal science" whose "conceptual foundation" does not take such fact-finding into account can-

[17] Cairns, *Legal Philosophy from Plato to Hegel* (1949) 476.

[18] See Frank, *Fate and Freedom* (1945) 194-201.

[19] Frank, "Mr. Justice Holmes and Non-Euclidean Legal Thinking," 17 *Cornell L.Q.* (1932) 568; Frank, *Fate and Freedom* (1945) 298-308. See further on this subject below, Chapter XXXI.

[20] See Cairns, *Legal Science* (1941).

[21] Cairns, *Legal Philosophy from Plato to Hegel* (1949) 501-02.

[22] *ibid*, 565. Stevenson reminds us that "the first principles are the last that can be obtained"; *Ethics and Language* (1944) 331.

not be anything but a ghost science, or dream science. It will furnish aesthetic satisfaction, but no more. And any legal theorizing which does take account of so inherently inconstant, so necessarily variable and subjective a matter as judicial fact-finding seems doomed never to resemble what ordinarily we call "science."

Many legal thinkers have tried to escape that conclusion, some bumblingly, some with acuity. On the bumbling efforts we need spend no time, if we can show that the more brilliant efforts have failed and are bound to fail. Among the brilliant, is that of Morris Cohen who tried to escape by employing, challengingly, a natural science analogy. In 1937, he wrote, "Using a method that has been most useful in the natural sciences, namely, ignoring perturbations or disturbances caused by other factors, and describing the ideal condition of our system when such disturbances are ignored, one can describe the ideal law as perfect certainty.[23] Now such an ideal is something which every lawyer, judge, or systematic jurist must employ if he is to make any order, system or meaning in the law." [24] Conceding that "disturbances" sometimes occur when judges or juries are moved "by passion," he continued: "The mere fact that there are disturbances . . . shows that there are *recognizable rules we normally expect to prevail.*" [25] That last sentence, examined in the light of the actual "operations" of our legal system, is fatal to Cohen's thesis.[26] If the "disturbances" interfering with the efficacy of the rules were few and peripheral, if they seldom occurred, one could legitimately say that there are rules we "normally expect to prevail." But my discussion of the difficulties of communication in trials, and of fact-finding by trial courts, shows that in those courts the "disturbances" tend to be "normal," not exceptional. Especially in jury trials are they notoriously "normal"; indeed, as we saw, defenders of trial by jury esteem it highly for the very reason that juries freely disregard the rules. What, then, can Cohen mean when he says that "we normally expect ["recognizable" rules] to prevail?"

[23] I shall later raise some doubts about that ideal; see Chapter XXVIII.

[24] He had previously said that it is necessary not to "forget that the real problem is to find the precise relation between the certain and the uncertain in law," and that "the significant issue is precisely . . . where to draw the line between legal rule and judicial discretion." Cohen, *Law and the Social Order* (1933) 359, 361.

[25] Cohen, "Legal Philosophy in America," in 2 *Law: A Century of Progress* (1937) 266, 310. (Italics added.)

[26] Which stems in part from his addiction to legal magic, previously noted in Chapter IV. The quotations from Cohen, there and here, show him to be what I have called a legal wizard of the second (semi-skeptical) class.

That is not the way a physicist talks of matters in his province. When he refers to the rule ("law") of the behavior of a freely-falling body, he knows and says that that rule holds good only in a vacuum. As observation teaches him that most bodies do not fall in a vacuum, he makes corrections of his rule to allow for "disturbances" affecting their ordinary non-vacuum behavior. He treats the "disturbances" as the usual, and vacuums as exceptional. He never believes or says: "We normally expect a vacuum to exist."

If Cohen had rigorously used the natural science analogy, I think he would have said something like this: "Recognizable legal rules would wholly govern most judicial decisions, if there were no fact-finding problem, if the actual facts of law-suits came into court neatly packaged, tailor-made. Let us provisionally take as an ideal a situation (resembling a legal vacuum) where the fact-finding problem disappears. Then let us ask whether that ideal is attainable. At once we see that usually it is not. Moreover, we see that, in the very trial-court process of attempting to 'find' the facts, the legal rules usually get inter-twined with the facts, that we encounter gestalts. In most law-suits, the 'ideal' is approximated—and then only in appearance—solely in the upper courts, on appeals, after the trial courts have packaged the facts." I say "only in appearance," because, of course, we can never be at all sure that those packaged facts are the actual facts.

Cohen's notion of what "normally we expect to prevail" describes, at best, the normality of the two-dimensional upper-court realm. Now there is nothing wrong with two-dimensional descriptions, provided that, in applying them to a three-dimensional context, one corrects them by adding the third-dimensional factors. Cohen's error, I think, was that he engaged almost exclusively in two-dimensional legal thinking, and forgot about the three-dimensional trial-court realm.[27]

Cohen, like many other legal thinkers, wanted (as he admitted) to make a rather simple "system" of the "law." Accordingly, he shut his eyes to the usualness of what he desired to think the unusual, and consequently could not break importantly new ground in legal theory. As William James said, "the great field for new discoveries is always the unclassified residuum," the "dust-cloud of exceptional observations," which "ever floats about" the "accredited and orderly facts . . . and which it always proves more easy to ignore than to attend to." When a "consistent and organized" system has been once made, then "phe-

[27] Note again my suggestion that the trial-court gestalt may perhaps be regarded as adding a fourth dimension.

nomena unclassifiable within the system are . . . paradoxical absurdities. . . ." James might have been describing a host of legal systematizers when he went on thus: "Facts are there only for those who have a mental affinity with them. When once they are indisputably ascertained and admitted, the academic and critical minds are by far the best fitted ones to interpret and discuss them . . . ; but on the other hand if there is anything which human history demonstrates, it is the extreme slowness with which the ordinary academic and critical mind acknowledges facts to exist which present themselves as wild facts, with no stall or pigeon-hole, or as facts which threaten to break up the accepted system." [28]

James Bryce once described an "ideal democracy" (resembling somewhat Cohen's ideal legal system). Bryce added, however, that it was "an ideal far removed from the actualities of any State." Graham Wallas tellingly commented: "What," he said, "does Mr. Bryce mean by an 'ideal democracy?' If it means anything it means the best form of democracy which is consistent with the facts of human nature. But one feels . . . that Mr. Bryce means . . . the kind of democracy which might be possible if human nature were as he himself would like it to be, and as he was taught at Oxford to think it was. . . . No doctor would begin a medical treatise by saying, 'the ideal man requires no food, and is impervious to the actualities of any known population.' No modern treatise on pedagogy begins with the statement that 'the ideal boy knows things without being taught them, and his sole wish is the advancement of science, but no boys like this have ever existed.'"

It is but fair to say that, in general, no one more emphatically inveighed than Morris Cohen against the belief that, in dealing with human affairs especially, a theory can hold aloof from practice. "No slogan," he wrote,[29] "is more productive of obscurantism than the cliché 'true in theory, but wrong in practice.' What is wrong in practice must be wrong in theory unless the theory itself is wrong. And if our theory is wrong it is certainly more intelligent to set it right by making appropriate qualifications than to attempt blindly to cling both to the theory and to the fact that contradicts it on the pretext that theories and facts belong to different worlds." Yet Cohen did stubbornly cling to his theory of a "legal science," a theory which made light of patent and observable "disturbances." Why? I think that perhaps Schlesinger,

[28] James, *The Will to Believe* (1896) 299-302. Compare the phrase, "the errors of the system," i.e., mistakes due to the way experiments are set up.

[29] *A Preface to Logic* (1944) 174.

in a recent review of a book by Cohen, found the answer. He said that the book disclosed a kind of liberalism which involves "a deep fear of acknowledging the emotional and destructive impulses of man," a liberalism which "in its rush to justify the beauties of reason and social organization . . . has underestimated the dark and subterranean forces of the human mind," so that it engages often "in fighting or denying the unconscious instead of trying to assimilate it."[30] Most of those who, thus far, have attempted to create a "legal science" have denied the "unconscious" in judicial fact-finding.

4

Their fault lies in over-simplification which, in physical science, is today a recognized danger. Bridgman says of theorizing in physics, "We have over-simplified our conceptual situations, and a necessary task before we can hope for adequate understanding is to recover some of the primitive complexity." Tocqueville warned against the tendency to arrange "hastily . . . under one formula." Francis Bacon had said much the same: "The human understanding, from its peculiar nature, easily supposes a greater degree of order . . . than it really finds. . . . The human understanding, when any proposition has been once laid down . . . forces everything else to add fresh support and confirmation; and although most cogent and abundant instances exist to the contrary, yet either does not observe or despises them, or gets rid of and rejects them by some distinction, with violent and injurious prejudice, rather than sacrifice the authority of its first conclusions. . . . It . . . is very slow and unfit for the transition to the remote and heterogeneous instances by which axioms are tried as by fire. . . ."[31]

All of us, of course, tend to over-simplify. Men, says Cornford, have a strong desire to "shape the chaotic world into some intelligible form" which they can "take in, in one survey." Faced with a baffling, complex world, men have always contrived simplistic "just-so stories,"[32] as if the confused phenomena they come upon must correspond to the

[30] 2 *Commentary* (1946) 290, 291. See, however, Cohen, *A Preface to Logic* (1944) 70: "And human wisdom consists in recognizing both the supreme claim of rational effort and its pathetic inadequacy."

[31] Compare Frank, *Fate and Freedom* (1945) 164-169, 327-28, 332-33.

[32] See Frank, *Fate and Freedom* (1945) 27, 88, 183; Frank, "The Place of the Expert in a Democratic Society," 16 *Phil. of Science* (1949).

Freud, in a letter written in 1932, observing that his own psychological theories seemed to amount to a "species of mythology," asked Einstein, "But does not every natural science lead ultimately to this—a sort of mythology? Is it otherwise with your physical science?"

human craving for simplicity. Employed cautiously, simplification is wise procedure. In natural science, it is called the "law of parsimony," although it is not a "law" but a man-made method, since, as Bridgman observes, "the overwhelming presumption is against the laws of nature having any predisposition to simplicity as formulated in terms of concepts, which is of course all that simplicity means. . . ."[33] Scientists and philosophers of science make much of "Occam's Razor," a principle stated in the 14th century by Occam: "Entities are not to be multiplied beyond necessity," i.e., as between alternative theories (to explain or account for a group of facts) that one is to be preferred which gives an explanation which uses the fewest assumptions. But Occam's Razor may be a dangerous weapon if it shaves too fine, cuts off too much. Kenneth Burke sagaciously remarks that, correlative with Occam's principle, we need another: "Entities should not be reduced beyond necessity."[34] That caution the advocates of legal science have not heeded.

5

There are two astute thinkers, Lasswell and McDougal, for many of whose views I have great respect,[35] who do not overlook the "unconscious," but who nevertheless believe in the feasibility of a science of legal prediction. In an article published in 1943,[36] they repudiate the notion that this "science" can be based upon materials "restricted . . . to the appellate court and the norms it announces." Yet they assert that is it possible to "lay a scientific foundation for prediction," to foresee "judicial behavior" in most specific cases. They speak of "the legitimate scientific goal of prediction." They admit that the job of thus "forecasting judicial behavior poses formidable problems," and refer to the "complexity of the task of making concrete forecasts." But they are undaunted in their conviction that the "skill to predict" court decisions "scientifically" can be taught and learned.

They grant that to predict the outcome of a trial, one must allow for "the personality characteristics of judges, parties, counsel, witnesses and juries. . . . What judges and juries do is 'human'[37] in the sense that

[33] See also quotation from Russell in Chapter XXVI.

[34] *A Grammar of Motives* (1945) 324.

[35] See Chapter XXVI.

[36] "Legal Education and Public Policy: Professional Training in the Public Interest," 52 *Yale L.J.* (1943) 203, 238, 241.

[37] Perhaps they are here referring to my article, "Are Judges Human?" 80 *Un. of Pa. L. Rev.* (1931) 17, 233.

it is affected to some extent by the impact of personalities upon one another. There are many patterns of personality, and the interaction of an aggressive claimant or witness upon judge and jury may produce different results than when submissive types are involved." Perceiving that the predicting lawyer is thus presented with a host of "variables," Lasswell and McDougal say that such a lawyer "must equip himself with skills appropriate to the task of evaluating" those variables. He must, accordingly, acquire "naturalistic skills of observation and analysis." Presumably he will then be able to prophesy "that a certain judge will decide a specific case for the defendant or the plaintiff," and to do the same concerning any particular jury. How? By knowledge of "the most significant variables, affecting judicial responses," by taking "into account all variables that may significantly determine" the "response" of any particular judge or jury.[38]

Now what do Lasswell and McDougal mean by "significant" and "significantly"? They do not explain. But I gather from their discussion that they mean that the trained predicting lawyer will take into account solely those "responses" of the judge or jurymen which accommodate themselves to generalizations, those "variables" which observably are likely often to recur. That surmise is strengthened when we find Lasswell and McDougal saying: "Truly scientific propositions can only rest on data of observation. Scientific prediction is based on the expectancy that past relations among variables will continue, and that, when a given list of variables occurs in the future, their inter-relations can be foretold on the basis of proper analysis of observations in the past." At that point my skepticism about the Lasswell-McDougal prediction program becomes almost boundless. For, when a trial judge is about to hear conflicting oral testimony by witnesses he has never previously seen—in an automobile accident case, or a will-contest case

[38] Lasswell and McDougal use the following formula to symbolize the decisional process:

$$R = \frac{E}{P}$$

E symbolizes "typical environmental factors," i.e., what goes on when a case is being tried—such factors as testimony, exhibits, briefs and arguments.

P symbolizes the "predispositions" of the court before the lawsuit began. The authors cite, as examples, a judge's bias for or against rich or poor, or attitudes towards legal rules and principles (e.g., the commerce clause of the Constitution).

R symbolizes the court's response to *E*. In other words, *R*, which results in the court's decision, derives from the impact of *E* on the court's *P*.

In the last analysis, this formula resembles the $S \times P = D$ formula (which I had suggested in 1931 before Lasswell and McDougal published theirs). I think it is equally useless for predictive purposes. Both formulas merely give names or symbols to unknowables. See Chapter XII.

involving undue influence, for example—can anyone have reliable observations of the "past relation among the variables" in the judge's previous conduct so as to be able to prophesy what will be his responses to those witnesses?

Perhaps Lasswell thinks so. For, in his interesting recent book, *Power and Personality,* he published "personality probes" of three judges. But no thoughtful reader of those judicial case-histories will be convinced that, with the assistance of those "probes," or of far more detailed studies, Lasswell or anyone else could foresee the reactions of any one of those three judges in a particular case to some particular witnesses that judge had theretofore never seen. And surely Lasswell cannot know in advance whether that judge on a particular day—because of a severe headache, a sleepless night, or aggravated domestic worries—will be inattentive to some vital testimony. Moreover, a predicting lawyer will often not know what judge will try a particular case, and will therefore be unable to use the Lasswellian divining method—unless "personality probes" of all trial judges are available. Let us assume, however, that all trial judges were psycho-analyzed, and that their psychoanalytic case histories were published. *Would not the very fact that a judge had been psycho-analyzed free him of most of his "compulsive" reactions and consequently render his responses less predictable than ever?*[39]

Think, too, of juries. Seldom is it knowable what men or women will compose a particular jury. Do Lasswell and McDougal believe that a lawyer can intimately know the "past relation among variables" in the responses of all those who may become jurors, can obtain "personality probes" of all or most prospective jurors? And would such "probes" tell when jurors would be attentive or inattentive to the testimony? Especially in small communities, painstaking lawyers now learn something of the background of each juror; our authors' proposal might lead to more intensive knowledge of that kind; but I doubt whether it would very substantially improve the guessing of jury verdicts in most cases. In some cases involving "dramatic" issues,[40] powerful group attitudes, for or against one side, shared by the trial judge or jury, will foreseeably outweigh all other considerations and dictate the decisions—e.g., a suit for assault by a Negro against a white man in some southern communities. Possibly studies, à la Lasswell and McDougal, would slightly enlarge our knowledge

[39] See Frank, *Law and the Modern Mind* (1930) 134.
[40] See Chapter XXV.

of issues of that sort. But the overwhelming majority of suits do not involve such issues.

Doubts about this science of legal prediction increase when Lasswell and McDougal say: "Our knowledge of causal connections is much greater if we can follow the entire sequence that begins with the occurrence of a disagreement" [which ripens into a law suit]. "Thus we can hope to predict the probable response of courts . . . to probable kinds of objective situations." This implies that the "objective situations," without the intervention of fallible testimony, ordinarily come before trial courts. Of course, our authors know better. Elsewhere in this article, they define the "objective facts" in a law-suit as the facts as they would look to "an objective, non-participant observer, who uses all available materials." Are "all available materials" usually brought into the trial courts? What of lost letters, missing or dead witnesses, witnesses who mistakenly saw or heard the past events or who mistakenly remember what they saw or heard? And are trial judges, and jurors, dispassionate "objective" observers?

Since Lasswell and McDougal use the label "science," they ought to follow good scientific procedure by telling us within what range of accuracy their prophesies have hit the target.[41] I suggest that they take up the challenge I issued to Felix Cohen, i.e., that they announce their predictions, reached through their techniques, of the decisions in a hundred ordinary law-suits, chosen at random, and now awaiting trial, in which the testimony will be oral and in conflict. If their predictions turn out to be even 80% correct, I think I will be able to show them how to make a huge fortune (which they can devote to further legal research).[42]

(On reflection, I think this challenge unfair to Lasswell and McDougal. They are probably not to be taken as saying that they now have in stock a legal prediction technique, but only that, working along their lines, one can be invented. Even so, I disagree: I think it predictable that none can.)

A good part of the answer to any such proposal as that of Lasswell

[41] Said Peirce: "In those sciences of measurement which are the least subject to error—metrology, geodesy, and metrical astronomy—no man of self-repute ever now states his result, without affixing to it its probable error; and if this practice is not followed in other sciences it is because in those sciences the probable errors are too vast to be estimated."

[42] Were their method wholly perfect, it would be foolish ever to try a law-suit, for the decision would be a foregone conclusion.

and McDougal was given (fourteen years before they wrote) by Keyser, a mathematician who interested himself in the possibility of creating a legal science. The subject matter of such a science, he said,[43] must be the distinctive behavior of judges, consisting of their decisions. "It is," he went on, "a familiar and just saying that . . . a genuine science makes it possible to predict. An attempt to predict based on legal science . . . employs the assumption or postulate that a given pattern of judicial behavior will repeat itself when the corresponding stimuli and conditioning circumstances repeat themselves. Is the postulate sound? It is a fact that stimuli and circumstances seldom or never do repeat themselves exactly. That fact being sufficient to explain why prediction of judicial behavior is impossible, we need not deny the validity of the postulate upon which attempted prediction depends. The fact is obvious that the cosmic stream, including the stream of human life, goes flowing on; the new is ever emerging without exact repetition of the old; and, inasmuch as judicial behavior is a part of the life of mankind, we should expect what we see to be a fact, that law [defined by Keyser as judicial behavior] is not an invariant somewhat but is a variable, changing with the time and place and the things that these involve. Law [i.e., judicial behavior] changes because the stimuli that evoke it and the circumstances that condition it do not remain the same and do not repeat precisely, but continually alter under the influence of new things emerging endlessly in the flux of life and the world. We are thus led to employ the scientific notion of functionality in the study of legal science. It is a well-known fact of observation that law [judicial behavior] depends upon and varies with a variety of more or less familiar variables. And so in functional notation we may write

$$L\ (v_1,\ v_2,\ v_3,\ \ldots\ v_X)$$

merely to indicate the thought that the law L is a function of certain variables v_1, v_2, . . . and undergoes changes due to change in them. . . . Given a set of v's, can the form of L be ascertained? It is almost certain that it cannot by any known means or in any time imaginable but that is not a good reason for failing or refusing to envisage the problem."

If we do envisage it, and if we add to the variables mentioned by Keyser that host of variables found in the idiosyncratic personalities of the individual trial judges and jurors, we see, I think, how futile is the pursuit of a science of legal prediction. The emptiness of legal pre-

[43] "On the Study of Legal Science," 38 *Yale L.J.* (1929) 413.

diction-formulas recalls Holmes' statement that "the only use of forms is to present their contents, just as the only use of a pot is to present the beer . . . , and infinite meditation upon the pot will never give you the beer." Those who forget the beer have (to borrow a phrase from Gibbon) "extended their knowledge without correcting their prejudices."

Nevertheless, I welcome the strivings of Lasswell and McDougal, because, in part, they are my allies, since they support an attitude toward the courts the adoption of which I have urged repeatedly during the past twenty years. For those who follow the lead of those authors will learn much about phases of court-house government, which most legal scholars have disregarded. I think the Lasswell-McDougal theory erroneous; but an erroneous theory has often turned up new facts. (Consider the revolutionary effects on physical science of the famous Michelson-Morley experiment.)

6

The recent amazing progress in developing machines which rapidly solve complicated mathematical problems,[44] suggests that a "logic machine" built on those lines could be the foundation of a "science of legal prediction." [45] Let us see.

It is conceivable that an "ultra-rapid" legal-logic machine [46] could promptly answer questions like these: (1) Given a specific state of facts, *F,* what possible alternative legal rules, *R*'s, will logically lead to a desired decision, *D*? (2) Given a legal rule, *R,* and a desired decision, *D,* what possible alternative states of fact, *F*'s, will logically yield that decision? (3) Given a specific legal rule, *R*, and a specific state of facts, *F,* what is the logically correct decision, *D*?

Anyone who believes such a machine can supplant the human process of judging is hoping to revert, in a scientific way, to the "mechanical" method of the ordeals. I, who have done my fair share of jeering

[44] See Wiener, *Cybernetics* (1948).

[45] In the 17th century, Leibniz, a lawyer, dreamed of a logic machine. See Wiener, *Cybernetics* (1948) 20; Cairns, *Legal Philosophy from Plato to Hegel* (1949) 300; Russell, *A History of Western Philosophy* (1945) 591-592. Such a machine, of sorts, was invented by Jevons in 1869, another by Venn in 1881, and another by Marquand in 1882. Professor Maguire has recently suggested a carding machine for assembling decisions in tax cases. See Proceedings of the Seventh Annual Institute on Federal Taxation (1949) 1008.

[46] I know too little of the subject to be sure, but I suspect it would resemble what Wiener calls an "analogy machine"; see Wiener, *loc. cit.* 154.

at "mechanical jurisprudence,"[47] have no such hope. Yet I think there is much merit in the idea of such a machine. I grant that its answers to the first two types of questions listed above might be singularly helpful to a trial judge who wanted to "fudge" his findings to produce a decision he deemed desirable, for good or bad reasons; whether in that respect the machine would be a boon may be doubted. But, that objection aside, it seems to me that judges and lawyers would benefit from having relatively simple problems—type (3)—speedily and correctly answered,[48] and from having put before them promptly all possible alternative solutions of more complicated problems, i.e., type (1) and (2) problems.[49]

But my previous discussion shows that such answers would not aid in predicting the outcome of any lawsuit where the testimony was oral and conflicting. In an assault-and-battery suit, for example, the possible *R*'s and *F*'s are few and easy to learn. It is seldom possible, however, to learn, and no machine can tell, what will be the *F*, and therefore the *D*, at which a particular trial judge or jury will arrive; more accurately, the gestalts cannot be thus foretold.

Such a machine would not reduce, but would increase, the need for legal intelligence: great skill would be necessary in formulating the questions put to the machine. Semantic difficulties would, too, in many instances, prove a stumbling block.[50]

Moreover, even were such a machine to disclose all possible available alternative legal rules, the judges (except when bound by statute or precedents) would still have to exercise "the sovereign prerogative of choice" between the rules, on the basis of the judges' conscious or unconscious notions of policy.[51] The machine might give judges the

[47] See Frank, *Law and the Modern Mind* (1930) 118-47.

[48] "It would be time-saving," I said in an opinion, "if we had a descriptive catalogue of recurrent types of fallacies in arguments presented to the courts, giving each of them a number, so that, in a particular case, we could say, 'This is an instance of Fallacy No. ——' ". United Shipyards v. Hoey, 131 F. (2d) 525, 526.

[49] Some judicial opinions could be very brief, stating only the buttons to be punched and the number of the particular answer selected by the court. Some lawyers' briefs might be written in the same abbreviated manner.

[50] See Chapters XIX and XXI.

[51] See Holmes, "Law in Science—Science in Law," 12 *Harv. L. Rev.* (1899) 493, reprinted in Holmes, *Collected Legal Papers* (1920) 210, 239: "But I think it most important to remember whenever a doubtful case arises, with certain analogies on one side, and other analogies on the other, that what really is before us is a conflict between two social desires . . . , and which cannot both . . . have their way. . . . Where there is doubt, the simple tool of logic does not suffice, and even if it is disguised and unconscious, the judges are called on to exercise the sovereign prerogative of choice." For a brilliant portrayal of such a situation, see Fuller, "The Case of Speluncean Explorers," 62 *Harv. L. Rev.* (1949) 616.

benefit of offering the alternatives clearly.[52] But it would not realize the hope of Leibniz who thought that, if there were such a machine, then "If controversies were to arise, there would be no more need of disputation between two philosophers [or lawyers, we may interpolate] than between two accountants. For it would suffice [for them] . . . to say to each . . . : Let us calculate." [53] Mr. Justice Douglas had in mind the judges' "sovereign prerogative of choice" when, in effect answering Leibniz, he said, "The law is not a series of calculating machines where . . . answers come tumbling out when the right levers are pushed." [54]

7

Loevinger, dissatisfied with the uncertainties of the traditional legal techniques, proposes, as a substitute, what he calls "jurimetrics," i.e., "the scientific investigation of legal problems" which will "put law on a rational basis." [55] He seems to hope, among other things, by such scientific investigation, to contrive a dependable lie-detector; to measure accurately the ability of witnesses to observe and recollect; to ascertain accurately the effect of bias upon witnesses' observations and recollection.[56] Would such investigations, if wholly effective, achieve those aims? Would they disclose that, in a suit for assault by Ho against Hum, a particular witness, Jennings, had a hidden bias, of which he himself was unconscious, against Ho or Hum? I doubt it. But assume that such a bias would be revealed, that due allowance could be made for that bias, and that we had measured Jennings' ability to observe and recollect. Would we then be able to learn just what he saw on the day when, according to Ho, Ho was hit in the eye by Hum? Suppose that, when examined by experts, the witness Jennings shows up as having virtually perfect sensory reactions and memory, and as being free of bias. Even so, it cannot be known that, at the time when Hum was supposed to hit Ho, Jennings' attention was not distracted or that he was not then so emotionally disturbed by a

[52] Compare Patterson, "Logic in the Law," 80 *Un. of Pa. L. Rev.* (1942) 874, 894-896.

[53] See Russell, *loc. cit.* But see Schrecker, 7 *J. of the History of Ideas* (1947) 107, 110.

[54] 23 *Amer. Jud. Soc.* (1948) 104, 105.

[55] Loevinger, "Jurimetrics," 33 *Minn. L. Rev.* (1949) 455. He defines "law" as "the words and actions of government agents, acting in their official capacity."

[56] In fairness to Loevinger, it should be noted that he does not say that he so hopes or expects. He does, however, state some of "the problems of jurimetrics," and the tenor of his article indicates that he hopes those problems will be solved.

breakfast quarrel with his son that his observations of the Ho-Hum quarrel were faulty? I am eager to have developed all possible devices for detecting witnesses' errors.[57] But I think it unwise to encourage the belief that thereby we can remove all obstacles, in the form of witnesses' fallibilities, to learning the actual past facts of cases.

Let us assume, however, that such devices some day will approach perfection. We then come to Loevinger's hope that there will be contrived "statistical measures" which will "summarize the behavior of individual judges in various categories of cases." The word "categories" exposes the Achilles' heel of his proposed "science." That "science" will have the fatal weakness of the Lasswell-McDougal scheme—the inability to foresee how a particular trial judge, on a particular future day, will react to, or how attentive or inattentive he will be to the testimony of, specific witnesses. Witnesses do not, for such predictive purposes, fall into categories; nor are such reactions of a trial judge constants or static. Similar but more biting criticism applies to Loevinger's notion that it will be possible, with respect to jurors, to "measure their reaction to evidence and instructions, and discover the determinant considerations in reaching verdicts." And so, too, of his hope that, "on the basis of inquiries relative to the behavior of witnesses," we "can construct . . . objective criteria for weighing testimony."[58]

8

Proponents of a "legal science" are up against many of the insolubles met by the believers in "social science." Yet, calling "law" one of the "social sciences," many would-be contrivers of a "legal science" hope to emulate the "social sciences." To expose the futility of the notion of a "legal science" it is important to show that the idea of a "social science" has itself been a will-o'-the-wisp.[59]

The idea began with the aim of constructing a "social physics" which

[57] See Chapters VI and XVII.

[58] He also hopes that we can "adapt the generally recognized scientific measures of probability to the problems of legal 'proof.'" As to this hope, see the discussion of "averages" in Chapter XXV.

[59] In this discussion of science and the "social sciences," I am borrowing from the following of my own earlier writings in which some aspects of the subject are considered more in detail: Law and The Modern Mind (1930) 285-288; Are Judges Human?, 80 Un. of Pa. L. Rev. (1931) 17, 233; Experimental Jurisprudence and The New Deal, 78 Cong. Rec. (1933) 12412; Fate and Freedom (1945) passim; Scientific Spirit and Economic Dogmatism, in the volume Science For Democracy (1946) 11, 12-13; A Plea For Lawyer-Schools, 56 Yale L.J. (1947) 1303, 1330-1340; Book Rev. 15 Un. of Chicago L. Rev. (1948) 462.

was to have "social laws." Those "laws," like those of physics, were to be based ultimately upon observation, and were to be formulations of "recurrent patterns or relatively constant configurations of repeatable elements" i.e., invariants, uniformities, regularities. No such "social physics" has as yet developed,[60] nor has a "social science" modelled on biology.[61] The subject matter of these social studies permits of so little exactitude that a "science of society" seems never likely to be invented. Certainly none is now on the horizon.[62]

The basic trouble is that all the so-called "social sciences" are but phases of anthropology: Their attempted generalizations relate to the customs and group beliefs (the mores, the folk-ways), matters which, especially in a changing modern society, are not readily predictable, because of the numerous elusive and accidental factors, including the fortuitous effects of forceful ("earth-quake") personalities.[63]

The hope of discovering reliable "social trends" through statistics has aroused much enthusiasm. Justification, or lack of justification, for that hope is pertinent to this book, for two reasons: (1) It is directly germane to the work of the courts, because of judicial reliance on such materials in connection with cases involving what I earlier referred to as "background" or "social and economic facts." (2) Also, some persons who talk of "legal science" mean, not the prediction of specific court decisions, but the social consequences of legal rules, whether those made by judges or by legislatures; such persons believe

60 "The social sciences . . . are notorious," says Horace Fries, "for their unscientific concern to emulate physics in an unscientific manner."

61 Social studies have been analogized not only to physics but to biology; and the biologists who, like the students of society, deal with living beings, are properly considered scientists. As, however, the biologists' field is far less distractingly complex than human society, far more submissive to scientific controls, it is now generally accepted as an error to pattern "sociology" on biology.

62 Note, for instance, the striking revaluative effects of viewing "economics" as but one aspect of cultural anthropology. "Economics," at best, has been descriptive of the social habits, and changes in such habits, of some particular groups in particular times and places, coupled with some rather inadequate guesses as to how other social groups will act under other circumstances. What our economists have done is this: They have observed some selected customary conduct, attitudes and beliefs of a society within a limited period, the selected conduct, attitudes and beliefs having what the economists call an "economic" character. The economists have generalized these observations and then have drawn logical inferences from these generalizations. Those generalizations and deductions they treat as the equivalent of the natural scientists' "laws." Their error should be plain: A society is not a static entity. It does not stay put. Customs and social attitudes are neither unchangeable nor consistent within any society, nor alike as between different societies. The generalizations about them and the inferences derived therefrom, if nicely logical, are almost certain to be importantly false. For the consequences of the operation of certain customs or group attitudes are often cancelled out by the consequences of other conflicting customs and attitudes.

63 See Frank, *Fate and Freedom* (1945) Chapter 4.

it possible accurately to predict the social effects, for instance, of a change in the patent statutes or of a new zoning law. Society, they say, is a "crowd" or "macrocosm," like the large aggregates of particles with which the physicist deals: Just as the physicist, unable to foresee the action of a single particle, can foretell the action of an aggregate, so the "social scientist," who cannot expect to predict the way any single law-suit will be decided, or how any single man will be affected by a new legal rule, can predict the general social effect of that rule.

Let us, then, consider the reliability, the "objectivity" of the social statistics, comparing them with the observations of natural scientists. At once it appears that social statistics which, to the unsophisticated, may seem indubitiably certain and "objective," always rest on someone's selection of "data," and that the selector's choice is seldom indisputably "objective" and reliable, for a variety of reasons. Chance, we are advised by able statisticians, frequently determines the statistical results. We are told that the investigator "may be compelled to employ data" which are fragmentary merely "because of their availability"; or that "his preconceptions" concerning the subject may lead him to believe that certain significant relationships existed, and, without sufficient verification, he may smuggle those preconceptions into both his "data" and his conclusions. "Disturbing" factors may be present but wholly undetectable, with effects that cannot be estimated or eliminated by the investigator's techniques. The undetected relationships may be more significant than those he can perceive. His "sampling" may not be representative, may involve the "fallacy of selection," the attribution, to an entire class of phenomena, of characteristics which pertain to the selected instances alone. His "data" are then not really "data," that is, "given"; and his inferences ("extrapolations") may thus be fatally mistaken guesses.

Dorothy Swaine Thomas, an eminent social statistician, says that even carefully chosen "data" will frequently allow of several reasonable alternative interpretations, that one who plots a curve of a social trend should "not fail to admit that the determination of the 'best' trend is largely subjective." Often, she confesses, "convenience has dictated" the statistician's procedure.

The "Brandeis briefs," using statistical and related "data," were, for a long time, used by government lawyers to win law-suits against private corporations. Those court victories were due largely to the fact that the opposing lawyers did not file briefs containing contradictory data of the same kind. A few years ago, the engineering firm of Ford,

Bacon & Davis published a pamphlet urging corporate executives to retain "experts" to prepare such briefs to favor corporations in litigation with the government. Whatever the cause, the fact is that now, in many such suits, both sides present material of that sort, and government victories have become less certain.

In such cases, or elsewhere, when "experts" with contrasting views collate statistics, each expert can often assemble figures which plausibly confirm his position. Referring to the "Brandeis briefs," Sigety, a teacher of statistical method, writes me, "There are ways of rigging your statistics so that almost any conclusion can be reached from the same basic information. . . . Just as the trial judge may sometimes first reach his *D,* and then, more or less unconsciously, 'fudge' his facts to justify that *D,* so the statistician may likewise 'fudge' his 'trend' curve." Of course, sometimes the "fudging" of a curve can be exposed; but frequently, for the reasons stated by Dorothy Swaine Thomas, it is difficult to prove the "objectivity" of one interpretation of figures as against another.

Hansen and Eldridge, expert social statisticians, in 1947 published an article, on future urban growth in this country, which is an admirable example of the modesty and circumspection needed in the use of such material. Their "estimates," they say, "are projections, not predictions," and are "presented . . . in accordance with varying assumptions" which represent "great oversimplification." They give this warning: "The one thing we can be certain about is that [our] assumptions will not hold."

The books are strewn with social predictions that went wrong. Burke scored a happy guess in 1790 when he prophesied that the lax relations of the French government with the French army would lead to the rise of a "popular general" who would become a dictator. But many wise men have made erroneous forecasts. Palmerston and Disraeli thought Germany would be defeated in the Franco-Prussian war of 1870; Morley believed Australia would never fight to aid Belgium. Many predictions of Marx and Engels misfired. Particularly in our dynamic society are long-range social predictions difficult, because today the time-span of continuity is shorter. New medicines can poke holes in the life-tables. Consider the accidental and unforeseeable origin of several major scientific discoveries which have revolutionized our society. (A banker once defined an invention as something which ruined his investments.) The utterly unexpected pops up to confound the predicter: No one in the nineteenth century, for example, foretold the coming of Fascism.

When "social scientists" recently asked Norbert Wiener to contrive rapid calculating machines for predicting social phenomena, he answered: "For a good statistic of society, we need long runs under essentially constant conditions. . . . [The] advantage of long runs of statistics under widely varying conditions is specious and spurious. Thus the human sciences are very poor-testing grounds for a new mathematical technique"[64]

Sometimes a short-range guess hits the target. Yet we have the example of John Maynard Keynes, an unusually sage and well-informed economist, who made one of the worst mis-guesses in history: He said on October 25, 1929, that the then precipitate stock-market break would liberate credit for non-speculative purposes and halt the deflation in world commodity prices. Precisely the opposite happened; the Great Depression was then just in its beginnings. Some of the ablest American economists went badly wrong in their prophecies of grave unemployment in 1946-1947. "Is there today," asks Sigety in June 1949, "an economist of repute who will squarely, and using no weasel words, make a prediction as to the number of unemployed six months from now, and what the price level will then be?"

The very fact of publishing a forecast of a future social happening may, indeed, have a transforming effect on that happening, so that it may turn out quite differently from what it would have been if the forecast had not been published. Thus, as J. M. Clark has suggested, the increased knowledge by businessmen of an expected business trend may undesirably hasten and intensify it.[65] If, says Neurath, a scientist were to publish a prediction that a meteorite would fall and kill some people at a certain time and place, the people might leave, and the prediction would be false; if he merely wrote the prediction in his notebook, it might be accurate; on the other hand if he published it, the people might think he had a selfish purpose in trying to induce them

[64] Wiener, *Cybernetics* (1948) 34, 189. Gabriel Tarde, an eminent French judge interested in statistics, smiled at the "special appetite which [the study of statistics] has whetted rather than satisfied, this thirst for social knowledge of mathematical precision and impersonal impartiality. . . .' Tarde, *Laws of Imitation* (1903) 133.

[65] See Cox, "Business Forecasting," 6 *Encyc. Soc. Sci.* 348, 352-353 (1931); Neurath, "Foundations of the Social Sciences," 2 *Encyc. of Unified Science,* No. 1, 28 (1944); Allen, "This Time and Last," 162 *Harper's* 193, 202 (1947); cf. Kuznets, "Time Series," 14 *Encyc. Soc. Sci.* 629 (1934); Seligman, "Are Businessmen Human Beings?," 2 *Commentary* 478 (1946); Katona, "Psychological Analysis of Business Decisions and Expectations," 35 *Am. Econ. Rev.* Pt. II (1945). See also Wiener, *loc. cit.,* 191.

to move and they might therefore remain, with the result that this prediction would be correct.[66] Johnson refers to "that inescapable irremovable factor that every logician faces when he assumes to deal with human beings. He may predict the movements of a planet or any electron for a thousand years with almost absolute accuracy. He may predict the development of fruit flies, or of guinea pigs, through many generations with a factor of error of negligible proportions. But the moment humanity enters the equation, mathematical calculation loses its authority. . . ."[67]

I could go on enumerating inescapable obstacles of a kind encountered by the "social sciences" (including "legal science") and not by natural science. But I must content myself with the following terse, crude, summary of the fundamental obstacle to the creation of a "science of society" (or a "legal science"): The natural scientist uses effectively the method of an "isolated system," one from which he can, for all practical purposes, exclude all but a very few variables. He thus arrives at fairly exact recurrent patterns." Restricting his attention to what are approximately repeatables—i.e., constants, regularities—and (on the "principle of indifference") ignoring the uniques, the non-recurrents, he is often able, with a sufficiently close approach to reliability, to trace the effects on the "isolated system" of modifying one of its components, and thereby to discover correlations which are definite within a high range of probability. In a social situation, however, usually the factors are so numerous and so complicatedly interacting, and there are so many unique non-repeatables, that the "isolated system" method becomes almost completely valueless. Seldom, therefore, can one at all accurately evaluate a change in terms of a single effect; thus nice controls and predictions are seldom possible.[68]

True, as the well-educated 20th century man knows, even the physical sciences are now recognized to be far less exact than they seemed to all but a few thinkers during the preceding three centuries. It might therefore be suggested that the difference between the natural sciences

66 Compare the physicist who, in the very act of observing tiny particles, affects them.

67 Johnson, *American Heroes and Hero Worship,* 64-65 (1943).

68 I have here, in part, drawn on three of Morris Cohen's articles: "The Social Sciences and The Natural Sciences," in the volume, *The Social Sciences and Their Interrelations* (1927) 437; "Law and Scientific Method," reprinted in Cohen, *Law and the Social Order* (1933) 184; "Philosophy and Legal Science," reprinted in *Law and the Social Order,* 219. His keen perceptions of the weaknesses of the "social sciences" make it the more surprising that he has been seduced by the idea of a "legal science."

and the "social sciences" (including "legal science") is but one of degree. That is a tricky suggestion: It has been said that the difference between a difference in kind and a difference of degree is not itself a difference of kind but one of degree—a violent difference, however.[69] The difference under discussion here is peculiarly violent. Vivas, who notes that apologists for "social science" sometimes "fall back on the utterly unhistorical excuse that they have not yet had time enough in which to try their ways," remarks, "They find it convenient to forget that in the short span between Galileo's birth and Newton's death, classical mechanics succeeded beyond the expectations of the most sanguine of the earlier scientists. . . ."[70]

Since "social" and "legal" sciences are but phases of cultural anthropology, necessarily, too, they are phases of psychology. Now psychology, in so far as it has attempted to ape physical science, has been singularly unfruitful. "If," says Professor Langer, "we follow the methods of natural science, our psychology tends to run into physiology, histology and genetics; we move further and further away from those problems which we ought to be approaching. That signifies that the generative idea which gave rise to physics and chemistry and all their progeny . . . does not contain any vivifying concept for the humanistic sciences. The physicist's scheme, so faithfully emulated by generations of psychologists . . . , is probably blocking their progress, defeating possible insights by its prejudicial force. The scheme is not false—it is perfectly reasonable—but it is bootless for the study of mental phenomena. It does not . . . excite a constructive imagination, as it does in physical researches. Instead of a method, it inspires a militant methodology."[71] Erich Fromm remarks that many social psychologists "believe that unless phenomena can be studied in a way which permits of exact and quantitative analysis, they must not be studied at all." Eager to be "scientists," they choose for study those problems that fit the laboratory method. "Their choice of problems is determined by their method instead of the method being determined by the problem."[72] Thereby, it should be added, they develop a "methodolatry,"[73] and "are drawn into social blindness by the glare of the laboratory."[74]

[69] Williams, "Law and Language," 61 *L.Q. Rev.* (1945) 172, 192.
[70] Vivas, "Two Notes on the New Naturalism," 56 *Sewanee Rev.* (1948) 477, 483.
[71] Langer, *Philosophy in a New Key* (Pelican ed. 1948) 18-19.
[72] Fromm, in the volume, *About the Kinsey Report* (1948) 46 at 49.
[73] Vivas, *loc. cit.*
[74] Dennis, in the volume, *Language, Culture and Personality* (1941) 259.

I do not mean that we should give up our efforts to make educated guesses about the social future and cautiously to plan that future in the light of those guesses. Constructive skepticism, I think, involves these two elements: (1) an eagerness to contrive, or to make operable, social inventions which will improve the workings of our democratic society; (2) an unceasing awareness of the difficulties of that undertaking (because of its complexity and inescapably guessy qualities) and of the consequent need ever to be tentative, experimental, in the formulation of ways and means. The old anarchistic regime of ultra-let-alone-ism can no longer serve our needs. Increased social cooperativeness, both domestically and on a planetary scale, has become imperative. Plan, then, we must. (Not to plan is a kind of planning, often the stupidest kind). As to our domestic future, our traditions and values put us in a position where we may have to choose either (1) chaos, or (2) civil war, or (3) some sort of totalitarianism, or (4) some sort of democratic planning inside a profit system, planning which seeks a working compromise, in which government would be efficient without being despotic, ensuring individual political freedoms without crumbling into anarchy. Democratic planning should be exceedingly flexible and circumspect. When someone says, "We know how to clarify values into blueprints for action," [75] we should answer, "Yes, we know a little about it."

But to call the making of social guesses a "science" has the disvalue of glossing over inescapable difficulties. I grant that anyone can define "science" (no one can stop him) so as seemingly to obviate my objections. Thus, for example, one can say that "science" is "intelligent observation guided by the best wisdom already in our possession" or "the method of dealing intelligently with all problems," or (more simply) "taking thought." But most persons will be misled when the word "science" is so used, for to them science means a fairly ponderable measure of exactness and of power to predict.[76]

As, in that sense, we do not now, and almost surely never will, have a "social science" or a "legal science," it also misleads, and raises false

[75] McDougal, 56 *Yale L.J.* (1947) 1349.

[76] Note once more that prediction may mean merely that, if stated operations are performed, stated phenomena will be observed. In some such way we may explain why geology is called a science. As the geologist studies the past, which cannot be predicted or made to occur again, geology might be considered not a science. But usually the geologist, under controlled conditions, can repeat many of the facts he studies. So to speak, he predicts the past. (Only the incautious, dogmatic, geologist denies the possibility that chance played a part in past happenings.)

hopes, to talk of "social" or "legal engineering." For "engineering" is a technology which consists of a body of techniques based on the relatively exact physical sciences that have no social or legal counterpart. What is more, "social engineering" invites treatment of human beings as non-human entities, parts of, or materials to be used by, a machine; and "legal engineering" encourages "mechanical jurisprudence."[77]

Demos, coming at the matter somewhat differently, arrives at a like conclusion.[78] He points out that an engineer, trained to analyze a relatively simple situation into its elements, and then to recombine them so as to reach a solution of a problem, can exhaust the variables because they are few; he can predict, and control, the result with comparative ease. If now you put to the engineer a problem in social relations, he finds that his techniques won't work, because the variables are too numerous and their inter-actions too complicated, while the evidence, according to his accustomed standards, is insufficient and often unreliable. The engineer, therefore, is likely to throw up his hands, muttering that, since science is inapplicable, the problem cannot be solved by intelligence. That pessimistic reaction—one which an engineering approach to society may well persuade—is frightening. For, writes Demos, "if you say that the complex questions of human policy—inasmuch as they do not lend themselves to scientific treatment—must be abandoned to instincts and sentiments, you are in effect turning the control of human affairs into the hands of fanatics and fuehrers."[79] A similar danger lurks in the idea of "legal engineering" or

[77] "It is necessary," said Chesterton, "to cease to be a man in order to do justice to a microbe; it is not necessary to cease to be a man in order to do justice to men. That same suppression of sympathies, that same waving away of intuitions or guess-work, which make a man preternaturally clever in dealing with the stomach of a spider, will make him preternaturally stupid in dealing with the heart of a man." Chesterton overstates his case: The able scientist does not wave away "intuitions or guess work."

It is worth noting that Pound, who coined the phrase "legal engineering," has not wholly given up the idea of "mechanical jurisprudence." See Chapter IV.

[78] "The Spectrum of Knowledge," 51 *Philosoph. Rev.* (1947) 237.

[79] Wise study of society requires a fusion of poetic imagination and the scientific spirit. As Demos puts it, "The dilemma—either science or sentiment, either strict logic or poesy—is false; over and above these two choices there is relational or complex thinking. This is thinking in a context, thinking which searches for cross-bearings between areas. . . ." The "scientific mode," the "mode of clarity," does "not exhaust the resources of intelligence. . . . Reason takes on various colors and is not limited to the scientific hue. . . . The false dilemma" which sharply splits off "poesy" from logic, "contains a threat to the existence of our society."

The brilliant writings of David Riesman point the way to valuable studies of society. Not only is his own approach full of "poetic" insights, but he frequently resorts for helpful clues to the writings of gifted literary artists, such as Tolstoy, Kafka, Joyce, Sartre and Farrell. Niebuhr, in a recent newspaper interview remarked: "The good poet and novelist have poetic insight into human ambiguities. . . . Lionel Trilling "legal science." It tends to distract attention from first-hand study of removable evils in the all-too-human conduct of court-house government.

We are suffering today from the consequences of that "religion of science," widely popular in the 19th century, which dogmatically asserts that faith in science must be man's only faith.[80] James[81] deplored this "religion of exclusive scientificism," as he dubbed it, with its over-emphasis on the virtues of "simplicity and consistency." He said that the "appetite for consistency," christened by "logicians . . . the 'law of parsimony,' . . . is nothing but the passion of conceiving the universe in the most labor-saving way." "It will," he warned, "if made the exclusive law of the mind, end by blighting the development of the intellect itself, quite as much as that of the feelings or the will." Our "moral, aesthetic and practical wants," wrote James, "form too dense a stubble to be mown down by any scientific Occam's razor. . . ." It frightened him that the "knights of the razor" were increasing in number, and that "their negations" were "acquiring almost as much prestige and authority as their affirmations legitimately claim over the minds of the docile public. . . ." That way, he felt, lay "mental barbarization." Ascribing to "scientificism" the motto, "Let science be done, though the world perish," James asked, "Was there ever a more exquisite idol of the den, or rather of the shop?," adding that, if all superstitions were to be wiped out, "let the idol of stern obligation to be scientific go with the rest. . . ." James's fears of such "scientificism" were justified. Too many students of human society, intoxicated with the idea that they must be "scientific," have followed a false trail. Where that trail may take them appeared in the boast, not long ago, of a leading sociologist. "Sociology as a science," he said, "is not interested in making the world a better place in which to live. . . ."[82]

With some legal thinkers, the idea of "law" as a "science" has had moral consequences similar to those observable among economists. Many economists, bent on achieving what they believed to be scientific dispassionateness and objectivity, have striven to cut themselves from ethics and politics. In producing "economics," they gelded "political

. . . has a poetic understanding of the endless complexities that you don't ordinarily find in the social scientists."

[80] See Frank, *Fate and Freedom* (1945) 14-05, 135, 13-64, 169-73, 293.

[81] *The Will to Believe* (1896) 111, 131-32.

[82] Ogburn, "The Folkways of a Scientific Sociology," 30 *Scientific Monthly* (1930) 301-03. Salomon says that sociology has become a dogmatic "religion of sociology"; 7 *Commentary* (1949) 594, 596.

economy"; and gelding, as usual, caused sterility. As Macdonald suggests, they have "confused scientific objectivity with disinterest in values." Worse still, in pretending a disinterest in ethical values and ideals, these economists and many "legal scientists" have concealed from themselves and others the ever-present activity, both in their thinking and their selection of "data," of their own social ideals, so that their buried and undetected ethical assumptions actually waxed the more pronounced. Asserting their dispassionateness, they have become peculiarly and partisanly passionate.

10

To reject the idea of a "legal science" does not mean rejection by lawyers of the use of the products of any science.[83] Nor does it entail their rejection of the "scientific spirit." It is, I think, a grave mistake, causing needless confusion, not sharply to differentiate the spirit, or attitude, of the physical scientist and his "scientific method." His method involves, increasingly, the use of mathematics as well as the search for, and contriving of, "scientific laws" which express "abstract universals dealing with repeatable elements." But the "scientific spirit" is another matter. That spirit entails the discipline of suspended judgment; the rigorous weighing of all the evidence; a consideration of all possible theories; the questioning of the plausible, of the respectably accepted and seemingly self-evident; a serene passion for verification; what I would call "constructive skepticism" (or what Fries calls the purpose of "doing one's damnedest to poke holes in one's own theoretical assumptions") [84] plus an eagerness not to be deceived.[85] With that spirit all students of our legal system should be imbued. If so, they will, I think, deny that they are or ever can be scientists—not because of any mental inferiority to the natural scientists (all of whom, by the

[83] Courts and lawyers, in dealing with patents, for instance, must acquaint themselves with the principles and products of the physical and biological sciences.

[84] Fries, "On the Unification of Science," 3 *Am. J. of Economics and Sociology* (1944) 193.

[85] One may agree with John Dewey when he describes the scientific attitude as "freedom from control by routine, prejudice, dogma, unexamined tradition, sheer self-interest," and the "will to inquire, to draw conclusions only after taking pains to gather all available evidence." But I think Dewey errs when he describes as the "scientific method" the "systematic, extensive and carefully controlled use of alert and unprejudiced observation and experimentation in collecting, arranging, and testing facts to serve as evidence." That, properly, I believe, describes not the "scientific method" but the "scientific spirit."

way, do not always have the "scientific spirit")[86] but because the subject-matter is far more complexly baffling.

A social ideal not yet realized, whether it concerns our legal system or anything else, represents an aspiration, a wish. It should be approached with the scientific spirit—the spirit which encourages the search for, or the invention of, means to a desired end. A man with that spirit will not use his ideal as a day-dream, but will try to ascertain what social changes must be made, if that ideal is to be actualized. He may discover that no changes can be made which will achieve his ideal. Such, I think, should be the conclusion of those who, in a scientific spirit, approach the ideal of a science of legal prediction. The astronomer Jeans says:[87] "The inventor who tries to devise a perpetual-motion machine may come to the conclusion that the forces of nature have joined in a conspiracy to prevent his machine from working, but wider knowledge shows that he is in conflict not with a conspiracy, but with a law of nature. . . ." For "a perfectly organized conspiracy of this kind differs only in name from a law of nature." Apply that conclusion to the efforts to create a science of nice legal prediction: Those efforts come up against an "organized conspiracy" resembling that which balks the hope of inventing a perpetual-motion machine; and that "conspiracy" may thus be regarded as a "law of nature." Those efforts have, then, this great value, that they have proved a negative.[88] We can now move on to more productive endeavors. There is much to be said for what Samuel Butler called the Art of Covery: "This is as important as Discovery. Surely the glory of getting rid of and burying . . . a troublesome matter should be as great as that of making an important discovery."[89]

We need not capitulate to the pessimism which stems from the false hopes engendered by "scientificism." To conclude that legal or social studies cannot be "sciences" does not commit us to desperation. To those who demand that we look upon science as Olympus, and all else

[86] That some of the greatest natural scientists have been most unpleasantly lacking in dispassionateness, have been selfish, jealous, vindictive, and have even shamelessly lied, see Frank, *Fate and Freedom* (1945) 180-181; Frank, "The Place of the Expert in Modern Society," 16 *Phil. of Science* (1949).

[87] 19 *Encyc. Britannica* (14th ed. 1909) 91.

[88] See Chapter XXV as to Underhill Moore.

That one who has the scientific spirit will welcome "an observed fact that does not square with" his theory, see Dewey in *The Philosophy of John Dewey* (1939) 576.

[89] *The Notebooks of Samuel Butler* (1917) 180.

as unworthy of respect, we should say with Tourtoulon, "There is no need to throw to the dogs all that is not fit for the altar of the Gods . . ." [90]

Wise physicians have always admitted that the practice of medicine, while using the sciences, is not a science but is and always will be an art.[91] So we should admit that all government, and court-house government in particular, is not and can never be a science, that it is and ever will be an art—and a difficult one.

[90] Tourtoulon, *Philosophy in the Development of Law* (1922) 347-48.

[91] Aristotle, son of a physician, so recognized. It would seem that the famous skeptic, Sextus Empiricus, espoused skepticism about scientific certainty in general because he feared the results of dogmatizing "scientifically" in the field of medicine. As to Sextus Empiricus, see, e.g., Frank, *Fate and Freedom* (1945) 149, 159, 208, 311-12, 331-32.

XV. THE UPPER-COURT MYTH

The difficulty of practicing an art is no excuse for practicing it stupidly, carelessly. To acquire absolutely reliable knowledge of the objective past facts of most law-suits is undeniably beyond human power. Yet, although those facts can only be approximated, we should strive to have that approximation, as nearly as possible, asymptotic. Of course, we must rely on probabilities. But there are degrees of probability, as Bishop Butler remarked two hundred years ago. What he said of medicine has relevance here: "Is it not a poor thing for a physician to have so little knowledge in the cure of diseases as even the most eminent have? To act upon conjecture and guesses where the life of man is concerned? Undoubtedly it is," replied the Bishop to his own questions, "But not in comparison of having no skill at all in that useful art, and being obliged to act wholly in the dark." So as to the judicial art: The facts as "found" in trials are inherently guessy; but we need not be content with the present guessing-in-the-dark techniques of our trial courts. Everything feasible should be done so that the probability of accuracy in discovering the true facts of cases will be as high as is possible. That trial-court fact-finding can never be completely objective, that unavoidably it involves conjectures, that often it is but one element in a gestalt—all this does not at all compel the conclusion that the traditional fact-finding methods are not capable of marked improvement. Today, to a shocking and needless extent, they are tragically bad. I now turn to one of the main obstacles to their improvement.

2

In legal mythology, one of the most popular and most harmful myths is the upper-court myth, the myth that upper courts are the heart of court-house government. This myth induces the false belief that it is of no importance whether or not trial judges are well-trained for their job, fair-minded, conscientious in listening to testimony, and honest. In considerable part, this belief arises from the fallacious notion that the legal rules, supervised by the upper courts, control decisions. But the false belief about the unimportance of the trial judge's activities is also encouraged by another tenet of the upper-court myth, i.e., that the upper courts on appeals can and will safeguard litigants against the trial judge's mistakes concerning the facts.[1] I think that by now the reader knows how delusional that notion is, knows that, when the oral testimony is in conflict as to a pivotal issue of fact, and when some of that testimony supports the trial court's (express or implied) finding on that issue, then the upper court ordinarily has to accept that finding. Usually it can refuse to do so only if it appears in the written or printed record of the trial that the finding was the product of the trial judge's incompetence, unfairness or dishonesty. Such matters, however, show up in such a record in but the tiniest fraction of cases. Because of the inherent subjectivity of the trial judge's decisional process, his deliberate or unintentional disregard or misunderstanding of honest and trustworthy oral testimony is ordinarily hidden from the scrutiny of the upper court.

Since, however, the upper-court myth creates and perpetuates the illusory notion that upper courts can offset all the failings of the trial judges, the public puts too much reliance on, and gives too much kudos to, upper-court judges. Note the consequences: In states where judges are elected, the politicos, responsive to public opinion, usually nominate, for upper-court positions, lawyers of distinguished ability and integrity. But, as the public is not onto the far greater importance of the trial courts, the politicos often (not always) are much less careful about whom they nominate to sit on the trial-court bench. I do not mean that many elected trial judges are not men of competence, character and ability. I do mean that the public tends to give relatively little attention to their qualifications.

Yet the duties of trial judges demand far more ability than do those of "higher" court judges. Concerned as the latter are primarily with the legal rules, knowledge of those rules and skill in dealing with them constitute the chief requisites for the performance of their task. Many lawyers possess such knowledge and skill, which can be acquired by an intelligent man through an education in a law school and a few years in practice. But neither in the law schools—as legal education goes today—nor elsewhere can a lawyer obtain any systematic training necessary to give him the peculiar skills a trial judge should have.

Writing of trial judges, Professor Morgan recently said: "Of course, no rules prescribed by legislation or judicial decision can create character or competence [in a trial judge]." "But," he continued, "it is

[1] I previously touched on this notion; see Chapter III.

equally true that no system of administering justice can be satisfactory if constructed on the hypothesis that the trial judge will be crooked or incompetent." Then he went on to say, "Inevitably some trial judges will be slippery, prejudiced or otherwise unfit for office." Please mark the word "inevitably." I grant the inevitability of some such misfortunes. But what are we doing to reduce them to a minimum? If the number of ill-equipped trial judges is larger than is inevitable, then we have negligently provided ourselves with a system of administering justice bound to be unsatisfactory to an extent that is not inevitable but evitable. I think we have been astonishingly careless in our haphazard method of educating and selecting men to serve as trial judges.

It may occur to someone that the upper-court myth would become a reality if every trial judge were required to state in writing why he believed or disbelieved witnesses, and to give a detailed report of their demeanor; for, in that way, the upper court could get rid of the subjectivity of the trial judge's reactions to testimony. But the upper court would still not know whether the trial judge's report was "objective."

A better device would be one I proposed in 1930:[2] Have a "talking movie" of each trial. It would completely reproduce the manner in which the witnesses testified, so that the upper court judges could form their own, independent, impressions of the trial. But these impressions would still be subjective reactions—those of the upper-court judges.[3] Each appeal would be but another trial in the upper court, a cumbersome procedure. At any rate, the upper-court judges would become trial judges, and they would then need training in trial judging.

[2] Frank, *Law and the Modern Mind* (1930) 110 note. See also my dissenting opinion in U.S. v. Rubenstein, 151 F. (2d) 915 at 921 note 5 (1945).

[3] Because of the subjectivity in the witnesses' testimony, it would still be impossible to be sure of knowing the actual past facts.

XVI. LEGAL EDUCATION

The upper-court myth and legal rule magic are plainly related. For the perpetuation of that myth, and for the widespread dissemination of the belief in that magic, American legal education must take considerable blame. And if the addiction to such magic indicates a core of somewhat neurotic attitudes, the explanation of the faults of legal education in this respect are not far to seek. For contemporary law-school teaching got its basic mood at Harvard, some seventy years ago, from a brilliant neurotic, Christopher Columbus Langdell.[1]

When Langdell was himself a law student he was almost constantly in the law library. He served for several years as an assistant librarian. He slept, at times, on the library-table. One of his friends found him one day absorbed in an ancient law-book. "As he drew near," we are told, "Langdell looked up and said, in a tone of mingled exhilaration and regret, and with an emphatic gesture, 'Oh, if only I could have lived in the time of the Plantagenets!' "[2]

After graduation, he practiced as a lawyer in New York City for sixteen years. But he seldom tried a case or went into court. His clients were mostly other lawyers for whom, after much lucubration, he wrote briefs or prepared pleadings. He led a peculiarly secluded life. A biographer says of him, "In the almost inaccessible retirement of his office, and in the library of the Law Institute, he did the greater part of his work. He went little into company."

Is it any wonder that such a man had an obsessive and almost exclusive interest in books? The raw material of what he called "law," he devoutly believed, was to be discovered in a library and nowhere else; it consisted, as he himself said, solely of what could be found in print. Practicing law to Langdell meant chiefly the writing of briefs, examination of published "authorities." The lawyer-client relation, the numerous non-rational factors involved in a trial, the face-to-face

[1] This chapter is based on several articles: Frank, "Why Not A Clinical Lawyer-School?" 81 *Un. of Pa. L. Rev.* (1933) 907; Frank, "What Constitutes a Good Legal Education," 19 *Am. Bar Ass'n. J.* (1933) 723; Frank, "A Plea For Lawyer-Schools," 56 *Yale L.J.* (1947) 1303. More detailed descriptions of Harvard Law School under Langdell will be found in the first two articles.

[2] Who reigned from 1154 to 1485.

appeals to the emotions of juries, the elements that go to make up what is loosely known as the "atmosphere" of a case—everything that is undisclosed in upper-court opinions—was virtually unknown (and was therefore all but meaningless) to Langdell. The greater part of the realities of the life of the average lawyer was unreal to him.

What was almost exclusively real to him he translated into the law-school curriculum when in 1870, at the age of forty-four, he became a teacher at Harvard Law School, and, soon after, its Dean. His pedagogic theory reflected the man. The actual varied experiences of the practicing lawyer were, to Langdell, improper materials for the teacher and the student. They must, he insisted, shut their eyes to such data. They must devote themselves exclusively to what was discoverable in the library. The essence of his teaching philosophy he expressed thus: "First that law is a science; second, that all the available materials of that science are contained in printed books." This second proposition, it is said, was "intended to exclude the traditional methods of learning law by work in a lawyer's office, or attendance upon the proceedings of courts of justice."

Langdell declared that "the library is to us what the laboratory is to the chemist or the physicist and what the museum is to the naturalist. . . . The most essential feature of the [Harvard Law] School, that which distinguishes it most widely from all other schools of which I have any knowledge, is the library. . . . Without the library the School would lose its most important characteristics, and indeed its identity." In the same vein, the President of Harvard commented, not long after, "The Corporation recognizes that the library is the very heart of the Law School." "What qualifies a person to teach law," wrote Langdell, "is not experience in the work of a lawyer's office, not experience in dealing with men, not experience in the trial or argument of causes, not experience, in short, in using law, but experience in learning law. . . ." In *The Centennial History of Harvard Law School* (published in 1918), it was said, "If it be granted that law is to be taught as a science and in the scientific spirit, previous experience in practice becomes as unnecessary as is continuance in practice after teaching begins."

This philosophy of legal education was that of a man who cherished "inaccessible retirement." Inaccessibility, a nostalgia for the forgotten past, devotion to the hush and quiet of a library, the building of a pseudo-scientific system based solely upon book-materials—of these Langdell compounded the Langdell method.

The neurotic escapist character of Langdell soon stamped itself on the educational programs of our leading law schools. Unavoidably, their acceptance of the Langdell-Harvard method meant that most of the university law-school teachers were men who had never practiced or had practiced for only a brief interval. Indeed, in 1931, Adolf Berle, then a Columbia Law School professor, but himself an exception to the rule, said to me that 90% of teachers in our leading law-schools had never so much as ventured into a court-room. There have been notable exceptions. I name, at random, former Dean (now Judge) Clark, Dean Sturges, Douglas, Arnold, James at Yale; former Dean Pound, Dean Griswold, and Professor Morgan at Harvard; Professor Hinton at Chicago; Professors Michael, Wechsler and Hays at Columbia. Since 1931, the number of law-teachers versed in court-house ways has increased. Yet it is, I think, still true that at many law schools the majority of the professors have never met and advised a client, negotiated a settlement, drafted a complicated contract, consulted with witnesses, tried a case in a trial court or assisted in such a trial, or even argued a case in an upper court.

The Langdell spirit choked American legal education. It tended to compel even the experienced practitioner, turned teacher, to belittle his experience at the bar. It tended to force him to place primary emphasis on the library, to regard a collection of books as the heart of the school. A school with such a heart is what one may well imagine. The men who teach there, however interested some of them may once have been in the actualities of law offices and court-rooms, feel obliged to pay but subordinate regard to those actualities. The books are the thing. The words, not the deeds. Or only those deeds which become words.

Langdell invented, and our leading law-schools still employ, the so-called "case system." That is, the students are supposed to study cases. They do not. They study, almost entirely, upper-court opinions.[3] Any such opinion, however, is not a case, but a small fraction of a case, its tail end. The law students are like future horticulturists studying solely cut flowers; or like future architects studying merely pictures of buildings. They resemble prospective dog-breeders who never see anything but stuffed dogs. (Perhaps there is a correlation between such stuffed-dog legal education and the over-production of stuffed shirts in my profession.)

[3] "Non-legal" matter, now incorporated in many "case-books," seldom relates to the out-of-court activities of lawyers.

In such a school, that which is not in books has become "unscientific"; it may perhaps have truth, but it is a lesser truth, relatively unreal; true reality is achieved by facts only when reported in books. To be sure, Dean Pound, many years ago, spoke of "law in action." That awakened hopes. But has Harvard been showing its students "law in action"? The students have had the opportunity to read in books and law review articles about some very limited phases of "law" in action. But that, at most, is "law in action" in the library.

At Harvard's law school the students are given courses in evidence, practice, and pleading. Close by, courts are in action, and especially trial courts, where one can observe evidence in action, practice in action, pleading in action. Are the students urged to attend the courts frequently? Do they spend many days there? Are they accompanied there by their professors who comment thereafter on what has been observed? Are the students familiar with the development of cases in those courts? Are they asked to speculate on the next move to be made in a trial—at a time when the results of that move depend on foresight and skill, instead of hindsight? Are the procedural possibilities of a real lawsuit shown to the students by their professors, together with the so-called "substantive law" formulae—or are the two split up into separate courses? Do they make any effort to watch, describe and interpret courts in action? I mention Harvard. I could as well refer to almost any of the leading university law schools.

"Law in action" was a happy phrase. It contained, to be sure, that miserably ambiguous word "law." Yet it was a pointer or guidepost; it seemed to indicate a new direction. But what university law school has followed the pointer? The phrase "law in action" has remained largely a phrase; at any rate, so far as legal pedagogy is concerned, the function of the phrase, psychologically, has been principally to substitute a new verbal formula for revised conduct. The contents of the bottle remained much the same, the label was changed. One is reminded of the scene in the Gilbert and Sullivan opera where the policemen march around and around the stage, promising the distracted father that they will rescue his daughters from the pirates who have abducted them. "We go, we go," shout the policemen as they continue to march in circles. "But they don't go," exclaims the father despairingly.

In 1937, when I was still a practicing lawyer, I spoke at Harvard Law School to some six hundred law students. I talked about government and "economics." One of the Harvard professors had previously objected, urging me, instead, to talk about my experiences in litigation. I told the students of that suggestion, but said I had refused to comply with it because, while what I might tell about litigation might be amusing to them, my remarks would be as remote from their knowledge as if I were to talk about head-hunting in the Solomon Islands. To test out the validity of that comment, I asked all those students who had ever been in a court-room to raise their hands. Ten of the six hundred did so. I then asked which of those ten had visited a trial since he had been in law school. Five raised their hands. I then asked how many had been urged by their professors to attend trials. Not a single student raised his hand. I made similar experiments recently at both Columbia and Yale, with substantially the same results.

If it were not for a tradition which blinds us, would we not consider it ridiculous that, with litigation laboratories just around the corner, law schools confine their students to what they can learn about litigation in books? What would we say of a medical school where students were taught surgery solely from the printed page? No one, if he could do otherwise, would teach the art of playing golf by having the teacher talk about golf to the prospective player and having the latter read a book relating to the subject. The same holds for toe-dancing, swimming, automobile-driving, hair-cutting, or cooking wild ducks. Is legal practice more simple? Why should law teachers and their students be more hampered than golf teachers and their students? Who would learn golf from a golf instructor, contenting himself with sitting in the locker-room analyzing newspaper accounts of important golf-matches that had been played by someone else several years before? Why should law teachers be like Tomlinson? "'This I have read in a book,' he said, 'and that was told to me. And this I have thought that another man thought of a Prince in Muscovy.'"

Legal practice, I have said, is an art, a fairly difficult one. Why make its teaching more indirect, more roundabout, more baffling and difficult than teaching golf? But that is what the Langdell method has done. Legal teaching would be no "cinch" at best. The Langdell method has increased the difficulties, has made the task of the teacher as complicated as possible. Even the teacher who is a genius cannot overcome the obstacles. When I was at law school I sat next to a Chinese student who had learned his English in Spain. As a consequence, when he took his notes on what the American professors said, he took them in Spanish. On inquiry, I ascertained that he actually thought them in Chinese. University law teaching today is involved in a process not unlike that. It is supposed to teach men what they are to do in courtrooms and law offices. What the student sees is a reflection in a badly-made mirror of a reflection in a badly-made mirror of what is going on in the work-a-day life of lawyers. Why not smash the mirrors? Why not have the students directly observe the subject-matter of their study, with the teachers acting as enlightened interpreters of what is thus observed?

As you will see in a moment, I am not advocating a plan for legal education which will produce mere legal technicians. It is imperative that lawyers be made who are considerably more than that. That "more" is alien to the Langdell spirit. That spirit, I grant, is somewhat weakened. The undiluted Langdell principles are nowhere in good repute today. But they are still the basic ingredient of legal pedagogy, so that, whatever else is mixed with them, the dominant flavor is still Langdellian. Our leading law schools are still library-law schools, book-law schools. They are not, as they should be, *lawyer-schools.*

The history of American legal education commenced with the apprentice system: The prospective lawyer "read law" in the office of a practicing lawyer. Daily he saw for himself what courts and lawyers were doing. Before his eyes, legal theories received constant tests in legal practice. Even if he did not always articulate the discrepancies between theory and practice, he felt them. The first American law school, founded by Judge Reeves in the 1780's, was merely the apprentice system on a group basis. The students were still in intimate daily contact with the courts and law offices.

To shorten a long story, legal apprenticeship, à la Reeves or otherwise, all but disappeared in the universities under the impact of Langdellism, as school after school quarantined its students in the library. Some twenty-five years ago, however, the university law schools began to have a troubled conscience. Why, they asked, does what we teach as "law" so little resemble "law" as practiced? The question and the troubled conscience yielded something labelled "sociological jurisprudence." Its watch-word was that "law" is one of the "social sciences." All, then, would be well if legal education meshed with sociology, history, ethics, economics and political science. That became the great new dispensation.

It was all to the good, as far as it went. But it did not bring the schools back on the track from which they had fatefully strayed under Langdell's neurotic wizardry. If you want to go from New York to San Francisco, you're not likely to get there soon by voyaging to Rio de Janeiro. Maybe you should go to Rio, even if your ultimate destination is 'Frisco; for, when you arrive in 'Frisco, you'll be a wiser citizen, thanks to the knowledge gained on that detour. But if your final goal is 'Frisco, then 'Frisco ought to be somewhere on your itinerary. On the itinerary of most university law schools you'll find no mention of a trip, not even of a side-trip, to the court-house or to real everyday lawyerdom. The student's travels consist almost entirely of detours.

The sole way for these law schools to get back on the main track is unequivocally to repudiate Langdell's morbid repudiation of actual legal practice, to bring the students into intimate contact with courts and lawyers. That simple, obvious step most university law schools have shunned as if such contact would infect the students with intellectual bubonic plague. These schools have been devising the most complicated ways to avoid taking that step; instead of marching straight up to lawyerdom, they have walked all around it. They have been like a man who reaches with his right hand around behind his neck to scratch his left ear.

I maintain that something of immense worth was lost when our leading law schools wholly abandoned the legal apprentice system. I do not for a moment suggest that we return to that old system in its old form. But is it not plain that, without giving up entirely the case-book method and without discarding the invaluable alliance with the so-called "social sciences," our law schools should once more bring themselves into close contact with what clients need and what courts and lawyers actually do? Should the schools not execute an about-face? Should they not now adopt Judge Reeves' 18th century apprentice-school method, modifying it in the light of the wisdom gained on the long detour?

Let me now be more specific. I present the following ideas for consideration:

First: A considerable proportion of teachers in any law school should be men with not less than five to ten years of varied experience in actual legal practice. They should have had work in trial courts, appellate courts, before administrative agencies, in office-work, in dealing with clients, in negotiations, in arbitrations. Their practical experience should not have been confined chiefly to a short period of paper work in a law office. I do not mean that there are not some highly capable teachers with little or no such practical experience; some such teachers, who are brilliantly intuitive, partially make up for their deficiencies by imaginative insight. Nor do I say that mere experience in legal practice will make a man a good law teacher. By and large, teachers are born, not made.

There is room in any school for the mere book-teacher. Part of the job of the lawyers is to write briefs for appellate courts. Brief-writing in part does employ "library-law." The exclusively book-lawyer is perhaps at his best in teaching such "library-law." But the "library-law" teacher should cease to dominate the schools. More than that, some of the teaching of the art of "persuasive reasoning" in briefs might well be done by men who have written many real briefs for real courts.

Unfortunately, attempted reform of legal pedagogy is frequently in the hands of the "library-law" teacher. With the best will in the world, such a teacher often finds it almost impossible to warp over the old so-called case-system so as to adapt it to the needs of the future practicing lawyer. So long as teachers who know little or nothing except what they learned from books under that case-system control a law school, the actualities of the lawyer's life are there likely to be considered peripheral and as of secondary importance. A medical school dominated by teachers who had seldom seen a patient, or diagnosed the ailments of flesh-and-blood human beings, or actually performed surgical operations, would not be likely to turn out doctors equipped with a fourth part of what doctors ought to know. But our law schools are not doing for their students even the equivalent of that shoddy job. Many of those schools are so staffed that they are best fitted, not to train lawyers, but to graduate men able to become book-law teachers who can educate still other students to become book-law teachers—and so on ad infinitum, world without end. They are, in large part, excellent book-law-teacher schools. Because many law school professors have cut themselves off from the realities of a lawyer's life, because viewing these realities from too great a distance, they are class-room lawyers, one might say that they teach what they call law "through a class darkly."

As I have already intimated, the spirit of Langdell so dominates many a university law school that even the practitioner who becomes a teacher in such a school often succumbs to that spirit and forgets the difference between the theory he is teaching and the actual practice he has previously encountered. In some instances, to be sure, this forgetfulness stems from the character of the individual teacher; he may have found practice distasteful and lacking in that certainty which he craved, so that he shifts with delight to a system in which far greater (but illusory) certainty seems to be a reality.

What I suggest, then, is not that all law professors should have had first-hand contacts with courts, lawyers and clients, but that a very large proportion of the professors should be men with such a past.

Second: The case-system, so far as it is retained, should be revised so that it will in truth and fact become a case-system and not a mere sham case-system. A few of the current type of so-called case-books should be retained to teach dialectic skill in brief-writing. But the study of cases which will lead to some small measure of real understanding of how suits are won, lost and decided, should be based to a very marked extent on reading and analysis of complete records of cases—beginning with the filing of the first papers, through the trial in the trial court and to and through the upper courts. A few months properly spent on one or two elaborate court records, including the briefs (and supplemented by reading of text-books as well as upper court opinions), will teach a student more than two years spent on going through twenty of the case-books now in use. In medical schools, "case histories" are used for instruction. But they are far more complete than the alleged case-books used in law schools. It is absurd that we should continue to call an upper court opinion a "case."

Third: Even if legal case-books were true case-books and as complete as medical case-histories, they would be insufficient as tools for study. At best, dissection of court records would merely approximate the dissection of cadavers which first-year medical students learn. What would we think of a medical school in which students studied no more than what was to be found in printed case-histories, and were deprived of all clinical experience until after they received their M. D. degrees? Our law schools must learn from our medical schools. Law students should be given the opportunity to see legal operations. Their study of cases, at the veriest minimum, should be supplemented by frequent visits, accompanied by law teachers, to both trial and appellate courts. The cooperation of many judges could easily be enlisted.

The "up-stage" attitude of the bookish-trained teacher towards instruction in the actualities of trial-practice is prettily illustrated in the following excerpt from *The Centennial History of Harvard Law School:* "Efforts have been made from time to time to give students some experience in the trial of cases by substituting a trial of the facts before a jury for the argument of questions of law, whether in the law clubs or in the . . . moot court. Interesting experiments have been made in acting out a legal injury and summoning the witnesses of the event to testify; and on the other hand in coaching witnesses on the points of actual testimony in their reported trial and having them reproduce the testimony in the Practice Court. Such experiments have been more successful in affording amusement than in substantial benefit to the participants. A fact trial now and then is well worth while, but only as a relief to the tedium of serious work."[4]

One cannot but agree, in part, with that writer. Such fake trials are poor substitutes for careful observation of actual trials. Would any medical school substitute pretend-surgical-operations for real operations as means for instructing students? Obviously such sham law school trials can do little more than "afford amusement" or serve "as a relief to tedium." They are not the equivalent of serious lawyer-work. It is interesting to note that Mr. Justice Douglas, formerly Professor Douglas, agrees with me on this score.

Fourth: Now I come to a point which I consider of first importance. I have stated that law schools could learn much from the medical schools. The parallel cannot be carried too far. But a brief scrutiny of medical education suggests the use of a device which may be employed as an adequate method of obtaining apprentice work for law students: Medical schools rely to a very large extent on the free medical clinics and dispensaries. There now exist legal clinics in the offices of the Legal Aid Society. Today, however, those offices are by no means the counterpart of the medical clinics and dispensaries. The ablest physicians devote a considerable portion of their time to medical clinics, while the Legal Aid Society is, on the whole, staffed by men who are not leaders of their profession. The Society, too, is limited in the kinds of cases it takes, and most law teachers have little, if any, direct contact with its efforts.

Suppose, however, that there were, in each law school, a legal clinic or dispensary. As before indicated, I think that a considerable part of (but not necessarily all) the teaching staff of a law school should consist of lawyers who already have varied experience in practice. Some of these men could run the law school legal clinics, assisted by the students. The work of these clinics would be done for little or no charge. The teacher-clinicians would devote their full time to their teaching, which would include such clinical work (although they

[4] *Centennial History of Harvard Law School* (1918) 84-5.

would also teach other matters). The law school clinics, however, would not confine their activities to such as are now undertaken by the Legal Aid Society. They would take on important jobs, including trials, for governmental agencies, legislative committees, or other quasi-public bodies. Their professional work would thus comprise virtually every kind of service rendered by law offices. The teacher-clinicians would disclose to their student assistants, both in and out of "office hours," the generalized aspects of the specific doctrines pertinent to the specific cases with which they dealt. Theory and practice would thus constantly interlace. The students would learn to observe the true relation between the contents of upper-court opinions and the work of practicing lawyers and courts. The students would be made to see, among other things, the human side of the administration of justice, including the following:

(a) The hazards of a jury trial: How juries decide cases. The irrational factors that frequently count with juries. The slight effect which the judges' instructions concerning the legal rules often have on verdicts.

(b) How legal rights are affected by lost papers, missing witnesses, perjury and prejudice.

(c) The effects of fatigue, alertness, political pull, graft, laziness, conscientiousness, patience, biases and open-mindedness of judges. How legal rights may vary with the judge who tries the case and with that judge's varying and often unpredictable reactions to various kinds of cases and divers kinds of witnesses.

(d) The student would learn that, except fictionally, in trials there is no such thing, for instance, as the "law of torts" as distinguished from specific decisions; and that all legal rules, including the "substantive" rules, in a fundamental sense are procedural, since, as we saw, they are only some among the many implements lawyers use in the court-room fights we call "litigation."

Participating in the preparation of briefs, both for trial courts and on appeals, the student, with the aid of his teachers, would learn legal rules and doctrines in the exciting context of live cases. The difference is indescribable between that way of learning and that to which students are now restricted in the schools. It is like the difference between kissing a girl and reading a treatise on osculation. Abstract theory divorced from concrete practical interests is usually dull. Montessori discovered that to teach half-witted children arithmetic became easy, if they were given practical activities, interesting to them, in which adding, subtracting and multiplying were necessary aids to the desired specific achievements. They learned by "doing." If that method is good for half-wits, why not for law students (who are presumably whole-wits)?

(e) Again, in a living context, the student in my sort of apprentice school would be instructed in the methods used in negotiating contracts and settlements of controversies.

(f) The nature of draftsmanship would become clearer. The student would understand how the lawyer tries to translate the wishes of a client (often inadequately expressed by the client) into wills, contracts or corporate instruments. The university law schools even now can, and some do, accomplish something in the way of teaching draftsmanship. That is, they can do something in the way of showing the students how to draft mortgages or wills or deposit agreements (or the like) which have a more or less stereotyped form. But "creative draftsmanship"—the use of novel fact-materials thrown at the lawyer by his client and sometimes worked out in negotiations with counsel representing the other party to the bargain—cannot be adequately taught in most university law schools as they are now conducted.

(g) In such a school, what I call the "enforcement approach" would soon dawn on the students. That is, they would perceive that in advising a client as to whether he should bring a suit, it may be well to begin with the projected end, to find out what the client wants, and then to ascertain whether by a law suit he can obtain it. For instance, if a man owes a client $5,000, but the man is hopelessly insolvent or all his assets are judgment-proof, litigation usually will be fruitless.

(h) Concern with the pressing practical affairs of clients would also induce close-up study of the legislative process in action. The student would be prodded into learning how legislation is made, would come to know the realities behind the "legislative intention" or the "purpose of the legislature." [5]

I will be told—I have been told—that the law schools at most have but three short years to train lawyers, and that these years are already so crowded that there is no time to spend on the sort of first-hand material to which I have been referring. I am not at all impressed by such talk. For in most university law schools the major part of the three years is spent in teaching a relatively simple technique—that of analyzing upper court opinions, "distinguishing cases," constructing, modi-

[5] See Chapter XXI.

fying or criticizing legal doctrines. Three years is much too long for that job. Intelligent men can learn that dialectical technique in about six months. Teach them the dialectic devices as applied to one or two legal topics, and they will have no trouble applying them to other topics. But in the law schools, much of the three years is squandered, by bored students, in applying that technique over and over again—and never with reference to a live client or a real law suit—to a variety of subject-matters; torts, contracts, corporations, trusts, suretyship, negotiable instruments, evidence, pleading, and so on. Of course, it is impossible in three years, or indeed in thirty-three years, to give or take courses, in all the subjects into which what is compendiously called "law" can be subdivided. If you measure the limited number of courses that can be covered in three years over against the totality of subject-matters which a lawyer, when engaged in general practice, will encounter, three years seem all too brief. But the point is that the able lawyer, if he has once mastered the dialectic technique in respect of one or two subject matters, can in short order become adept in coping with a great variety of subject-matters. Teach a man the use of precedent-distinguishing devices with respect to the so-called law of contracts or trusts, and he will have little trouble in applying those devices with respect to corporations, insurance, or what-not.

The myopic "case-system" necessarily limits the student to study of a limited portion of a very few subjects. It seems absurd to me that students should not be required to read textbooks and legal encyclopedia articles, not only on those few subjects, but on several dozen others. By that means they will attain a general nodding acquaintance with the leading concepts and peculiar vocabularies of a variety of special topics. Thus they will, for example, overcome that silly dread, experienced by many a graduate, of legal problems concerning patents, copyrights, and admiralty.

Some eighteen years ago, Judge Crane of the New York Court of Appeals characterized the typical graduate of a university law school as follows: "With the practical working of the law he has little or no familiarity. He may come to the bar almost ignorant of how the law should be applied and is applied in daily life. It is, therefore, not unusual to find the brightest student the most helpless practitioner, and the most learned surpassed in the profession by one who does not know half as much. Strange as it may seem, there were some advantages in the older methods of preparation for the bar. As you know, the law school is relatively a matter of recent growth. Formerly, a student, working in the office of a practitioner, combined the study of law with its daily application to the troubles and business of clients. He had an opportunity of hearing the story at the beginning, of noticing how it was handled by his preceptor, of reading the papers prepared to obtain a remedy; he accompanied the lawyer to court and became acquainted with the manner of the presentation of the case to the judge or to the jury. . . . You know much more law after coming out of a university [law school] than these former students ever knew, but you know less about the method of its application, and how to handle and use it."

Is not that a shocking state of affairs? Think of a medical school which would turn out graduates wholly ignorant of how medicine "should be applied and is applied in daily life." In this connection it is important, to note that, according to Flexner, in the best-equipped medical schools, the student "makes and sees made thorough physical examinations, painstaking records, varied and thoroughgoing laboratory tests, at every stage in the study of the patient; the literature of the subject is utilized; at one and the same time medicine is practiced and studied—teachers and students mingling freely and naturally in both activities." In this manner, said Flexner, there has been "effected the fusion of bedside and laboratory procedures alike in the care of patients, in teaching, and in research. . . . From the standpoint of training, fragmentariness, if stimulative and formative, is desirable rather than otherwise. . . . The student must . . . acquire a vivid sense of the existence of breaks, gaps, and problems. The clinics I am now discussing carry him from the patient in the bed to the point beyond which at the moment neither clinical observation nor laboratory investigation can carry him. There he is left, in possession, it is to be hoped, of an acute realization of the relatively narrow limits of human knowledge and human skill, and of the pressing enigmas yet to be solved by intelligence and patience."[6] Here is much that law schools should ponder carefully. The Langdell system is their albatross. They should cast it off.

The core of the law school I propose would be a sort of sublimated law office. Those who attended it would learn by "doing," not merely by reading and talking about doings. But such a school would not limit itself to instruction in legal techniques. It would consider "strictly legal

[6] A. Flexner, *Medical Education* (1925) 269-70.

problems" in the light supplied by the other social studies (miscalled "social sciences")—history, ethics, economics, politics, psychology and anthropology. Mere pre-legal courses in those fields, unconnected with the live material of human actions with which lawyers must cope, have proved a failure. The integration ought to be achieved inside the law schools. Some of the teachers who give these courses need not have been practicing lawyers, indeed not be lawyers at all. Most of the synthesis, however, between the instruction in legal techniques and in those other wider perspectives should occur in the courses relating to legal subjects. Accordingly, all the teachers should be men who have themselves made that synthesis.

I may say that, more than twenty years ago, I was one of a group of alumni who pleaded with the University of Chicago Law School thus to widen its curriculum. Far, then, from rejecting the notion of teaching subjects not directly "legal," I would extend such teaching. I would, in addition, show (as I try to do in my own teaching) the connections between legal philosophy and other phases of philosophy. Noting that a trial judge or jury is a kind of historian, I would also show the resemblances and differences between the methods—the logics—of the natural scientists, the historians and the lawyers. I would give a first-rate course in logic and semantics. For example, apropos of the distinction between so-called "substantive law" and "procedure," I would explore the concept of "substance" in philosophy and science. I would have students study the several varieties of psychology as related to the problems of lawyers and judges, including the psychology of judges, juries, witnesses and litigants. If I had my way I would have the schools point to the error of determinism, economic or otherwise,[7] and severely criticize "behaviorism." I would have them indicate the lack of foundation for cyclical theories of history, such as Toynbee's and Spengler's;[8] I would show the intertwining of the legal notion of "natural law" and the notion of "laws of nature"; and I would lay much stress on legal theory.

It is a pleasure to report that many of the law schools today give marked emphasis to the role of lawyers as policy-makers or policy-advisers, and bring home to the students the need for embodying democratic ideals and values in the legal rules. But a law school which really means business about democratic ideals should interest itself mightily,

[7] See, e.g., Frank, *Fate and Freedom* (1945) passim.
[8] *ibid.* 37-38.

as most of our schools do not, in the problem of thoroughly overhauling our trial methods, and in the problem of the inability of many litigants to obtain justice because of lack of money to meet the expense of obtaining crucial testimony.

Of course, the lawyer's interests should roam far beyond the courthouse aspect of government; yet to say that is not to say that he should submerge his interest in that aspect. Without doubt, the "full role of the lawyer in the community" compels recognition of "his impact on policy-advising and policy-making," and he should therefore give imaginative consideration" to "the whole range of institutions . . . that can be created, improved, or rearranged for community values." [9] But, in our democracy, prominent among the vaunted community values is the right to a fair trial; and a legal education which does not vigorously stimulate the interests of the future lawyers in that direction, while they are still youthfully idealistic, although it may deserve high praise for its general educational worth, is not a democratic education for lawyers. For, I ask once more, if lawyers do not cherish the values of which courts peculiarly should be the guardians, who will or can?

The schools should also concern themselves with the problem of the effect of judicial corruption. Of that problem, law students learn little or nothing. If one inquires why, he is told that dishonest judges and purchased or "fixed" decisions are "abnormal." That answer does not content me. I share the hope that all crooks will be driven from the bench; but that hope, alas, is not yet a reality—and probably will never be if the law schools maintain their present policy of failing to discuss the subject in class-rooms. What would one say of an engineering school where students heard nothing of wind pressure? Such an obstacle to engineering is deplorable from an ideal point of view. But is it to be called "abnormal" and therefore ignored? Engineering students properly study frictionless engines; but they will do injury to mankind unless they are also taught much about friction. Should not law students be taught about judicial "friction?" What would be thought of a college course in city government in which no mention was made of "graft" and "pull?" How can we afford to have men practice law who have been educated to shut their eyes to the effect of those factors on decisions? [10]

[9] McDougal, "The Law School of the Future," 56 *Yale L. Rev.* (1947) 1345, 1348.

[10] In the case of Root Refining Co. v. Universal Oil Products Co., decided in 1948, 169 F. (2) 514, the court held that, in two earlier cases, the decisions had resulted from the bribery of a judge. That judge, on the bench for many years, had decided a multitude of cases. All those decisions are now, necessarily, under suspicion of having

Not of course, in order that they may learn how to use bribes or political pull,[11] but for these obvious reasons: (1) A lawyer should know which judges are corrupt, or susceptible to political influence, so that, when possible, he may keep his clients' cases from coming before those judges. (2) Lawyers should do what they can to help the public eliminate such blights on the judicial process. But lawyers engaged in practice before the courts find that a most perplexing problem: If some particular lawyers try to cause the removal of a judge they suspect of corruption, and if they fail, that judge probably will, in roundabout ways, visit his wrath on their clients. For that reason, practicing lawyers usually hesitate to initiate such removal proceedings. Moreover, most busy lawyers tend to lose a keen interest in reforms. Here is a problem, which, if it is to be solved, should be discussed in the schools with the law students who, still in their formative years, are generally rife with idealism.

It is objected that public reference to any judicial dishonesty may create the incorrect and unfair belief that many judges are dishonest. The answer is to say—as I do say unequivocally—that fortunately most of the judiciary is honest, that but a very few scamps manage to get on the bench, and that the best way to avoid unfairness to the vast majority of judges is to oust the few rascals.

"Policy" teaching will be fruitless if "policy-minded" lawyers are not trained to protect policies when under fire in the trial courts. Let me give an illustration of the way such lawyer's know-how, or its lack, may vitally affect policies. In 1935-1937, the constitutionality of the PWA statute was under attack in litigation in the federal courts. When I entered that litigation for the government, I found that the cases were on appeal. They had not been tried on evidence, because my book-lawyer predecessor had "demurred" to the complaints, thereby admitting the truth of the allegations of fact made by the plaintiffs in those complaints. Those admitted allegations were to the effect that the PWA Administrator, Harold Ickes, had, in dozens of ways, shockingly misused his powers under the statute. The Solicitor General, Stanley Reed (now Mr. Justice Reed), and I agreed that, with those facts admitted,

---

been purchased. It would be instructive to have law students track down those decisions to see which of them became precedents that lower courts were obliged to and did follow.

[11] Professor Kantorowicz, in a much-quoted article, deplored the notion that law students should be told of the existence of dishonest judges; he said that such class-room discussions would amount to teaching the "art of bribing judges." Kantorowicz, "Some Rationalism About Realism," 43 *Yale L.J.* (1934) 1240, 1252.

the defense of the statute's validity was in danger, since there would be such a bad "atmosphere" as to arouse marked hostility on the part of even the most liberal Justices when the cases were argued in the Supreme Court. Through considerable maneuvering, we managed to have the suits remanded, by several upper courts, to the lower courts for trial. We won those trials, obtaining findings of fact, based on the evidence, which flatly contradicted the plaintiffs' factual allegations, thus completely dissipating the bad atmosphere. Then in the Supreme Court we were victorious. I strongly suspect that, but for those trial tactics, PWA and the valuable policy it represented would have been judicially destroyed.

Although no lawyer should be unversed in the way courts function, it is true that many lawyers never get into court. They advise clients, draft their contracts and wills, attend corporate directors' meetings, help to negotiate business transactions, settle disputes without recourse to litigation, engage in arbitrations.[12] Most university law schools do not even hint at the skills such lawyer activities demand. For instance, some of Columbia's graduates, honor men in their day at school, and now, experts in such skills, successfully practicing in New York City, have told me they would be delighted to talk about their experiences to Columbia law students. Yet Columbia never thinks of inviting them to do so. Such talks would have some slight educational value. But the only way for students really to learn those skills would be to see them in operation and to participate in those operations. Near at hand to every law school are those laboratories known as law offices, where students could learn the relation of their theoretical studies to the realities of a practicing lawyer's life. A few university law-school teachers now do take their students to look inside those laboratories. Such visits are indeed desirable. But they are pale substitutes for the real thing. The real thing would be to have such laboratories inside the law school. I do not mean the so-called "Practice Laboratory," now in vogue in some schools, where students draft documents for suppositious or paper clients. I mean, as I've said, law schools which are themselves, in part, law offices dealing with flesh-and-blood clients.

To altogether too many law teachers are applicable the comments of Anatole France: "There are bookish souls for whom the universe is but paper and ink. The man whose body is animated by such a soul

[12] See further, Chapter XXV.

spends his life before his desk, without any care for the realities whose graphic representation he studies so obstinately. He knows of the labors, sufferings, and hopes of men only what can be [found in books] sewn on to tapes and bound in morocco. . . . He has never looked out of the window. Such was the worthy Peignot, who collected other people's opinions to make books out of them. . . . He conceived of passions as subjects for monographs, and knew that nations perish in a certain number of octavo pages." Such an attitude, on the part of law-teachers, means, I think, moral irresponsibility.[13] It induces in many a law-student when he emerges from school a bitter, cynical, disillusionment like that described by Silone in the following passage: "Don Paolo went back to his room to reflect on the peasants and their lives. . . . The idea occurred to him of using his remaining time at Pietrasecca to finish his essay on the agrarian question. He took his notebook from his bag and started reading the notes he had started. . . . He read them through, and was astonished and dismayed at their abstract character. All these quotations from masters and disciples on the agrarian question, all those plans and schemes, were the paper scenery in which he had hitherto lived. The country which was the subject of those notes of his was a paper country, with paper mountains, paper hills, fields, gardens, and meadows. The great events recorded in them were mostly paper events, paper battles, and paper victories. The peasants were paper peasants."

It is often said that it will do no harm to leave the law student ignorant of a large part of the facts in the legal world he will later enter, that he can learn those facts after his graduation. That argument comes to this: Have the student spend three long years being mis-educated—i.e., receiving erroneous impressions about the ways in which many courts and lawyers behave—because he will be able to dissipate those impressions subsequently.[14] Dr. Brickner gave an apt reply to a similar argument: "It is a horrible thing to picture what is involved in the customary idea that . . . we have about many an adolescent, 'Oh he is being disillusioned, he will soon be all right'—the idea that it is a

13 Their attitude recalls the story of Maxwell and Todhunter: Maxwell, having contrived an experiment which disclosed a new optical phenomenon, asked Todhunter to examine it. Todhunter refused. He explained that he had been teaching the subject of optics all his life, "and I do not want all my ideas upset by seeing it."

14 In 1840, when Prussia was under the Code of 1794 which had displaced the earlier Roman-derived "law," Savigny, at the University of Berlin, continued to base his legal teaching entirely on the Roman "law." He said that there was no occasion for telling law students about the existing code, because, for "the needs of subsequent practice, [post-school] experience suffices."

customary thing for people who grow up in our society to have to go through a stage of disillusionment. That means we have been illusioned. What kind of education is it that has to be undone?" If, said Bentham, in his *Comment on the Commentaries,* "there be a case in which students stand in need of instruction, it is where the generality of books that come into their hands represent things in a different light from true ones. True it is, that after many errors and disappointment, observation and practice may let a beginner into the bottom of these mysteries; but what sort of an excuse is it to give for feeding him with falsehood, that some time or other he may chance to find it out?"

When Langdell counseled against having law teachers experienced "in dealing with men" or "in the trial and argument of causes," he said that properly equipped teachers should have "not the experience of the Roman advocate [court lawyer] or of the Roman praetor [magistrate] but the experience of the Roman jurisconsult." That reference to the "Roman jurisconsult" shows the defect of the Langdell method which still too much pervades legal education. For the jurisconsult was a man who seldom, if ever, tried a case or went to court. It was his business to give answers to legal questions based upon assumed states of fact. He did not bother about the means of convincing a court, through testimony, that those were the facts, or the method by which the court would reach that conclusion. Such matters were beneath the dignity of the jurisconsult; he left them to trial lawyers and judges.

Professor Max Rheinstein of Chicago, in a recent letter to me, referring to my attempt to explain, by way of legal magic, the dominant law-school aversion to observation of trial courts, offered a supplemental explanation. "To me," he wrote, "the reason seems to be rooted in history. In Rome, 'legal' activities were divided up among three groups of men; the jurisconsults; the orators; and practical politicians, statesmen, and, during the late empire, bureaucratic officials. The jurisconsults busied themselves exclusively with the rules of law; the practical administration of justice remained outside of their field. Yet, their work has become the foundation of all legal science ever since, not only in the countries of the so-called Civil but also in the Common Law orbit. The style of Common Law legal science was determined when Bracton [15] started out to collect, arrange, and expound the rules of the Common Law of his time in the very style of the Roman classics

[15] Bracton was a 13th century English judge.

and the corpus juris.[16] All the law books since his time . . . have adhered to the pattern thus determined. Legal education built upon these books has been equally limited; from Pavia and Bologna [17] to Harvard, law schools have regarded it as their task to impart to their students a knowledge of the rules of law and hardly anything else. Of course, for practical work in the administration of justice such a training is far from being complete."

Rheinstein, commenting on my notions of a revised law-school curriculum, says that I am calling for the development of the "science of administration of justice." Change the word "science" to "art," and I agree. Instruction in such an art would include first-hand observation of all that courts, administrative agencies, and legislatures actually do. Such instruction would serve three purposes. First, it would aim to equip future lawyers to cope with courthouse realities, no matter how ugly and socially detrimental some of those realities are; for a lawyer cannot competently represent his clients if he is ignorant of the devices which his adversaries may utilize on behalf of their clients. Second, such instruction would stimulate the contrivance of specific practical means by which existing trial-court techniques can be improved, in order that justice may be judicially administered more in accord with democratic ideals. Third, it would train men to become trial judges.

A law school which turns its back on the observable happenings in the trial courts inevitably does what Langdell intended: It devotes itself basically to the *R*'s. It teaches students little about those elusive characteristics of the *F*'s on which I have been dwelling. And an *F*-less study of the judicial process necessarily yields a magical attitude towards the courts.

Our law schools, being principally library schools, do an admirable job of producing library-lawyers. Such lawyers function well in upper courts, since those courts are largely library-courts. A first-rate graduate of a first-rate law school, after a few years, will therefore make a first-rate upper-court judge. But our law schools do practically nothing to educate men to become trial judges. Yet, as I said, the role of the trial judge is far more important, and his task far more difficult, than that of the appellate judge. To educate a future trial judge adequately,

16 The collective title of the body of Roman "law" as promulgated by the Emperor Justinian in the 6th century.

17 Pavia and Bologna were celebrated Italian law schools in the Middle Ages. In the 12th century at Bologna a renaissance of "Roman law" began.

it would be necessary to train him elaborately in the skills of fact-finding. One of the principal reasons for the backwardness of judicial fact-finding is that the law schools have shirked their obligation to teach those skills. Moreover, thanks to their disregard of the trial court, the legal profession is not sufficiently alive to the need of improving fact-finding.

In defense of much of conventional method of legal pedagogy, some one might perhaps quote Abe Martin's aphorism: "Nobuddy kin talk half as interestin' as the feller that aint hampered by facts or infermashun"; or the comment of Ho Hum, the sage of Chinatown, that "if no man talked of that which he did not understand, the silence would be unbearable." [18] But I think little of that defense.

However, let me say again, emphatically, that all university law schools and all their teachers do not deserve my criticism. Yale Law School, for example, is coming ever closer to grips with lawyers' realities; and all the schools have professors who are outstanding exceptions to my description of the genus "law-teacher." Bradway, at Duke University Law School, has been using clinical teaching methods for some years.[19] Not long since, I received a letter from Professor Lon Fuller of Harvard in which he said that he, for one, had become convinced that "one of the major deficiencies in American legal education is in dealing with facts," in its over-emphasis on the work of upper courts. If all legal pedagogues soon adopt that point of view, the reign of legal magic, before long, may be doomed. But, alas, that reign is still unfortunately powerful in many law schools.

[18] I borrow this aphorism from Wilson, Book Review, 17 *Cornell L. Q.* (1932) 538.

[19] See Bradway, *Clinical Preparation for Law Practice* (1946). In large part, Bradway's methods supply what I consider wanting in most university law schools. I say "in large part," because it seems that the clinical work at Duke (1) comes late in the student's law-school career, (2) is not closely integrated with the "social studies," psychology, philosophy, history and ethics, and (3) does not stress the importance of policy-making in general and of reform of trial-court fact-finding in particular.

XVII. SPECIAL TRAINING FOR TRIAL JUDGES

I SUGGEST that we should at once set about contriving methods of avoiding the avoidable tragedies caused by lack of systematic training of trial judges. Here are my tentative ideas on the subject:

Such a man should be specially educated for that job. In law school, he should be taught not only what a law student now learns—that is much about upper courts, the legal rules, the values, policies, and ideals which are or should be expressed in those rules—but also what no law school now teaches. He should be shown, in great detail, the problems, relating to the facts, which confront a trial judge, as they do not confront a higher court judge. He should learn all that is now known about psychological devices for testing the trustworthiness of witnesses as to their individual capacities for observation, memory and accuracy in narrating what they remember. He should be taught to be alert to the possibilities of using such devices, as they become improved, in trials.

We saw how much weight the courts give to the trial judges' observation of witnesses' demeanor traits as clues to their trustworthiness. To be valuable as clues, those traits need to be wisely interpreted. Occasionally there are astonishing revelations of absurd rules-of-thumb some trial judges use, such as these: A witness is lying if, when testifying, he throws his head back; or if he raises his right heel from the floor; or if he shifts his gaze rapidly; or if he bites his lip. Every psychologist knows how meaningless as signs of prevarication any such behavior may be. The skilled perjurer may have no such indicia. I suggest that the future trial judge should learn what there is to learn about the interpretation of demeanor. He should also see at first hand, in trial courts, how trials are conducted, thereby becoming thoroughly acquainted with trial lawyers' wiles. He ought, too, himself, when still in law school, act as an assistant to lawyers at some actual trials.

At a minimum, he should learn what it means to keep his mind open, to be receptive to new impressions, to be patient and attentive. In short, he should not be naively intuitive. His should be a carefully trained intuition. He should learn the value of "perhapsing." "I prefer," said Montaigne, "those words which tone down and modify the hastiness of our propositions: 'Perhaps,' 'In some sort,' 'Some,' 'They say,' 'I think,' and the like." This is what Johnson calls "to-me-ness," a conscious recognition that, when one says "This is," he usually is reporting merely his own personal evaluations. Related is what Johnson describes as "ventriloquizing," as when the judge purports to speak dogmatically as if he were The Law Speaking. These tendencies, which all men share, are abused by those who are not clearly on to them.[1] Of course, simply to use words of self-reference will not suffice; a man may vocabularize "to-me-ness" and yet be convinced that his every "is" has thorough objectivity; the "perhapsing" should eat into his very thinking processes.

Some nineteen years ago, I said that judges should "come to grip with the human nature operative in themselves. What this implies," I added, "is that the judge should be . . . well trained in . . . the best available methods of psychology. And among the most important objects which would be subject to his scrutiny . . . would be his own prejudices . . . not only in connection with attitudes political, economic and moral, but with respect to more minute and less easily discoverable preferences and disinclinations."[2] I earnestly renew that suggestion: The future trial judge, while in law-school, should, through work with psychologists, engage in a voyage of intensive self-exploration, so that he will be sensitively aware of many of his own hidden biases and antipathies to divers kinds of persons; then he will be able to control or modify many of his biases with respect to the witnesses who will appear before him. To quote Montaigne again, "If everyone would closely watch the effects and circumstances of the passions that sway him . . . , he would see them coming, and would a little break their course and impetuosity."[3]

Such self-study, however, may be no complete solution of the problem: The psychiatrists, much concerned with self-evaluation, or "insight," believe that merely "verbal" or "intellectual" insight may yield little real self-knowledge. One psychiatrist remarks that often alleged "insight" means "only the ability to use a lot of fancy terms in describ-

[1] Johnson, *People in Quandaries,* (1946) 61, 65, 85, 123, 145, 223. Johnson suggests the use of such phrases as "it seems to me," "as I see it," "apparently," "seems," "from my particular point of view."

[2] Frank, *Law and the Modern Mind* (1930) 147.

[3] That was said in 1580. In 1736, Bishop Butler said that "many men seem perfect strangers to their own characters. . . . Hence it is one hears people exposing follies which they themselves are eminent for; and talking with great severity against particular vices . . . they themselves are notoriously guilty of."

ing [one's] feelings"; another observes that "we cannot say that the illiterate individual may not have the higher degree of insight." These views suggest that a judge's knowledge of his own undesirable prejudices, and his ability to nullify them, are not necessarily to be measured by the extent to which he verbalizes such knowledge.[4]

Especially is that true of deeply-buried destructive aggressive tendencies. The subject of such aggressiveness has been much discussed by psychiatrists of recent years. From the abundance of utterances concerning it, I choose some comments by Ranyard West, because, in this respect, he disagrees with Freud who seemed to consider aggression the primary component of human nature, and because (as I noted earlier) West is a psychiatrist who has carefully studied legal matters. Aggressiveness, he writes, "which harmonizes so ill with our social selves, yet which will out, is a cause without rival at once of blindness to our own faults and prejudice against those of others. And naturally enough, the more firmly we demand a high standard of social virtue of ourselves, the more complete has a self-deception to be in order to allow the egress of our cruel, selfish . . . lusts." The "whitewashing" of our own aggressiveness takes the form of "projection"—the "blackening of others by foisting upon them, in our imagination, our own unconscious feelings." We use the method of "repudiating our own aggressiveness" by "imagining it to be in others."[5] The uncovering to a man of his own destructive aggressiveness thus "projected" is none too easy. Verbalizing that tendency will not suffice. Yet that tendency, operative in a judge, may produce hideous consequences in sadistic decisions which he will self-deceptively rationalize.

[4] Herbert Spencer was often unusually dominated by his prejudices, in spite of the fact that he wrote: "The only reasonable hope is, that here and there one may be led, in calmer moments to remember how largely his beliefs about public matters have been made for him by circumstances, and how probable it is that they are either untrue or but partially true. When he reflects on the doubtfulness of the evidence which he generalizes, collected haphazard from a narrow area—when he counts up the perverting sentiments fostered in him by education, country, class, party, creed—when, observing those around, he sees that from other evidence selected to gratify sentiments partially unlike his own, there result unlike views; he may occasionally recollect how largely mere accidents have determined his convictions. Recollecting this, he may be induced to hold these convictions not quite so strongly; may see the need for criticism of them with a view to revision; and, above all, may be somewhat less eager to act in pursuance of them." Spencer, *Study of Sociology* (1873) 356-57.

[5] West, *Conscience and Society* (1945) 163. For an important study of the subject by a brilliant lawyer, see Sharp, "Aggression, A Study of Values and Law," 57 *Ethics* (1947) Part II. He points to two mistakes to be avoided: (1) To curb overt forms of aggression may be merely to drive destructive aggression underground where, in concealed form, it may play social havoc. (2) In curbing the destructive types of aggression, care should be taken not to impair socially valuable, constructive aggression.

To speak bluntly, I urge that each prospective judge [6] should undergo something like a psychoanalysis. I say "something like," because the theory and techniques of the art of psychoanalysis are being constantly revised,[7] and some adequate, less prolonged and complicated, substitute may soon appear. I do not believe that, through such self-study or otherwise, any judge will become aware of all his prejudices or always able to control those of which he is aware. But such self-knowledge, I think, can be of immense help in reducing the consequences of judicial bias.

The judge's voyage of self-exploration should, indeed, not end even after he is on the bench. For, as old Sir Thomas Browne said, a man should "understand not only the varieties of men, but the variations of himself, and how many men he hath been. . . ." In 1946, I made a suggestion which is relevant here: "Why," I asked, "should not those holding major administrative posts in government be required periodically to consult government psychiatrists? For unconscious fears, aggressions, and frustrated, anti-social impulses, of a kind which psychiatrists discover to be factors distorting the judgments and distressingly affecting the conduct of their patients, also often influence, although to a smaller extent, the views and behavior of persons who do not display symptoms sufficiently grave to induce them to become patients or to justify intensive psychiatric treatment. My experience in government leads me to believe that a very considerable part of the friction between government departments, if one peered behind the rationalizations, could be traced to personality difficulties of one or more of the disputants. Under severe pressure, the best of men become the creatures of inner drives and obsessions of which they have no awareness. An occasional chat by an overworked official with a government psychiatrist might make government run more smoothly." [8] Those remarks fully apply to court-house government.

The future trial judge should become aware not merely of his prejudices, but also of the factors which peculiarly affect his capacity for sustained attention, so that he can avoid inattention when witnesses testify before him. Burtt, noting that hunters and scouts have developed an unusually good capacity for observing minute details, through

[6] I would not limit this suggestion to trial judges.

[7] I have elsewhere expressed my belief that psychology (including psycho-analysis) is by no means a science but only an art, and still in its early infancy. See Frank, *Law and the Modern Mind* (1930) 21 note, 163, 359-60.

[8] Frank, "The Scientific Spirit and Economic Dogmatism," in the volume, *Science for Democracy* (1946) 11, 20-21.

habits of attention, proposes that detectives and policemen, by training, could acquire such habits. That suggestion might well be applied in the education of trial judges. The student should come to know, too, his own peculiar hindrances to good vision and good hearing, so that he can remedy or make allowance for such defects.

After his graduation from law-school, he should function as a trial lawyer in a large number of trials. He should then, for a considerable period, serve as an apprentice to a trial judge. Before he is nominated for election to, or appointed to, the office of trial judge, he should be required to pass a stiff examination and be officially certified as fit for that office.

Perhaps any such program will seem absurd to the reader. It seems good horse-sense to me. We would not allow a man to perform a surgical operation without a thorough training and certification of fitness. Why not require as much of a trial judge who daily operates on the lives and fortunes of others? We would not dream of permitting an engineer to run a train, or a pilot to fly a passenger-plane, unless he demonstrated his ability to do his job. Is the job of a trial judge less exacting, less important?

Of course, I do not mean that mere training will endow a man with the character and native capacities a first-rate trial judge ought to have. Nor do I mean that, in spite of the fact that they received no adequate systematic training, many of our present trial judges, men of the highest character, have not, through years of experience, acquired the requisite competence. But it is too much a matter of chance that they have done so. Moreover, it is unfair to have a trial judge attain his competence through operating on litigants in his first years on the bench. For that reason—because I feel my own lack of equipment—I hesitate now to sit as a trial judge, although, as a member of the SEC, for a period I did something like trial-judging.

To avoid misunderstanding, I shall restate something I said in Chapter XIV: The trial judge who has not engaged in intensive self-exploration sometimes has some gross prejudices which lawyers can discern and which at times assist them somewhat in guessing his decisions. Probably, then, decisions by trial judges educated according to my program would be less, not more, predictable.[9] So my program would increase, not diminish, the obstacles to a "science of legal prediction."

[9] See Frank, *Law and the Modern Mind* (1930) 134.

2

Even as matters now stand, many a trial judge is superior to most juries. After a few years on the bench, the judge has gone through a long series of trials, as most jurors have not. He knows, better than most jurymen, how to size up witnesses, to make allowance for the effects on them of the strangeness of testifying in court, to see through the lawyer's stratagems, to minimize his own prejudices, and how to apply the legal rules. Were we to provide and require special training for trial judges, the superiority of judge-trials would markedly increase.

To be sure, the trial judge is, and will be, a sort of jury, for his gestalts will usually be the crucial factors in his decisions. We must trust some human beings to make court decisions by appraising the evidence. It is, I think, wiser to trust a competent, honest judge, with a trained intuition, than twelve inexperienced laymen.

I urged, you recall, that, when juries sit, special or fact verdicts should be required. Such a verdict has one feature which, in the light of my subsequent discussion, may seem undesirable to you: Since a special verdict separates the *F* and the *R*—assigning the one to the jury and the other to the judge—it may mean that the decision will not result from a gestalt. The decision may thus be too artificial, too "logical," in Professor Langer's terms. I confess that this problem puzzles me.

If we want to have laymen participate in the decisions of some kinds of cases, perhaps we should adopt the practice (now employed in several European countries and in some of our states) of having a few laymen sit with the trial judge; if those laymen acted solely in an advisory capacity with respect to the facts, the judge's decision would stem from his gestalt.

3

Our procedures on appeal are today excessively formal. The trial judge is walled off from the upper-court judges. They may not consult him. They learn about the trial only from a formal printed record. This practice complicates and artificializes appeals. I think that, at any rate whenever the upper-court judges deem it desirable, the trial judge should sit with them on the hearing of an appeal, but that he should have no vote. He could then point to facts in the record to which neither litigant had directed the upper court's attention.[10] This is not a new idea. It means a return to a practice which once prevailed in some English and in some American courts.

[10] Service on an upper court has taught me that sometimes an important record fact, to which the trial judge would have directed attention, is overlooked by the upper court.

XVIII. THE CULT OF THE ROBE[1]

An important deterrent to public comprehension of the human characteristics of judges is the curious way in which they dress. The pretense that judicial reactions are uniform manifests itself in the demand that judges wear uniforms.

In the service of our federal government, no one other than judges wears a uniform except members of the armed forces, elevator-starters and operators. The costumes of the servicemen and of the elevator-workers have utility. The robe of the judge is an antique garment, awkward, impractical, and, to the dispassionate eye, of no aesthetic value. It is of a piece with the "Hear ye! Hear ye!" that opens court sessions, and the quaint medieval Latin and the obsolete Norman French often incorporated in judicial opinions.

Robes and such court-house verbiage symbolize the notion that courts must always preserve the ancient ways; that the past is sacred, and change impious. According to this notion, what has heretofore been done must be right; improvements, and experimentation in novelties are always unwise; the populace must never profanely seek to modify inherited customs and institutions. While this idea prevailed, the courts tended to frown upon the work of the legislatures. In innumerable decisions, the judges did what they could to whittle down new statutes, regarding them with ill-concealed contempt as alien to the Common Law and presumptively wrong. This attitude was anti-democratic. For our legislators, elected for relatively short terms, reflect popular views. The legislature is, par excellence, the democratic instrument. Happily, of recent years, we see a new judicial attitude emerging. Many judges now give legislation proper consideration, believing, not without cause, that the legislature is the voice of the people. Unfortunately, however, too many judges still resent legislation. Robe-ism is still too much with us.

Judicial conservatism, to be sure, should not be scorned. Tradition, it should be remembered, is the prime support of social stability. Like those of the single individual, the bulk of society's actions must be semi-automatic. Tradition is economical, a saver of minds and time. It has

1 Part of this chapter was published, under the title, "The Cult of the Robe," in 28 *Saturday Review of Literature* (1945) 41.

been wisely said that, where no great principle is involved, "the trite way is generally the short way." Too, the trite way often means the sensible acceptance of old solutions; about taken-for-granted issues there is danger in raising too many questions at once.

But an intelligent judiciary must be alert to discern the difference between stability and paralysis. Not that the judiciary should itself avidly innovate. "Judge-made law" there has always been and always will be, but it should have a relatively narrow range.[2] The matter is basically different, however, when it comes to legislative "law"-making by statutes. The Constitution sets wide bounds to legislation, and enactments that stay within those bounds wise judges will not frustrate. If we believe in democracy, the courts must not be used to prevent democracy from working out new adaptations.

The judge's vestments are historically connected with the desire to thwart democracy by means of the courts. Characteristically it was democratic Thomas Jefferson who opposed any distinctive judicial raiment for federal judges, while it was aristocratic Alexander Hamilton, his eye on the 18th-century English mode, who advocated both robes and wigs. (Incidentally, as a federal judge, I am glad, when the mercury is high in the column, that Hamilton's judicial head-gear lost out.) In most state courts, however, the judges did not deck themselves out in the atavistic robe until the last decades of the 19th century—at a time when, significantly, conservative lawyers were hoping to utilize the courts as a bulwark against the rising Populist movement.

The judges were oracles of an impersonal "higher law," a body of "law" absolute and infallible—so believed many who sponsored the judge's gown. Therefore, this garment of sacerdotal origin was appropriate, clothing its wearer with the dignity that befits the augur. Others, more skeptical of the law's divinity, nevertheless appreciated the public effect of priestly trappings. They were astute in this perception. In the minds of altogether too many persons the judicial garb inspires excessive awe. Hughes, as Secretary of State, was fallible; Van Devanter, as Solicitor for Interior, was not beyond criticism. But, as judges, clad in their solemn black silk, they automatically became (for much of the public) if not as sacred as once was Japan's Emperor, at least brushed with divinity.

Of course, no such change occurs in a man with the mere donning of a robe. At least in my case it didn't. When I woke up one morning a federal judge, I found myself just about the same person who had

[2] See further, Chapters XIX and XXI.

gone to bed the night before an SEC Chairman. My intimate acquaintance with judges confirms my impression that the robe works no major transformation. Public knowledge of that fact will be all to the good.

An American President or Senator has no garment to betoken dignity; if he has true dignity, all will know it. So of the man on the bench: If he deserves respect, he will receive it, although he be dressed in a business suit. But, unfortunately, the bigoted judge, the ignorant judge, can often effect a false show of dignity. Become a judge, the mediocre lawyer can avail himself of the robe to conceal his incompetence: The robe will cover up the man. Worse, his false pomp often nourishes pomposity, and he browbeats the laymen who appear before him.

His robe, we say, gives him prestige. But remember that "prestige" derives from a word meaning delusion, and from the same root as "prestidigitator"—a sleight-of-hand performer who "puts things over" by trickery on his audience. Long ago, Pascal sensed this fact. To compel respect for judicial decisions, "august apparel" is necessary, he wrote. Curiously enough, defenders of this judicial apparel cite Pascal as authority—forgetting to note that this philosopher added, "If magistrates had true justice," they would require no such paraphernalia. Pascal touched the nerve of the matter. The robe, as ceremonial costume, functions as part of a rite, and rites have deep roots in the tabu. An institution ritually protected by tabu is fenced off from the attack of critical reason. So the robe serves to shield the judges and their ways from rational inquiry. Unintelligibility, so anthropologists tell us, far from invalidating a rite, "positively supports it by deepening the atmosphere of mystery."

A "priestly tribe" some lawyers have called the judges. One legal writer has described them as persons into "whose hands are confided the ark of the covenant of our fathers." Tocqueville said that the American legal profession constitutes an aristocracy, forming "the most powerful, if not the only, counterpoise to the democratic element" in our society, and that American judges have "the instincts of a privileged class"—and Tocqueville has been quoted with approval by many of our ultra-conservative lawyers. One such lawyer has written of "an inner Republic, formed of the Bench and Bar." To these anti-democratic legalists, the robe is a welcome symbol. It announces in impressive terms that the judge is a member of a caste at once mysterious and aristocratic.

The robe, as I have suggested, also gives the impression of uniformity in the decisions of the priestly tribe. Says the uniform black garment to the public mind: Judges attain their wisdom from a single, superhuman source; their individual attitudes must never have any effect on what they decide. Patently that belief is delusional. Else no judge would ever write a dissenting opinion—a practice not of recent vintage, as many persons believe, but in the Supreme Court dating back to 1793, three years after that Court's creation.

Defending the American judicial robe, a distinguished lawyer has said, "It has always been a custom in Great Britain for the judges to wear a wig and gown, and if in that country these adjuncts to dignity were laid aside the country would receive a jolt and look for the beginning of a revolution." A strange argument: Judges in America should dress themselves antiquely because an English revolution would occur if English judges ceased to do so. Moreover, that argument would logically require American judges to wear not only gowns but wigs, which none has done since the close of our American Revolution.

The story of the English judicial wig is illuminating. Until the latter part of the seventeenth century, wigs were not generally used. Then, imported from France where a bald king had created the vogue, they suddenly became popular. Each social class, except the peasantry, adopted a distinctive type of wig: the clergy, the nobility, soldiers, lawyers, businessmen, coachmen. Early in the 18th century reign of George III, the general fashion began to wane, but the professions still retained their uncomfortable headgear. Then the physicians and the military relinquished the style. At the coronation of William IV, the weather being hot, the king permitted the bishops to take off their wigs, which they never put on again. At present the only group to wear the strange head-covering is the British legal profession, the barristers and judges.

Lovers of antiquity will perhaps remark that I am captious. The judges' sartorial distinction, they will say, is but a harmless relic of the past—a pleasant romantic touch, like the open fireplace in a modern steam-heated house. But the robe is no mere romantic survival. It has adverse effects on the administration of justice. An ordinary, honest, citizen, unaccustomed to court-house ways, is often disquieted by the strange garb of the judge and his elevation above the court-room throng; called as a witness, this honest citizen may testify in a manner so constrained and awkward that he gives the impression of not telling the whole truth. For like reasons, the younger lawyers, instead of being properly impressed, are often unduly ill at ease. Recognizing those facts, the late Judge Julian Mack, one of our ablest federal trial judges, refused to wear a robe when presiding at a trial. He went even further, frequently holding trials in his chambers, where he sat at his desk on a level with the witnesses and lawyers.[3] With the formal judicial trappings absent, he found that he could more quickly and easily get at the facts. This also has been the experience of the judges in the Domestic Relations Courts, and was indubitably my own when I participated in holding hearings as an SEC Commissioner.

As unfortunately concealing as the robe is much of the esoteric judicial vocabulary. It is a fundamental democratic principle that no part of government should be secret, that the acts of all government officials should be made public, and should be understood, so far as possible, by the citizens. We have come a long way from the days of the 18th century English aristocracy, when it was a crime to publish Parliamentary debates. Today, except for a few "executive sessions," what ever is said in Parliament or in our own Congress is promptly disclosed. Similarly, almost all trials are public. Judicial secrecy and a free press cannot be reconciled. On that account, judges often publish opinions, statements purporting to reveal their reasons for their decisions. The public, it is said, has the right to learn the grounds upon which cases are decided, and to evaluate their soundness. Yet, as we've seen, judicial opinions usually omit many of the "real reasons," the factors which, to use Rohrlich's description, "dare not be written down." The conventions of judicial opinion-writing—the uncolloquial vocabulary, the use of phrases carrying with them an air of finality, the parade of precedents, the display of seemingly rigorous logic, bedecked with "therefores" and "must-be-trues"—lend an air of thorough certainty, concealing the uncertainties inherent in the judging process. Close examination discloses, as most court opinions do not, that our legal concepts often resemble the necks of the flamingoes in Alice in Wonderland which failed to remain sufficiently rigid to be used effectively as mallets by the croquet-players.[4]

Moreover, the average judicial opinion is so worded that, at best, only lawyers can comprehend it. As Sir Henry Maine noted many years ago, most English and American lawyers believe that the "law" belongs as much to the class of exclusively professional subjects as does the practice of anatomy. There results an esoteric lawyers' jargon. Diplomats

[3] Perhaps he recalled Montaigne's words: "Much good does it do us to mount on stilts, for on stilts we must still walk with our legs; and on the loftiest throne in the world we sit only on our buttocks."

[4] The reference to the flamingoes I have borrowed from Edmund Wilson who used it in connection with literary criticism.

have their cant; so, too, do baseball-players, physicists and philosophers. Wherefore some legal jargon is inevitable. But we have too much of it. The excess helps to keep alive the notion that the springs of decision in judges wholly differ from the springs of decision in other men. It prevents laymen from seeing what judges are doing, prevents them from tuning in.

The publicity given to judicial opinions will, then, remain a good deal of a mockery as long as "law" is regarded as the private possession of a professional guild. This attitude is slowly beginning to break down. It is an idea that should be rejected in toto. The courts should feel obligated to make themselves intelligible to the men on the street or the subway.

Here the robe has its effects: Unfrock the judge, have him dress like ordinary men, become in appearance like his fellows, and he may well be more inclined to talk and write more comprehensibly. Plain dress may encourage plain speaking.

In 1898, Mr. Justice Brewer called it a mistake to suppose that the Supreme Court is either honored or helped by being considered beyond criticism. "On the contrary," he said, "the life and character of its Justices should be the objects of constant watchfulness by all, and its judgments subject to the freest criticism. The time is past in the history of the world when any living man or body of men can be set on a pedestal and decorated with a halo." But many lawyers and judges did not agree with him. Believing in a judicial aristocracy, they believed also in judicial immunity from freedom of the press, a basic principle of a democratic America. Recurrently, a judge has jailed, or fined for "contempt of court," not someone creating a disturbance in the courtroom or refusing to obey a court order, but a newspaper writer who had the temerity to publish a criticism of that judge's official conduct in trying a case. Published criticism in the course of a trial interferes with the proper discharge of judicial duties—such was the excuse given for such a "contempt" sentence. "Liberty of the press," so the argument ran, "is subordinate to the independence of the judiciary." Yet there is no press immunity for a President, a Senator, a Congressmen, Governor or Mayor in the midst of performing his official duties. None of these officials can summarily fine or jail his critics; the most he can do is to institute suit for falsehood or malice. Nor will such a suit, as in the case of the judge, be decided by the maligned official himself. The unique right of the judge to be insulated from adverse comment must rest on the belief in his peculiar sanctity, and his consequent protection from the ordinary democratic processes.

Happily, in 1941, the United States Supreme Court did away with that kind of judicial insulation. In the Bridges contempt case, that Court decided that the Bill of Rights was violated by a judgment of contempt of court for publication of a newspaper article. The founders of our government said the Court, "intended to give to liberty of the press . . . the broadest scope that could be countenanced in an orderly society. . . . The assumption that respect for the judiciary can be won by shielding judges from published criticism wrongly appraises the character of American public opinion. For it is a prized American privilege to speak one's mind, although not always with perfect good taste, on all public institutions. And an enforced silence, however limited, solely in the name of preserving the dignity of the bench, would probably engender resentment, suspicion and contempt much more than it would enhance respect. . . . Legal trials are not like elections, to be won through the use of the meeting-hall, the radio and the newspaper. But we cannot start with the assumption that publications . . . actually do threaten to change the nature of legal trials, and that to preserve judicial impartiality, it is necessary for judges to have a contempt power by which they can close all channels of public expression to all matters which touch upon pending cases."

By this decision, the Supreme Court went far in undermining the myth of judicial divinity. A judge can still legitimately keep order in his court-room. He can still adjudge in contempt for an inflammatory publication likely to create court-room disorder. But he can no longer stifle the rights of free speech and free press when exercised merely to his discomfort.[5] Judges must now recognize that the Supreme Court regards them as no better than other public servants.

Interestingly enough, Mr. Justice Black, who wrote the majority opinion in the Bridges case, a short time later, due doubtless to a lapse of memory even an amateur psychologist could explain, appeared on the bench minus his robe.

The time has come, I think, for all judges to discard their ancient trappings. The robe as a symbol is out of date, an anachronistic remnant of ceremonial government. An immature society may need or like to fear its rulers, but a vital and developing America can risk full equality. A judge who is part of a legal system serving present needs

[5] There is some reason to question whether criticism should be permitted, when trial is by jury, until the final decision is rendered.

should not be clothed in the quaint garment of the distant past. Just as the robe conceals the physical contours of the man, so it needlessly conceals from the public his mental contours. When the human elements in the judging process are covered up, justice operates darklingly. Now that the Supreme Court has declared the judiciary a part of candid democratic government, I think that the cult of the robe should be discarded.

XIX. PRECEDENTS AND STABILITY

Recall, once more, the crude formula which I have used to schematize the conventional description of how courts arrive at their decisions: $R \times F = D$. A court decides a case, it is said, by applying a legal rule (R) to the facts (F) of the particular case. I have heretofore dealt chiefly with the F's, with fact-finding. I shall in this chapter dwell on the R's, assuming, for the present, that the actual facts of any case are readily discoverable.

A legal rule, as I have remarked, may be roughly defined as a statement, in general terms, of allowable or forbidden conduct. It says that, if certain kinds of facts occur, then the courts will attach specified consequences to those facts. For example, a rule says that, if a man steals, a court will order him jailed; if he breaks a contract, it will order him to pay damages.

Analytically, the making of any such rule is an act of legislation, or, as it is often ambiguously put, of "law-making." Now the judicial function, in this country, some suppose, is solely that of deciding disputes by applying to particular cases the legal rules which are the products of legislation. One might think, then, that our courts, being judicial bodies, never make any of the rules. For, under our Constitutions, the function of legislating seems to be assigned solely to legislatures—to Congress in our national government, to state legislatures in our state governments. These legislatures make rules embodied in what are called statutes. If a court attempted to enact a statute, it would be acting in violation of the Constitution.

Nevertheless, although many of the legal rules, which courts apply, come from statutes, yet a vast number of such rules can be found in no statute. They have been made by the judges. In other words, if we define rule-making as legislation, the courts have extensively engaged in legislation, in what is called "judicial legislation." We thus have two kinds of legislation, which might be termed, respectively, "legislative legislation" and "judicial legislation." In the second category, that of judge-made rules, are most of those rules relating to so-called "torts"— the rules concerning negligence or intentional harms, such as give rise to "accident" cases, or to suits about assaults, or about libel and slander. Also among judge-made rules are those stating what constitutes a binding contract, when a contract is broken, how much damages must be paid for a breach of contract.

"No intelligent lawyer would in this day pretend that the decisions of the courts do not add to and alter the law," said Pollock, a distinguished English jurist. "Judge-made law is real law," wrote Dicey, another famous legal commentator, "though made under the form of, and often described by judges . . ., as the mere interpretation of law. . . . Whole branches, not of ancient but of very modern law have been built up, developed or created by action of the courts." "I take judge-made law as one of the realities of life," said Cardozo. And again: "Hardly a rule of today but may be matched by its opposite of yesterday. . . . These changes or most of them have been wrought by judges. The result has been not merely to supplement or modify; it has been to revolutionize and transform." Judge Young of New Hampshire said in 1917: "It is idle to say that the court does not legislate, that the constitution forbids it; for even a casual reading of the reports will show that it makes rules and applies them to determine the rights of the parties. . . ."

Yet, during the 19th century, most American judges and lawyers stoutly maintained the contrary. The story they told was this:[1] The body of legal rules go to make up something called "Law," or the "Common Law." Judges never have and never will make Law—that is, legal rules. Those rules pre-existed all court decisions. The judges merely find or discover these pre-existing rules, just as Columbus discovered America. The courts no more invent new rules than Columbus invented the new world when he found it. If a rule announced in a former case is later rejected by a court, it is an error to say that a new rule has been contrived. One must say that the old rule never existed. It was a false map of the "Law"—just as a pre-Columbian map was false. The judge who announced the rule in the former decision must have had bad eyesight, for he had made a mistake in "finding" the "Law." Calvin Coolidge, expressing the prevailing 19th century attitude, wrote, "Men do not make laws. They do but discover them. . . . That state is most fortunate in its form of government which has the aptest instruments for the discovery of laws."

As Sir Henry Maine put it, "When a group of facts comes before a court for adjudication, . . . it is taken absolutely for granted that there is somewhere a rule of known law which will cover the facts of the

[1] I am borrowing from my book, *Law and the Modern Mind* (1930) 32-33.

dispute now litigated, and that, if such a rule be not discovered, it is only that the necessary patience, knowledge or acumen, is not forthcoming to detect it. The uninformed listener would conclude that court and counsel unhesitatingly accept a doctrine that somewhere, *in nubibus,* or *in gremio magistratum,* there existed a complete, coherent, symmetrical body of . . . law, of an amplitude sufficient to furnish principles which would apply to any conceivable combination of circumstances."

Gray punctured this absurd notion when he asked, "What was the law in the time of Richard Coeur de Lion on the liability of a telegraph company to the persons to whom a message was sent?" Previously Austin had referred to the "childish fiction employed by our judges, that judiciary or common law is not made by them, but is a miraculous something made by nobody, existing, I suppose, from eternity and merely declared from time to time by the judges."

This fiction—or, rather, this myth—works harm. It misleads. Judge Young regarded it as "impolitic and calculated to discredit the courts." Roscoe Pound has said that the vice of pretending that judges never create but merely discover pre-existing rules of law is that sooner or later men will "insist upon knowing where the pre-existing rule was to be found before the judges discovered and applied it, in what form it existed, and how and whence it derived its form and obtained its authority. And when, as a result of such inquiries," the truth comes out, the public concludes that "the courts are exercising a usurped authority." The public grows distrustful of judicial double-talk.

There is this much of truth to the myth: When a court makes a legal rule, it does not do so by a statute. It does so in this way: A court decides a law-suit. The court sometimes gives its reasons for its decision. It says that, with the facts as it finds them, certain legal consequences follow. It states the consequences of those facts in terms of a generalization, that is, a rule. Then another law-suit occurs. The facts, as there found, are much like, but not exactly the same as, those in the previous suit. Nevertheless, the court applies the same generalization or rule. In a third suit, the facts seem sufficiently different to require a different generalization, or an exception to the former rule. Thus, by case-to-case decisions, the courts evolve the legal rules. The particular "suits are controlled by the rules," says Walton Hamilton, but "in the aggregate the rules are determined by the suits." The courts contrive those rules. Without possible doubt, they are judge-made.

These judge-made rules, at least when first made, reflect the views of the judges as to desirable social policies. Or rather, in those rules, said a great lawyer, Thayer, the judges should seek to express "the opinion of the community as to what is just and expedient." The word "expedient" is significant. It directs attention to the fact that, although the judges have often been only dimly aware of it, initially most of the judge-made rules represent judicial compromises or adjustments between conflicting social interests, and thus express judgments of value or policy. That is what Holmes meant when he said that "the growth of the law," though the work of the courts, is "legislative" in that it is "traceable" to the judge's "convictions" or "intuitions" of "public policy."[2] Just as legislative bodies, in enacting statutes, work out adjustments between rival interests, so have judges done in making the judge-made rules.[3] Each court, when making or revising such a rule is, so to speak, a sort of miniature legislative assembly, Congress, or Parliament.

2

In each of our states, and in the federal government, there exists a hierarchy of courts: There are trial courts; (usually) intermediate courts of appeal; and a highest court of appeal.[4] Judge-made legal rules announced by a court ranking higher in any judicial system are binding upon and usually followed by courts lower in rank. On the whole, the contriving of such rules is a function not of the trial courts but of those above it, the upper courts, especially the highest courts.[5]

Now suppose that, having contrived a rule, based upon its conscious or unconscious conception of social policy, a court, when a later similar case arises, reconsiders that rule and believes it made a mistake, believes that the policy behind that rule is undesirable, socially harm-

[2] See Stone, "Fallacies of the Logical Form," in the volume, *Interpretations of Modern Legal Philosophies* (1947) 696.

[3] This idea, going back to Aristotle, forcibly stated in the 19th century by Jhering, was popularized in this country by Dean Roscoe Pound. It permeates the Restatements of "law," published by the American Law Institute, an organization composed of eminent judges, lawyers and teachers of law. Many of those men were by no means radical; prominent among them were such as former Senator George Wharton Pepper. For a fiery attack, nevertheless, on the idea of judicial balancing of interests as heretical and subversive, see Thornton, "Balancing of Community Interests," 35 *Amer. Bar Ass'n. J.* (1949) 473. As to Pound, see Patterson, "Pound's Theory of Social Interests," in the volume *Interpretations of Modern Legal Philosophies* (1947) 558.

[4] In the federal system, the trial courts are the District Courts, the intermediate appeal courts are the Courts of Appeal, and the highest court is the Supreme Court.

[5] See Chapter XXI as to the limited scope of intermediate appeal courts.

ful, "unjust" if you please—believes that newly emerging or previously submerged interests or moral values should receive legal recognition and protection in a new or altered rule. Will the court, should the court, abandon or modify that rule, substituting one which it thinks more desirable, more "just?"

Here we come to the problem of following precedents. "A precedent," as its name discloses, is what has preceded, what has been done in the past. Ought a court follow one of its precedents which states a legal rule, even if, on reconsideration, it thinks that rule should not have been so stated, or should now be revised? The conventional answer is generally yes. This answer is known as the doctrine of precedents. Sometimes it is labeled by the Latin words *stare decisis* which come from the maxim, *Stare decisis, et non quieta movere,* meaning, "Adhere to the decisions and do not unsettle things which are established." If that were the unvarying practice, the judges would resemble a kind of caterpillar called "processional" because "the larvae have the instinct of moving in single file, . . . touching one another head to tail. The experiment has been made of so directing the front caterpillar of such a procession that its head came to touch the tail of the last one, a closed ring being thus formed. For a whole week these caterpillars continued to walk round and round, after one another." [6]

For, if actually and rigorously adopted, the precedent doctrine would mean this: No matter how absurd or unwise or unjust a legal rule, once announced by a court, may turn out to be, that court must not, cannot properly, change it, but must go on endlessly applying it until the legislature, by a statute, intervenes. As the legislature often does not intervene, the precedent doctrine, as avowed by some of the courts and generally praised by the lawyers, has led to severe criticism of the legal profession by many non-lawyers. "It is a maxim among lawyers," wrote Swift, "that whatever has been done before may legally be done again, and therefore they take special care to record all the decisions formerly made against common justice and the general reason of mankind. These, under the name of precedents, they use as authorities to justify iniquitous opinions, and the judges never fail to direct accordingly." In like vein, Voltaire referred to lawyers as "the conservators of ancient barbarous usages."

If you listen to what many judges have *said,* and disregard what they have *done,* you will probably feel that such strictures are justified. For

[6] Fox, *The Personality of Animals* (1947) 105.

judges, in their opinions, have repeatedly affected a "hard-boiled" air, a sadistic manner. "The courts," one will find them declaring, cannot depart from an old rule "to do justice in a particular case." "The court is governed by the principle of law, and not by the hardship of any particular case." "It is better for the public that courts should adhere to general established rules, than that those rules should yield to circumstances of compassion in particular cases, however strong." "The court is not permitted to indulge its feelings at the expense of unsettling the law, or to break with the decided cases to sympathize with the petitioner's misfortune." "The case, perhaps, may be hard, but the law has made it so."

These statements of compelled, but rather proud and dignified cruelty, are seemingly of the essence of the *stare decisis* doctrine. "When a question has once been judicially considered and answered," we are advised, "it must be answered in the same way in all subsequent cases in which the same question again arises." A writer, in 1929, describing the precedent doctrine, said: "It is founded on the . . . theory that it is essential for the law to be certain, and that to attain that certainty it is worthwhile to sacrifice justice in occasional cases."

In sum, the doctrine of *stare decisis* seems to mean that certainty outweighs justice: Let certainty be achieved though injustice be done and the heavens fall. Since to follow precedents will presumably produce certainty, some courts say that they feel obligated to consecrate their former blunders. "Stability and certainty in the law are of the first importance," said an Ohio court. "Hardship may sometimes result from a stern adherence to general rules. This is unavoidable. . . ." It is "of more importance that a rule should be fixed and stable than it should be strictly just." Said another judge, "Where things are settled and rendered certain, it will not be so material how, so long as they are so, and that all people know how to act." "The natural tendency of a well-trained judge," wrote Dicey, "is to feel that a rule which is certain and fixed . . . promotes justice more than good laws which are liable to change or modification."

3

Several arguments have been advanced in support of this harsh doctrine. (1) The first is an argument of justice. Justice, it is said, requires equality of treatment. It would be intolerable, so the argument goes, if the rule applied when Mr. Wiseman sues Mr. Simple were not applied when the same question arises subsequently in a suit of Mr. Bold against Mr. Timid. To prevent such a result, it is said to be necessary that a court, deciding a particular case, should not act on its sense of fairness, in the case before it, but should consider what has heretofore been decided in like cases. Only so can caprice and subjectivity be precluded. Through following precedents, courts achieve uniformity, continuity, objectivity, and, thereby equality. Via the courts' respect for precedents, says Salmond, the "law" is rendered impartial. "It has no respect of persons. Just or unjust, wise or foolish, it is the same for all. . . . In the application and enforcement of a fixed and predetermined rule, alike for all and not made for or regarding his case alone, a man will willingly acquiesce."

That is indeed a powerful argument. "Equality before the law" is a properly cherished principle. Yet it ought not to be pushed to ridiculous limits. Merely because a court was outrageously unfair to Mr. Simple in 1900 is a poor reason for being equally unfair to Mr. Timid in 1947. Thus to perpetuate a markedly unjust rule seems a queer way of doing justice. Even if "justice" did so command, it would seem wise that a bad rule should not endure forever. As Wigmore remarked, "Equality is something desired for persons *now*" before the courts; "it does not call for sameness of treatment between those of the present and those of the past or the future generation. Allowing, therefore, a short time before and after now, as necessary for the consequences of equality with our own generation, equality calls for no longer period of stare decisis." [7]

(2) A more powerful argument for *stare decisis* rests on the need for stability. Only if rules are certain and stable, it is said, can men conduct their affairs with safety. This argument assumes that most men do conduct their affairs relying on certain legal rules. However, one of America's greatest lawyers, John Chipman Gray, expressed skepticism on that score. He had in mind that, all too often, a man does not know his legal rights until after a decision in a law-suit involving those rights, that those rights are thus not knowable until that decision, and that the decision is therefore retroactive. "Practically, in its application to actual affairs, for most of the laity, the law," Gray said, "except for a few crude notions of the equity involved in some of its general principles, is all *ex post facto*. When a man marries, or enters into a partnership, or engages in any other transaction, he has

[7] *The Science of Legal Method* (1917) Editorial Introduction.

the vaguest possible idea of the law governing the situation, and with our complicated system of jurisprudence, it is impossible it should be otherwise. If he delayed to make a contract or do an act until he understood exactly all the consequences it involved, the contract would never be made or the act done. Now the law of which a man has no knowledge is the same to him as if it did not exist." Cardozo, somewhat more cautiously, said much the same: "No doubt there is need to consider whether men have acted in good faith on the assumption that the rule will be continued. If they have, retrospective change may be forbidden. . . . Such cases of legitimate reliance upon established wrong . . . are rarer in my judgment than some of us suppose."

However, some men sometimes do consult their lawyers before embarking on business ventures. Those men sometimes can fairly be said to have relied on the precedents. But if such reliance is advanced by a litigant as the reason why a court should refuse to abandon an unjust or unwise rule, then the court might well declare, "Prove to us that, in actual fact, you did thus rely. If you did not, we will not hestiate to over-rule this undesirable precedent. If you did rely on it, then we'll follow it in your case; but we hereby serve notice that we will not follow it in any other subsequent cases unless actual reliance is also proved in those cases." Some few courts have taken that position.[8]

But without any proof of actual reliance, most courts say that, in any event, they will not reject a precedent establishing a "rule of property," no matter how unjust or foolish it may now appear to be. The courts declare that they feel far more free to depart from a rule relating to evidence, procedure, or negligence.[9] That distinction is somewhat questionable. A change in a rule of evidence or procedure, or as to negligence, may cause a litigant to lose a case which he would otherwise have won. As the money he pays as loser comes out of his property, the change in the rule, whatever its label, adversely affects his property. Or a new rule of evidence or negligence may drastically affect the earnings of an insurance company; and the value of that company's "property" rests almost entirely on its earnings. So it is arguable that the real test should always be actual reliance—that, if such reliance is shown, if a litigant has substantially changed his position because he relied on an old rule, then it ought not to matter what kind of rule it

[8] See my dissenting opinion in Commissioner v. Hall's Estate, 153 F. (2d) 172 at 175, and my concurring opinion in Aero Spark Plug Co. v. B. G. Corp. 130 F. (2d) at 298.

[9] Recall Pound's distinction, referred to in Chapter IV, between "property" or "commercial" cases and negligence cases.

is, but he ought to be able to have it applied, unaltered, in his case. Congress has so provided by statute with reference to some rules of an administrative agency, the SEC.[10] Why should not the courts do much the same as to their own rulings?

Absent such actual reliance on a rule, the stability argument seems to be irrational:[11] Assume that a judge-made rule embodies a court's past view of social policy. Why should a view of policy once expressed by a court be beyond recall by that same court? Why should the policy be frozen? Why should the judicial power to formulate a policy be exhausted by an erroneous exercise of that power? The judicial practice of adhering to a rule embodying an unjust policy seems itself to be a policy—a policy of doing injustice.

Courts, when they apply *stare decisis* in hard cases, say, "We regret our inability to avoid this unjust rule. But we can do nothing to be rid of it. The legislature alone can undo it." Why should that be so? Why wait for the legislature? The underlying assumption is that the legislature should and will promptly rectify the unjust judge-made rule. In truth, legislatures sometimes are extremely tardy in doing that job. But, aside from that difficulty, note the inconsistency of the court's position: It refuses to alter its own admittedly unjust rule for fear of causing instability. Yet it invites the legislature to wipe out that rule. Will not the legislature, if it accepts that invitation, cause as much instability? Why, then, should a court look to the legislature to remove an injustice created by the court itself? Legislatures repeal rules which legislatures have made. Why should not courts do the same with rules they have made?

I would differentiate to this extent: In some instances a legislature may rescind a rule on which men have relied. *If I could revise the precedent doctrine, it would require that a court should never change a rule, retroactively, in its application to any person when the court has reason to believe that he actually relied on that rule and would be harmed substantially by the change; but the court would be free to change an unjust rule as to all other persons, both retroactively and prospectively.*

When judges, refusing to depart from an unjust precedent, on which

10 See the Public Utility Holding Company Act: "No provision of this chapter imposing any liability shall apply to any act done or omitted in good faith in conformity with any rule, regulation, or order of the Commission, notwithstanding that such rule, regulation, or order may, after such act or omission, be amended or rescinded or be determined by judicial or other authority to be invalid for any reason."

11 See Frank, *Law and the Modern Mind* (1930) 213, note, second paragraph; Commissioner v. Hall's Estate, 153 F. (2d) at 175.

there has been no reliance, say that "hard cases make bad law," I think that, instead, they usually should say, "Bad 'law' makes hard cases. If an unjust decision is the logical result of a rule, then that rule should be changed." (I shall note some exceptions later).

(3) Still another argument for *stare decisis* is that, without it, the "beauty and symmetry" of the legal system would be destroyed. The preservation of the aesthetic proportions of a legal system seem to me a ridiculous excuse for working injustice.

(4) Another argument, seldom openly expressed but not entirely without influence, was assigned by a famous English judge, Lord Ellenborough: "If," he said, "this rule were to be changed, a lawyer who was well stored with these rules would be not better than any other man without them." In other words, the judge was taking care of his brothers at the bar, the lawyers' guild or labor union. Surely lawyers ought to have no vested interest in injustice. Ellenborough's reasoning would serve as a permanent obstacle to a change of bad rules even by statutes. I confess I don't think much of it.

(5) Still another argument is the convenience of the judges. When they have grown accustomed to applying a rule, they find it irksome to readjust their habits. I suspect that something of that sort is what judges have in the back of their minds when they say that, regardless of the hardship which ensues, bad rules must not be changed else "the law ceases to be a system." For a settled system is easier for judges to operate than a set of variable and mutable rules. But this argument, too, is largely untenable. I happen to be a judge sitting in an upper court where application of legal rules is my daily job.[12] But I regard my convenience of trifling importance as compared with injustice to citizens caused by bad rules. I think that, if the precedent system means the perpetuation of judge-made rules, shown to be unjust or undesirable, rules on which no one has been proved to rely, then usually the courts, when they accept that system, are not performing their function—the administration of justice. They are administering injustice.

4

Let me now, instead of justifying, try to explain the precedent system. First and foremost is habit. Every institution—a telephone company, an athletic club, a debating society—builds up habit patterns, precedents. It could not get on without them. Routines save time.

[12] But see Chapter XXI as to the limited scope of the court in which I sit.

In more general terms, some acceptance of precedents stems from inevitable inertia. In all aspects of life, individual or social, there is resistance to change. Men have a feeling of pleasure in identification with customary ways.[13] There seem to be deep-lying physiological and psychological bases for hostility to change.[14]

Innovations call for adjustments which may cause emotional disquietude. "All experience hath shown," says our Declaration of Independence, "that mankind are more disposed to suffer, while evils are sufferable, than to right themselves by abolishing the forms to which they are accustomed." Men often dread the new. It seems dangerous: "Not to venture is not to lose." Many of us today are not very different from "primitive" men; and often a man in "primitive" society, writes Read, "exposes himself to serious trouble who . . . thinks of substituting a new track, even though it be shorter and more suitable, for the usual one. The fact is that a track has its own secret potencies. One has had experience of it, and, so long as this experience is not unpleasant, one preserves the track: what would happen with a new road? Is it not the wisest course to pass with the utmost care by the places by which everyone else has already passed?" Fear, then, seems to play a role in adherence to precedents. We see, again, symptoms of that "institutionalizing of a fear neurosis" which I called legal magic.

In part, that fear is a hangover from the anxieties of early childhood. The young child fears the unknown, the uncertain, the changeable; he craves the security which complete stability seems to promise.[15] Emotional immaturity in adult years perpetuates these childish attitudes. Inquiry into the rightness of established ways and scrutiny of new alternatives, demand an open mind, suspended judgment. But, as I have suggested, there is "pain involved in suspended judgment" because of the "drag of childish nostalgia for the over-secure and the impossibly serene," so that most men, most of the time, prefer routines, thus "avoiding the pain of suspended judgment."[16]

Especially are professional or other groups of specialists addicted to set ways. Even the natural scientists, presumably inspired by the spirit of intellectual adventuring, are by no means free of stick-in-the-mud-

[13] See Aristotle, *Politics* 1448b, 5-19; *Rhetoric,* 1371b, 5-9.

[14] For expansion of this theme, see Hoffman v. Palmer, 129 F. (2d) 976, 996-97, citing the interesting work of Stern. See also Rignano's views summarized in Frank, *Law and the Modern Mind* (1930) 323.

[15] See Frank, Law and The Modern Mind (1930) 13-19, 165, 248ff., 361.

[16] Frank, *Law and the Modern Mind* (1930) 160-67; see also Chrestensen v. Valentine, 122 F. (2d) 511 at 521 as to "judicial anguish."

ism.[17] The medical profession is almost as much precedent-ridden as the legal. Partly such devotion to past ways involves a sort of ancestor-worship; veneration for one's predecessors is often given as a reason for sticking to precedents. Partly it involves pride: Judges, like doctors and others, are reluctant to admit they made mistakes. Then, too, there is plain old-fashioned animal laziness. It's a nuisance to revise what you have once settled. Out of such laziness comes what Holmes called "one of the misfortunes of the law," that "ideas become encysted in phrases and thereafter for a long time cease to provoke further analysis."[18]

But, I repeat, don't be too harsh in your criticism of the judges. "If," says Walton Hamilton, "businessmen, university faculties, baseball players or debutantes were forced to set down the . . . reasons for the decisions which make up their streams of conduct," the result "would resemble the" judicial process. George, writing of the "scientist in action," says that man is a "patterning animal" with a dislike of the tension he experiences when something is seen as an "uncompleted pattern." There is in all human beings a desire to "tidy things up," to put coins in a row or books on shelves. The scientist is often impatient to reach a pattern, to complete an over-neat theory. Bridgman, a scientist, observes in all men an impulse to consistency which is "often elevated into an end and a good in itself," regardless of its practical value. He makes a comment to which judges should attend: "This impulse to consistency springs [often] from mental limitations, not from mental strength . . . It may be evidence of mental caliber of the very highest order to be able suddenly to stop running in one direction and at once start running in the other under the impact of a new idea." But, he adds, "there is a ludicrousness in the sight of such a performance" which usually inhibits it. The unwillingness to look ludicrous may, in some measure, explain that judicial eagerness to appear consistent which accounts partially for stare decisis.

To that extent, precedent-following merits no great praise. Nor does it, in so far as it has its roots in emotional immaturity. For with emotional adult-hood, "doubt and inquiry should no longer be unpleasant, but should, rather, become a source of . . . satisfaction. The constant effort to achieve a stable equilibrium, resembling sleep, is . . . immature. The . . . welcome of new doubts, the keen interest in probing into

[17] Frank, "The Place of The Expert in a Democratic Society" (Brandeis Lawyers' Society, 1944, reprinted in 16 *Phil. of Science,* 1949).

[18] 225 U.S. at 391.

the usual, the zest of adventure in investigating the conventional—these are life-cherishing attitudes. . . . If justice is to be capably administered, judges must be trained to put a premium on their dynamic tendencies. . . . Such men will not talk of 'rules' and 'principles' as finalities while unconsciously using them as soporifics to allay the pains of uncertainty." [19]

Yet, other things equal, a smooth-running habit system has its advantages. The administrative convenience of judges is not to be ignored, for, somewhat legitimately, they do not want to be swamped with too many novel problems. "A court," writes Green, "will not knowingly enter upon a course of dealing which may bring down upon it an increase in business or a mass of problems which it is not prepared to handle. On the other hand, even though a rule or practice has become antiquated and no longer meets the requirements of business, ethics, or justice, if it works easily, and judges understand its operation, they will hesitate to discard it for some improved practice not yet accepted generally even though the latter promises much greater utility. The caution of courts is due primarily to this influence rather than to that over-stressed . . . notion represented by *stare decisis*. Or, stated differently, the doctrine of precedent is weighty, not so much because courts either dislike improvement or feel themselves bound by prior decisions, but because changes require all sorts of adjustments that cannot be anticipated. . . . It is little wonder that opposition is encountered when the integrity of the court's scheme of things is threatened by some new doctrine or new practice, or new demand for relief."

But the result has not been all that was expected. The precedent system perhaps causes increased work for judges. Green thinks so. "It creates," he says, "infinitely more difficulties than it renders benefits. For one thing a court's scheme of things may become so ponderous in the course of time that the succeeding judges cannot possibly know what their predecessors have done. Courts . . . doubtless spend more time trying to maintain a consistency of decision than on any other one problem. Moreover, this feeling that a court must drag along the dead part of itself creates a psychological deadweight of tremendous import." [20]

[19] Frank, *Law and the Modern Mind* (1930) 166.
[20] See Wigmore, *loc. cit.*

5

The precedent system, as I have thus far described it, seems to cause much injustice and to impede desirable social change. Yet its bark is worse than its bite. It does not really bite when a court follows a precedent which it considers just or wise; or when the judge-made rule it accepts is of a neutral kind, neither just nor unjust, wise nor unwise; or when a court consults and heeds its own or other judges' earlier opinions because those opinions contain sagacious solutions of difficult problems. As I suggested several years ago, "To find 'authority' for a position which they [have already] reached, is . . . pleasing to all men. Precedents often aid thinking; often, too, they allay inner doubts, and help, as rationalizations, to persuade others." [21] The precedent system really bites viciously only when a court, regarding a precedent as undesirable, nevertheless refuses to deviate from it.

There are such cases, without question. But not so many as a superficial observer may think. For the judges know how to get rid of an obnoxious judge-made rule. In 1810, when our Supreme Court was still a young institution, it explicitly over-ruled one of its decisions made two years before. And, ever since, that Court has recurrently indulged in that practice. However, out of deference to the precedent doctrine, direct repudiation is not too frequently utilized. But judges have other ways of sterilizing an obnoxious rule.[22]

(1) *The "Distinguishing" or "Precise Question" Device.*

One such "out" is this: Courts often say that what they decided in some earlier cases must be limited to the "precise question" there involved. At once the query arises, What is a "precise" question? Since the rule announced by a court is, to use Austin's phrase, "implicated with the peculiarities of the specific case," it follows that seldom, if ever, can it be said that one case is so completely identical with another that there is no possible ground for differentiation, that one case, without any conceivable doubt, "runs upon all four feet" with another. To apply the rule laid down in one case to the facts of another case therefore involves "reasoning by analogy," i.e., reasoning that the cases are sufficiently alike so that differences may be ignored. Now the courts have held that, in reasoning by analogy, great care must be exercised that the analogy shall be "close, true and perfect," and that an analogy is rendered inapplicable "by the intervention of material circumstances,

[21] Frank, *If Men Were Angels* (1942) 235.
[22] See Frank, *Law and the Modern Mind* (1930) 148 note; Stone, *loc. cit.*

modifying the case, and bringing it under the application of a different rule of law." The courts maintain that they are at liberty to choose between "competing analogies" when such "modifying circumstances" intervene. "Minute differences in the circumstances of two cases," said a well-known English judge, "will prevent any argument being deduced from one to the other."

Thence arises the interesting lawyers' technique of "distinguishing cases." There are many valuable implements available for that purpose. The most useful is the maxim that it is the decision in a case, and not the language of the opinion of the court, which makes the precedent. "It is a maxim not to be disregarded," said Chief Justice Marshall, "that general expressions in every opinion are to be taken in connection with the case in which those expressions are used. If they go beyond the case, they may be respected, but ought not to control the judgment in a subsequent suit when the very point is presented for decision." An opinion, the courts remark, often "outruns the decision." The United States Supreme Court has stated that an "opinion must be read as a whole in view of the facts on which it was based. The facts are the foundation of the entire structure, which cannot with safety be used without reference to the facts."

That position is sensible. As I said in an opinion:[23] "In formulating the reasons for their decisions, judges often adopt rulings made in previous decisions in which the facts were somewhat similar, saying, in effect, 'This situation is sufficiently like those which we previously considered so that we can disregard the differences and restrict ourselves to the resemblances.' And, thus ignoring—for the purpose immediately at hand—the unlikenesses, the situations are, frequently, spoken of as identical. But elliptical discussions of cases partly alike, as if there were complete identity, is merely for convenience. There is present, although it may be unexpressed, an 'as if,' a 'let's pretend'—a simile or metaphor. Such 'as-if' or metaphorical thinking is invaluable in all provinces of thought (not excepting that of science). However, some of the greatest errors in thinking have arisen from the mechanical, unreflective, application of old formulations—forgetful of a tacit 'as if'—to new situations which are sufficiently discrepant from the old so that the emphasis on the likenesses is misleading and the neglect of the differences leads to unfortunate or foolish consequences. In governmental or business administration, such neglect, when it occurs, provokes justifiable irritation at 'bureaucracy'; in judicial administration it deserves criticism as unen-

[23] United Shipyards v. Hoey, 131 F. (2d) 525, 527.

lightened precedent-mongering." So Judge Cuthbert Pound cautioned lawyers and laymen that "the decision consists in what is done, not what is said by the court in doing it . . . The courts state the general principles but the force of their observation lies in the application of them, and this application cannot be predicted with accuracy."

For the purposes of "sterilizing" earlier decisions, there is available, too, much learning about the distinction between a decision and a "dictum." A "dictum" is defined as "an expression of opinion in regard to some point or rule of law, made by a judge in the course of a judicial opinion, but not necessary to the determination of the case before the court." Such an expression is not to be considered as creating a precedent. But the significant point is that able lawyers often disagree concerning the portions of opinions which are dicta. What one judge calls the "true rule" employed in a decision, another judge may describe as "dictum."

(2) *Verbal Stability.*

A second way of getting around *stare decisis* is to pretend to preserve an old rule by retaining it verbally, while so stuffing the words of the old rule with new meanings that, in practical effect, it becomes a new rule. Many lawyers and judges in the past have resorted to that method, striving "to cover up the transformation, to deny the reality of change, to conceal the truth of adaptation [to new circumstances] behind a verbal disguise of fixity. . . ."[24] As Max Radin says, when a court, "in its desire to secure a just decision," does "homage to stability by forcing the result into an established category in which the decision does not really fit," the stability is "not a real stability."[25] It is but "a stability of words," that "of making merely the same statement" with a different content. Such verbalisms, on careful inspection, sometimes turn out to be hollow. Rignano compares them with the shell which a lobster sheds, but which continues to resemble the lobster that no longer inhabits it: So a word, emptied of all intellectual content, may still be mistaken for a live thought which once dwelled in it.

True, as Radin observes, verbal stability is not without its uses: "To keep the words stable has a value for lawyers because it facilitates the organization of the enormous mass of legal material they must remember. . . ." But even that use of verbal stability may be illusory. For many rules are phrased in "weasel words," loose words with vague meanings—like "due care," "fair dealing," "unfair competition," "in

[24] Frank, *Law and the Modern Mind* (1930) 293.
[25] Radin, "The Trail of the Calf," 32 *Cornell L.Q.* (1946) 137.

the public interest," "reasonable man." They supply a seemingly stable support for unstable, inexact, and fluctuating conceptions. To those who would otherwise be too much distressed by their inability to achieve real legal certainty, such words furnish emotional satisfaction. Yet, for the most part, the satisfaction is but emotionally compensatory, hallucinatory.[26]

Indeed, as I have said elsewhere, "The leaky character of words is not always an unmixed evil. Isn't it lucky that 'democracy' was not frozen in its meaning in 1800? Where would we be if the words in our Constitution had been given inflexible definitions?"[27] Often the instability concealed by ambiguous words cannot be downed. As Kenneth Burke notes,[28] "men's linguistic behavior . . . reflects paradoxes in the nature of the world itself—antimonies that could be resolved only if men were able, not in thought, but in actual concrete operations, to create an entire universe." Many verbal ambiguities are inevitable and thus unavoidable; "instead of considering it our task to 'dispose of' any ambiguity by merely disclosing the fact that it is an ambiguity, we [should] rather consider it our task to clarify the resources of ambiguity." Similarly, Richards says: "The systematic ambiguity of all our most important words is first a cardinal point to note. But 'ambiguity' is a sinister word, and it is better to say 'resourcefulness.' "[29]

(3) *The "Ratio Decidendi" Device.*

There is another device—which seems inconsistent with the "precise-fact" device—often said to be employed in the technique of distinguishing cases. The courts often say that the authoritative part of a decision is neither what was decided nor the rule on which the court based its decision, but is something (lying back of both the decision and the rule) called the *ratio decidendi,*—the "right principle upon which the case was decided."

According to this notion, it is not the decisions that are binding. A much respected English judge, Jessel, phrased it thus: "The only use of . . . decided cases is the establishment of some principle which the judge can follow in deciding the case before him." Or, as Jessel put it, another time, "The only thing in a judge's decision binding as an authority upon a subsequent judge is the principle upon which the case was decided; but it is not sufficient that the case should have been decided on a principle, if that principle itself is not a right principle,

[26] Frank, *Law and the Modern Mind* (1930) 57-63.
[27] Frank, *If Men Were Angels* (1942) 313.
[28] Burke, *A Grammar of Motives* (1945) Introduction and p. 56.
[29] Richards, *How to Read a Page* (1942) 22.

or one not applicable to the case; and it is for a subsequent judge to say whether or not it is a right principle, and, if not, he may himself lay down the true principle."

As depicted by Jessel and some other legal writers, this idea has a delightful vagueness which makes it most helpful in "sterilizing" an awkward precedent. For, if those writers are correct, a court need pay scant heed (a) to the *decision* of the court in any given previous case; or (b) to what the judges who decided a previous case *stated* in their opinion as the *"rule"* of that case; or (c) to what the judges who decided a previous case stated in their opinion as the *"principle"* or as the *ratio decidendi* of that case.

"It is," says Allen, "for the court, of whatever degree, which is called upon to consider the precedent to determine what the true *ratio decidendi* was." That means that the authoritative part of an earlier decision is not the rule announced by a judge in the earlier case, nor what that judge then thought was the principle back of the rule which he thought he was applying. What binds a judge in any present case is what that judge now determines was the "true" principle or "juridical motive" involved in the earlier decision.

For precedential purposes, a case, then, means only what a judge in any later case says it means. Any case is an authoritative precedent only for a judge who, as a result of his own reflection, decides that it is authoritative. "We say that a judge is 'bound' by the decisions of higher courts," remarks Allen. "But the judge is bound only at his own discretion, according to his own judgment. Nothing can make the process of 'binding' merely automatic and mechanical, for the judge has first to decide, according to his lights, whether the illustration is really apposite to the principle he is seeking."[30] "In this way," Green notes, "the same case may be a precedent for as many holdings as there are judges who differ . . . as to the 'principles' involved in the decision." We are, it has been said, "driven . . . to the unsatisfying conclusion that the whole matter ultimately turns on impalpable and indefinable elements of judicial spirit or attitude." A German observer, Gerland, reaches much the same conclusion. Our Anglo-American precedent system, he says, "cannot but lead to subjectively arbitrary judgments." Thus, if these writers are correct, the *stare decisis* doctrine

[30] Allen, *Law in the Making* (1927) Chapter 4. In a third edition (1938), Allen says that I had misinterpreted him in my comments in *Law and the Modern Mind* (1930) 148 note. But see Stone, *loc. cit.* 710.

contributes to that uncertainty-breeding subjectivism, the preclusion of which is the supposed outstanding virtue of that doctrine.

The foregoing is an overdrawn picture of the vagueness caused by the *ratio decidendi* device. But that some of the sort of subjectivity to which Gerland refers does exist is shown by the differences between judges of the same court, as to the meanings of many precedents, evidenced in dissenting opinions.

Stare decisis does not prevent such differences. So, by now, I think you'll see that the precedent doctrine, the precedent theory, is very different from the precedent practice. The theory, at first blush, seems gruesomely cruel. The practice is far less so. Holdsworth, the noted English legal historian, explained that English judges have never followed precedents as slavishly as the theorists have made out.[31] The same is true of American judges. But, because the lawyers and judges go on talking a theory which does not jibe with their practice, the truth about the practice is obscured, and the practice made needlessly difficult.

6

The resultant elaborated over-subtle explications of the judicial precedent system, by lawyers and judges, may seem to you to be unique. It is not. Much the same characteristics can be observed in theological interpretations of sacred texts.[32] In the development of many a religion, there has been a period in which sacred writings, taken as guides for daily living, have been understood by going behind the apparent meanings to the "real" meanings.[33] Especially when the literal meanings clashed with changing moral attitudes, have the theologians had recourse to "secondary meanings," representing the true doctrines, a method resembling that of lawyers who search for the "right principles" underlying the precedents. The theological result has often been a vast structure of subtle interpretations with considerable disagreement among the interpreters.

A. D. White reports that, towards the end of the 17th Century "Voetius declared, 'Not a word is contained in Holy Scriptures which

[31] See also Stone, *loc. cit.*

[32] Radin says: "The problem of what to do with words has been fought out in western culture chiefly in the domain of theology." Radin, "A Short Way with Statutes," 56 *Harv. L. Rev.* (1942) 388, 400.

[33] Radin says that "the theologians did not hesitate to interpret even sacred texts conter les parolles, if reason and justice required." Radin, 38 *Ill. L. Rev.* (1943) at 39.

is not in the strictest sense inspired, the very punctuation not excepted,' and this declaration was echoed back and forth from multitudes of pulpits, theological chairs, synods and councils. Unfortunately it was very difficult to ascertain what the 'authority of Scripture' really was. To the great number of Protestant ecclesiastics it meant the authority of any meaning in the text they had the wit to invent and the power to enforce." Here theological theory approximated legal-precedent theory as depicted by some legal writers. For you will remember what Allen said as to a judge's estimating the worth of a precedent "according to his lights," and Gerland's comment on the individual subjectivism which stems from *stare decisis.* Note again that too much should not be made of this kind of legal subjectivism, for our highest courts do have the same power to utter authoritative interpretations of the precedents, just as in some churches one person or body is empowered to settle theological doctrines.

At another point, too, legal and theological theories seem to coincide: In many religions, at some stage, the theologians regard all parts of a group of separate sacred writings as "interpenetrating, every statement in each fitting exactly into each statement in every other; and each and every one, and all together, literally true to the fact, and at the same time full of hidden meanings." Many lawyers exhibit a similar tendency to find a harmonious unity among judicial precedents regardless of their respective dates. They try to reconcile, as consistent with one another, decisions made, say, in 1710, 1840, 1890 and 1949, ignoring the differences in the social environments of those decisions. In this way, they reach the conclusion that what they call "law" is a logically coherent system of principles based on the immense multiplicity of precedents.

It is of interest to observe that, according to Philo and Josephus, those who wrote the Scriptures "were passive instruments in the hands of God." This view, known among writers on theology as "the mechanical conception of inspiration," was once generally adopted by the Church. It finds an almost complete parallel in the older traditional judicial theology according to which the function of the judges was purely passive. The Law, it was thought, spoke through them. Thence developed the conception of "mechanical jurisprudence." But just as, we are told, some students of theology "perceived that divine inspiration did not override the personalities of prophets or evangelists," so recently some students of "sacred" legal utterances have urged a similar view with respect to judicial opinions.

Resemblances between some theological and some legal methods have caught the attention of several lawyers. Doubtless thinking of the undesirable sort of theologizing, Holmes warned against the idea that legal development consists in the "theological working out of dogmas"; and Dean Leon Green has criticized the "theology of precedents," accompanied by word rituals. An English judge once referred to the judicial repetition of some rules as a cantilena, a kind of pious chant.[34]

7

"Mechanical jurisprudence," or the "theological working out of dogmas" in the courts, takes this form: A court, deciding a case, has laid down a rule; another case arises in which the facts somewhat resemble those in the previous case; extending the rule by analogy to the new case, the court "logically" arrives at its decision of that case. Still another case occurs, and again the court extends the rule in the same way, but without much reflection. Finally a point is reached where this unreflective, "mechanical," process promises to bring about an absurd or unjust decision. Then the court balks. As Holmes once said: "the whole outline of the law is the resultant of a conflict at every point between logic and good sense—the one striving to work fiction out to consistent results, the other restraining and at last overcoming that effort when the results become too manifestly unjust."[35] Holmes' description is admirable, although his use of the word "logic" was not too happy, for the fault usually is not one of logic but rather that of selecting, mechanically, an unwise premise.[36]

8

Perhaps, in the light of what I have said, you will perceive why the precedent system has sometimes been praised for its "flexibility." Curiously, however, some of those who praise it on that account also assert that it ensures certainty, stability and reliability. The patent inconsistency of such a thesis suggests that these defenses of *stare decisis* are not entirely rational, that they are, rather, partially rationalizations.

[34] See Radin, "The Trail of the Calf," 32 *Cornell L.Q.* (1946) 144.

[35] Holmes, "Agency," 4 *Harv. L. Rev.* (1891) reprinted in Holmes, *Collected Legal Papers* (1921) 49, 50.

[36] See Hoernle, Book Review, 31 *Harv. L. Rev.* (1918) 807, 810-811; Frank, "Cardozo and The Upper Court Myth," 13 *Law and Contemp. Problems* (1948) 369, 371-72. For a defense of Holmes's use of the word "logic," see Stone, *loc. cit.*, 721-22, 735 note 216.

Noting the numerous ways of circumventing precedents, it is not difficult to comprehend why some critics say that *stare decisis,* as it actually operates, yields not certainty but uncertainty. "*Stare decisis* is said to be indispensable for securing certainty in the application of the law," wrote Wigmore. "But the sufficient answer is that it has not in fact secured it. Our judicial law is as uncertain as any law could well be. We possess all the detriment of uncertainty, which *stare decisis* was supposed to avoid, and also all the detriment of ancient law-lumber, which *stare decisis* concededly involves—the government of the living by the dead as Herbert Spencer has called it." "Under modern conditions," says Dillon, "it has by some been doubted whether the rule of precedent, in the broad scope and imperativeness which we have given it, is the source of more certainty than uncertainty in law. . . . What is a like case, and whether the precedent is considered erroneous, can often be known only after the judgment of the court in the very case in which the question arises." Judge Cuthbert Pound, one of the most respected of our judges, reported in 1929: "The courts . . . state this doctrine of stability with repetitious and tedious emphasis. Yet it is not infrequently reasoned away to the vanishing point. One may wade through a morass of decisions only to sink into a quicksand of uncertainty."

That *stare decisis,* even in the days when it was most stoutly asserted by the courts, did not breed certainty, can easily be demonstrated by the fact that, even then, hundreds of cases were appealed each year on the ground that the wrong legal rules had been applied in those cases. Most of those appeals would have been absurd if the precedent system abolished legal uncertainty.

Many years ago, when a strict theory of *stare decisis* was in high favor, John Austin, a lawyer with a searching mind, wrote as follows: "A system of judiciary law (as every candid man will readily admit) is nearly unknown to the bulk of the community, although they are bound to adjust to the rules or principles of which it consists. Nay, it is known imperfectly to the mass of lawyers and even to the most experienced of the legal profession. . . . By the great body of the legal profession (when engaged in advising those who resort to them), the law (generally speaking) is divined rather than ascertained. And whoever has seen opinions even of celebrated lawyers must know that they are worded with a discreet and studied ambiguity which, whilst it saves the credit of the uncertain and perplexed adviser, thickens the doubts of the party who is seeking instruction and guidance. And as to the bulk of the community—the simple-minded laity (to whom by reason of their simplicity the law is benign)—they might as well be subject to the mere arbitrium of the tribunals, as to a system of law made by judicial decisions. A few of its rules or principles are extremely simple, and are also exemplified practically in the ordinary course of affairs. Such, for example, are the rules which relate to certain crimes, and to contracts of frequent occurrence. And of those rules or principles, the bulk of the community have some notion. But those portions of the law which are somewhat complex, and are not daily and hourly exemplified in practice, are by the mass of the community utterly unknowable. Of those, for example, who marry, or of those who purchase land, not one in a hundred (I will venture to affirm) has a distinct notion of the consequences which the law annexes to the transaction. . . . Unable to obtain professional advice, or unable to obtain advice which is sound and safe, men enter into transactions of which they know not the consequences, and then (to their surprise and dismay) find themselves saddled with duties which they never contemplated."

In considerable measure, this uncertainty is an inherent part of any healthy legal system. For, even in a stable simple society, cases are sure to arise which are covered by no precedents; and, in our dynamic society, social, economic and political conditions, and values, are constantly changing, and the changes throw up new legal problems. If, in our society, the legal rules remained static, we would be straitjacketted. Some pliancy and fluidity are essential. Much—not all—of the instability of the rules should therefore be deemed not a misfortune but a blessing.[37]

Llewellyn and others suggest that the value of the precedent system lies in this very pliancy of the precedents. Under that system, intelligent judges often can limit or nullify an unfortunate precedent; but such judges, also, by reading former opinions, can learn of the wise formulations made by their predecessors, and can then intelligently expand those rules to decide unprovided cases or to meet newly emerging problems. Much can be said for that defense of stare decisis. But the precedent system so considered—as a sort of accordion—comes far from supplying legal uniformity and certainty. To shift the metaphor, if we regard precedents as premises, one might say that often there are many vacant premises.

[37] See *Law and the Modern Mind* (1930) 6-7, 10-11 and note, 223-25. For references to numerous, highly respectable lawyers who had previously said the same, see Frank, *If Men Were Angels* (1942) 303-04. See also Stone, *loc. cit.*

Such uncertainty stems in part from the fact that the courts, as Holmes said, must work out compromises between the policies or principles behind the legal rules. Legal principles cannot dwell, à la Robinson Crusoe, or in anarchic "state of nature" where there is a war of all against all; they must learn to live together, socially, in a sort of democracy of principles in which none is dictator.[38] Only absolutists object to compromises between principles. As Morley said, "The disciples of the relative may afford to compromise. The disciples of the absolute, never." But the necessary viable adjustments, when principles clash, sometimes are not too satisfactory. For example, the policy of immunity of citizens from unreasonable searches and seizures, guaranteed by the Constitutional Fourth Amendment, runs, head on, into collision with the policy of facilitating the detection and punishment of criminals. In accommodating those policies one to the other, the Supreme Court, to date, has left them both uncertain; it has at times prevented the conviction of guilty men, but also has made loopholes in the constitutional immunity which, practically, may soon destroy it.[39]

9

Some of my students, I find, have an idea that judges are at liberty to and do decide all cases as they please. Of course, that is not true of conscientious judges, mindful of their duties. For all that I have said about *stare decisis,* you must not believe that such judges feel wholly unconstrained by precedents. *Stare decisis,* despite all its numerous loopholes, has its effects. (1) In the first place, it is foolish to change a rule that does no harm. Such a rule, in itself, may be neither good nor bad, but indifferent—like the rule about driving on the right side of the road. To have some rule on such a subject is good, but the particular choice is unimportant. Therefore many rules of that kind remain fixed for a long period. (2) Then there are established rules which the judges may think unwise, but to which a majority of the community is deeply attached.[40] (3) Moreover, there are many rules as to which the judges have a strong hunch that they have become deeply entrenched in community ways of acting, so that the judges, despite

[38] See my dissenting opinion in Chrestensen v. Valentine, 122 F. (2d) 511 at 522.

[39] I have in mind particularly the rulings that a federal prosecutor may introduce evidence obtained unlawfully by persons not in the service of the federal government, provided only that it cannot be proved that any federal employee connived in the illegal obtaining of that evidence. Usually it is impossible for a defendant to procure proof of such connivance.

[40] See Hoffman v. Palmer, 129 F. (2d) 976 as to the hearsay rule.

the fact that they think those rules unjust or unwise, hesitate to change them, although there is no specific proof of reliance in any particular case. This hesitation has its warrant: The judges are poorly equipped to investigate the actual past social consequences of old rules or to form competent surmises as to the probable future consequences of new ones.[41] (4) Most important are the cases in which there has been actual reliance upon the precedents, so that it would be unjust to change them, retroactively, as to persons who have thus relied. *For all these reasons, although many persons (myself included) believe that the theory of precedents ought to be restated so as to conform more nearly with precedent practice, no sensible person suggests that stare decisis be abandoned.*

To indicate my own attitude, for what it is worth, I quote remarks I made a few years ago:[42] "I do not believe that there is any inherent virtue in mere change, that every change is praiseworthy. The new is not necessarily desirable, of course. Boredom, the tedium of the usual, and neurotic as well as healthy-minded impulses, often account for the pressure for novelty. Laymen are often more eager for change than the specialist. They may long for change for the mere sake of change. That longing sometimes needs to be resisted. And susceptibility to change may be but a fashion."[43] To show you my own views a propos of legal change in particular, I quote from an opinion I wrote for our court a few years ago: "Of course, courts should be exceedingly cautious in disturbing (at least retrospectively) precedents on which men have importantly changed their positions."[44] In another opinion, I said that "undeniably . . . it is important, generally, that a court should not deviate, except prospectively, from its own decision in a prior case, even if that decision was in error, especially where that decision will harm persons who acted in reliance on that decision. . . ."[45]

But I have also, in another opinion, referred to another aspect of judges' rule-making which needs to be considered: "Excessive concentration of attention, by some upper court judges, on the formulation

[41] See Chapter XXV.

[42] Frank, "The Place of The Expert in a Democratic Society" (1944), reprinted in 16 *Phil. of Science* (1949).

[43] See also Frank, *Law and the Modern Mind* (1930) 249-52. See Frank, *If Men Were Angels* (1942) 165: "With respect to change, men, roughly speaking, can be divided into three groups: Those to whom anything new is inherently wrong; those to whom anything new is inherently right; those to whom novelty is a badge neither of rightness nor wrongness."

[44] In re Barnett, 124 F. (2d) 1005, 1011.

[45] Dissenting opinion in In re Marine Harbors Properties, Inc., 125 F. (2d) 296, 299-300.

in their opinions of . . . legal rules, with an eye chiefly to the impact of those rules on hypothetical future cases not yet before the court, sometimes results in their allotting inadequate attention to the interests of the actual parties in the specific existing cases which it is the duty of courts to decide. Such judges never quite catch up with themselves; for, in cases which actually occur, they are deciding future cases that may never occur. Legal history shows that such an attitude leads to judicial pronouncements which, at times, are none too happy in their effects on future cases. For the future develops unanticipated happenings; moreover, it does not stay put, it refuses to be trapped. The intended consequences of efforts to govern the future often fail; the actual consequences—which may be good or evil—are, frequently, utterly different. Results are miscalculated; there is an 'illusion of purpose.' Of course, present problems will be clarified by reference to future ends, but . . . such ends, although they have a future bearing, must obtain their significance in present consequences, otherwise those ends lose their significance. . . . 'Tomorrow today will be yesterday.' Any future, when it becomes the present, is sure to bring new and unexpected problems. There is much wisdom in Valery's reference to the 'anachronism of the future.' And the paradox is that when judges become unduly interested in the future consequences of their rulings, they are . . . doing precisely what they say they must avoid—they are deciding not real but hypothetical cases, with no one to speak for the imaginary contestants. The interests of the parties actually before the court are thus sacrificed to the shadowy unvoiced claims of supposititious litigants in future litigation which may never arise; and the judicial process becomes the pursuit of an elusive horizon which is never reached. No doubt it expands the ego of a judge to look upon himself as the guardian of the general future. But his more humble yet more important and immediate task is to decide individual, actual, present cases. . . . Such judicial legislation as inheres in formulating legal rules is inescapable. But courts should be modest in their legislative efforts to control the future, since they cannot function democratically, as legislative committees and administrative agencies can, by inviting the views of all who may be affected by their prospective rules. And, because they do not learn those views, and must largely rely on their own imaginations, they should be cautious about attempting, in present cases, to project their formulations too far and too firmly into the days yet to come. To cope with the present is none too easy, in part because the present is only a moving line dividing yesterdays and tomorrows, so that reflections on what will happen are unavoidable elements of current problems. But, although continuity, both backwards and forwards, is to some extent a necessity, judges should not shirk the present aspect of today's problems in favor of too much illusory tinkering with tomorrow's. The future can become as perniciously tyrannical as the past. Posterity-worship can be as bad as ancestor-worship."[46]

10

When a court engages in extinguishing a precedent by "distinguishing" it, or by giving a wholly new meaning to the words of an old rule, sometimes—not always—it purposely acts obliquely, evasively. Some lawyers prefer that technique to a forthright judicial pronouncement that the old decision has been killed off. I can't agree. Judicial candor with the public, I think, is the only practice consonant with democracy. For that reason, I admire the way in which our present Supreme Court Justices often straightforwardly over-rule precedents instead of chloroforming them by indirect methods, as their predecessors were more inclined to do. No greater real instability results from the direct than from the oblique methods. In the 19th century, in what some lawyers now call the "good old days," Pollock, writing of American courts, said that their decisions were little more than expressions of opinions of individual judges. General Benjamin Butler, in 1887, wrote to Holmes, complaining that the Supreme Court was abandoning the precedents "to make new law." In 1911, a lawyer, in an article in the *Harvard Law Review,* lamented the "decadence of the system of precedent." He severely criticized the judicial decisions "of the past ten years." The courts, he deplored, although still pretending to abide by *stare decisis,* had grown excessively interested in "which side ought to win." This had left little of "our much vaunted system of deciding cases in accord with the rules laid down in prior opinions." That system had become "a mere mirage." The courts, he lamented, "lay less and less stress" on what "the law" has heretofore been declared to be, and "more and more"—note this—on the "merits" of a case as "they appear in the facts presented." Former Attorney General Wickersham, in 1935, before the Roosevelt court fight, said, "It is always hazardous to attempt a prediction concerning a decision by" the Supreme Court. Thus the evasive ways of the "good old days" yielded no more certainty

[46] Concurring opinion in Aero Spark Plug Co. v. B. G. Corporation, 130 F. (2d) 290.

than the more direct approach. But the current candid method of obliterating undesirable precedents is, I submit, more democratic.

A few months ago, Mr. Justice Douglas said, in the course of a brilliant discussion of changes in some rules recently made by the Supreme Court, "It is sometimes thought to be astute political management of a shift in position to proclaim that no change is under way. That is designed as a sedative to instill confidence and allay doubts. It has been a tool of judges as well as other officials. Precedents, though distinguished and qualified out of existence, apparently have been kept alive. The theory is that the outward appearance of stability is what is important. . . . But the more blunt, open, and direct course is truer to democratic traditions. . . . The principle of full disclosure has as much place in government as it does in the market place. A judiciary that discloses what it is doing and why it does it will breed understanding. And confidence based on understanding is more enduring than confidence based on awe."[47]

Here is a good place to answer those who clamor that the present Supreme Court, as the Texas Bar Association said in 1944, has unduly "over-ruled decisions, precedents and landmarks of long standing." In truth, many of those "landmarks" were not at all of "long standing." Most of them were judge-made rules, made a few decades earlier, in Supreme Court decisions which had themselves over-ruled still earlier cases. The recently over-ruled cases were the innovations of "conservative" Justices who had upset preceding landmarks, established by more "liberal" Justices a short time before.[48] The recent revitalization of the previous "liberal" precedents has offended some lawyers whose clients had vested interests in the rejected conservative innovations. That fact, plus the increased honesty of the Court, explains a recent editorial which said, "Because of the packing of the courts with leftists, New Dealers, bigots and political hacks, there is no law today. . . . Precedent is only a word in the dictionary." When you read that sort of editorial, please remember the lawyer who, in 1911, more than twenty years before the New Deal, had deplored the "decadence" of the precedent system.

[47] "Stare Decisis," 49 *Col. L. Rev.* (1949) 735, 754.
[48] See Douglas, *loc. cit.*

XX. CODIFICATION

This notion that the effects of the man in the judge can be eliminated is hard to down. Recurrently men say, "Why tolerate the uncertainties in the rules which come from the vagaries of judges? Why not make the rules clear and certain by a simple device? Enact, once and for all, a code, a complete body of rules, prescribed by the legislature, to settle all future legal problems, thereby putting an end to lawyers' quibbles." This method was once popular on the continent of Europe. Frederick the Great tried it. Napoleon did the same. So, too, did Germany at a later date.

This plan has never succeeded.[1] No code can anticipate every possible set of facts. Moreover, when social conditions change and social attitudes alter, many portions of any code act as an intolerable strait-jacket. Resort is necessarily had to judicial interpretations. These interpretations, or "glosses" as they are sometimes called, take the place of the letter of the code. Judge-made glosses possess all the uncertainties of judge-made rules. Indeed, some persons have suggested that elaborate codes increase judicial legislation.

Recognizing the fatuousness of the conception of a detailed judge-proof code, the more modern European codes have abandoned the effort to procure precision, and have aimed, instead, at flexibility. The Swiss Civil Code has been described as an "outline of legal principles." Thus the legislative role of the judge is frankly accepted as an inescapable fact.[2]

Bentham in England, and Livingston in Louisiana, both enthusiastic codifiers, thought they had invented a method of keeping judges from tampering with a code: Provide that, whenever a court finds a gap in the code, the judges must so report to the legislature, which will then promptly fill the gap. Something like this method has been unsuccessfully attempted on the European continent. And, owing to the tardiness of legislation, one may doubt whether it could ever be satisfactory. Yet there is in this idea the germ of a workable notion which, to some

[1] For a more extensive discussion of codification, see Frank, *Law and the Modern Mind* (1930) 186-95, 310-11.

[2] In countries "governed" by codes, the courts, without so acknowledging, use precedents much as do our courts. See Usatorre v. The Victoria, 172 F. (2d) 434, 439 and notes.

extent, has been exploited in several of our states, notably New York. In that state, several officially-created bodies each year recommend legislation to the legislature in order to "modify or eliminate antiquated and inequitable rules, . . . and to bring the law of the state . . . into harmony with modern conditions." It has been wisely suggested that all the states and the federal government create such agencies and coordinate their work.

This device, unquestionably important, is no panacea. Legislatures, busy with pressing duties, do not promptly respond to all such suggestions. Moreover, these advisory bodies have shown a tendency to stay away from highly controversial issues. In New York, the Law Revision Committee has done little to acquaint the public generally with its activities—so little that few laymen know that such a body exists, and most lawyers are largely ignorant of what it has done. In Sweden, apparently some legislation is enacted for only a short period, during which its effects are carefully studied. Perhaps we should experiment with that method, for it would tend to keep legislatures from losing interest in a statute after its enactment.

Lobingier [3] recently made a more daring proposal which he apparently borrowed from Roman procedure: Have the upper court of each jurisdiction appoint a committee, staffed with researchers, to bring to the court's attention judge-made rules which, as indicated by their practical social consequences, are obsolete or gravely unjust.[4] Let the judges, on the basis of this advice, if they agree with it, and without waiting for legislative action, reject or modify undesirable judge-made rules, as cases arise in which the courts are asked to apply them. I think this proposal worthy of earnest consideration. It puts it up to the courts to undo their own past errors. It means that relief to citizens from judicial mistakes will not need to wait on the often tardy action of legislatures. If the advisory committees invited advice from all sources, and held hearings, the judges would learn much concerning the wisdom of the policies embodied in the existing judge-made rules.[5]

[3] "Precedent in Legal Systems," 44 *Mich. L. Rev.* (1946) 955, 986-989.

[4] I would supplement this proposal by authorizing a court to ask the committee to do such research.

[5] But see Chapter XIV as to the limits of such knowledge.

XXI. WORDS AND MUSIC: LEGISLATION AND JUDICIAL INTERPRETATION

THE moderate stability of the judge-made rules, however, as I have already indicated, can be disrupted at any moment by the legislature. A statute—except in the few instances where it is unconstitutional—can change any judge-made rule.

In most countries other than England and the United States, the source of the rules has been statutes, a network of legislation called a code. But in England and here, that has not been true. So that when legislatures changed the rules, our courts, until quite recently, resented it, treated statutes as intrusions and therefore to be so interpreted as to do the least possible to alter the judge-made rules. "Here," the judges felt, "is a stable body of rules which create legal certainty. We, ourselves, seldom change any of them, and then only after the most careful consideration. But the legislature makes new rules, frequently without adequate consideration, which upset legal certainty. The legislatures do their work capriciously, superficially, on the basis of the limited subjective impressions of a few members of a legislative committee. Why should we greatly respect such shoddy products?"

If the extreme *stare decisis* theory were sound, much could be said for that attitude. For, if and in so far as adherence to precedents finds its support in men's reliance on them, a statute which destroys a relied-on judge-made precedent does seem unjust. Yet, within wide limits, legislatures may, and often do, wipe out such rules.

However, even if this position were otherwise cogent, and even if criticism of legislative workmanship were invariably correct, yet the anti-legislative bias of judges would be untenable for reasons previously stated: To the legislatures the Constitutions assign the power of enacting statutes; and the legislatures come closest to reflecting popular desires. When a court, then, fails wholeheartedly to enforce a statute, it sets itself against our constitutional scheme, acts undemocratically. It then incurs the danger of arousing popular wrath. To be sure, American courts have always pretended to accept willingly the legislature's directions. But, in actual fact, until the last few decades, they were often resistant.

At first glance, the result, when a statute prescribes a rule, seems simple. You probably think that the existence of a statutory rule on any subject has these effects: It wipes out any previous inconsistent judge-made rule and stops all future judicial legislation on that subject. But the situation is not, by any means, so simple. The complications have these principal roots: (1) Statutes are often carelessly worded. The legislature, through inadvertence, uses language the meaning of which is highly ambiguous. The courts then have the task of ascertaining that meaning as best they can.

(2) Frequently, the ambiguity does not result from careless draftsmanship, but from the fact that it is impossible to anticipate with precision the multitude of particular circumstances which later arise, and which, although not within the literal words of the statute, can be argued to have been within its general scope. Sometimes a court can easily conclude that an unexpected state of facts was not meant to be covered by the legislation. Sometimes that conclusion is more doubtful. For instance, was a statute relating to innkeepers meant to apply to a company operating sleeping cars? Or was a statute, passed in horse-and-buggy days, which spoke of "vehicles," intended to include automobiles? Does the word "person" or "citizen" include a corporation? When does "may" mean "shall?" What effect should be given to a comma, separating two phrases in a sentence? [1] A glib answer may defeat the purpose of the legislature. The courts sometimes adopt this attitude: Would the legislature, had it thought of this set of facts, have explicitly applied the statute to them?

This is an age-old type of problem. Thousands of years ago, Aristotle discussed it, and lawyers have discussed it ever since Gray, several decades ago, with not much advance beyond Aristotle,[2] put the problem this way: "Interpretation is generally spoken of as if its function was to discover what the meaning of the legislature really was. But when the legislature has had a real intention, one way or another on a point, it is not once in a hundred times that any doubt arises as to what its intention was. If that were all that the judge had to do with the statute, interpretation of the statutes, instead of being one of the most difficult of a judge's duties, would be extremely easy. The fact is that the difficulties of so-called interpretation arise when the legislature has had no meaning at all; when the question which is raised on the statute

[1] Justice Johnson, in United States v. Palmer, 3 Wheat. 610, 636, pointed out the lives of the defendants "may depend upon a comma."

[2] See Frank, "Words and Music," 47 *Col. L. Rev.* (1947) 1259; Usatorre v. The Victoria, 172 F. (2d) 434, 439-41 and notes.

never occurred to it; when what the judges have to do is, not to determine what the legislature did mean on a point which was present to its mind, but to guess what it would have intended on a point not present to its mind had the point been present."

The problem is, in part, one of what today we call "semantics." Words serve as symbols. As such, necessarily they are somewhat compressed, condensed. Does the legislature's compression which omits some particulars, indicate an intention to omit them? The judges must determine the proper limits of expansion of the condensed symbols. Judges often differ among themselves as to the appropriate amount of such expansion.

The varieties of human experiences are legion. They cannot be dealt with in mathematically exact terms. What, for instance, does the word "value" [3] or the word "employees" mean when found in a statute? Were a legislature to try always to tie down the courts by over-precise words, it would often defeat itself. Consequently, the legislature, not infrequently, uses words that are purposely vague, intending that the courts should work out the meaning as specific cases arise.[4]

Legislative legislation thus often calls for interpretation which compels judicial legislation necessary to carry out the legislature's purpose. That explains the following statement by Gray to which some lawyers object: "It has sometimes been said that the Law is composed of two parts—legislative law and judge-made law, but in truth all the Law is judge-made law. The shape in which a statute is imposed on the community as a guide for conduct is that statute as interpreted by the courts. The courts put life into the dead words of the statute. To quote . . . from Bishop Hoadly: 'Nay, whoever hath an absolute authority to interpret any written or spoken laws, it is He who is truly the Law Giver to all intents and purposes, and not the Person who first wrote and spoke them.' " [5]

[3] See Andrews v. Commissioner, 135 F. (2d) 314, 317: " 'Value' is not a single purpose word. Men have all but driven themselves mad in an effort to definitize its meaning. . . . The answer is obviously a guess. Much cerebration has been wasted in the vain hope that some assemblage of some letters of the alphabet would eliminate the uncertainty inhering in such guessing."

[4] Sometimes, because of a political stalemate, the legislature deliberately leaves the statute vague; it then "passes the buck" to the courts. See Jaffe, 47 *Col. L. Rev.* (1947) 359, 361, 366-367, 371. See also 1 *Mass. L.Q.*, No. 2 (1916) at 13-15.

[5] Hoadly wrote in the 18th Century. "By the craft of an Interpreter," Hobbes had said in the 17th Century, "the Law may be made to bear a sense, contrary to that of the Sovereign; by which means the Interpreter becomes the legislator."

A sixteenth-century legal treatise had said: "For the Sages of the Law, whose wits are exercised in such matters, have the interpretation in their hands, and their Authority

2

As I noted, the doctrine of precedents has been extolled for its aesthetic value. Legal rules, it is said, should be worked out so as to give "symmetry" to a legal system. The Roman lawyers delighted in the "elegantia juris," the artistic beauty of "the law." Blackstone, an amateur poet, indulged freely in legal aesthetics. An amateur architect as well, he absurdly extolled the beauty of the English legal system,[6] comparing it often to a well-constructed building.[7] A California court, justifying its refusal to abandon an unwise precedent, said that to do so would be to mar the "beauty and symmetry" of the "law." Sir Frederick Pollock years ago spoke of the "law" as a "work of art"; Llewellyn in 1942 wrote at length on the Beautiful in Law;[8] Wolfson in 1945 published some sprightly suggestions in his paper, *Aesthetics In and About the Law;*[9] and many others have touched on that theme.

I am therefore not unjustified in exploiting the fine-art metaphor. I suggest a comparison between (1) the interpretation of statutes by judges and (2) the interpretation of musical compositions by musical performers.[10] I know that Llewellyn in his essay rejected the musical analogy, and (although without obeisances to Blackstone) insisted that "the aesthetic phase of a legal system is cognate to architecture." But, as on a few other occasions, I dare here to disagree with Llewellyn, while always admiring him.

Krenek, a brilliant modern musical composer, criticizes those musical

---

no man taketh in control: wherefore their Power is very great, and high, and we seek those Interpretations as Oracles from their mouths."

[6] See, *e.g.*, Frank, "Sketch of an Influence," in *Interpretations of Modern Legal Philosophies* (1945) 189.

[7] Radin suggests that the notion of legal "stability" has its aesthetic appeal, architecturally derived. Radin, "The Trial of the Calf," 32 *Corn. L.Q.* 137, 147 (1946).

[8] "On the Good, the True, and the Beautiful in Law," 9 *Un. of Chi. L. Rev.* 224 (1942).

[9] 33 *Ky. L. J.* 33 (1945).

[10] In 1945, Maurois read a paper, "The Role of Art in Life and Law" (Brandeis Lawyers' Society, 1945) in which, *inter alia,* he briefly compared the opinions of great judges with the works of musicians. A very brief suggestion comparing musical and statutory interpretation appeared in 1947 in an article by Cossio, "Phenomenology of the Judgment," in *Interpretations of Modern Legal Philosophies* 85, 97 (1947).

I want, therefore, to assert my claim to priority: The comparison first occurred to me when, in December 1944, I read an article by the musical composer, Ernest Krenek, "The Composer and the Interpreter," 3 *Black Mountain Coll. Bull.* (1944). I wrote him on January 8, 1945, calling his attention to the analogy. In his reply of January 15, 1945, he suggested that I read his book, *Music Here and Now* (1939). In the summer of 1945, I began writing an article on the theme I am here exploiting, which was published in 1947; see Frank, "Words and Music," 47 *Col. L. Rev.* (1947) 1259.

"purists" who insist on what they call "work-fidelity." The performer of a musical piece—an individual pianist, violinist, or an orchestra-leader—should, say the purists, engage in "authentic interpretation" which eliminates the interpreter altogether, by "the actual rendition" of the musical symbols just as they were written, in order to "serve the true intention of the composer." Krenek shows that often such literalism is absurd. He agrees that the "romantic" school went to excesses when they improvised freely, on the basis of their individual moods. But Krenek says that "the honest efforts" made today "to get as close as possible at the originals may involve as great a number of errors as the innocent enthusiasts of the romantic school committed," in their attempt to "serve the true intentions" of composers.

Even literalism cannot wholly prevent varieties of musical interpretation. How "in spite of declared work-fidelity," Krenek asks, "does it happen that the 'Seventh' as read by Furtwaengler will differ considerably when Toscanini conducts? How can this happen, when each claims to be an infallible executor of the composer's will?" Abject literalism fails to discriminate between major elements and those of subordinate significance.

There are, Krenek observes, composers who regard interpreters as "their natural enemies." They insist that there is "only one single way of interpreting their music." But some great composers have a different view. They know that the process of interpretation is not mechanical, automatic. Wagner, Krenek relates, after some disappointing experience with interpreters who followed faithfully his metronomic markings, decided to dispense with that kind of indication altogether.[11] And the same is true of directions that a certain phrase is to be played "with determination" or "with tenderness." Even careful indications cannot help leaving "a substantial margin for the interpreter." The attempt at "work-fidelity which sticks to the letter of the score leads to an unbearable caricature of the composition." The trouble with such an attitude is that the literal "interpreters are trying too hard to suppress their own imagination." Another composer, Darnton, reports that "the written notes are at best only an approximation to the composer's intention, no matter how fully they are supplemented by verbal directions." It "makes nonsense of the music to play it as if the truth, the whole

[11] "Wagner parodied the tendency to regard the printed notes as 'sacred and inviolable' when he created the character of Beckmesser . . . who knew all about rules, nothing about inspiration." Herbage, "Brains Trust," 1 *Penguin Music Magazine* 75 (1946).

truth and nothing but the truth reside in the notes and such directions," for "all kinds of nuances and inflections, variations of tempo and dynamics are essential to the music. . . . The result varies with the musical insight and interpretative skill of the interpreter." [12]

Krenek urges a mean: There is a middle ground, between disregarding the composer's intention and being intelligently imaginative. Interpretation of a score usually "allows for a great number of equally good . . . and satisfactory variants." The composer legitimately wants to "get his message across . . . in undistorted and unadulterated fashion." But he must recognize that he cannot completely control the performer, that he is "practically helpless," and becomes a "passive onlooker," as "soon as he has handed his music over to the interpreter." Nor is this merely a counsel of despair. The composer should have sufficient confidence in human nature to "enjoy rather than to fear the medium of personal life through which his message is filtered. . . . The personality of the interpreter is not necessarily a stumbling block on which the work . . . goes to pieces." Unfortunate cases there are. In "the good cases, which ideally should be the rule, that personality vouchsafes an increment of vitality that is not only desirable but truly necessary in order to put the message across." The wise composer expects the performer to read his score "with an insight which transcends" its "literal meaning." He does not deplore the performer's creative activity, does not denounce it as "caprice" or "subjective tricks." The attempt to eradicate the "human element . . . merely shows," writes Krenek, "distressing cynicism and distrust," similar to that which, in the political sphere, "has resulted in the rise . . . of dictators."

You now see the bases for my comparison of art interpretation and statutory interpretation. Sometimes a literal interpretation of a piece of legislation is indubitably correct. Often, however, so to construe a statute will yield a grotesque caricature of the legislature's purpose. A famous case in point was decided in 1892. Congress in 1885 had passed a statute which expressly prohibited "the importation . . . of foreigners . . . under contract . . . to perform labor in the United States." Trinity Church, in New York City, made a contract with an English minister, who having agreed to become its pastor, came to this country. The government sued the church for violation of the statute. The Supreme Court admitted that the act of the church was "within the letter" of the statute. But it held that it was not within the purpose Congress intended. The Court said it was not substituting the judges'

[12] Darnton, *You and Music* 40, 161-62 (1946).

will for that of the legislature, for "frequently words of general meaning are used in a statute, words broad enough to include an act in question, and yet a consideration of the whole legislation, or of the circumstances surrounding its enactment, or of the absurd results which follow from giving such broad meaning to the words, makes it unreasonable to believe that the legislator intended to include the particular act. . . . The common sense of man approves the judgment mentioned by Puffendorf, that the Bolognian law which enacted 'that whoever drew blood in the streets should be punished with the utmost severity,' did not extend to the surgeon who opened the vein of a person that fell down in the street in a fit."

When, not so long ago, some judges were anti-democratic, they often obstructed the democratic will voiced by the legislature. This they sometimes did by obstinately construing a statute narrowly, without real regard to its intention. Let me illustrate. You will recall that, in 1936, the Supreme Court, in an opinion by Mr. Justice McReynolds, interpreted the famous "commodities clause" of the Interstate Commerce Act, enacted in 1906, designed to stop railroad favoritism to certain kinds of shippers.[13] Mr. Justice Stone, in a dissenting opinion, showed that this interpretation gutted the legislation. He said that if the Court's construction were correct, "one is at a loss to say what scope remains for the operation of the statute," and that it brought about its "reduction . . . to a cipher in the calculations of those who control the railroads of the country."[14]

At the time, no protest came from a certain well-known columnist. But now that the majority of the Supreme Court has adopted Stone's democratic perspective, this columnist, in purist fashion, editorializes that the present Court "insists on writing legislation by employing the fiction that it is merely interpreting legislation."[15] He forgets that, long before the New Deal existed, Charles Evans Hughes (later to

[13] United States v. Elgin, J. & E. Ry., 298 U.S. 492 (1936).

[14] An English court observed: "It is not enough to attain to a degree of precision which a person reading in good faith can understand; but it is necessary to attain a degree of precision which a person reading in bad faith cannot misunderstand." In re Castrom, (1891) 1 Q.B. 149, 167.

[15] This same columnist, severely criticizing the recent decision of our court in NLRB v. Clark Bros., 163 F. 2d 373, said that the court "considers itself obligated to write a law or promulgate legislation which the Congress did not adopt. . . . As long as New Deal judges sit on the bench and legislate, Congress will have to grow more instead of less legalistic. . . ." It happens that the court in that case consisted of Judges Swan, A. N. Hand and myself, the opinion of the court being written by Judge Swan. Judges Swan and Hand were appointed to the circuit court in 1927 by President Coolidge.

become Chief Justice) in some lectures remarked that the meaning of "a federal statute is what the (Supreme) Court says it means." [16]

Factory workers can commit sabotage effectively by failing to use intelligent imagination in complying with the management's rules, i.e., by literally following them. So, too, we learn from Krenek, can orchestra-leaders. Similarly, some judges, like Justice McReynolds, sabotaged legislative purposes by sticking to the exact words of statutes. When judges, however, use their imagination in trying to get at and apply what a legislature really meant, but imperfectly said, they cooperate with the legislature.[17]

The non-lawyer, when annoyed by the way judges sometimes interpret apparently simple statutory language, is the victim of the one-word-one-meaning fallacy, based on the false assumption that each verbal symbol refers to one and only one specific subject. If the non-lawyer would reflect a bit, he would perceive that such an assumption, if employed in the non-legal world, would compel the conclusion that a clothes-horse is an animal of the equine species, and would make it impossible to speak of "drinking a toast." Even around the more precise words, often there is a wide fringe of ambiguity which can be dissipated only by a consideration of the context and background. The literalist should also consider that essentially the same problem arises in construing private writings, such as contracts, trusts and wills.[18] One wonders whether the columnist I mentioned has never had a dispute as to what he meant by a letter or an editorial.

He is, it must be confessed, dreaming a dream some lawyers have dreamt. Thayer wrote of "that lawyer's Paradise where all words have a fixed, precisely ascertained meaning; where men express their purposes not only with accuracy, but with fulness; and where, if the writer has been careful, a lawyer, having a document before him, may sit in his chair, inspect the text, and answer all questions without raising his eyes." [19] There is no such paradise. The serpent in the imagined garden of Eden is the irrepressible semantic problem.

[16] Hughes, *The Supreme Court of the United States* 280 (1928). The "demolition of the purpose of Congress, through stingy interpretation, is the most emphatic kind of judicial legislation." M. Witmark & Sons v. Fred Fisher Music Co., 125 F. 2d 949, 967 (dissenting opinion).

[17] See Hoffman v. Palmer, 129 F. 2d 976, 986 as to the need of judges to avoid excessive "generosity" with "other people's words." cf. Slifka v. Johnson, 161 F. 2d 467, 470 (concurring opinion).

[18] Compare the "objective theory" of contractual interpretation. For criticism of over-extensions of that theory, see concurring opinion in Ricketts v. Pennsylvania R.R., 153 F. 2d 757, 760-64.

[19] *A Preliminary Treatise on Evidence* (1898) 428-429.

Judge Learned Hand has often spoken of the way in which literalism in interpretation can thwart the purpose of Congress. The courts, he wrote some thirty years ago, by "scrupulousness to the written word," had at times so interfered with the intention of the statute-makers that the courts fell under public suspicion, and recourse was had, excessively, to administrative agencies.[20] Again and again he has criticized the dictionary theory of statutory construction. It is, he said in a recent opinion, "one of the surest indexes of a mature and developed jurisprudence not to make a fortress out of the dictionary, but to remember that statutes always have some purpose or object to accomplish, whose sympathetic and imaginative discovery is the surest guide to their meaning.[21] Here he was following Holmes who had said: "The Legislature has the power to decide what the policy of the law shall be, and if it has intimated its will, however indirectly, that will should be recognized and obeyed." [22] Holmes added that "it is not an adequate discharge of duty for courts to say: We see what you are driving at, but you have not said it, and therefore we shall go on as before." Does not this sound like Krenek's criticism of "work fidelity" with respect to music?

No more than in the case of music, can differences in interpretation be prevented. Yet the wise legislature will be in accord with Krenek's attitude towards musical performers: A judge with an imaginative personality supplies "an increment of vitality that is . . . desirable . . . and truly necessary in order to put" the legislative "message across," for only such a judge can read a statute "with an insight which transcends its literal meaning."

The legislature is like a composer. It cannot help itself: It must leave interpretation to others, principally to the courts. In a recent article, Herbage says that "music does not exist until it is performed." [23] Perhaps that comment applied, a la Bishop Hoadly, is too sweeping. But it contains a large part of the truth.

Those who today complain of any "judicial legislation" in statutory interpretation are complaining of the intrusion of the judges' personalities. However, just as Krenek shows that the effect of the performer's personal reactions cannot be excluded, so legal thinkers, in increasing numbers, have shown that the personal element in statutory construc-

20 Hand, "The Speech of Justice," 29 *Harv. L. Rev.* (1916) 617, 620; cf. Wyzanski, "Judge Learned Hand's Contribution to Public Law," 60 *Harv. L. Rev.* 348, 362 (1947).

21 Cabell v. Markham, 148 F. 2d 737, 739.

22 Johnson v. United States, 163 Fed. 30, 32.

23 Herbage, *loc. cit.*, at 76.

tion is unavoidable. Yet Krenek's mean, too, has its judicial parallel: The creativeness of the judges should always be limited; but, within proper limits, it is a boon not an evil.[24]

There is a story of Miss Goodlooks, the chorus-girl, who, in an emergency, acted Ophelia. In the players' scene (according to the text then being used), Hamlet asks Ophelia, "Are you chaste?" [25] and she answers, "My Lord?" But Miss Goodlooks said, "Chaste? My Lord!" When chided, she remarked, "Well, that was my interpretation of the part." Of course, no judge should thus let his personality run unrestrained. Nevertheless, there are many legitimately differing ways of reading some texts. Apposite here is the opinion of a great American, both a lawyer and an artist: Thomas Jefferson, in his *Thoughts on English Prosody,* said that there is "a modulation in tone of which it is impossible to give a precise idea in writing," that there are "different shades of emphasis which . . . judgment dictates," so that "the difference" in interpretation "exists in the judgment. . . . No two persons will accent the same passage alike. . . . Perhaps two real adepts who should utter the same passage with infinite perfection, yet by throwing the energy into different words might produce very different effects." [26] So we find Holmes writing that "the meaning of a sentence [in a statute] is to be felt rather than to be proved." [27] Nonetheless, what Krenek says of the musical performer holds good of a judge. He "should put himself in the place of the composer, trying to reconcile the impulses of his (own) imagination with the principle," and he must "obey the prescription of the composer as well as he can." In that vein, Wurzel properly protested against the unqualified suggestion that statutory interpretation is "exclusively an art" in which the judge gives free play to his fancy as if he were a poet.[28]

Here it is important to observe that the proper latitude of judicial construction should vary with the nature of divers statutes. (1) When

[24] cf. Herbage at 76: If a musical "conductor does not interpret a work with every atom of understanding and expression of which he is capable, I consider he has failed as an artist. I would never have him restrain himself out of 'reverence' to a composer's supposed wishes. If he does not feel, and is not convinced, he had better leave the music alone. I need hardly add that any attempt to focus attention upon himself rather than the music is pure charlatanism."

[25] The usual text uses the word "honest" which, in Shakespeare's day, meant "chaste" or "virtuous." The modern adapter had apparently, therefore, substituted "chaste" for "honest."

[26] Quoted in Padover, *The Complete Thomas Jefferson* (1943) 832-846.

[27] United States v. Johnson, 221 U.S. 488, 496.

[28] Wurzel, "Methods of Juridicial Thinking" (1904) translated in *The Science of Legal Method* 286, 326-32 (1917).

a court strives to ascertain the legislative purpose, the judges should try to eliminate as far as possible their own personal views of policy. For the legislative purpose is the resultant of the pressure of conflicting interests in the legislature. In 1942, answering a litigant's suggestion that we should ignore both the language and purpose of a tax statute "to achieve what we might regard as a more just result," I said for our court:[29] "Such a remaking of the legislation would require consideration of questions of legislative policy bearing on fiscal and economic matters and on administrative convenience; to discharge that task efficiently we would be obliged to hold a sort of Congressional Committee hearing, at which all interested persons would be heard, so as to be sure that our amendments would not entail unforeseen and undesirable results. We have no power to embark on such an enterprise."[30] (2) But the problem is different when the legislature uses words which, by their nature, leave to the courts the job of applying broad vague standards. Required to apply the phrase "in restraint of trade" in the Sherman Act, Learned Hand said, in 1943, in the *Associated Press* case: "Certainly such a function is ordinarily 'legislative'; for in a legislature the conflicting interests find their respective representation, or in any event can make their political power felt, as they cannot upon a court. The resulting compromises so arrived at are likely to achieve stability, and to be acquiesced in: which is justice. But it is a mistake to suppose that courts are never called upon to make similar choices: *i.e.,* to appraise and balance the value of opposed interests and to enforce their preference. The law of torts is for the most part the result of exactly that process, and the law of torts has been judge-made, especially in this very branch. Besides, even though we had more scruples than we do, we have here a legislative warrant, because Congress has incorporated into the Anti-Trust Acts the changing standards of the common law, and by so doing has delegated to the courts the duty of fixing the standard for each case."[31]

Pekelis brilliantly illuminated this subject. He pointed to the fact

[29] Commissioner v. Beck's Estate, 129 F. 2d 243, 246.

[30] The courts properly look to the "legislative history" for light concerning the legislature's purpose.

As even such light may not be sufficiently strong, courts may sometimes go astray in construing intricate statutes, like the federal Revenue Acts. See Eisenstein's brilliant article, "Some Iconoclastic Reflections on Tax Administration," 58 *Harv. L. Rev.* 477 (1945); Paul, "The Place of the Courts in the Taxing Process" (an address before the National Tax Conference, June 6, 1946); McAllister v. Commissioner, 157 F. 2d 235, 237, 240 n. 6 (dissenting opinion).

[31] United States v. Associated Press, 52 F. Supp. 362, 370.

that today statutes abound with words such as "reasonable," "fair," "equitable," "proper." Those words, he said, invite, they require, judicial legislation.[32] Those judges who, neglecting such court-house legislation, reiterate the "accepted folklore" that the legislature "necessarily had a specific intention with respect to every case which subsequently invites consideration of the statute," that the legislative intention has a "Platonic existence before the Courts discover it in the words of the statute,"[33] are not to be taken too seriously.

Musical interpreters often face a problem much like that which courts sometimes face. When a modern performer plays Bach, it is all but impossible to reproduce the exact mood of that composer (who lived in a period in which the general mood was substantially different from ours), to recreate the "taste" of that period. So, too, a court, when called upon to interpret a statute enacted in the 17th century, or in 1789, or even in 1830. Often the judges cannot be at all sure that they have recaptured the purpose of the composers of the legislation, who lived in an era with a quite different outlook.

Some particular interpretation of a Beethoven sonata may become a convention; that interpretation takes the place of whatever Beethoven may have intended. Then this interpretation is itself interpreted. But a new musical interpreter may revolt against the convention, and may go directly to the musical score, trying to rediscover the composer's original meaning. So with a statute: The judges having interpreted it, that interpretation—the "gloss on the statute"—is substituted for the words the legislature used,[34] and the interpretation becomes the subject of further interpretation. However, a court may some day spurn that interpretation and try to recapture the original legislative meaning, as the Supreme Court has recently done with the patent laws.[35] When a court thus scrapes off the "gloss," it acts like one who uncovers the original text in a palimpsest (a manuscript on which early writing has been covered over by a later writing).

I have referred to what judges should do in applying statutes. Not all judges, however, have the brilliant sympathetic imagination of a Learned Hand. Some are sure to be dull-witted. Others will not be as

[32] Pekelis, "The Case for a Jurisprudence of Welfare," 11 *Soc. Research* 312 (1944).

[33] Eisenstein, *loc. cit.*

[34] Montaigne wrote: "Who would not say that the glosses increase doubt and ignorance. . . .? It is more of a business to interpret the interpretation than to interpret the things."

[35] That the recent interpretations of the patent statutes have not been as revolutionary as some persons believe, see Kenyon, "Patent Law," 35 *Am. Bar Ass'n. J.* (1949) 480.

conscientious. When asked by the legislature to legislate judicially, some will shamelessly exploit their personal prejudices, instead of trying to base their solutions on their honest estimates of the community's sense of values. Even, however, if all judges had Learned Hand's qualities, yet agreement among them, as to statutory interpretation, would not be invariably assured. For here, as in the case of the judge-made rules, sometimes there exists, not one community notion of policy, but several such notions; and, here again, the judges, obliged to choose, sometimes disagree.

A legislature can make plain when it wants literalness, and when it wants to authorize judicial legislation. It can, in effect, say to the courts, "Play this statute with tenderness," or that statute "with determination." It can give unequivocal directions to the courts. The composer Stravinsky asked his interpreters to be wholly unimaginative. Krenek says that this is possible "in the case of the highly mechanized music that Stravinsky writes." Likewise, a legislature can write a highly mechanized statute.

Unfortunately, legislation sometimes is so worded as not to disclose whether the legislative composer wants literalness or *ad lib.* interpretation.[36] The drafting of statutes can be much improved. I agree with Conard who in a recent article says that "many ways of making laws more readable" exist and should be employed.[37] He is, nevertheless, somewhat over-sanguine. Words often are unruly. To overcome that obstacle, a statute sometimes contains an "interpretation" or "definition" section, a sort of special dictionary or glossary defining the words used in the statute. That device does not always work. The definitions often themselves are ambiguous. "These interpretation clauses," said an English judge, "are often the most difficult to be understood."

Krenek, you will recall, said that the aim of the musical purists to eliminate the interpreter altogether, to eradicate the "human element," was a symptom of "distressing cynicism and distrust," similar to that which "resulted in the rise of . . . dictators." It is significant that two despots, Frederick the Great and Napoleon, each attempted to forbid judges to interpret statutes. Those attempts failed. It is significant, too, that, in the decades preceding fascism, even the so-called liberals on the

36 "The composer can never explain himself enough. And the trouble is that he does not even try. When Shaw complained that Ibsen's plays were unintelligible, unless they were produced on the stage by a man of genius, Ibsen's reply was: 'What I have said, I have said.' To which Shaw promptly retorted: 'Precisely. But what you haven't said, you haven't said.'" Darnton, *loc. cit.*

37 "New Ways to Write Laws," 56 *Yale L.J.* 458 (1947).

European continent had a similar aim. When in charge of a democratic government, they had, said Pekelis,[38] "out of distrust . . . of the discretion of judges, . . . engaged in the pursuit of that legal blue bird, . . . the perfect statute" that "would foresee, classify and judicially regulate in advance every possible case." In so doing, Pekelis later perceived, they had paved the way for fascism. In this country we have done far better, he concluded, by our reliance on the "common sense, decency and skill" of judges in the handling of individual cases.

I briefly note some other resemblances between musical and statutory interpretation: Krenek writes that the "number of possibilities in which a work of art may be interpreted convincingly is an indication of its greatness. Only small and insignificant things have only one aspect, allowing only a single interpretation." Krenek's has been the approach of all our great Supreme Court Justices in construing the Constitution.

Another parallel: At one time, every composer was the sole performer of his compositions. So, at one time, English judges actively participated in enacting the statutes which they interpreted. And, just as later there was a dissociation of the functions of composing and performing, so there developed in America a pronouncedly American version of the doctrine of separation of governmental powers—the differentiation between statute-making and judicial interpretation. American courts, however, have been given the power to promulgate their own rules governing procedure. In that respect, they openly engage in a kind of statute-making. The judges then interpret those rules. So, to that extent, modern courts differ from most modern composers: The courts both compose and perform; they play their own compositions.

Another difference is noteworthy. Many a musical performer strives to make the music sound as if he were creating it in the act of playing it. But our courts, until recently, have tried to conceal their limited creativeness, have attempted to make their conduct appear as if there were no judicial "law-making." While the musical composer is a definite known person, when judges speak of the legislature's intention or purpose, they have difficulty in ascertaining to what persons they refer. Sometimes the sole purpose which can be definitized is that of a single member of a legislative committee.[39] Thus a Senator once said of a

[38] Pekelis, "Administrative Discretion and the Rule of Law," 19 *Soc. Research* 22, 34-35 (1943).

[39] See Wigmore, "The Judicial Function," in *The Science of Legal Method* (1917) xxvi.

tax measure that "even Senators who worked upon the bill for months do not understand it," and another Senator remarked that "there are many sections of the bill which it is almost humanly impossible for a man who is not an expert to understand or comprehend." [40]

The legislature cannot itself enforce statutes. It must delegate that task to other governmental agencies—to the chief executive and his subordinates, or to administrative bodies, or to the courts. When the delegation is to the executive or to administrative agencies, usually the aid of the courts is also invoked; and when the job is assigned directly to the courts, often they must call in the executive to assist them. We do not usually speak of "delegation" to the judiciary, but the fact of such delegation is undeniable, whatever the label. As Jaffe says, "Indeed, every statute is a delegation of law-making power to the agency appointed to enforce it [since] 'jurisdiction,' the power to declare the law applicable to a case, is the power to apply a general formula to a specific situation. This delegated power, when exercised by the judiciary, is ordinarily called interpretation or discovery of the legislative intention." [41] Although "we must not take lightly the objection to indiscriminate and ill-defined delegation"—an objection which "expresses a fundamental democratic concern"—we should not "insist that 'lawmaking' is the exclusive province of the legislature." We should, according to Jaffe, demand no more than that in the total process we achieve government by consent.[42]

But that consent can scarcely be said to have been given voluntarily if the consenters do not know that they have given it. Wherefore the courts should not conceal from the public their delegated power of sub-legislation, but should make every effort to inform the citizenry of how that power is exercised. Correct advice to our citizens about the courts necessitates telling them the difference between "legislative legislation" and "judicial legislation." To make that difference popularly understood may not be easy, but it will seem impossible only to those who undemocratically distrust our citizens. It is, then, the job of judges and lawyers to let the public know that judges, like violinists and pianists, are often creative interpreters—because they must be.

Awareness and public acknowledgment by judges of their legislative power may well induce restraint in exercising it. A judge who publicly

[40] Eisenstein, *loc. cit.*
[41] Jaffe, *loc. cit.* at 360.
[42] See Guiseppi v. Walling, 144 F. (2d) 608, 620-622.

admits that at times he cannot help legislating, is likely to be far more restrained when doing so. Such a judge will do his best to enforce the policy of a statute even when he detests its aim. If he is a so-called conservative, he will not try to frustrate a distastefully liberal statute; if he is a so-called liberal, he will deal similarly with what he considers perniciously reactionary legislation.

Some judges say that when doubt exists whether a statute was meant to be broadly construed, the safer and appropriate course is for the court to construe it narrowly, leaving it to the legislature, if it disagrees with the court, to amend the statute. This sounds reasonable. But there are those who argue that to play safe may be the means of negating the statute's purpose; for often much legislative inertia must be overcome to bring about an amendment: the legislature has to relearn the problem; and new, pressing matters may crowd out for years a consideration of an existing statute narrowed in scope by the courts.

There is an important difference, usually overlooked by commentators, between the interpretive latitude of the highest courts and that of lower courts. A court like that on which I sit, an intermediate appellate court, is, vis-à-vis the Supreme Court, "merely a reflector, serving as a judicial moon."[43] Judges on such a court usually must, as best they can, cautiously follow new "doctrinal trends" in the court above them.[44] As their duty is usually to learn, "not the congressional intent, but the Supreme Court's intent,"[45] their originality is often inadvertent.[46]

The conscientious, intelligent judge will consider government a sort of orchestra, in which, in symphonies authorized by the people, the courts and the legislature each play their parts.[47] The playing may sometimes be bad.[48] There may, occasionally, be some disharmonies.

[43] Choate v. Commissioner, 129 F. (2d) 684, 686.

[44] See Perkins v. Endicott-Johnson Corp., 128 F. (2d) 208, 217-218 (C.C.A. 2, 1942); Picard v. United Aircraft Corp., 128 F. (2d) 633, 636 (C.C.A. 2, 1942).

[45] Surrey, "The Supreme Court and the Federal Income Tax," 35 *Ill. L. Rev.* (1941) 779, 808.

[46] See Choate v. Commissioner, 129 F. (2d) 684, 685 (C.C.A. 2, 1942). Montaigne wrote: "It is more of a business to interpret the interpretations than to interpret the things. . . .; we do nothing but gloss one another." *Essays,* Bk. III, c. 13.

[47] See Shakespeare, *Henry the Fifth,* Act I, Scene 1: "For government, though high and low and lower, Put into parts, doth keep in one consent, Congruing in a full and natural close Like music."

[48] "When there are several performers, as in the case . . . of orchestras, the number of things that can go wrong is terrifying. The astonishing thing is not that the generality of performances is bad, but that it is so good." Darnton, *You and Music,* (1946) 40-41.

But, after all, modern music has taught us that a moderate amount of cacophony need not be altogether unpleasant.

I might summarize the foregoing: Just as, perforce, the musical composer delegates some subordinate creative activity to musical performers, so, perforce, the legislature delegates some subordinate (judicial) legislation—i.e., creative activity—to the courts.

3

The fact that courts must interpret private contracts as well as statutes, suggests this startling idea: private persons, by their contracts, often make legally binding rules. In other words, private persons "legislate."

This thesis seems first to have been enunciated by Bentham in a book written in 1782 but not published until 1945. The thesis was independently developed, without knowledge of Bentham's book, by several American writers in this century.[49] That thesis, briefly stated, is this: The government, by committing itself through court orders, to enforce contracts, delegates to private citizens the power to make contracts which bind the parties to the contracts and which also create legal rights that other persons must (within limits) respect. As long as the contract-makers do not violate any legal rules (judge-made or legislature-made or contained in Constitutions), they may thus establish effective legal rules of their own contriving. For the courts, if necessary, will direct the public force to be put behind the enforcement of those rules arising from those contracts. In other words, the government

[49] As to Bentham, see *The Limits of Jurisdiction Defined* (Everett ed. 1945) 35, 37, 38, 49, 50, 55, 61-63, 67-68, 73, 106-11.

Outstanding among the American writers mentioned in the text is Commons, *Legal Foundations of Capitalism* (1924) 6, 13, 14, 34, 36, 52-53-54, 59, 120-121, 128, 215, 297, 304, 320, 365; Commons, "Legislative and Administrative Reasoning in Economics," 26 *J. of Farm Economics* (1942) 369, 379; cf. Parsons, "John R. Commons' Point of View," 17 *J. of Public Utility Economics* (1942) 246. See also Commons, "Bargaining Power," 2 *Encyc. of Soc. Sciences* (1930) 459. Commons acknowledged his debt to Veblen's *Theory of Business Enterprise* (1904); see especially chapter VIII of Veblen's book.

Similar ideas were expressed by others. See Hale, "Coercion and Distribution in A Supposedly Non-Coercive State," 38 *Pol. Sc. Q.* (1923) 475; Hale, "Force and the State," 35 *Col. L. Rev.* (1935) 563; Cohen, "Property and Sovereignty," 13 *Cornell L.Q.* (1927) 8, reprinted in Cohen, *Law and the Social Order* (1933) 41, and Cohen, "The Basis of Contract," *ibid.*, 69; Lippmann, *The Good Society* (1937) 186-191, 222, 269-76.

See Standard Brands v. Smidler, 151 F. (2d) 34 at 38 note 6 (concurring opinion); M. Witmark & Sons v. Fred Fischer Music Co., 125 F. (2d) 949 at 963 (dissenting opinion).

delegates governmental power to persons who hold no governmental office. Contracts constitute a sort of "sub-legislation."[50]

However, as we have seen, the courts, before they enforce contracts, must interpret them. In so doing, the courts frequently say they are carrying out the "intention of the parties." Holmes called that statement a "humbug." So, often, it is, for these reasons: The real intention is not always clear; and many courts look solely to what they term the "objective" intention, i.e., what the parties appear to a reasonable third person to have intended.[51] Moreover, the courts, as a matter of policy, attach to contracts many obligations of which the contracting parties never thought,[52] so that a contract, supposed by many persons to be the antithesis of a "status," is, in large measure, but the means of creating a "status," i.e., a relation between the parties carrying with it duties of a kind neither party actually contemplated.[53] So, in a sense, the courts have the last word about the "law-making" powers delegated to private persons.

[50] See Allen, *Law In The Making* (1927) 303ff. He there discusses the "sub-legislation" made by corporations and associations.

An interesting sort of sub-legislation consists of rules made by "public utility companies," rules which bind their customers and which the courts will enforce.

[51] See criticism of the "objective" theory in Ricketts v. Pennsylvania R. Co., 153 F. (2d) at 760-764 (concurring opinion).

[52] See, e.g., Kulukundis Shipping Co. v. Amtorg Trading Corp., 126 F. (2d) 978, 990-991; Beidler & Bookmyer v. Universal Ins. Co., 134 F. (2d) 828, 830-831.

[53] See, e.g., Beidler & Bookmyer v. Universal Ins. Co., 134 F (2d) 828, 830; Martin v. Companaro, 156 F. (2d) 127, 130 note 5.

XXII. CONSTITUTIONS—THE MERRY-GO-ROUND

OUR national government, and each of our states, long ago adopted a sort of code—a written constitution. But a written constitution is a peculiar kind of code. Generally speaking, it does not go into details. It lays down broad basic principles, setting forth how the government is to function, and prohibiting it from doing certain types of things.

Our American Constitutions are characterized by one feature which renders them unique. For the most part, the final power to decide what the Constitution means is vested in one branch of the government—the judiciary. The strange fact is that this unique feature—found in virtually no other country—is not explicitly set forth in any provision of our Constitutions. There has been much debate as to whether the framers of our federal constitution had it in mind. I am strongly inclined to believe they did. At any rate, the Supreme Court decades ago said they did, and this view is now generally accepted. Since our government consists of separate states and a national government, it was essential to survival that the power be vested in some one body to decide how far any particular state could go in passing laws which might disrupt the union. Conceivably, this authority could have been given to Congress or the President. But, almost surely, such a scheme would have proved unworkable. Consequently, it is all but imperative that the Supreme Court of the United States should have the authority to decide that a law of a state violates the federal constitution and is therefore void.

Is it equally imperative that the Supreme Court be able to deal similarly with the conduct of Congress? Mr. Justice Holmes said, No. "I do not think," he remarked, "the United States would come to an end if we lost our power to declare an Act of Congress void." But, ever since John Marshall's day, the Supreme Court has asserted that power.

Although once it was strenuously denied, today almost every intelligent student concludes that, when that Court decides that a congressional statute is invalid, "unconstitutional," the Court is not acting as courts have done traditionally, but is, in reality, exercising a veto. No English court does anything like the equivalent. No English judge would dream of holding void an Act of Parliament. Now a judicial veto by our Supreme Court is unlike that of the President, in several respects. The President can veto an Act because he thinks it unwise; and his veto can be over-ridden, if a sufficient number of the members of Congress disagree with him. The Supreme Court, in theory, vetoes a statute only if it decides that it violates the Constitution. Moreover, this veto is not exercised except in deciding a particular law-suit in which the statute is involved. Nevertheless, when the court strikes down (i.e., vetoes) a statute, it does not, then, function in the usual judicial manner. The considerations which affect its decision are primarily those of policy. The judicial veto power thus is basically political.

Many persons have so maintained. Even so conservative a lawyer as James M. Beck spoke of "this extra-ordinary political-judicial tribunal." Perhaps most striking is the statement, made in 1931, by Professor Felix Frankfurter, now Mr. Justice Frankfurter, "The stuff of constitutional law," he wrote, "differs profoundly from ordinary law. . . . The Court exercises essentially political functions. . . . Constitutional adjudication has always been statecraft." In 1928, Frankfurter had said that "no other country in the world leaves to the judiciary the power which it exercises over us."

This thesis has been expounded in a delightful book, by Charles Curtis, *Lions Under the Throne,* recently published. With respect to constitutional questions, the Supreme Court, he says, is not a court. Its power to nullify legislation compels it, he asserts, to be primarily a peculiar kind of political agency, although legal tradition requires it to talk as if it were a judicial tribunal. Thanks to Mr. Justice Holmes, this approach to constitutional decisions is now openly accepted by the Supreme Court Justices, even if, on the bench, they do not expressly avow it. This candid recognition of the nature of this function is all to the good. It is democratic, since it means honest dealing with our citizens. The older, now abandoned, way of the Court in concealing what it was doing, has been described by Llewellyn as "prudery" which, he says, "reminds one of some Victorian virgin tubbing in a nightgown." Such prudery was unwholesome; we may be thankful that the Court has ceased, in that sense, to be Victorian, old-maidish. For such prudishness meant that the real issues in constitutional cases were not squarely faced. Now the Court and the lawyers proceed directly to a discussion of the proper confines of the court's political power.

Let me here recall my comparison of musical and statutory interpretation. It has been asked whether a performer may legitimately play on a modern piano a piece written by Bach for the well-tempered clavichord, considering the pronounced differences between the piano and Bach's harpsichord. May a conductor adapt to a large orchestra a composition written in the 18th century for a small orchestra? Some musicians say emphatically No. They would say the same of playing Hamlet in modern clothes. They call such conduct a "sacrilege." Krenek disagrees. There has been the same sort of disagreement among lawyers as to the interpretation of our 18th century national Constitution. Some insist that it is virtually sacrilegious to put our Constitution in modern clothes. Mr. Justice Holmes emphatically took the other view. When "we are dealing with" the words of the Constitution, he wrote in 1920, "we must realize that they have called into life a being the development of which could not have been foreseen completely by the most gifted of its begetters. It was enough for them to realize or to hope that they had created an organism; it has taken a century and cost their successors sweat and blood to prove that they created a nation. The case before us must be considered in the light of our whole experience and not merely in that of what was said a hundred years ago." Earlier, in 1914, Holmes commented of the provisions of the Constitution: "Their significance is vital not formal; it is to be gathered not simply by taking the words and a dictionary, but by considering their origin and the line of their growth." Subsequently, Chief Justice Hughes declared, "If by the statement that what the Constitution meant at the time of its adoption it means today, it is intended to say that the great clauses of the Constitution . . . must be confined to the interpretation which the framers, with the conditions and outlook of their time, would have placed upon them, the statement carries its own refutation." (These remarks are probably not applicable to the highly specific, unambiguous, provisions of the Constitution.)

Owing to Holmes's influence, and to the impact of F.D.R.'s famous "court fight," the Supreme Court now uses its veto power sparingly. It accords the strongest presumption to the validity of legislation. Chief Justice Stone, however, articulated one notable exception: When a statute relates to the privileges contained in the Bill of Rights—to "civil liberties"—the presumption is apparently against the statute. In some measure, the Court seems to have adopted that exception.

The Supreme Court has said that, because of the difficulty of amending the Constitution, it is more willing to over-rule precedents interpreting the Constitution than those dealing with other subjects; and a statute held unconstitutional as applied to one person or a particular state of facts may be held constitutional as to another person on another state of facts.

As the Supreme Court's veto function compels it to engage in a political undertaking, this function—plainly legislative in character—is substantially different from the Court's function when it interprets a statute. True, even there, as we saw, some judicial legislation and some consideration of policy cannot be excluded. But the policy factor should, in that respect, be far less extensive than in constitutional cases. There can and should be a sharp difference of degree between the legitimate scope of judicial concern with policy when, for instance, the Supreme Court interprets a statute and that Court's far greater legitimate scope when it determines, in the name of the Constitution, whether to veto a statute.[1] Because of the danger that the mood necessary in the latter field may carry over to the other field, it has been suggested that we have two Supreme Courts, one devoting itself solely to solving constitutional problems.[2] I doubt, however, whether that suggestion will soon be adopted.

2

In the modern era in the occidental world, there have developed successive efforts of divers kinds to be rid of the human component in the making and application of laws. At one time, and markedly in the period of the powerful monarchs, the promulgation of legal rules, their judicial interpretation, and their execution or administration, were all three largely centered in the Crown, through the king's subordinates subject to his commands. Then there arose the idea of sharply separating the exercise of those powers or functions. The notion of the sharp separation of government powers into executive, legislative and judicial got its vogue in the 18th century largely through Montesquieu. He purported to find it in actual existence in England. He erred. For in England in those days, the powers were intertwined, although, to

[1] Curtis errs in neglecting that difference.

[2] Hexner, Studies in Legal Therminology (1941) 90, refers to Joseph-Borthelemy, Droit Constitutionel for examples of special courts to examine such issues alone.

an extent, the judiciary had become separated from the other branches, and the legislature, Parliament, was beginning to be independent of the Crown. Later, in England, Parliament became and is today supreme.

In America, however, Montesquieu's idea was, in considerable measure, embodied in our Constitutions adopted after the Revolution began. The cleavage never was as clear in fact as the theory suggested to some persons. But, at first, through fear of royal power, the executive, and even the judiciary, were subordinated to the legislature. This experiment frightened the economic conservatives, who feared the liberal tendencies of elected representatives. In our national Constitution, subsequently adopted, the powers of the President and of the courts were strengthened at the expense of Congress.

Yet Congress remained, in the popular view, the voice of the people. And, for another reason, by no means entirely economic, its utterances were regarded as peculiarly important; many men longed for definite general rules to be equally applied. In the interpretation of laws by judges, in their execution or administration by the President and his subordinates, individual differences in application of the general rules appeared; they seemed symptoms of a dreaded capricious "government of men." But the legislature, the Congress, was the Constitutional author of the general rules; limited though Congress was by constitutional restraints, it, as the general rule-maker, stood forth as the symbol of what seemed to be a "government of laws, not of men."[3]

The conservatives, however, perceived that there could be caprice in the making of laws by a majority in Congress. And, when, by constitutional amendments, Congress came to be more democratically elected, the conservative minority, fearful of popular legislation inimical to their interests, and fearful, too, of Presidents more and more responsive to popular desires, turned to the courts.[4] For a long period, the courts, on the whole, played a conservative role. They declared popular statutes unconstitutional; they interpreted others in such ways as to thwart the purpose of Congress. But when, of recent years, changes in the personnel of the courts induced a judicial attitude more friendly to legislation, the conservatives began fiercely to criticize the courts. They now look to the legislature to restrain the other branches.

[3] See Chapter XXX as to this phrase.

[4] As our courts have the power to declare statutes invalid, Max Radin cogently notes that "the fact that constitutional decisions use the language of adjudication does not change the fact that we have in this respect fused governmental functions on a new pattern after having taken some centuries to differentiate them."

I can't stop here to tell this story in detail. But I've said enough to make this point: Partly in order to protect conservative, economic vested interests, and perhaps more largely because of a desire—unrelated to economic interests—to have a government devoid of the effects of human personalities, men have sought a sort of human-less government. Distrust of human-ness, then, centers at times in distrust of the legislature; at times, of the executive or administrative branch; at times, of the judiciary. There has been a sort of merry-go-round of fear of the human factor in government.

Today, much of the animosity stemming from that fear is directed at the judiciary, particularly because its human characteristics, always present, have now been made more apparent. We had apotheosized the judges, especially, our Supreme Court judges. The immediate reaction to the disclosure that they were human, resembled that of the natives in Kipling's story when they discovered that the soldiers they had deified could bleed: They fell on them, crying, "Neither Gods nor devils but men." So today we hear charges that the judges do not literally adhere to the rules laid down in statutes, and demands that they do. I have tried to show you how futile, in part, is that demand—how, beyond certain limits, judicial legislation, even as to statutes, cannot be avoided.

XXIII. LEGAL REASONING

THE reader may now be wondering whether trial-court fact-finding does not affect the precedent doctrine and the interpretation of statutes and the Constitution. It does indeed. I think the best way to explain how it does will be to consider what has been said by some distinguished "rule-skeptics" who seem to think otherwise.

2

I have tried to show that, absent a statute, the legal rules are judge-made and therefore frequently mutable; that, even when rules are proclaimed in statutes by the legislature, still judicial legislation, with its resultant destruction of complete certainty, must often intervene; that, consequently, the legal rules, whether judge-made or statute-made, are by no means always clear and dependable. Many rules which seem certain are surprisingly vague when examined at close range. Numerous gaps and many "unprovided cases" then show up. The legal specialist in any particular field—for instance, patents, copyrights, real estate, "commercial law"—is far less sure of the completeness and precision of the rules than one who eyes them casually. Yet, making all due allowance for their uncertainty, vagueness, instability, and flexibility, nevertheless, as to a very considerable number of matters, the rules, at any point of time, are precise. On that account, most lawyers say, with Cardozo, that much of what they call "law" is fairly certain.

With that view many "rule-skeptics" agree. They maintain that legal uncertainty is restricted, for the most part, to the growing points in the rules, to the cases where the facts present novel situations or where, under the impact of newly emerging social needs or altered policy attitudes, the courts change the rules.

Professor Walter Wheeler Cook, a leading rule-skeptic, illuminated that subject.[1] He differentiated between (1) "routine" cases and (2)

[1] See the following articles by Cook: " 'Substance' and 'Procedure' in the Conflicts of Law," 42 *Yale L.J.* (1933) 333; "Scientific Method and the Law," 13 *Am. Bar Ass'n. J.* (1927) 303; Cook, "The Logical and Legal Bases of the Conflicts of Law," 33 *Yale L.J.* (1929) 457, 467-487; "An Unpublished Chapter," 37 *Ill. L. Rev.* (1943) 418; " 'Facts' and 'Statements of Fact,' " 4 *Un. of Chi. L. Rev.* (1937) 233, 238-39.

those involving "new and unusual situations." He said that "many of the cases which present themselves to a trial judge are so much like other cases already passed upon that they are disposed of in a more or less routine way without much thought," and are decided "automatically" or by "habit." A "system of rules and principles . . . can be expected to provide 'certainty' and 'predictability' of decisions . . . in routine cases that fit into the existing pattern without any real thought." The legal generalizations "will give us the answer" in "the vast bulk of human transactions . . ."

But not so, said Cook, when "new and unusual situations" arise which do not fit into the existing legal rules. Then a judge must engage in "reflective thinking," must act creatively. He must then treat the rules as working tools. For, "whatever else they may be, generalizations are not fixed rules for deciding doubtful cases, but instrumentalities for their investigation, methods by which the net value of past experience is rendered available for present scrutiny of new perplexities . . . ; they are hypotheses to be tested and revised for their further working. To call a generalization a tool is not to say it is useless; the contrary is patently the case. A tool is something to use. Hence it is something to be improved by noting how it works."

With this view of the function of legal rules I concur. But I think there is something naive in Cook's conception of "routine cases," for it blithely assumes that the facts in any such a case come before the judge at a trial in a manner requiring no "real thought" on his part. This attitude is the more surprising since Cook, elsewhere, disclosed a singularly alert awareness of the protean nature of "facts" and of the way in which human purposes affect the very determination of what "facts" are. When, he wrote in 1937,[2] we look at the "external world," it "presents itself to us as a shifting, varying series of changing patterns of color, sound, odor or what not," which may be called "brute, raw events. . . . If we try to describe . . . these 'crude, raw events,' we discover . . . that there are an infinite number of aspects of any 'situation,' and that, in order to talk about it at all, we have to select, from among these infinitely varied aspects, those which for some reason or other we are going to talk about. In the second place, we discover that in talking about the selected aspects, we have to relate them in such a way as to put them under some category, some class, for which we have (or perhaps create) a verbal symbol or name. . . . In other words, in

[2] Cook, "'Facts' and 'Statements of Fact,'" 4 *Un. of Chicago L. Rev.* (1937) 233, 238-39.

making a 'statement of facts' about the 'given' situation . . . , so as to state 'what it is,' I have in every case necessarily selected certain aspects, thereby [bringing] all the selected 'data'. . . under some category. Then and then only can I say 'what it is'—that is, make a 'statement of fact.' " The "facts," Cook concludes, "are the product first of 'abstraction' from the concreteness [of the] 'brute, raw events,' [and] then of interpretation of the elements abstracted. . . ."

Strangely, Cook overlooks this analysis when he explains the difference between "routine" cases and others. There he writes as if, for a court in all kinds of cases, the first step—the initial "selection" ("abstraction") from the "brute, raw events"—is "automatic," and as if, except in "unusual" cases, the court effortlessly puts the facts, thus "automatically" selected, under some legal category (a legal rule or principle). Cook assumes that the court receives the winnowed "data," that they are "given," and that the court engages solely in their "interpretation." As a result, Cook's description of the decisional process is too simple. In a law-suit, the "selections" are more numerous and complicated.

Here I must revert to what I said in earlier chapters. There are three steps in the selection: (a) First the witnesses make their selections from the "brute, raw events" of the past about which they testify. What they pick out depends not only on their individual capacities for seeing, hearing, touching or smelling, but also on each witness' individual emotional condition at the time when he "selects"; similar factors, plus bias or lying, affect the witnesses' "selections" when asked to recollect what they originally observed, and again when they testify. (b) Second, when the testimony is oral and the witnesses tell differing stories, the trial court (omitting, for the moment, its gestalt) makes a "selection": it chooses to believe some and to disbelieve other testimony. (c) Only after the completion of this second step does there occur the kind of selection which Cook describes. The trial court must now, from the previously selected facts, cull out those facts which are "relevant," i.e., those which fit into some well-settled rule or some new rule the court contrives.

Cook's discussion of legal reasoning in the process of deciding a law-suit relates exclusively to this last step of "selection," i.e., to the "interpretation" of the "data." Cook says nothing of the difficulties and uncertainties involved in the witnesses' "selection" and in the trial court's first stage of "selection" from the witnesses' testimony.[3] More

[3] In 1933, in his article, " 'Substance' and 'Procedure,' " he said that when one

serious is Cook's disregard of the gestalt factor in the trial court's decision, a factor which often means that the trial court (jury or judge) made no real selection of facts to be fitted into a rule, but reached the decision by way of an undifferentiated, unarticulated, reaction to the oral testimony. Accordingly, Cook leaves unexamined the most baffling and disturbing aspects of the decisional process. To phrase my criticism more sharply, he does not observe that there is no knowing, before a suit is begun, whether the case will appear to the trial court to be a "routine" case or one which is "unusual."

An illustration will help. Suppose that the Acme Auto Company, which manufactures Acme automobiles, sells some of them to Tompkins, an independent dealer. Tompkins, in turn, sells one of these Acme cars to Mr. Meek. Meek sues the Acme Company. He asserts that, while driving his car carefully, one of the wheels broke, the car went into a ditch, and as a result he broke his hip. At the trial, he and several other witnesses so testify; and others testify that the Acme Company was careless in manufacturing the wheel. Some witnesses for Acme, however, testify that it was not thus careless; and others swear that Meek was not injured in any automobile accident but had fractured his hip when he slipped on a rug in his house. The trial court, believing Meek's witnesses, "finds" the facts accordingly,[4] and gives Meek a judgment against the Acme Company for $10,000.

The Acme Company appeals. The upper court, as usual, accepts the facts as found by the trial court. But, until 1916, any upper court would have held that those facts lacked legal significance, and would have reversed that judgment on the ground that, under the applicable legal rule, an automobile manufacturer owes no legal duty to a man who bought a car, not from the manufacturer, but from an independent dealer like Tompkins. It was a "routine" case.

However, beginning in 1916, most upper courts changed the legal rule, and have held that the manufacturer is liable to such a buyer. Through that change in the legal rule, the "facts" as found in a case

speaks of a "right," one is but predicting what action officials will take. In a footnote he added, "Of course all statements as short as this oversimplify and tend to ignore the fact that if the case is contested one can never be sure, for example, what verdict the jury may bring in, etc. For the purposes of the present paper, this always present uncertainty is of no importance." But in no other writings did Cook discuss that "always present uncertainty."

[4] Remember that, if the trial is by jury, usually no express "finding" is made, and that, in a judge-trial, the trial judge may not publish any finding; in either of those circumstances, the "finding" is but a guess by the upper court that the trial court intended so to "find." Remember also that even a special finding by a trial judge may be merely a product of his somewhat artificial *ex post facto* analysis of his gestalt.

like Meek's become "relevant." That change called for "reflective thinking." The courts in 1916 came to regard such facts as presenting a "new situation." Now that the changed rule is established, a court, without much "real thought," will slide such a case under that rule—once the "facts" are "found" to be like those in Meek's case.

It is this sort of categorization of "facts" which Cook and many other legal thinkers describe when they write of "facts" as presenting either "routine" or "new situations." But those legal thinkers disregard the process by which the trial court arrives at the facts, i.e., the choice of some part of the oral testimony as correctly depicting those facts and the trial court's gestalt. Consequently, these thinkers seriously err in saying that, when a court employs a previously formulated rule, the decision is "routine," is a product of "habit" requiring no "real thought."

That legal rules frequently intertwine with the "facts," that a rule often gets its meaning in its "application" to "new" fact situations, is an idea, once unorthodox, but now increasingly accepted, thanks largely to the efforts of the legal skeptics.[5] In a searching study of "legal reasoning," recently published, Professor Edward Levi goes beyond that idea.[6] Legal reasoning, he says, "has a logic of its own." He criticizes the much repeated "doctrine" that "the legal process" is a "method of applying general rules of law to diverse cases. . . . If this were the doctrine, it would be disturbing to find that the rules change from case to case and are made from case to case. Yet this change in the rules is the indispensable dynamic quality of law. . . . Not only do new situations arise, but in addition peoples' wants change. The categories used in the legal process must be left ambiguous in order to permit the infusion of new ideas. . . . In this manner the [rules] come to express the ideas of the community." We do have "a system of rules," but they are "discovered in the process of determining similarity or difference" in "fact situations." The "rules change as the rules are applied. More important, the rules arise out of a process which, while comparing fact situations, creates the rules and then applies them." The changes occur "because the scope of a rule of law, and therefore its meaning, depends upon a determination of what facts will be sim-

[5] Most of them have neglected Wurzel's pioneering treatise, "Juridical Thinking," published in Vienna in 1904, and, as translated, published in this country in the volume, *The Science of Legal Method* (1917) 286.

[6] Levi, "An Introduction to Legal Reasoning," 15 *Un. of Chicago L. Rev.* (1948) 501.

ilar to those present when the rule is first announced. The finding of similarity or difference is the key step in the legal process. . . . The problem for the law is this: When will it be just to treat different cases as though they were the same? A working legal system must therefore be willing to pick out key similarities and to reason from them to the justice of applying a common classification."

Granted the "facts," Levi's exposition admirably answers many questions which have puzzled lawyers and non-lawyers concerning "legal logic." But, like Cook, Levi hurdles the chief difficulty to an understanding of the decisional process. He sees it as one of "comparing fact situations," of the "finding of similarity or difference" in facts, involving the ability to "pick out key similarities." One who reads Levi would think that the facts of a case appear in court ready-made, waiting only to be compared with those of some previous cases. Levi is debonnaire in his unconcern with all the pain and anguish of giving birth to the facts which are compared with those in earlier cases. Levi, although for a considerable time a successful practicing lawyer, is a "rule-skeptic," not a "fact-skeptic."[7] He by-passes the chief work of trial courts.

Professor Fred Rodell, in his coruscating book, *Woe Unto You Lawyers!*, published ten years ago, a book which deserves careful reading,[8] gives a satirical account of how courts sometimes draw fine distinctions based on slight differences of fact. The lawyer, says Rodell, "will tell you . . . that fact situations, by reason of their similarity or dissimilarity, fall naturally into groups; one group will be governed by one legal principle, another group by another or possibly a contradictory principle. In short, each new case or problem that comes up is enough like some batch of cases . . . that have come up before to be controlled by the same principle that was used to control them. . . . The joker in the theory is the assumption that any two, much less twenty, fact situations or legal problems can ever be sufficiently alike to fall naturally

[7] Paul's article, "Dobson v. Commissioner: The Strange Ways of Law and Fact," 57 *Harv. L. Rev.* (1944) 753, scintillatingly discusses the interplay between rules and facts. "The law . . . has set the pace for the facts," he writes. "But the facts perform a similar pace for the law, since a principle must rest upon the facts from which it is deduced." Yet, almost entirely neglecting "fact skepticism," Paul somewhat oversimplifies. See Frank, Introduction to Paul, *Studies in Federal Taxation* (1927) 3-4; Cahn, Book Review, 2 *Tax L. Rev.* (1947) 289-90.

[8] I recommend its reading because it raises many questions which should be seriously pondered. I think, however, that (perhaps unintentionally) its condemnations of lawyers and courts are sometimes excessive and seem to ascribe far too much in the way of willfully selfish aims and hypocrisy to the legal profession.

—that is, without being pushed—into the same category. The very existence of two situations or problems means that there are differences between them. And here, perhaps, the lawyer defending his craft may pop up . . . to say that the differences can be major or minor, important or unimportant. It is when the 'essential' facts are the same, he will tell you, that the same general principles apply. But which facts in any situation or problem are 'essential' and what makes them 'essential'? Somebody must pick the 'essential' facts of any situation from the unessential ones. Who? Well, who but the lawyers and the judges? And the picking of the 'essential' facts, which are going to determine the 'similar' group of old cases, which group in turn is going to determine the appropriate legal principles, then becomes . . . arbitrary and wide-open. . . .

"Suppose, to take a simple example, a man driving a 1939 Cadillac along the Lincoln Highway toward Chicago runs into a Model T Ford, driven by a farmer who has just turned onto the Highway from a dirt road, and demolishes the Ford but does not hurt the farmer. The farmer sues, and a local judge, on the basis of various principles of Law which are said to 'control' the case, awards him $100. A week later, another man driving a 1939 Cadillac along the Lincoln Highway toward Chicago runs into a Model T Ford driven by another farmer who has just turned onto the Highway from the same dirt road, and demolishes the Ford but does not hurt the farmer. This farmer also sues. The facts, as stated, seem to make this case quite similar to the previous case. Will it then fall into the same group of fact situations? Will it be 'controlled' by the same principles of Law? Will the second farmer get $100? That all depends. For of course there will be other facts in both cases. Some may still be similar. Others, inevitably, will be different. And the possibilities of variation are literally endless. Maybe the first Cadillac was doing sixty miles an hour and the second one thirty. Or maybe one was doing forty-five and the other one forty. Or maybe both were doing forty-five but it was raining one week and clear the next. Maybe one farmer blew his horn and the other didn't. Maybe one farmer stopped at the crossing and the other didn't. Maybe one farmer had a driver's license and the other didn't. Maybe one farmer was young and the other was old and wore glasses. Maybe they both wore glasses but one was nearsighted and the other farsighted. Maybe one Cadillac carried an out-of-state license plate and the other a local license plate. Maybe one of the Cadillac drivers was a bond salesman and the other a doctor. Maybe one was insured and the other wasn't.

Maybe one had a girl in the seat beside him and the other didn't. Maybe they both had girls beside them but one was talking to his girl and the other wasn't. Maybe one Cadillac hit its Ford in the rear left wheel and the other in the front left wheel. Maybe a boy on a bicycle was riding along the Highway at one time but not the other. Maybe a tree at the intersection had come into leaf since the first accident. Maybe a go-slow sign had blown over.

"The point is, first, that no two fact situations anywhere any time are entirely similar. Yet a court can always call any one of the inevitable differences between two fact situations, no matter how small, a difference in the 'essential' facts. Thus, in the second automobile accident, any one of the suggested variations from the facts of the previous accident might—or might not—be labelled 'essential.' And a variation in the 'essential' facts means that the case will be dumped into a different group of cases and decided according to a different legal principle, or principles.

"When the second accident case came to court, the judge might call entirely irrelevant the fact that a caution sign along the highway had blown down since the week before. Or he might pounce on that fact to help him lay the legal blame for the smashup, not on the Cadillac driver this time, but instead on the farmer, or on both of them equally, or on the state highway department—according, of course, to accepted principles of Law. Moreover, the mere fact that one driver was doing forty-five miles and the other forty might easily be enough to induce the judge to distinguish the second accident from the first and group it instead with a bunch of cases involving railroad trains that had run over stray horses and cows. The 'essential' facts being similar, the judge would put it, the same principles of Law are 'controlling.'

"As with the two automobile accidents, so with any two legal disputes that ever have come up or could come up—except that most legal disputes are far more complicated, involve many more facts and types of facts, consequently present the judges with a far wider selection from which to choose the 'essential' facts, and so open up a much greater range of legal principles which may be applied or not applied. And since no two cases ever fall 'naturally' into the same category so that they can be automatically subjected to the same rules of Law, the notion that twenty or thirty or a hundred cases can gather themselves, unshoved, under the wing of one 'controlling' principle is nothing short of absurd."

Rodell's description of "legal reasoning," less flattering to courts than

Cook's or Levi's, is perhaps, as to some decisions, more accurate. But it suffers from the same disregard of the process of "finding" the "facts," manifests the same unconcern with that process. Rodell does not mention, for instance, how in the automobile accident cases, the judge reached his determination that one of the cars travelled at thirty or sixty miles an hour, or that one driver did, or did not, have a license. Clearly Rodell, too, is not a fact-skeptic but a rule-skeptic (although a radical one).

3

As portrayed by such writers as Cook and Levi, the "selection" of facts turns on their "relevance" in terms of the legal rules; the selection, these writers would have it, widens or narrows only as the courts expand or contract those rules. This subject of "legal relevance" needs exploration.

Holmes once discussed that subject. "The reason," he wrote, "why a lawyer [in stating his case to a court] does not mention that his client wore a white hat when he made a contract, while Mrs. Quickly would be sure to dwell upon it along with the parcel gilt goblet and the sea-coal fire, is that he foresees that" a court "will act in the same way whatever his client had upon his head."[9] Despite my profound respect for Holmes, I think that in this instance he wrote somewhat misleadingly. Of course, he did not mean that a person's apparel is always irrelevant in a trial. That a woman wore a distinctive white hat may be relevant testimony when it is a method of identifying her, as, for instance, when some witnesses swear that they saw a woman with such a hat leaving the scene of a murder, and other witnesses say that they saw the accused, Miss Glamor, thus appareled, not far from that scene a few minutes earlier.

What does contradict Holmes is that "irrelevant" testimony is often given because the opposing lawyer does not object to its reception,[10] and that such testimony may have telling effects. "Irrelevance," says Judge Bok,[11] "can be highly enlightening. The witness who starts with what she ate for breakfast and remembers it was Thursday because her husband's sister came down with the measles when she shouldn't

[9] Holmes, "The Path of the Law," 10 *Harv. L. Rev.* 457 reprinted in Holmes, *Collected Legal Papers* (1920) 166, 167. To the same effect see Patterson, Book Review, 41 *Col. L. Rev.* (1941) 562, 564; Llewellyn, *The Bramble Bush* (1930) 41-42.

[10] An experienced trial lawyer will often refrain from objecting to such testimony because the objection may prejudice the jury against his client.

[11] Bok, *I Too, Nicodemus,* (1946) 322.

if she had only gone to the doctor, the one with glasses—should be a delight to the judge's heart and make the jury feel at home. Behind this leisurely sweep of incident they can follow her as they please, and it will give them at least her barometric pressure at the time when she signed the note at the bank without reading it. After listening to enough of it, any idiot would know that she was an accommodation endorser who had done it to help her husband and had got nothing out of it herself. . . ."

More than that, even when a party's attire in the past, before the trial, may be unimportant, nevertheless her appearance—sartorial or otherwise—at the trial may markedly affect the attitude of the trial judge or jury towards her testimony. In terms of the legal rules, that appearance lacks legal significance (i.e., is irrelevant); but when it induces the court to accept that testimony as true, it may influence the "finding" of the facts and thus determine the decision. Experienced trial lawyers do not overlook such factors which are omitted from treatises on "legal reasoning" because the writers of those treatises disdain to consider those subjective elements in trial courts' "selections" of the "facts."

XXIV. DA CAPO

The truth is that, were all the legal rules contained in statutes, and were all statutory rules so worded that they each permitted of but one exact meaning, nevertheless the personal element in the work of the courts would still operate.

Da Capo. I am back once more to my oft-repeated theme. In the light of my discussion of precedents and interpretation of statutes, I shall, for convenience, briefly restate what, in my earlier chapters, I said of fact-finding.

The *R,* in the $R \times F = D$ equation, is only one of the components of a court's decision. Take the most rigid and specific rules you can think of—say the rule that one must drive on the right side of the road, or the rule that for breach of a contract a court will give damages. Such a rule doesn't get into action, will not yield a decision, unless the necessary facts are proved. Mr. Shadrach sues Mr. Abednego, claiming that Abednego injured Shadrach in an automobile collision, because Abednego drove on the left side of the street. Shadrach can't win his suit unless he proves that fact. What does "prove" mean? It means that Shadrach must not only produce witnesses who swear to that fact, but also that the trial judge or jury must believe those witnesses. Maybe Shadrach's witnesses were faulty in their observation of the accident or that their memories have weakened. Maybe the trial court will think they lie or are mistaken. Then Shadrach will lose his suit.

But even that statement is inaccurate. Maybe the trial court will believe those witnesses, and will nevertheless say (expressly or impliedly) that it does not believe them. The facts of a case, remember, are not what actually happened but, at best, what the trial court says it thinks happened. For decisional purposes, the facts are therefore "subjective." They consist of the personal, individual, reactions of the trial judge or jury to the testimony of the witnesses.

As I observed earlier, the formula should be, not

$$R \times F = D$$

or

$$R \times OF \text{ (i.e., the objective facts)} = D$$

but

$$R \times SF = D$$

The "subjective" facts, in other words, are the things that count. The effects of that subjectivity on the supposed workings of the precedent system should now be plain. Under that system, cases the actual facts of which are alike should usually be decided alike, in the interest of objectivity, uniformity and equality. But how, when the testimony is oral, can anyone know whether the facts of two cases are alike? We can only know whether the facts as "found" in the two cases are similar. They may be so "found" that they seem similar, when in truth they were markedly different. If the same rule is applied to both, then there is no true equality of treatment, only a seeming equality. And if the facts as found are different, but in truth the facts were identical, then the decisions will be different, and equality will be denied.

Note, too, the effect of subjectivity on reliance: If a man, advised by his lawyer, enters into a transaction relying on a well settled, crisp and definite legal rule, but the court mistakenly finds the facts of that transaction—that is, finds that a different transaction occurred—then the court will not apply the rule on which the man relied. Mistakes in finding the facts, by a trial judge or a jury, may be deliberate or may be inadvertent. The consequences, in either event, frustrate the application of the correct legal rule to the actual facts. It follows that incorrect fact-finding frustrates both the precedent system and legislation. Studies of those subjects which neglect trial-court fact-finding use a scissors minus one blade, and end in futility. For fact-findings by trial courts often affect stare decisis and the interpretations of statutes and Constitutions.[1] Since fact-finding is a subjective matter, the legal rules, whether judge-made or statute-made, and the social policies the rules embody, are at the mercy of the personal subjective reactions of trial judges or juries. The fact-findings of trial courts—the products of those inescapable personal factors—thus show up as perhaps the most important element in court-house government.

You should bear that in mind when you hear it said that precedents serve as "a chart to govern conduct," that, without them, "the law" is "but a game of chance," so that men "will not know whether to litigate or settle, for they will have no assurance that a settled rule will be followed,"[2] and will be unable "safely to conduct [their] affairs in reliance upon a settled body of court decisions."[3] Remember the trial

[1] For instance, the Supreme Court may hold unconstitutional the action of state officials if performed in one way but not if in another way. Which way it is performed becomes a question of fact to be determined by a trial judge or jury.

[2] Roberts, J., dissenting in Mahnich v. Southern S.S. Co., 321 U.S. 96.

[3] Roberts, J., dissenting in Higgins v. Smith, 308 U.S. 473.

court's immense "fact discretion," and the subjectivity of that discretion, when a judge says: "But, in my view, liberty to decide each case as you think right without regard to any principles laid down in previous similar cases would only result in a completely uncertain law in which no citizen would know his rights or liabilities until he knew before what judge his case would come and could guess what view the judge would take on a consideration of the matter without any regard to previous decisions." [4] Is there not often just such uncertainty, despite the "previous decisions," because of uncertainty in fact finding?

Many legal thinkers have deceived themselves in this matter through their failure to distinguish between the functions of trial courts and upper courts. For, ordinarily, in an upper court, no fact-finding problem exists, because the facts are beyond dispute, having been "found" by the trial court. The usual questions for the upper court are then only these: [5] Do the facts of the case now before the court sufficiently resemble those of an earlier case so that the rule of that case is applicable? If there is such a resemblance, should that rule now be applied or should it be modified or abandoned? Although able lawyers cannot always guess how an upper court will answer those questions, the educated guesses of those lawyers are good in the majority of instances. When, in a trial court, the parties agree on the facts, so that they are undisputed, that court faces only those same questions; and again, usually, able lawyers can answer those questions. But (to repeat what I have often observed) in most cases in the trial courts, the parties do dispute concerning the facts, and the oral testimony is in conflict. In any such case, what does it mean to say that the facts are substantially similar to those of an earlier case? It means, at most, only that the trial court regards the facts of the two cases as about the same. Since, however, no one knows what the trial court will find as the facts, no one can guess what precedent ought to be or will be followed either by the trial court or, if an appeal occurs, by the upper court. This weakness of the precedent doctrine becomes the more obvious when one takes into account the gestalt factor, the intertwining of rules and "facts" in the trial court's decision.

The uniformity and stability which the rules may seem to supply are therefore often illusory, chimerical. No rule can be proof against the subjectivity inherent in fact-finding. Ordinarily the human element

[4] Hill v. Aldershott Corp. [1933] 1 K.B. 259, 263-264. Compare that statement with the ruling about a trial judges' fact-finding in Powell and Wife v. Streatham Manor Nursing Home [1935] A.C. 243.

[5] I omit here cases raising questions of errors in "procedure."

in judging cannot be escaped by resort to legal rules. In the last analysis, the legal rights of any man—to his property, to his means of earning a living, or not to be jailed or hanged when innocent of crime—if that man's rights become involved in a law-suit, usually depend on that human element. Don't let anyone persuade you to believe otherwise, to believe that, by any system of precedents or by legislation, you ordinarily can, when you go to court, get away from the reactions of some fallible human beings, if the facts are in dispute.

Experienced trial lawyers know better, even if they do not explain why, to themselves or others. For that reason, older lawyers are often more daring than recent law-school graduates.[6] "After you have been in practice a few years," wrote Henry Taft, "you will be surprised to find how many desperate cases can be won. . . . Speaker Reed once said to me that some of the notable forensic victories he had were in cases where he had been advised that success was impossible; and Sir Matthew Hale in the earlier years of his practice had misgivings about undertaking causes which he believed could not be sustained, but he became less conservative when case after case had been decided contrary to his prediction." I think of such remarks when I read a statement that the present Supreme Court's recent over-rulings of precedents have bred "the take-a-chance attitude towards litigation."[7] Surely that "take-a-chance attitude" would persist, and justifiably, if all courts were forever to abide by all the rules and precedents.

I must say once more that this much of truth there is in the conventional theory: When the facts are undisputed in the trial court, frequently a settled legal rule will determine the decision. Moreover, the rules announced by the upper courts have effects as sermons, sometimes influencing the community's customs and moral attitudes;[8] and constitutional decisions may prevent legislatures from enacting statutes which the legislators think the courts will strike down.

[6] See Frank, *Law and the Modern Mind* (1930) 31, 63.
[7] Kennedy, in 13 *Ford. L. Rev.* (1944) 8, note 44.
[8] See, however, Chapter XXV.

XXV. THE ANTHROPOLOGICAL APPROACH

We saw that some "primitive" societies, dreading the variable personal or human element in the judging process, with its resultant chanciness and uncertainties, resorted to what were regarded as the impersonal magical ordeals. We saw, too, that we have our own brand of legal magic—unverified beliefs by which we conceal the difficulties arising from that ever-present personal element in the decisional process, and that we create an illusory appearance of impersonality.

One of the most persistent of magical beliefs of that sort is this: Legal rights and duties, it is said, correspond to the customs of the community. The customs (the mores, the folkways, the habits of society) translate themselves, it is asserted, into court decisions, so that to know those social regularities is to know what the decisions will be. Since anthropology is the art concerned with such social regularities, I shall label this notion the "anthropological approach" to decisions.

This magical idea, which often has bobbed up in the past, is today entertained by many persons (including many "rule-skeptics") who, aware of the frequent unreliability of the formal legal rules as legal-prediction-instruments, seek a substitute in uniformities back of those rules. The key to those uniformities, they claim, may be found in so-called "social forces," such as modes and forms of business, customs, public opinion, and the like. These "social forces" are sometimes referred to as if they were discoverable objective entities. It has even been intimated or implied, with varying degrees of hopefulness, that some day we may be able to plot a curve, showing the effect of the confluences of these "social forces," so that, by using the proper ordinates and abscissas, the decision in any given lawsuit can be exactly foretold.

The anthropological thesis about the predictable effect of the mores on the courts is so often encountered, in some form or other, that it deserves detailed criticism. First let me restate it thus: Community attitudes—the customs, or folkways, or the mores—we are told, express themselves in decisions. It is possible, before a case is tried, to forecast the decision, if you know the community attitude towards the facts of the case. Indeed, to foresee that decision, one need not know the legal rules. Consider the layman, Jones, about to do an act. He feels, or "senses," the folkways. Accordingly, he acts with a "feeling of rightness," because it is a feeling which reflects the current mores, a feeling which therefore fairly accurately anticipates what a court will decide if that act ever comes before it for abjudication. If those mores are changing, the layman, while acting, "senses" the change. Usually he does not think about the legal rules relative to his action, nor does he usually contemplate future litigation affecting it; and even if he attempted to formulate that act in terms of legal rules he would probably err. But, if a court is later called upon to consider that act, its judgment will often (as Llewellyn puts it) "jump with the layman's prior non-legal expectation." The layman can therefore, before acting, says Llewellyn, often "plan safely, counting on the law, although not knowing it." Llewellyn also says that "the ordinary layman guides his conduct not by legal norms but by social norms. . . . Legal certainty . . . for the layman [the non-lawyer] . . . consists in the fact that the transaction he has entered into, if it gets into litigation, will be adjudged as a prudent man [that is, a prudent layman in the particular circumstances] would have foreseen, if he had in mind, at the beginning, the unforeseen suit."

Let me state that thesis somewhat more specifically. Here is a non-lawyer, Mr. Ordinary. He lends someone his automobile, or agrees to invest some money, or signs his name to a note. He has not the faintest notion that what he does is, in lawyer's jargon, making a "bailment," or "entering into a joint adventure," or becoming an "anomalous endorser." Those words would be gibberish to him. He knows only, and often but semi-consciously, that what he does is "right and proper" according to some accepted social norm, some customary way of behaving approved by his society, what has been called a "non-litigious custom." Unknown to him, his conduct fits into a legal rule which matches that custom according to which he acted. Because that legal rule and that custom do match, it follows that, if later he "goes to law" (becomes involved in a law-suit) about his conduct, Mr. Ordinary will win the suit, because the court will apply the legal rule which corresponds to the social norm, the "non-litigious custom," in accordance with which he acted. For, as the matter is sometimes put, a rule of conduct which, from one point of view, is a custom, from another is a legal rule; many non-legal uniformities spell themselves out as legal uniformities which control the courts in deciding cases.

It will be convenient to schematize this notion. Let N represent the social norms (the "non-litigious customs"). Then, as according to this thesis, every N is matched by a definite legal rule (an R) we can change our $R \times F = D$ formula, by substituting N for R, and say:

$$N \times F = D$$

We may refine that formula as follows: Instead of referring merely to F, we may call any particular act or transaction an Fa or Fb or Fc, etc. Now the anthropological thesis maintains that, for many a particular act or transaction—an Fa or Fb—there is a particular N—an Na or Nb. But, ex hypothesi, this Na or Nb is often matched by a particular R—an Ra or Rb. Also, any particular R, an Ra or Rb, will usually yield a particular D—a Da or Db. Consequently, we may say

$$Fa = Na = Ra = Da$$

or

$$Fb = Nb = Rb = Db, \text{ etc.}$$

We are now in a position to poke holes in this thesis. It involves several untenable assumptions:

(1) It assumes that, ordinarily, as to any particular set of facts, there is a fairly precise and knowable social norm, group habit, "non-litigious custom," or customary attitude. But that is untrue even in the most "primitive" societies; it is far less true in so shifting and changing a society as that of the U.S.A. today.

However, even in our society, it is more or less true with reference to some fundamental issues I have labelled "dramatic" issues. The views of the majority, or the views of the group of which many judges are members, are not too difficult to know when these "dramatic" issues are up for judicial consideration. Murder will stir up known reactions. Even as to some somewhat less dramatic issues than murder, much the same can be said at any given moment, for there are judiical "trends": It is moderately obvious what the present majority of the United States Supreme Court will do about some kinds of labor cases and utility-rate cases. But, with respect to innumerable non-dramatic problems of conduct, group-habits are not definitely crystallized in our society. If the dispute does not involve "capital and labor," or major crimes, often there can be found no ready-made group attitude which will predictably translate itself into a decision.

Moreover, many disputes activate, not one definite community attitude, but conflicting community attitudes—economic attitudes, racial attitudes, religious attitudes, etc. Thus a "property" attitude may collide with a Roman Catholic or Methodist attitude or a State-Rights attitude or with a women-in-business attitude. Holmes said in 1899, "I think it most important to remember whenever a doubtful case arises, with certain analogies on one side and other analogies on the other, that what really is before us is a conflict between two social desires, each of which seeks to extend its dominion over the case, and which cannot both have their way. The social question is which desire is stronger at the point of conflict." Which of those "social desires" will win out it is often not easy to know in advance. Nor is the guessing made simpler by referring to terms like "interests," "interest-groups," "pressure-groups," and the like. "Interests" or groups push and pull and fight with one another. The outcome is often a compromise, the result of a sort of (subjective or objective) log-rolling

(2) In the next place, the customary attitudes or social norms do not, in "pure" form, pass through the minds of judges. The "personalities" of the individual judges sometimes refract and bend the mores in unforetellable ways. As Cardozo said in 1921: "In every court there are likely to be as many estimates of the 'Zeitgeist' as there are judges on its bench."[1] "Current mores," says John Dickinson, ". . . are things about which there is room for difference of opinion and . . . , when it is a question of their writing themselves into the law, the opinion which prevails is the judge's opinion." He also comments: "It is, of course, possible to speak in a figurative sense of 'authority' as attaching to the operation of impersonal forces like tradition or public opinion. There is always, however, the possibility that contending individuals will hear the pronouncements of such impersonal authorities differently." And the divers judges, too, may differ among themselves in their "hearing" of such pronouncements.

(3) But ignore these criticisms. Assume, for the moment, no matter how unjustifiably, that to a given set of facts, an *Fa,* there will usually correspond a precise and ascertainable social norm, an *Na.* Assume that, when *Fa* is believed to exist, it will automatically evoke a corresponding *Na* in the mind of every judge or juryman, and will therefore indubitably lead to decision *Da.* The layman, Mr. Ordinary, has participated in facts *Fa;* he knows those to be the actual facts; he has a sense of rightness about his participation in those facts because he

[1] Yet Cardozo also wrote in 1932 as if he thought the "law" could usually be "made to conform to [the layman's] reasonable expectations," through its accommodation to "the mores of the times."

senses the existence of the corresponding social norm, *Na,* which clicks with his sense of rightness. In participating in facts *Fa,* Mr. Ordinary (according to the anthropological thesis) could plan his acts with safety, "counting on the law"—the legal rule, *Ra*—"although not knowing it." If he "goes to law," the decision will be in his favor—it will be *Da,* for it will inevitably result from the rule *Ra.*

Unfortunately, it happens, time and again, in such a case, that the trial court, after hearing the witnesses, does not believe that the facts (the facts as they actually happened) are *Fa.* For any one of a number of reasons or unreasons, the trial judge or jury mistakenly believes the facts are *Fb.* Now, on the assumptions of the "anthropological approach," if the trial judge or jury does mistakenly take the facts as *Fb,* that *Fb* will usually evoke in the mind of the trial judge or jury a corresponding social norm, *Nb*—which is not the social norm, *Na,* according to which Mr. Ordinary acted. And, if the anthropological thesis is correct, this evocation of *Nb* is bound, through a matching *Rb,* to produce a decision, *Db,* against Mr. Ordinary, which is not the favorable decision, *Da,* that he anticipated.

You see what happened to the layman who was "counting on the law although not knowing it." The court's decision did not "jump with his prior non-legal expectation." Where he went wrong was in "sensing" that the acts which he performed would be correctly reproduced in the mind of the judge or the jury. When he acted, he could not know or sense or guess what the court would find to be the *F.* From his standpoint, the wrong social norm was applied. Or, to put it differently, the "right" social norm was applied, but it was applied to facts which never happened.

When, in Shaw's play, the sheriff's jury, in advance of hearing the evidence, decided to hang Blanco Posnet, the accused objected, and the sheriff replied that, if he did not like that jury, he "should have stole a horse in another town." The folk-notions of what to do with a horse-thief were well known. Blanco Posnet complained because he had not been proved to be the thief. Conscientious judges do not knowingly pick out the wrong defendant, but, through their misapprehension of the facts, their decisions are often not justified by the actual past events.

Even, then, if the formula, $Fa = Na = Ra = Da$, were otherwise adequate, the *F,* in any case which involves conflicting oral testimony, would still be at large, on the loose, unguessable and unpredictable. For, to repeat, that *F* in such a case is an *SF*—i.e., "subjective," idiosyncratic, varying with the peculiar reactions, at the trial, of the particular judge or jury trying the case. Consequently, even in a lawsuit involving the more dramatic issues, where the group reactions to conduct, the social norms, are (1) precise, (2) easily ascertainable, and (3) sure to slide right through any trial court's mind without friction, still there is no knowing what the decision will be, because of the unknowability of what the trial court will believe was the conduct of the parties to the lawsuit. Thus, Thulin's admirable study indicates that judges in the several states feel about the same towards reckless automobile driving, and will interpret the language of differently-worded statutes to arrive at substantially similar penalties for that offense. The social norms in Iowa and Georgia, on that subject, are virtually identical. But there is no telling whether a particular judge in Iowa will think that, in fact, a particular defendant transgressed that norm. In other words, neglecting all other criticisms, the frequent inaccuracy of the judicial *F*—because it is an *SF*—suffices to vitiate the thesis that, generally, a specific decision in a specific "contested" case reflects the community attitude towards the actual facts of that case. Cultural anthropology will not render predictable most specific decisions in such cases.

Not very long ago, a federal trial judge, towards the end of his long career on the bench, publicly revealed for the first time that he had always counted as a liar any witness who rubbed his hands while testifying. That judge must have decided hundreds of cases in which he arrived at his *F*'s by applying that asinine test for detecting falsehoods. Even if the *R*'s in those cases were but reflections of precise, community attitudes, nevertheless the *D*'s were at the mercy of those absurdly constructed *F*'s.

What is more, the decision of the trial judge or jury is not the product of an *R* and an *F*, but, as we saw, often is a gestalt, a composite, the analysis into *R* and *F* being somewhat artificial. However, for present purposes, we may overlook that artificiality, since, even supposing that the *F* were a distinctly separable ingredient of the decision, yet its subjective, unpredictable character would destroy the anthropological thesis, which rests on the assumption of knowable uniformities.

2

Cutting deeper into the anthropological thesis, we can detect a basic fallacy: Let us assume, for the sake of the argument, that social habits and customs, smooth-running, non-legal, social regularities, are usually closely correlated with, or clearly reflected in, some legal regularities, some "substantive" legal rules, or some "real rules" lying back of the "paper rules" the courts utter. But (as some sponsors of the "anthropological approach" fully recognize) litigation signifies a critical breakdown of the smooth-running, non-legal social regularities. Using the metaphor of social health, litigation has been called "pathological," a sort of social sickness, and law-suits have been referred to as "hospital cases." Now this "pathological" nature of litigation should alone suffice to throw doubt on the validity of the anthropological thesis. For one should seriously doubt whether what happens in the event of social sickness (i.e., what happens in a law-suit) closely corresponds to what had happened previously during the period of social health (when the non-legal, social regularities were smoothly working). Observation confirms that doubt. For (to say nothing of the disturbances caused by "procedural" blunders of one or another of the lawyers or by missing evidence) the vagaries of trial-court fact-findings and gestalts play havoc with the assumed correlation of (1) pre-litigation, out-of-court, regularities with (2) in-court results. Once again, ability to predict the rules ("paper" or "real" rules) which a trial court will use in deciding a case, or which the upper court will use on an appeal from the trial court, does not mean ability to predict the decision when witness' credibility is crucial, as usually it is.

In our day, those (like Llewellyn) who have espoused the anthropological approach have been men who know and care little about trials and trial courts. Consequently they have deceived themselves about these correlations. Their anthropological researches, to be sure, may show some correlations between the social norms and those "substantive" legal rules which are either expressly stated in, or inferable from, upper-court opinions. For, accepting the *F*'s as stated in those upper-court opinions as if they were the actual facts, one may be able to discover in the *R*'s—contained in (or lurking behind) those opinions—more or less direct manifestations of the usual social responses to those facts. In that way, study of courts' opinions may be useful to the anthropologist and to the anthropologically-minded lawyer, by furnishing them with samples of, or clues to, the mores and folkways, and also by showing how the legal rules influence customs and how the customs affect the legal rules. Such anthropological studies, however, will not help the lawyer or the anthropologist or anyone else to foresee the subjective *F*'s, or the gestalts—and therefore the *D*'s—in most lawsuits in the trial courts. The anthropologist, and others, should therefore be warned that it is far easier to detect manifestations of the mores in courts' opinions than in their decisions.

The basic fallacy in this anthropological thesis appears in some of Walter Wheeler Cook's writings. Statements of the "law" of a given country, he said, are "true," if "they accurately and as simply as possible describe the past behavior and predict the future behavior" of "certain officials of society" such as judges. "So, a statement that, by the law of New York, A has, under given circumstances, a 'right' and that B is under a correlative 'duty', is a conventional way of asserting that, on the basis of certain past behavior of certain New York officials, we now predict that New York officials will behave in a certain way if specified events happen and the officials are set in motion in the appropriate way by the injured party." Cook added, "To be entirely accurate we must add that the assertion that A has a 'right' and B is under a 'duty' is an assertion that not only the officials but also the members of the given political community are in the habit of reacting in certain ways to certain stimuli. It is because these habit-patterns exist that we can safely predict; and the total prediction must be as to the reaction of the vast majority of the inhabitants of the country as well as of the judges, or we cannot speak of law as 'existing.' If, for example, a majority of the community were not in the habit of acquiescing in the acts of the officials, there would be not law but the absence of law. This conduct of the rest of the community is commonly assumed and we devote our attention to the probable action of the officials." You see that this thesis rests on the knowability of the operation of "habit-patterns," defined as "the habit of reacting in certain ways to certain stimuli." But how can one know with any accuracy, in any particular law-suit, before it is begun, (1) what will be the stimuli—the words and gestures of the witnesses—or (2) how the officials—the trial judge or jury—will react to those stimuli. The operation of the "habit patterns" in such circumstances is often hopelessly unforeseeable.

Underhill Moore, generally in an admirably tentative way, has employed the "anthropological approach." Perhaps the following is his best statement of his thesis: "It has been observed that the litigation-situation is a complex of innumerous variables of which the aspect of the behavior of the parties referred to as 'the facts,' and the aspect of the behavior of the court referred to as the decision are but two. What some of these other variables are is easily suggested. First, there are the aspects of the behavior of the court and the parties which are isolated for study by the biological sciences including psychology. They range from the processes of physical heredity to the data of psychiatry. Secondly, there are the aspects of the physical environment whose causal relation with human behavior is the study of anthropogeography. Thirdly, there are the elements of human culture as distinguished from human nature. These are the tools and the tangible equipment which is their product, the established patterns of behaving with this equipment and toward other men, and the propositions which are the sciences, philosophies, and religions. It is the study of the correlation between these cultural elements and particular human behavior which is, to those without curiosity, the ultimate end of anthropology, economics and sociology.

"Even if the litigation-situation were to be narrowed by the exclusion of those aspects which on the basis of a tentative judgment were not causally related to decisions, the psychological and cultural factors would remain. Even if techniques were at hand for the study of the causal relation of each factor to decisions, the joint manipulation of all is out of the question. It would be absurd to attempt to state a litigation-situation in terms of all the variables in causal relation with the decision. The formulation of such an equation is a day-dream. Short of such a formula the forecast of a particular decision can be no more certain than the forecast of tomorrow's weather in New Haven. . . . But observation of the relation between any group of variables including the decision makes the sphere of intuitional judgment smaller; and the study of any one or more variables may disclose that their correlation with decisions is a useful index. The forecast of the course of decisions or even of a particular decision in some fields at least may perhaps be made as probable as the prediction of the meteorologist. The same course which was open to the weather prophet of the seventeenth century is open to the lawyer and the student of government today. The rigorous application of a defined method to measure defined variables in units as invariable as may be, and to state in terms of those units a relation between those variables is as available a procedure now as it was then. Is it not conceivable that the time will come when the lawyer in making his judgments will take into account the results of the methodical study of a few cultural and psychological factors as well as his law books and his intuitive valuations of such factors as he happens to think of, just as today the American farmer in making his judgments takes into account the weather forecasts as well as the Farmers Almanac?

"If a piecemeal exploration of the litigation-situation is to be undertaken, at what point should the beginning be made? Should it be directed at the causal relation between some aspects of the native psychological equipment of the court or at the correlation of cultural factors and decisions? It is believed that the most profitable beginning is a study of cultural factors. . . . The hypothesis which does underlie this study is that the institutions of a locality are among the cultural factors in a litigation-situation significantly connected with the decision and that the semblance of causal relation between future and past decisions is the result of the relation of both to a third variable, the relevant institutions in the locality of the court. It is probable that the notion of a court as to the just, reasonable, fair, and convenient way for a customer and bank to behave and also the just, reasonable, fair, and convenient consequence which the court should attempt to attach to the way the parties did behave is related to the more frequent and therefore regular behavior in such situations in the locality. Though behavior which is frequent and regular may not have impinged, frequently or at all, upon the court yet, in part, its attitudes and ideas are molded by a cultural matrix whose patterns are engraved by frequency. Put in another way, if the court is not conditioned by frequent contact with the behavior itself, it is conditioned by verbal behavior which will be found, on last analysis, to be causally related to the patterns or institutions."

Note that, despite all the cautiousness displayed in the earlier part of this quotation, the last three sentences seem to abandon that caution. Is there evidence to support the theses there stated? So far as I know, Moore offers none. Absent such evidence, there is much reason to be skeptical as to whether the "regular behavior," out of court (especially in the dealings of a somewhat technical kind studied by Moore) of a sub-group in a particular locality, has often either come to the knowledge of the judge or "conditioned" his "verbal behavior."

But the criticism of Moore's thesis must go deeper: So far as can be ascertained, he has never faced these difficulties: (1) Behavior, when it becomes the issue in a law-suit, is a past fact; (2) there is an inherent "subjectivity" in the judical effort to ascertain the past "facts" of a case; (3) there result many contingencies which block prediction of any specific decision in any "contested case," no matter how completely the "regular behavior . . . in the locality" with respect to the specific situation involved in the suit, has carried over to the judge or jury. However, having in mind Moore's dominant mood of tentativeness, probably he is to be taken as saying no more than this: "(1) Among the variables in the decisional process are those which I have studied. (2) My studies of even that limited kind of variables show how difficult it is to obtain reliable prediction-data. (3) My work thus tends to prove a negative—to prove that a science of legal prediction will probably never be contrived." That is no mean accomplishment. As Morley remarked, "the negative truth . . . leads us away from sterile and unreclaimable tracts of thought and emotion, and so inevitably compels the energies which would otherwise have been wasted, to feel after a more profitable direction."[2]

3

Related to the "anthropological approach" is the notion that we should look at average results, and that, if we do, most of the differences between specific decisions will wash out, with the consequence that regularities will be discovered, which will make possible the prediction of future trial-court decisions. That notion has some cogency, if restricted to upper-court decisions and to their generalized ingredients, i.e., the formal *R*'s or some discernible uniformities lying behind the *R*'s. But any average, to be helpful in predicting most trial-court decisions, would have to be based on knowledge by the person constructing the average, of at least this: The relation between (1) the unknowable actual past facts of each case, the decision of which is included in making up the average, and (2) the facts as "found" by the trial court in each such case. I submit that no one can acquire such knowledge. The average, therefore, will usually furnish predictions that have little practical value: It will enable one, at best, to say merely that, if a trial court thinks that the facts of a case are of a certain kind, then probably it will decide in a predicted way. Omitting the gestalt problem, there remains all the uncertainty about what the trial court will think are the facts of a case, where the testimony is oral and conflicting. In such a case, the "average" factors—the regularities—combine with the unpredictable, non-average, reactions to the testimony of the trial judge or jury to balk prediction of the decision.

The method of averages is, of course, related to the theory of probability. In 1877, Jevons, in his *Principles of Science,* wrote: "Attempts to apply the theory of probability to the results of judicial proceedings have proved of little value, simply because the conditions are far too

[2] *Compromise,* 59.

intricate." He quoted La Place who earlier had said, "All the emotions, the most diverse interests and circumstances, complicate questions relating to such a subject, to the point where" in terms of probable decisions, "they are almost always insoluble." Jevons continued, "Men acting on a jury, or giving evidence before a court, are subject to so many complex influences that no mathematical formulas can be framed to express the real conditions." As to judges and jurymen, he remarked that "there are subtle effects of character and manner and strength of mind which defy analysis." [3]

4

Although I believe the "anthropological thesis" unsound, I would not have you think that the lawyer should be unconcerned with anthropology. As I previously suggested, the so-called "social sciences" are but phases of cultural anthropology. Since the competent lawyer needs to know much about the subjects with which those alleged "sciences" deal, undoubtedly it will repay him to give some heed to the divers sorts of cultural anthropologists known as "social scientists." But the lawyer should keep in mind the fact that his occupation is not primarily that of an anthropological observer or anthropological practitioner. As an amateur anthropologist, he will be interested to note the effects of court decisions on laymen's conduct (to see how groups of laymen react to what courts have done) and in the effects on courts of what groups of laymen have done. But the wise lawyer will be wary in his guesses as to whether the courts will give effect to lay reactions. Every practicing lawyer has frequently been told by clients that certain ways of doing things must be lawful because a multitude of persons do business in these ways; the intelligent lawyer does not glibly advise that those ways can safely be considered "legal."

[3] It has been suggested, however, that, in some fields of business, there is an unusually close congruence between the legal rules and the out-of-court ways of non-lawyers, at least whenever every step of a business transaction is guided by lawyers. That may be measurably true. But what of it? In litigation involving such lawyer-guided transactions, are the courts' facts less subject to the infirmities in fact-finding which I've described? The answer to that question—which I previously discussed when I spoke of lawyers' "paper-work"—runs thus: Not infrequently the documents lawyers write provoke lawsuits; the holes in the parol evidence rule often let fact-uncertainty pour into lawsuits in cases relating to lawyer-made documents; while court-room disputes about the facts are probably somewhat reduced by careful lawyer-draftsmanship, nevertheless no one really knows the quantum of such reduction. More to the point, the great majority of human acts are not, and probably never will be, lawyer-guided affairs.

Yet the practical lawyer cannot dispense with anthropology. It is true, as I said earlier, that usually a client, when he asks what are his "legal rights" in a particular matter, is not asking his lawyer to function as an anthropologist, that, ordinarily, the client really wants a prophecy of a future court decision should litigation occur, not an answer concerning the out-of-court "behavior patterns." But that statement needs qualification. Some lawyers, "office lawyers," have relatively little to do with litigation directly. Such a lawyer advises his clients about business transactions of such a nature that, if disputes arise, they will probably be adjusted out of court, more or less in line with the customs of some trade. Such a lawyer is indeed, in part, a practicing anthropologist. He must handle negotiations and give counsel involving knowledge of trade habits and customs. Almost every lawyer, these days, does some of that sort of negotiating and counselling. Lawyers also advise government administrators, legislators, business executives, or labor leaders, in the making of policies. Such activities, again, call for knowledge of the mores, for wisdom as to how the mores should be desirably modified, shrewd judgment as to what changes are likely to be socially accepted.

It might be said that the lawyer's special training, his legal knowledge, gives him no special skills in such matters, that a non-lawyer could as well serve as a practicing anthropologist. But the lawyer has some advantages not possessed by the non-lawyer in such anthropological undertakings. First, litigation may always break out, and the lawyer's guess about its outcome, dependent in part on knowledge of the legal rules and surmises as to the judges' reaction to the mores (i.e., the anthropology of the judiciary), is likely to be better than that of a layman. Second, the non-litigious customs are affected by the legal rules as enunciated in court opinions: What society, or some social subgroup, believes the courts have decided or will decide will often influence out-of-court behavior. The lawyer may therefore be more efficient than a non-lawyer as a working anthropologist. For the lawyer probably has a keener awareness of the mutual interaction of the legal rules and the non-litigious customs.

The courts, as accurately as possible, should evaluate existing or proposed legal rules in terms of their actual or potential social consequences, respectively.[4] Courts sometimes talk glibly about those con-

[4] Llewellyn has said that the principal function of courts is not to settle disputes but to formulate legal rules which, if sufficiently precise, regulate out-of-court be-

sequences. So in 1895, the Supreme Court, in holding unconstitutional the federal income tax law, was patently frightened by the prediction that such a tax would usher in communism, a prediction which proved absurd after the adoption of the income tax amendment in 1913 and the subsequent imposition of federal income taxes. Such, too, was the fate of the prophecy, made by many judges, that, without the "fellow-servant rule," the country would be ruined. When judges indulge in such glib soothsaying, they generally resort to "judicial notice," which may be roughly defined as what everyone is supposed to know but which sometimes consists of wholly unverified impressions—recalling Gibbon's remark that a man who refers to "the opinion of the world at large" means "the few people with whom I happened to converse."

I do not suggest that courts never correctly evaluate the consequences of legal rules. I do say that, unfortunately, the judges seldom have any means of obtaining reliable information of that kind. Indeed, no one has much of it. I therefore heartily favor the kind of research once conducted at the now defunct Johns Hopkins Law School and which the University of Chicago Law School, I think, is about to undertake—research in the social effects of legal rules. Such anthropological explorations—which should cover the reciprocal interaction of legal rules and social habits—deserve approbation and encouragement. Lobingier's proposal for the establishment of official staffs of researchers, attached to the courts,[5] is pertinent here.

For the reasons canvassed in my discussion of the "social sciences,"[6] the products of any such anthropological research should be most circumspectly received. The courts should not, however, cease trying to learn how legal rules affect society, even if the results of such efforts will often be crude. But those results will seriously mislead, if we ignore the impact of trial-court fact-finding on the court-room operations of the legal rules.

---

havior by becoming "working rules" of society. The "settlement of disputes, large though it bulks to a lawyer or disputant, is but a minor function of law," he wrote in 1925. "Each case has a value chiefly for the light it sheds on the rights of ten or ten thousand people not in court." When "custom has not crystallized, rules can really regulate conduct, prevent evils and disputes," but "only where the approved rules are known to men before they act" and are not vague. "Not that knowledge means obedience," but, "given knowledge, our general mores of obeying law—when not too bothersome—join with whatever enforcement may exist to make enforcement superfluous." In that way, the legal rules serve as "working rules which will prevent . . . disputes." Llewellyn, "The Effect of Legal Institutions Upon Economics," 15 *Am. Ec. Rev.* (1925) 665, 671. I think those statements point to part of the truth, but that they are far too unqualified.

[5] See Chapter XX.

[6] See Chapter XIV.

5

Many communists, socialists, and other economic determinists (of whom Laski is typical) resort to a special kind of anthropological thesis. They assert that judicial decisions are invariably nothing more or less than the expression of dominant-class biases.[7] The judge, they say, as a member of the economically superior class, always (unconsciously or consciously) shapes his decisions so as to favor that class.[8] I shall assume, merely for the sake of the argument, the following as unquestionably true, although I disagree with the assumptions: (1) Class bias shapes most of the legal rules;[9] (2) whenever a case arises involving issues between members of different economic classes (or involving the interests of differing economic classes), the judge is certain to decide in favor of his own class. But in the bulk of the law-suits in our courts—the numerical majority of cases affecting the lives of ordinary citizens—those class motives are absent or neutral. For most cases are between members of the same economic class: If Mr. Rockefeller's automobile while occupied by Mr. Rockefeller were to collide with Mr. Ford's Lincoln, and Mr. Rockefeller were sued by Mr. Ford, would the decision be one determined by "exploiting-class" prejudices? When two giant corporations litigate about the title to a lead mine, then what? Or suppose there is a back-fence quarrel between the wives of two members of the proletariat (Mrs. Schumulski and Mrs. Moriarity) which ripens into a law-suit. The great majority of cases which come before trial courts in this country today are, I repeat, of that kind—that is, between members of the same class.

Ask yourself whether the problems relating to fact-finding, to the personal element affecting the *F*'s in judicial decisions, have disappeared or are likely to disappear in such cases in our country or in any cases in Soviet Russia. Disputes in Russia between individuals will surely never cease. Nor disputes between economic or administrative units: The Russian Government railroad department must certainly be unable to agree at times with the Russian Government department having charge

[7] I shall deal with that thesis summarily here. I have elsewhere discussed and criticized economic determinism at length. See Frank, Save America First (1938) 185-231; Frank, Fate and Freedom (1945) 45-53, 64-75, 78-80, 223-256, 271-272.

[8] That economic factors do sometimes affect decisions is undeniable. Cf. Frank, If Men Were Angels (1942) 60-62.

[9] The economic factors are among the important influences in the mores; and, as we saw, the mores do affect the legal rules.

of oil production. Some officials must settle those disputes; and the process of official dispute-settlement gives rise to all the problems, concerning the facts, we have been considering. The Russian legal rules differ from ours. But the uncertainties about the facts in litigation are basically the same in Russia as in the United States.

XXVI. NATURAL LAW[1]

In the age-old search for objectivity, uniformity—for escape from subjectivity and caprice—in the operations of legal systems, men have often turned to the idea of Natural Law, a "higher law" or "law behind law." I must therefore discuss that idea. At the outset of my discussion, I want to bring out a point to which later I shall recur: The most optimistic adherents of the Natural Law idea promise objectivity and uniformity in the legal rules and principles, seldom if ever in court decisions. Those adherents have evaded the problem arising from the variable and subjective factors in that trial-court fact-finding which is unavoidably necessary in most law-suits. For when those Natural Law adherents speak of "law," they identify it not with specifics but with generalizations.

2

Most expositors of Natural Law draw a distinction between (1) man-made legal rules ("law as it is," often called "positive law")[2] and (2) Natural Law, "higher law" principles (or "law" as it "ought to be"). The man-made rules, in contradistinction to the Natural Law principles, are often described as "artificial" or "conventional." Some expositors maintain that the Natural Law principles set a standard or ideal of morals or justice, to which the man-made legal rules should conform, as nearly as possible; others say that any rules which do not so conform have no legal validity (i.e., are not "law").

Although the phrase, Natural Law, throughout its long history, has labeled the greatest variety of attitudes, implicit in most of these attitudes has been this notion: There exists a body of fundamental, unalterable, basic principles, uniformly applicable to all mankind, for the

[1] In this discussion of Natural Law, I am, in part, borrowing from some of my previous writings. See *Fate and Freedom* (1945) Chapters 10 and 11; *Law and the Modern Mind* (Preface to 6th printing, 1949); "A Sketch of an Influence," in the volume, *Interpretations of Modern Legal Philosophies* (1947) 189, 222-25, 234-37.

[2] The word "positive law" as a label for man-made legal rules first came into use through the Stoics. The Roman lawyers did not use the phrase, but the theologians did, and from them it was borrowed by the medieval jurists who popularized it. See Radin, "Early Statutory Interpretation in England," 38 *Ill. L. Rev.* (1943) 16, 25-26.

just governance of society; those principles inhere in Nature; as these principles are rational, it follows that men, by the use of reason, can discover them. "There is," said Cicero, usually hailed as a leading expositor of Natural Law, "a true law—namely right reason—which is in accordance with nature, applies to all men, and is unchangeable and eternal. . . . It will not lay down one rule at Rome and another at Athens, nor will it be one rule today and another tomorrow. There will be one law, eternal and unchanging, binding at all times upon all people."[3] If, then, man lives according to "right reason," he lives "naturally." Natural Law, in this sense, seemingly symbolizes a belief in uniform rules or principles which prevent the intrusion of the variable personal element into the legal realm.[4] There is an opposing view typically expressed by Roscoe Pound who once wrote of "the purely personal and arbitrary character of all natural law theories."[5]

The Natural Law concept has often involved the use of three words: (1) Law, (2) Nature and (3) Reason.[6] Each of them is ambiguous. Over the centuries, each of these words has received varying and conflicting interpretations. What, for instance, does one mean by Nature? Does it refer to all of nature, or primarily to human nature? If the latter, then what aspects of human nature? Does Reason designate the reason of the Deity or man's reason? If God's reason, then who is to discern and declare it? If human reason, then the reason of which men? And what does human reason signify? Some Natural Law advocates say that Reason is the logical reasoning of the best trained minds; others say that it is the untutored intuition of the multitude. . . . The combination of the three ambiguous terms —Law, Nature, Reason—produces, necessarily, a composite of exquisite ambiguity.

Natural Law is sometimes praised as a revolutionary force. Undeniably, at times it has been the fighting slogan of those who have fought oppressive laws and governments. Undeniably, also, however, many exponents of Natural Law have exploited it to defend the status quo, maintaining that the existing government or existing laws

[3] Strictly speaking, Cicero here was referring to what he called "heavenly law" (*lex caelestis*). See Cairns, *Legal Philosophy from Plato to Hegel* (1949) 135-143.

[4] I think that Cicero did not so maintain, that he regarded the higher law as an "ought," not as an "is." But there are others who differently interpret Cicero.

[5] He so wrote in 1908. In later writings, he seems to have shifted his position.

[6] Not all Natural Law theories center on reason; some derive Natural Law from intuition or feelings.

represented the best possible approximation of the ideal, the "natural." The ambiguity of the words makes possible either interpretation: If what is reasonable is natural, then the natural may be said to mean what men should do, thereby inducing protests against the existent. But "natural" may be said to mean what it has been customary to do, thereby inducing acquiescence in, and glorification of, the existent; thus needed reforms have been decried as presumptuous efforts to defeat the "designs of Providence" or "Nature's laws."

Natural Law has given emotional aid and comfort to rigid authoritarians and, antithetically, to philosophic anarchists. With Plato, Natural Law stood for dictatorial government by a select few; and, since then, it has often been the watchword of oligarchs and political absolutists. In the 18th century, revolutionaries espoused Natural Law. Yet, at the very same time, Blackstone, an eager anti-revolutionary, smugly proclaimed that the laws and government of England substantially matched Natural Law and must be little altered. In this country, Natural Rights, an offspring of Natural Law, inspired the wording of the Declaration of Independence which speaks of the "Laws of Nature and of Nature's God." The Declaration was penned by Jefferson, who denounced Blackstone as a vicious reactionary. In this denunciation he was joined by James Wilson, one of the Founding Fathers, a much-quoted teacher of Natural Law doctrines, who proclaimed as a "natural right" the "right of revolution." But later, during the 19th century, some American judges, in the name of Natural Rights, made extreme extensions of laissez-faire doctrines to maintain the status quo; these judges succeeded in upsetting, as opposed to Natural Rights, much humane social legislation. As recently as 1930, the handful of white men in Northern Rhodesia deplored, as "contrary to natural law," a proposed subordination of their selfish interests to aid "the development of other races," that of the black natives of that land.

In short, because of its convenient vagueness, the Natural Law idea lends itself to either side of almost any cause. In the long struggle between Emperors and Popes, each of the two factions invoked Natural Law. During the English controversy about the Reformation, Catholics and Protestants each pleaded their case in terms of that concept. As Chroust says, it "has, at different times, assumed and relinquished every and any philosophic standpoint." It has been all things to all men. It has helped to promote liberty, democracy, wars against tyrants. It has also served the purpose of despots and bigots.

When Henry VIII, in his controversy with the Pope, defended his position regarding his first divorce on the basis of Natural Law, Cardinal Pole remarked that that concept could as easily be used to assail that position. Often Natural Law has been called upon to justify slavery; in modern times, slavery has been denounced in its name. Rutherforth reasoned from Natural Law that polygamy is inherently evil; but some learned Catholic expositors of Natural Law have said that, in appropriate circumstances, it is not incompatible with plurality of wives. The Catholic Church sanctifies Natural Law; yet, in respect of legal institutions, Natural Law has been called a "kind of legal Protestantism." From Natural Law, Bodin deduced the rightness of absolute monarchy; but later political thinkers deduced from it the rightness of popular sovereignty and democracy. Extreme nationalists and extreme cosmopolitan internationalists have alike preached Natural Law. Little wonder that someone has said, "Natural Law is simply that law of which the person using the phrase approves."

Lovejoy, exploring the history of ideas, has made some illuminating comments:[7] "All these trouble-breeding and usually thought-obscuring terms, which one sometimes wishes to see expunged from the vocabulary of the philosopher and the historian altogether, are names of complexes, not of simples—and of complexes in two senses. They stand, as a rule, not for one doctrine, but for several distinct and often conflicting doctrines held by different individuals or groups to whose way of thinking these appellations have been applied, either by themselves or in the traditional terminology of historians; and each of these doctrines, in turn, is likely to be resolvable into simpler elements, often very strangely combined and derivative from a variety of dissimilar motives and historic influences. . . . In the whole series of creeds and movements going under the one name, and in each of them separately, it is needful to go behind the superficial appearance of singleness and identity, to crack the shell which holds the mass together, if we are to see the real units, the effective working ideas, which, in any given case are present." There is need for "an inquiry which may be called philosophical semantics—a study of the sacred words and phrases of a period or a movement, with a view to a clearing up of their ambiguities, a listing of their various shades of meaning, and an examination of the way in which confused associations of ideas arising from these ambiguities have in-

[7] Lovejoy, *The Great Chain of Being* (1936) 5-6, 14.

fluenced the development of doctrines, or accelerated the insensible transformation of one fashion of thought into another, perhaps its very opposite. It is largely because of their ambiguities that mere words are capable of this independent action as forces in history. A term, a phrase, a formula, which gains currency or acceptance because one of its meanings, or of the thoughts which it suggests, is congenial to the prevalent beliefs, the standards of value, and tastes, because other meanings or suggested implications, not clearly distinguished by those who employ it, gradually become the dominant elements of its signification. The word 'nature,' it need hardly be said, is the most extraordinary example of this, and the most pregnant subject for the investigations of philosophical semantics."

In the light of history, it is remarkable that a learned American lawyer, McKinnon, should write that "the doctrine of a higher or natural law transcending man-made laws . . . has served man's cherished ideals of freedom and justice. . . ."[8] It is peculiarly surprising that he should use Plato's political views as illustrative, and yet should assert that a belief in Natural Law helps to shield against personal government and deprivation of individual liberty. For Plato, in his *Republic,* described as an ideal government one in which a few would govern autocratically.

To abandon the Natural Law idea, we are sometimes told, is to breed cynicism. Yet so frequently has Natural Law been adopted as a mask for the sheerest expediency, the crassest and most unlovely opportunism, that its espousal may also induce cynicism—as when, for instance, one saw a well-known Italian champion of Natural Law become, with the advent of Mussolini, an eager apologist for fascism. I, for one, find it a bit difficult to repress cynicism when Cicero's philosophic utterances are held up as notable examples of Natural Law preachments, for I recall his self-confessed wily conduct as a practicing lawyer. A few years before he prosecuted Catiline, he had thought of defending him, although then believing that Catiline's guilt was as clear as noon-day. Again, before assailing Catiline as a man of unmitigated vile character, Cicero had said publicly that Catiline had in him undeveloped germs of the highest virtues, and that it was the good in him that made him dangerous. Subsequently, Cicero persuaded the Senate to over-ride the constitution by ordering the death of Catiline's conspirators without according them

[8] McKinnon, "The Higher Law," 33 *Am. Bar. Ass'n. J.* (1947) 106, 203 note 52.

the trials to which they were constitutionally entitled.[9] He boasted that in one case he had successfully cast dust in the eyes of the jury.

One may perhaps answer that the ideals Cicero proclaimed have nobility and deserve to be followed,[10] despite his behavior. That suggestion does not lack force (although those who advance it should remember, too, that many men who repudiated Natural Law doctrine have led the most exemplary lives).[11] The striking discrepancy between Cicero's pronouncements and his acts shows that eloquent verbal adherence to Natural Law gives no assurance of moral practices, may indeed furnish a smoke-screen for highly questionable activities.[12] Verbal devotion to Natural Law does not prevent "pharisiasm." Pragmatically, such devotion is no guaranty against injustice and immorality. It is well here to note Peirce's remark that pragmatism "is only an application of the sole principle of logic which is recommended by Jesus: 'Ye may know them by their fruits. . . .'"

3

The historical origin of the Natural Law concept is a fascinating theme. I cannot here explore it in detail. Let me, somewhat tersely, suggest that the story as usually told is almost surely wrong. That usual story runs thus: The early Greek philosophers observed that, back of the restless changes in the physical world, there was an order of things, there were uniformities, laws of nature. Employing this conception of physical or natural laws, they explained the disturbing fact of diversities in man-made laws and customs, both in and out of Greece. "The Greek philosophers," we are told, "noted that, while the phenomena of nature were uniform, that the sun rose and set, fire burned and water flowed in Greece, Persia and at Carthage, on the

[9] He was quick to appeal to the "higher law" as a substitute for the Constitution he purported to admire. Thus he said of Cassius' patently illegal conduct in raising an army that Cassius had acted by a decree of Jupiter.

[10] See Corwin, *Liberty Against Government* (1948) Chapter II. Among other things, Corwin applauds Cicero's notion of liberty, and praises Cicero for bringing into prominence the Stoic conception of equality as an attribute of Natural Law. For another version of Cicero's view of liberty, see Ortega, *Concord and Liberty* (1946) 28-32.

[11] Compare Clarence Darrow and Cicero as practicing lawyers. Compare also Judge Learned Hand, who does not believe in Natural Law, with Judge Manton, who professed to.

[12] Many of those who write of Cicero—e.g., writers such as Corwin, Cairns and Wilkins—give no hint of the seamy side of his activities. Good correctives will be found in Cicero's own letters, and Haskell's book, *This Was Cicero*. Haskell brings out Cicero's lack of concern with the grave economic plight of the Roman masses.

other hand human laws and customs and observances were as diverse as possible. . . ." Behind these human diversities, this changing element in human laws and customs, there existed, they concluded, a Natural Law consisting of universal, immutable principles of justice. Human laws, they said, were artificial. They were just by convention; the truly just was just by nature. Such, I say, is the usual story.

But the fairly clear indications are that this carry-over to the social realm of the conception of laws of nature governing the physical realm was a late development.[13] Originally, so it seems, the thought processes worked just in reverse:[14] In "primitive" Greek religion, the notion of an ideal, moral, just, regular and stable human society arose first, and was then transferred to ideas concerning the non-human part of the universe. This naive conception of the primacy of the social order reappeared in more sophisticated form when the Greeks began to philosophize. And, in the beginnings of Greek scientific thinking about the physical universe, the quest for physical regularities was often a search for something like a justly ordered physical system. One might almost say that, at that time, an ideal well-run human society was taken as the model of physical, non-human nature. Then, however, as Greek science progressed, the concept of universal, unchanging, physical laws came to be dominant. The thought process was now turned around. Scientific thinking now stimulated thinking about society: The physical world, conceived as governed by "laws of nature," now became the model for an ideal human order.

This leap-frogging, this back-and-forth interaction of views of physical nature and of human affairs, has often subsequently recurred. Zilsel suggests that, in the 17th century, the somewhat despotic ideal of a perfect well-governed state, in which government was omnipotent and the police omniscient, with all the laws always obeyed, affected the way in which the natural scientists approached their problems. In turn, when, as a result of this approach, Isaac Newton contrived his picture of a law-controlled physical universe, and it was popularized in the 18th century, it became widely accepted as the norm of wise social organization. Typical was a book bearing the title, *The Newtonian System of the World the Best Model of Government.* Probably in that way the theory of governmental "checks and balances" acquired an immense impetus. For, if the physical

[13] I am discussing here solely the development in occidental thought. Something like the Natural Law idea is to be found in other cultures. That subject deserves more attention than it has received.

[14] See Frank, *Fate and Freedom* (1945) Chapters 10 and 11, for a fuller discussion.

world was a self-operating machine, so, too, it was thought, should government be.

So, also, in respect to the relations between government and economics: Newtonian physics encouraged the sentiment expressed by Pope, "Thus God and Nature linked the general frame, And bade Self-Love and Social be the same." These Newtonian-derived sentiments, aided by Adam Smith and Ricardo, helped to give birth to the Manchester School of political economy with its worship of ultra-laissez-faire as "natural" and therefore inevitable, to the doctrine of an "order of nature" economics, the motive power of which was individual, selfish striving, only minimally to be restricted by government. And, when Darwin published his "natural selection" thesis, there developed so-called Social Darwinism, the thesis that, as Nature works its way through the survival of the fittest, so, similarly, unchecked, ruthless rivalry must be the way of human progress, that crass individual selfishness must be the basis of social morality. Like Newtonian economics, Social Darwinism, purporting to use Nature as a model, strenuously opposed all social legislation which aimed to better the common lot.

4

It is high time that we put an end to the device of referring to Nature as the justification for any particular social or economic program or method of government. That device has always led to the worst kind of casuistry. It is oblique, indirect, lacking in forthrightness. The candid approach is to say: "Here is my program. Whether or not it is 'right' depends upon whether it is in accord with, and will effectively promote, values and ideals which you think both desirable and possible of accomplishment. Here are the values and ideals which I favor. And here are my reasons for believing that they will be furthered by my program, and that that program is feasible." In that way one presents, most effectively for intelligent consideration, any proposal—whether it concern labor legislation, world government or rent control. To argue that any such proposal is sanctioned by Nature—in any other sense than that nothing in nature will prevent its fulfillment—does not clarify but clouds the issue. Of course, neither in "economics" nor in government can nature tell us what to do.

There have been men bold enough deliberately to break away from the fashion of reasoning in terms of the "natural" about a desirable social order. Civilization, they declare, represents a human achievement resulting from man's changing what would otherwise have been the course of nature.

Thus, in 1874, John Stuart Mill said that it had never been settled "what particular department of nature shall be reputed to be designed for our moral instruction and guidance; and accordingly each person's individual predilections or momentary convenience has decided what parts" of Nature should be regarded as an analogy. "One such recommendation must be fallacious as another." And Mill continued: "Nearly all the things for which men are hanged or imprisoned for doing to one another, are nature's everyday performance. If it is a sufficient reason for doing one thing that nature does it, why not another thing? If not all things, why anything? . . . It cannot," he concluded, "be . . . moral to guide our actions by the analogy of the course of nature. . . . Nature impales men, breaks them on the wheel, casts them to be devoured by wild beasts, burns them to death, . . . starves them with hunger, freezes them with cold, poisons them . . . , and has hundreds of other hideous deaths in reserve, such as the cruelty of a . . . Domitian never surpassed. Even the love of 'order' which is thought to be a following of the ways of Nature, is in fact a contradiction of them. All of which people are accustomed to deprecate as 'disorder' and its consequences, is precisely a counterpart of Nature's ways. Anarchy and the Reign of Terror are over-matched in . . . ruin and death by a hurricane and a pestilence. . . . Either it is right that we should kill because nature kills; torture because nature tortures; ruin and devastate because nature does the like; or we ought not at all to consider what nature does, but what it is good to do. . . . Conformity to nature has no connection whatever with right and wrong. . . . The duty of man is" not to proceed "by imitating but by perpetually striving to amend the course of nature—and bringing that part of it over which we can exercise control more nearly into conformity with a high standard of justice and goodness."

Subsequently, Thomas Huxley, himself a leading expositor of Darwin's views of nature, vigorously protested against Social Darwinism. "Let us understand, once and for all," he said, "that the ethical progress of society depends not on imitating the cosmic process, still less on running away from it, but in combatting it. . . . The history of civilization details the steps by which men have succeeded in building up an artificial world within the cosmos. Fragile reed as he may be, man, as Pascal says, is a thinking reed; there lies within him a fund of energy, operating intelligently and so far akin to that which pervades the universe, that it is competent to influence and modify the cosmic process. Laws and moral precepts are directed to the end of curbing the cosmic process, and reminding the individual of his duty to the community, to the protection and influence of which he owes, if not existence itself, at least the life of something better than a brutal savage. . . . The practice of that which is ethically best—what we call goodness or virtue—involves a course of conduct which, in all respects, is opposed to that which leads to success in the cosmic struggle for existence. In place of ruthless self-assertion, it demands self-restraint; in place of thrusting aside, or treading down all competitors, it requires that the individual shall not merely respect, but shall help his fellows; its influence is directed, not so much to the survival of the fittest, as to the fitting of as many as possible to survive. It repudiates the gladiatorial theory of existence. . . . Cosmic nature is no school of virtue, but the headquarters of the enemy of ethical nature. . . ." We have "command over the course of non-human nature greater than once ascribed to the magicians. . . . And much may be done to change the nature of man himself."

Surely that is sound thinking. Aided by Huxley's analysis, we must agree with Fouillée that we should not speak of "natural rights," but of "ideal rights," since "nature knows nothing of rights, which appear only in the thoughts of man."

Nature is no copybook containing precepts for civilized man. Nor is human nature, unartificialized, a sound foundation for a beneficent social structure. Millions of Nazis recently disclosed what human nature can be. The rules of civilized behavior cannot operate, of course, if they demand that which physical nature makes impossible, or that to which human nature cannot conform. But those rules are not the products of the unguided mechanical workings of nature, human or otherwise. They are the glorious accomplishments of original, inventive, enterprising, noble-spirited, civilized men.

To say that is not to reject religion. Man is part of the universe, which, because of his finiteness, he cannot fully comprehend. His achievements, his ideals—both the good and the evil ones—are in one sense "artificial." But, in another sense, they are natural because he and they are parts of nature. If, then, ideals, which some men regard as noble, are realized, they will become "natural." Man does not find his "oughts," his "should-be's," spelled out for him in nature: he puts them there. Religion means faith that man's ideals are achievable and will be achieved, his hope that the universe, of which he understands but a portion, will not prevent those ideals from being actualized and from, in some part, surviving.

5

Sometimes, due to its stress on regularity, Natural Law theory has over-valued similarities among men, an over-valuation inconsistent with respect for human dignity, which calls for a high valuation of differences between human beings. Starting with the tenet that human nature is always and everywhere the same, much Natural Law philosophizing concludes that moral values must be unchanging, that there is and always has been a universal moral conscience, possessed by an immutable mankind. That there are a few uniformities among men, of all times and climes, cannot be doubted. But they are minimal. Above the very few basic human needs and characteristics are others of amazing flexibility and variety.

Man's nature is in part immutable, but in large part astonishingly changeable. Even the most uniform biological actions take on different meanings in different cultures. "It would be idle," says Malinowski, "to disregard the fact that the impulse leading to the simplest physiological performance is . . . highly plastic . . . and determined by tradition." As Sidney Hook suggests, "Since the changes that men undergo are part of their nature, it is absurd to argue from a definition of the term 'human nature' that human nature through its long historical pilgrimage has not changed and cannot change." Those who insist on the universal constancy of human nature often use that phrase with "systematic ambiguity."

In the 16th century, Montaigne said, "The laws of conscience, which we say are born of Nature, are born of custom. . . . What is off the hinges of custom we believe to be off the hinges of reason. . . . But those people amuse me who, to give some certainty to laws, say that there are some that are fixed, perpetual and immutable, which they call laws of Nature, and which, by the very condition of their being, are imprinted in humankind. And of these some say there are three, some four, some more, some less; a sign that it is a mark as doubtful as the rest. Now, they are in such a hapless case (for what else can I call it but haplessness, that out of so infinite a number of laws there does not happen to be one at least that has been permitted by Fortune and the heedlessness of chance to be universally accepted by the consent of all nations?), they are, I say, so unhappy, that of those three or four selected laws there is not one that is not rejected and disowned, not by one nation, but by many. . . . There is nothing in which the world varies so much as in customs and laws. Many a thing is abominable here that is commended elsewhere. . . . The murder of infants, the murder of fathers, community of wives, traffic in robberies, license in all sorts of pleasures; nothing in short is so outrageous but it may be allowed by the custom of some nation or other."

In the 17th century, Pascal enlarged on this theme. "We see," he wrote, "neither justice nor injustice which does not change its nature with change in climate. Three degrees of latitude reverse all jurisprudence; a meridian decides the truth. . . . A strange justice that is bounded by a river! Truth on this side of the Pyrenees, error on the other side." Some men say that "justice . . . resides in natural laws, common to every country . . . ; but the farce is that the caprice of men has so many vagaries that there is no such law. Theft, infanticide, parricide, have all had a place among virtuous actions."

In our own century, Sumner asserted, with a wealth of illustrations, that the mores of a group can make almost anything seem right or wrong for the members of that group. Ruth Benedict writes that the cultural patternings "take the raw material of experience and mold it into fifty different shapes among fifty different peoples," that these "patterns of behavior set the mold and human nature flows into it." We "might suppose," she says, "that in the matter of taking life all peoples would agree in condemnation. On the contrary, in a matter of homicide, it may be held that one is blameless if diplomatic relations have been severed between neighbouring countries, or that one kills by custom his first two children, or that a husband has right of life and death over his wife, or that it is the duty of the child to kill his parents before they are old. It may be that those are killed who steal a fowl, or who cut their upper teeth first, or who are born on a Wednesday. Among some peoples a person suffers torments at having caused an accidental death; among others it is a matter of no consequence. Suicide also may be a light matter, the recourse of anyone who has suffered some slight rebuff, an act that occurs constantly in a tribe. It may be the highest and noblest act a wise man can perform. The very tale of it, on the other hand, may be a matter for incredulous mirth, and the act itself impossible to conceive as a human possibility. Or it may be a crime punishable by law, or regarded as a sin against the gods."

All such anthropological observations are too extreme; beneath the diversities some uniformities exist. The modifiability of man's characteristics has its limits. Yet, too little is now known to make possible any convincing statement as to those limits. The meager knowledge we have does not deserve the high-sounding name, Natural Law. The inescapable evidence of un-uniform characteristics, and of the resultant multiplicity of, and changes in, moral standards, has led to the somewhat question-begging revised title: "a Natural Law with a variable content," a label for a relativistic Natural Law.

To be sure, some defenders of Natural Law claim that the diversities of views about just and proper laws show merely that men, being fallible, err in their efforts to reach perfection, and that those diversities constitute a necessary means for the unfolding of the perfect Natural Law. But that contention, I submit, involves the fallacy of employing one's conclusion as the premise of one's reasoning. It comes close to asserting, too, that the less apparent the evidence of moral uniformity, the more one should believe in it.

6

Sponsors of the Natural Law idea almost always cite Aristotle as one of the first and ablest expositors of that idea. I think that, in several ways, they have misinterpreted his position.

Those sponsors usually quote certain passages from his book, the *Rhetoric*. They fail to note that that book is, in considerable part, a manual on how to win a law-suit in which, repeatedly, Aristotle says that, whether one likes it or not, victory in court requires all sorts of appeals to the prejudices of the judges or jurors. We should argue to the court, he admonishes, "whichever way suits us." In that spirit, he suggests that if "the written law tells against our case, clearly we must appeal to the universal law, and insist on its greater equity and justice. We must argue that the juror's oath, 'I will give my verdict according to my honest opinion,' means that one will not simply follow the letter of the unwritten law. We must urge that the principles of equity are permanent and changeless, and that the universal law does not change either, for it is the law of nature, whereas written laws often change. This is the bearing of the lines in Sophocles' *Antigone,* where Antigone pleads that in burying her brother she had broken Creon's law, but not the unwritten law: 'Not of today or yesterday they are, But live eternal: none can date their birth. Not would I fear the wrath of any man And brave God's vengeance for defying these.' We shall argue that justice indeed is true and profitable, but that sham justice is not, and that consequently the written law is not, because it does not fulfil the true purpose of law. Or that justice is like silver, and must be assayed by the judges, if the genuine is to be distinguished from the counterfeit. Or that the better a man is, the more he will follow and abide by the unwritten law in preference to the written." This does, indeed, sound like advocacy of Natural Law.

But the Natural-Law-ites never quote what Aristotle says a very few lines later, namely: "If, however, the written law supports our case, we must urge that the oath 'to give my verdict according to my honest opinion' is not meant to make the jurors give a verdict that is contrary to the law, but to save them from the guilt of perjury if they misunderstand what the law really means. Or that no one chooses what is absolutely good, but every one what is good for himself. Or that not to use the laws is as bad as to have no laws at all. Or that, as in the other arts, it does not pay to try to be cleverer than the doctor; for less harm comes from the doctor's mistakes than from the growing habit of disobeying authority. Or that trying to be cleverer than the laws is just what is forbidden by those codes of law that are accounted best. . . ."

It is true that, a few pages earlier, Aristotle also said: "Particular law is that which each community lays down and applies to its own members. . . . Universal law is the law of nature. For there really is, as every one to some extent divines, a natural justice and injustice that is binding on all men, even on those who have no association or covenant with each other. It is this that Sophocles' Antigone clearly means when she says that the burial of Polyneices was a just act in spite of the prohibition: she means that it was just by nature. 'Not of today or yesterday it is, But lives eternal; none can date its birth.' And so Empedocles, when he bids us kill no living creature, says that doing this is not just for some people while unjust for others, 'Nay, but, an all-embracing law, through the realms of the sky, Unbroken it stretcheth, and over the earth's immensity.' "

This passage seems unequivocal. Yet in a still earlier part of the *Rhetoric,* Aristotle said: " 'Law' is either special or general. By special law I mean that written law which regulates the life of a particular community; by general law, all those unwritten principles which are supposed to be acknowledged everywhere." Note the word "supposed." Reading all those passages together, it becomes doubtful whether Aristotle in this treatise was sponsoring Natural Law, except as an ideal.

To be sure, in his *Nicomachaean Ethics* he said: "Of political justice part is natural, part legal—natural, that which everywhere has the same force and does not exist by people's thinking this or that; legal, that which is originally indifferent, but when it is laid down is not indifferent. . . . Now some people think that all justice is of this sort, because that which is by nature is unchangeable and has everywhere the same force (as fire burns both here and in Persia), while they see change in the things recognized as just. This, however, is not true in a sense; or rather, with the gods it is perhaps not true at all, while with us there is something that is just even by nature, yet all of it is changeable; but still some is by nature, some not by nature. It is evident which sort of thing, among things capable of being otherwise, is by nature; and which is not but is legal and conventional, assuming that both are equally changeable. And in all other things the same distinction will apply; by nature, the right hand is stronger, yet it is possible that all men should come to be ambidextrous. The things which are just by virtue of convention and expediency are like measures; for wine and corn measures are not everywhere equal, but larger in wholesale and smaller in retail markets. Similarly, the things which are just not by nature but by human enactment are not everywhere the same, since constitutions also are not the same, though there is but one which is everywhere by nature the best." Here Aristotle comes closer to a statement of a belief in Natural Law as a fact; but the statement is by no means free of ambiguity.

I must confess that I am an amateur in philosophy and no Greek scholar. But my reading of Aristotle leads me to agree with Ritchie who, in his book *Natural Rights* (1895), says that Aristotle was not consistent in his use of the words "natural" and "by nature" as applied to matters human, that sometimes Aristotle meant innate or inherited human impulses, sometimes the ideal, what ought to be. Ritchie believes that generally Aristotle had in mind that there are principles which should be acceptable to all educated civilized men, but that he regarded such acceptance as an ideal which could never be completely realized.

7

Aristotle, unlike Plato, believed in the objective reality of unpredictable chance in the physical universe. Very likely for similar reasons, he opposed the regimenting legal and political theories of Plato, and favored, as both necessary and desirable, some free play in any legal system, some unruly individuality—some "anarchy" one might say. His attitude towards government, his recognition of the reality and desirability of individual spontaneity, is at odds with one of the most unfortunate features of many Natural Law theories—an insistence upon social inevitabilism, determinism, fatalism. Even many of those whom Natural Law theories have incited to revolt against injustice were, paradoxically, fighting to bring about what they deemed to be inevitable. The stars in their courses, they thought, were on their side. Such fatalism, or social determinism, is, I think, bad medicine, especially for Americans.

It is indeed bad medicine in the field of international relations. International lawyers have frequently spoken in Natural Law idiom. But a healthy, global order is not predestined, nor is it patterned in Nature. We must earn it through a combination of intelligence, goodwill, and earnest striving.

In the 19th century, most scientific philosophizing—underscoring the alleged existence of universal, undeviating laws of physical nature—was enthusiastically deterministic, an interesting fact when one recalls, as I've just said, that often the idea of Natural Law, in its social applications, has encouraged fatalism. Reflecting the views of the physical scientists, much of 19th century history-writing and economics was deterministic, fatalistic. Today, however, many natural scientists speak of chance as an objective part of the physical world, and look upon unpredictable spontaneities as a reality. Chance, to these scientists, is not a name for human ignorance, but a real factor at play in the universe.[15] This idea (which goes back in philosophic thought at least to Aristotle and Epictetus) has its modern philosophic spokesman in our great American scientific philosopher, C. S. Peirce.[16]

There are still some eminent physicists (like Einstein, for instance) who reject that idea, who believe that the world is an ordered and comprehensive entity. As I have suggested elsewhere, Einstein—as a philosopher, not as a scientist—longs for a tidy universe, a sort of old maid's paradise, with everything in its place and a complete inventory of the world's contents. But Bertrand Russell reports that "most modern physicists . . . show a preference for" a picture of the physical world as one full of "caprice and whim." He adds: "Such orderliness

[15] For a more extensive discussion, see Frank, *Fate and Freedom* (1945) Chapters 12 and 13, and Appendix Five.

[16] See Chapter XIV as to the "crowd" or "average" natural laws which modern physicists employ.

as we appear to find in the external world is held by many to be due to our passion for pigeon holes." Noting that "academic philosophers . . . have believed that the world is unity," he says, "The most fundamental of my intellectual beliefs is that this is rubbish. I think the universe is all spots and jumps, without unity, without continuity, without coherence or orderliness or any of the properties that governesses love." [17]

Physical Nature, as we now know it, is, then, no model, for an ordered or orderly society. Nor, if taken as a model, does it inculcate fixity, unalterability, in matters human. More than ever today, we are justified in following Thomas Huxley's lead. Men can and should be socially inventive. Social welfare calls for no worship of the status quo. Desirable deviations from the past, social novelties designed to promote justice and human well being, are, if you please, "natural." For Nature does not tell us to remain chained to the present or to seek a return to the past. If Nature has any lesson for us, perhaps it is this: As Nature is replete with spontaneities, we need not fear spontaneities in social development. We must make our own way into the future, through social contrivances devised by free inventive men. We must take account of Nature, for she sets limits to our achievements. But those limits are indeed wide.[18]

8

As previously noted, some believers in Natural Law have said that any man-made rules which flatly contradict Natural Law principles and precepts lack legal validity (i.e., are "not law") and consequently need not be obeyed. Other believers depict Natural Law as meaning merely that such faulty man-made rules are immoral or bad rules which should be changed or abandoned but which men meanwhile must accept as legally binding. Some Natural Law adherents have maintained that from the Natural Law principles men can logically deduce a detailed code of legal rules valid forever and everywhere.

[17] Russell, *The Scientific Outlook* (1931) 94-96. See also Frank, *Fate and Freedom, loc. cit.*

[18] See Feibleman, Book Review, 23 *Tulane L. Rev.* (1949) 427, 429: "Legal philosophy in the hands of professional philosophers divides chiefly into theories which seek to establish law as a conventional, man-made affair, more or less arbitrary, and theories which hold law to be natural, on the assumption that 'finding nature' is possible in human affairs as well as in physical or chemical events. The commonest error of the former is to insist that all postulates or first principles are subjective, and the commonest error of the latter is to argue that all candidates for natural law are for that very reason absolute. Certainly a synthesis of the truth contained in both theories, purged of their errors, is at least possible."

That last notion is rejected in the Roman Catholic conception of Natural Law. That conception merits high respect from non-Catholics. Formulated in the 13th century by St. Thomas Aquinas, it is often called the Scholastic or Thomistic version of Natural Law. In briefly describing, as follows, this Thomistic version, I shall, for the sake of simplicity, borrow from its recent popular exposition by McKinnon.

Inherent in man, as a rational being, is an "intuitive awareness" of a few basic, universal and eternal principles of justice, such as, "Seek the common good," which may be subdivided analytically into, "Live in society,[19] do good to others, avoid harming others, and render to each his own." These principles, deriving from human nature, implanted there by the Creator, are, say the Thomists, basic principles of Natural Law. From these basic principles, there can be deduced, logically, rationally, some secondary principles or precepts, such as, for instance, that one should not kill or steal. But these precepts, being highly general, must be applied more concretely, to determine, for example, the difference between illegitimate and legitimate killing (as in self defense). These applications take the form of the man-made, legal rules of "positive law."[20] While the principles and precepts are immutable, the applications, the legal rules, are not. They are tentative, uncertain, contingent and changeable. They vary with time, place and circumstance;[21] also they involve fallible human choices of means to give effect to the precepts. The principles and precepts, however, do help in appraising the "positive" legal rules as just or unjust. They assist in measuring the rules that exist by the standard of what they ought to be.

Father Lucey, an eminent Catholic law teacher, takes pains to explain the error of envisaging Natural Law as "an absolute development of immutable principles by an absolute process in such a way as to produce, by deduction, a body of absolute, immutable law adequate to every place, time and situation." What "is morally good today," says Fr. Lucey, "may be morally bad tomorrow, and vice versa, because, while the few basic principles of morals do not change, others do. . . . Countless human actions are neither good nor bad in themselves" but "get their goodness or badness from circumstances of time, place, ob-

19 Here Aquinas took over from Aristotle the invaluable conception of man as a social being. See, further, Chapter XXIX; see also Frank, *Fate and Freedom* (1945) 213-214, 259-60 as to the "communalist" ideal of the Roman Catholic Church.

20 There are said to be other man-made rules not derived from Natural Law principles and to which Natural Law is indifferent except to admonish that those rules should not contradict these principles.

21 Maritain refers to a "geology of the conscience." Maritain, "The Meaning of Human Rights," an address before the Brandeis Lawyers Society (1949).

ject and intent." This sounds surprisingly like pragmatism; indeed, Brendan Brown, another Catholic law professor, suggested, a few years ago, the teaching of what he termed "Scholastic pragmatism." In sum, Catholic Natural Law doctrine recognizes not only that Natural Law is not designed to govern each particular case but also that the basic principles and precepts it proclaims do not operate mechanically. Their applications, their particularizations, through man-made rules, necessarily vary. Moreover, those rules, the work of fallible men, cannot be free of human errors.

The Catholic doctrine, therefore, is not open to the criticism which should be leveled at the thesis of those dogmatic advocates of Natural Law who maintain that it supplies such clear, objective, guides that, if followed, it will prevent the intrusion of the "personal" or subjective factor into the judicial process, even as to the rule component of court decisions. The enlightened Catholic will not expect uniformity in judicial formulations of the legal rules even by judges who believe in Natural Law and earnestly attempt to apply it.

But the more dogmatic (non-Catholic) Natural Law theorist should be disquieted when he sees that judges who accept the same basic Natural Law principles are frequently not in accord with one another concerning what changes of circumstances require changes in the applications. There was such a spectacle at a time when virtually all American judges were wont to speak of Natural Law, yet often disagreed about what legal rules it entailed in specific cases.

As the enlightened Catholic acknowledges, a notable characteristic of Thomistic Natural Law is that it is not concrete. No one has ever been able to work out anything like a complete set of legal rules, deduced from Natural Law principles, acceptable to all honest and just lawyers, or non-lawyers, even in a given time and place.

9

Some non-Catholics balk at calling the Catholic Natural Law principles and precepts "eternal" or divine in origin. Indeed, to such persons—mindful of man's finiteness, his limited capacity for comprehending, intellectually or emotionally, all that goes on in the vast stretches of the universe beyond his ken—it seems presumptuous to assert that man should know what is eternal, or what constitutes order or regularity, present or future, except within his own small span of experience.[22] But no decent non-Catholic can fail to accept

[22] See Frank, *Fate and Freedom* (1945) 310-311.

the few basic Natural Law principles or precepts as representing, at the present time or for any reasonably foreseeable future, essential parts of the foundation of civilization.[23]

There is little sense in quarreling about a name, a label. But the name, Natural Law, does confuse many non-Catholics. Surely a name can be found that is less confusing to them. At its best, Natural Law has symbolized the unquenchable, human desire for norms or standards of justice by which to evaluate existing, legal rules, contrasting the "is" with the "ought to be." We need a symbol for the demand that statutes should be repealed, and judge-made rules abandoned or modified, when they obstruct valued moral aims, for the demand that human institutions be altered when they work injustice. I suggest Justice as a better symbol than Natural Law. It will fully as well inspire men to manifest their dissatisfaction with governmental accomplishments which do not satisfy their ideals. Of course, the word Justice has no great precision. But it does not have the misleading connotations and embarrassing historical associations of the words Natural Law, which today must be translated to be understood by most non-Catholics. If Natural Law signifies the quest for justice, why not speak of Justice directly? If you want a waiter to bring you a glass of water, you do not think of telling him, "Please bring me a transparent brittle container nearly full of aqueous fluid."

10

The discussion of Natural Law thus far has, I hope, demonstrated the unavoidability of considerable diversity in the man-made legal rules, no matter how much agreement there may be about basic principles and their logical corollaries. Even more unavoidable is diversity in most trial-court decisions when the man-made rules are applied to the facts. There, Natural Law, neither in its Catholic nor in any other version, assures us of uniformity; and it is exactly there that justice in the courts must get its practical meaning. Justice in the abstract—gen-

[23] Maritain is not wholly satisfied with such agreement. One reason for his dissatisfaction apparently is that he holds that the Church, under Natural Law, has the right (held in reserve at the present time) to "mobilize the State against heretics," a "right" which non-Catholics, of course, do not recognize. See Maritain, *loc. cit.*

With his discussion of the powerlessness of rational justifications to create agreemet, compare Stevenson, Ethics and Language (1944).

For the view that men with differing theoretic approaches can often well afford to agree upon practices concerning important practical matters, see McKeon, 59 *Ethics* (1949) 155, 159.

eral principles of Natural Law, if you prefer that phrase—can have little worth if justice is wanting in specific instances. The devotees of Natural Law, who regard it as so important to extol its virtues that they take no interest in the reform of present, miserably inadequate and unjust trial methods, are in danger of impeding that reform. Thus sincere preoccupation with Natural Law—that is, with generalities—may actually foster injustice by neglecting one of its major sources.

I stand subject to correction by better informed persons, but as I read Thomas Aquinas, he stopped short of grappling with the problem of justice in specific trial-court decisions. True, he wrote, "The practical reason is concerned with practical matters, which are singular and contingent . . . , wherefore human laws cannot have that inerrancy that belongs to the demonstrated conclusions of science.[24]. . . Consequently, although there is necessity in the general principles, the more we descend to matters of detail, the more frequently we encounter defects." But there he was talking of the defects in detailed rules, not of details of fact-finding in specific litigation.

To be sure, he did say "A judge's sentence is like a particular law regarding some particular fact";[25] and he did briefly discuss the task of the trial judge when dealing with conflicting testimony. In some situations, he said, when the witnesses disagree, the judge must use his "prudent discernment," his "discretion."[26] But Aquinas did not ex-

[24] Here he was borrowing from Aristotle. One may doubt whether either he or Aristotle, if alive today, would so write of science.

[25] See *The Summa Theologica of St. Thomas Aquinas* (translated by the Fathers of the English Dominican Province, 1929) Part II, Second Number, Question 67, Art. 1.

[26] *ibid.* Question 70, Art. 2. The passage reads: "If the witnesses disagree in certain principal circumstances which change the substance of the fact, for instance in time, place, or persons, which are chiefly in question, their evidence is of no weight, because if they disagree in such things, each one would seem to be giving distinct evidence and to be speaking of different facts. For instance, if one says that a certain thing happened at such and such a time or place, while another says it happened at another time or place, they seem not to be speaking of the same event. The evidence is not weakened if one witness says that he does not remember, while the other attests to a determinate time or place. And if on such points as these the witnesses for prosecution and defence disagree altogether, and if they be equal in number on either side, and of equal standing, the accused should have the benefit of the doubt, because the judge ought to be more inclined to acquit than to condemn, except perhaps in favorable suits, such as a pleading for liberty and the like. If, however, the witnesses for the same side disagree, the judge ought to use his own discretion in discerning which side to favour, by considering either the number of witnesses, or their standing, or the favourableness of the suit, or the nature of the business and of the evidence. Much more ought the evidence of one witness to be rejected if he contradict himself when questioned about what he has seen and about what he knows; not, however, if he contradict himself when questioned about matters of opinion and report, since he may be moved to answer differently according to the different things he has seen and heard. On the other hand, if there be discrepancy of evidence in circumstances

plain how the exercise of this discretion was to be made "objective": A particular trial judge who happens to be sitting in a particular case employs this discretion so that he decides for the defendant. Suppose another judge had happened to sit and had heard the same witnesses. What means exist for guaranteeing even approximate uniformity (objectivity) in such matters? Aquinas does not answer that question. Nor do non-Catholic Natural-Law adherents. Without an answer, Natural Law, in the great majority of lawsuits, encounters insurmountable subjectivity—and subjectivity of a kind not relative merely to time, place and general circumstances.

This point has been so much overlooked that it is worthwhile to restate it:[27] Natural Law yields, at best, a standard of justice and morality for critically evaluating the man-made rules, and, perhaps, for ensuring a moderate amount of certainty in those rules; but it furnishes no helpful standard for evaluating the fact-determination of trial courts in most law-suits, and no assistance in ensuring uniformity, certainty, or predictability in such determinations. Natural Law aims at justice, and at moderate certainty, in the man-made rules, that is, in the more or less abstract, generalized human formulations of what men may or may not lawfully do. To be practically meaningful, however, judicial justice must be justice not merely in the abstract but in the concrete—in the courts' decisions of the numerous particular, individual, cases. A general rule against forgery, or a general rule against breaking contracts, is eminently just and fairly certain. But a court decision that a particular man, Campbell, committed forgery, or a court decision that a particular man, Wilcox, broke a contract, is surely unjust if in truth he did not so act, yet a trial court mistakenly believes he did, because of its belief in the reliability of oral testimony which does not match the actual facts. Thence arises the problem of achieving justice, and uniformity, in trial-court ascertainments of facts in divers individual lawsuits, a problem which can be solved, via Natural Law, only to the extent that Natural Law principles operate on and control the subjective,

---

not touching the substance of the fact, for instance, whether the weather were cloudy or fine, whether the house were painted or not, or suchlike matters, such discrepancy does not weaken the evidence, because men are not wont to take much notice of such things, wherefore they easily forget them. Indeed, a discrepancy of this kind renders the evidence more credible, as Chrysostom states, because if the witnesses agreed in every point, even in the minutest details, they would seem to have conspired together to say the same thing: but this must be left to the prudent discernment of the judge."

Aquinas here, unlike Cardozo, clearly recognized "fact discretion."

[27] I am here plagiarizing from my Preface to the sixth printing (1949) of my own book, *Law and the Modern Mind.*

un-get-at-able, often unconscious, and un-standardized ingredients of trial-court fact-findings, when oral testimony is in conflict as to crucial issues of fact. I see no signs that those principles do so operate and control. So far as I know, Natural Law adherents—whether or not Catholics—have considered neither that problem nor the puzzling problem of coping with the gestalt in trial-court decisions.

For that reason, all other difficulties aside, there is a latent error, which needs to be exposed, in the pronouncements of those who now say that Natural Law supplies a basis of judgments which "is objective, and therefore free from the inevitable variations and the inconsistencies of purely subjective standards," is not "subject to the whims of personal caprice."

11

Before I go further into that subject, I want to say a few words about the attitudes toward Natural Law of non-Catholic American legal thinkers. Among them, in the early part of this century, the Natural Law idea was in general disrepute. Recently, however, some of them have urged its revival. They suggest that the courts should invoke some sort of Natural Law to assist in revising the legal rules they employ.

Typical is Professor Friedrich Kessler. He criticizes as naive any Natural Law philosophy which maintains that "propositions of positive law can be deduced from natural law principles." But, he says, the Natural Law "way of looking at the legal system expresses a profound insight with regard to the constant interaction of law and morality." "Laws," he writes, "in order to command obedience, must live up to the 'ethical minimum' of a community." Moreover, he remarks, "our legal system" is not "closed and complete. In reality, due to the elasticity of the case law system, the courts are given a considerable leeway in shaping the law according to their sense of justice, which in turn is influenced by the cultural patterns of the community and the moral tradition. Thus, the ideal is constantly becoming the positive."

In a similar vein, Max Radin, although he does not mention Natural Law, insists that the judges' sense of justice operates, and should operate, in their decisions, and that this sense of justice does and should reflect community ideals. "There is nothing subjective," he says, "about applying a standard of conduct which the overwhelming majority . . . would at once recognize." The late lamented Pekelis, although similarly he did not use the term Natural Law, urged something equivalent under the name of a "jurisprudence of welfare." Judges, he maintained, have a duty openly to consider and discuss the effects of their opinion on the general welfare, on "what is good for society." There is already in this country, he said, as to a large number of issues, a "state of articulate opinion," so that a "considerable degree of unanimity may be found"; and unanimity is likely to emerge as to many other issues, if, conscientiously, the courts publicly canvass them. In that way, he argued, the moral norms of the community can, as they should, write themselves into court decisions. Professors Lasswell and McDougal, who, at Yale Law School, urge their students to look to the policies behind the legal rules, and to help in the revision of the rules to make them accord with democratic ideals and values—those men, too, might well be classified as advocates of a revival of Natural Law.

I am entirely in agreement with the essential aims voiced by Kessler, Radin, Pekelis, Lasswell and McDougal. But I think you see that their aims run up against the difficulties we previously considered in connection with the "anthropological approach." The first difficulty is that, at any given time in any community, there are warring community ideals which translate themselves, warringly, into differing judicial decisions. A sign of those clashes can be observed in the dissenting opinions in our Supreme Court.

Another difficulty we find by searching into the meaning of "lawlessness." [28] Every society violates not only the rules that other groups consider important but even some of its own rules. All groups have their pseudo-standards, their "pretend rules"; it is part of the mores of any group to break some of its own legal rules. Greeks and Trobrianders, New Yorkers and Hottentots, not only preserve but currently produce apparently significant rules which they circumvent or openly violate but which they refuse to abandon. Since the violation of some laws is a normal part of the behavior of every member of every group, "lawlessness" often reduces to a charge of a mistaken selection of the existing laws which are to be ignored. The notions of what constitutes such a mistaken selection not only vary from society to society but are not uniform even within any particular society. Religious, political and economic stratifications cut across each community; the attitudes of any individual are conditioned by a complex of influences impinging upon him from his various relationships. His conception of what laws may be violated or ignored without serious hurt to his "moral sense" is likely to be a resultant of these influences. By appropriate selection any sub-group can prove that some other sub-group is lawless. Thus the "law-

[28] See Frank, "Lawlessness," 9 *Encyc. of Soc. Sciences* (1933) 276.

lessness" of the so-called "lower classes" is apt to run in terms of crimes of violence, that of the so-called "upper classes" in terms of crimes involving fraud.

Let us, however, forget the objection that there are many differences within our society as to proper moral behavior. Let us assume, with Pekelis, that, as to many questions, a very substantial amount of unanimity of moral ideals does prevail or can be made to prevail. We still must face the problem I have so often stressed—the problem caused by the variations in findings of the facts in thousands of mine-run law suits. As I've said repeatedly, the facts of a case, when the oral testimony is conflicting, consist, for court purposes, of the trial judge's or jury's belief as to what those facts are. Assume that all judges and all juries have the same general sense of justice,[29] resulting from the impact on them of the unanimous general moral ideals of the community. That identity in the general sense of justice will not, however, produce identity in beliefs about the facts of particular contested suits. Those beliefs are markedly affected by the individual predilections, prejudices, of judges or jury men of which they are often themselves not cognizant. Those prejudices—for or against witnesses who are Irish or Polish, or Republican or Democrats, or swarthy-faced men or red-headed women or men or women who rub their hands while testifying—would, if known and articulated, spell out as moral (or immoral) attitudes. But those moral attitudes are both hidden and idiosyncratic. They vary from judge to judge, from jury to jury. How, then, can it be said that trial court decisions, which result from such varying concealed and publicly unscrutinized moral attitudes, express relatively uniform community ideals? And especially, how can that be said of decisions in jury trials? How, then, can Radin assert, with any degree of assurance, that "there is nothing subjective about applying" acknowledged moral standards? [30] Surely there is not much uniformity in the translation of community ideals into most of such decisions.[31] We can perhaps inject a uniform sense of justice into many of the legal rules. But can we inject it into findings of fact when the orally testifying witnesses disagree? [32]

29 Cahn, borrowing from Aristotle, prefers to speak of a "sense of injustice."

30 Radin's position on this subject is the most surprising. For, in several of his writings, he has been unusually mindful of the difficulties of accurately ascertaining the "facts" in lawsuits.

31 Cahn, Book Review, 49 *Col. L. Rev.* (1949) 286, 289, says it is not enough to list "jural postulates". . . without "showing how men execute the leap from the abstract assumptions to the positive decision."

32 "The internal standard of the individual will always be separated in practice

The point is that these neo-Natural-Law advocates base their thesis on generalized factors in the decisional process, on some uniformities or "constants" operative in the reactions of judges and juries at a given time and place. But they overlook the variable and subjective factors inherent in fact-finding—to say nothing of the gestalts—in the numerous cases where the credibility of witnesses is crucial.

For the sake of the argument, suppose we accept, without qualification, the notion that there exist some general, immutable and eternal principles of morality or justice. Or, if that notion disturbs you, assume that, in a particular place at a particular time, there are, as "temporary absolutes,"[33] such general principles. Assume further that these principles can be fairly reliable guides to concrete and definite legal rules. Still we will not have justice done, in specific lawsuits, in accord with those principles and those subsidiary rules, unless we can eliminate the numerous variable "subjective" elements in fact-finding. So that, if you accept Natural Law, in some form or other, nevertheless, unless those subjective elements are under control, you cannot be assured that the natural law principles will be applied in particular "contested" cases.

Here we corner our real problem—the problem of "subjectivity" in fact-finding. That problem will not be solved by a resort to Natural Law, whether under that name or under the label of a Jurisprudence of Welfare.

If Natural Law symbolizes the quest for justice, then those lawyers who claim to be adherents of Natural Law, or its equivalent, should not be content with improving the legal rules the better to reflect moral values. Those lawyers should also assiduously devote themselves to reforming our methods of trying cases, of training of future trial judges, of using the jury. For in our trial courts today "is" and "ought to be" remain too far apart. To separate ethics from the judicial process is to pervert the latter. We must ethicize the work of the courts. But that aim will come to relatively little unless we do so at the trial-court level.

I would recommend to devotees of Natural Law that they carefully

---

from the general standard of his society by the measure of his own peculiar fantasy life. . . . Each man sees his relationship to others differently and feels his obligations differently from what other men would see and feel them to be if they were in his place. He will consequently be liable to act differently wherever his acts are not stereotyped for him by convention, wherever, in fact, they require his individual judgment. . . . It should be noted that, upon the whole, man does . . . follow his conscience. But he follows it always in the light of his own peculiar interpretation of fact." West, "A Psychological Theory of Law," in the volume, *Interpretations of Modern Legal Philosophies* (1947) 779.

[33] See Frank, *Law and the Modern Mind* (1930) 252.

re-read Aristotle's *Rhetoric*. For there he alone, of all who have considered the Natural Law concept, comes close to honestly confronting the subjectivity problem. He explains that legal rules are necessarily "prospective and general," but that all lawsuits are "definite cases," each of which relates to "past events." The legislature has to leave to the judge "questions as to whether something has happened or has not happened," i.e., questions which relate to specific facts that happened in the past, "things already done." If a judicial system were perfect, each side in a suit would "in fairness fight (his) case with no help but the bare facts," and "nothing should matter except the proof of those facts." But, says Aristotle, "other things affect the result considerably." He notes that "unscrupulous practices" are often employed. It seems wrong "to pervert the judge by moving him to anger or pity," since the arousing of such "emotions has nothing to do with the essential facts, but is merely a personal appeal to the man who is judging the case." Yet such appeals to the emotions are made: Judges "often have allowed themselves to be so much influenced by feelings . . . that they lose any clear vision of the truth." Consequently, the litigant must know the ways of "working on the emotions of the judges." And Aristotle goes on to tell in detail the means used "to excite prejudice." Among other things, one should aim at stimulating the judge's "good will, or at arousing his resentment, or sometimes at gaining his attention to the case, or even at distracting it—for gaining it is not always an advantage," and, on that account, one should sometimes "try to make him laugh." [34]

12

Although Aristotle honestly faced the subjectivity problem, he did not indicate a solution. The problem exists, whether or not one conceals or evades it. *Strangely enough, if we look for a constant in all mature human societies, we will discover at least this one: the constancy of the inconstancy in judicial fact-finding. No legal system, no matter what may be the economic or political set-up, can escape it. It constitutes a universal element of social organization. In that sense it could*

[34] That Aristotle was also aware of the problem of witnesses' fallibilities, appears from his discussion, elsewhere. "The organ which perceives color," he says, "is not only affected by its object but reacts upon it. . . . We are easily deceived respecting the operations of sense perception when we are excited by emotions, and different persons according to their different emotions; . . . and the more deeply one is under the influence of emotion, the less similarity is required to give rise to illusory impressions. . . . Thus, too, both in fits of anger, and also in all states of appetite, all men become easily deceived, and the more so the more the emotions are excited."

be described as a "natural law" or "law of human nature." It poses a major question to every man who reflects on the legal aspects of human affairs. Yet, with perhaps the single exception of Aristotle, the men who have thus speculated, lawyers and non-lawyers alike, have not unflinchingly faced it.[35]

13

Erich Fromm[36] outlines a universal ethics which prizes spontaneities and represents a goal, not a certified destiny. He says that man's nature gives rise to universal ethical norms of conduct; their "aim is the growth and unfolding of man," the achieving of all the "unique potentialities" of each person "which it is the task of mankind to realize"; the "ethical systems of all great cultures show an amazing similarity in what is considered necessary for the development of man, of norms which follow from the nature of man and the conditions necessary for his growth." He gives as examples, "Love thy neighbor as thyself" or "Thou shalt not kill." But the universal norms will not prevail until "mankind becomes united culturally" and until humanity "has succeeded in building a society in which the interest of 'society' has become identified with that of all its members." For, presently at odds with the universal norms, are relative ethical norms, "socially immanent" norms, i.e. necessary for the functioning and survival of particular societies as they now exist. These norms express what is good or bad for men within each society. These "historically conditioned social necessities clash with the universal existential necessities of the individual."

Fromm's conception points to what might be deemed a sort of Natural Law. It is profoundly wise. Dynamic, broad in its premises, and laying a foundation for individual uniqueness, it affords valuable tests for justice. But those tests are too vague to furnish much aid in deciding specific lawsuits or in evaluating most specific decisions.

35 This will be obvious to the reader of Cairn's recent excellent book, *Legal Philosophy from Plato to Hegel* (1949).

36 *Man for Himself* (1947) 238-44.

XXVII. THE PSYCHOLOGY OF LITIGANTS

In an earlier chapter, I criticized the "fighting theory" of trials with the artificial "litigious man" as its key figure; and I urged that we move towards the realization of the "truth theory," i.e., that a trial court should do everything feasible to ascertain the actual past facts which are in dispute. That proposal, however, impliedly assumes that when men "go to law," it is invariably desirable that the true facts be discovered. It also assumes a standard litigant who will feel frustrated if the court fails to find the facts accurately.

I must now raise some doubts about the second assumption. It does not fully accord with actualities so far as all litigants are concerned: There is no one type of litigant; the motivations of all litigants are not identical; nor are the motivations of any one litigant necessarily constant and unmixed. This subject of the psychology of litigants has never been properly investigated.[1] I hope, some day, to write extensively on the scope of such an investigation. Here I can do no more than throw out a few hints.

When a man feels that another has grievously wronged him, he sometimes wants relief for his injured feelings in the form of some signal vindication. He wants to win a fight; and the sublimated courtroom fight may therefore furnish the means of relief. He may be neurotically aggressive, destructively so, quick to take out his aggressions on someone who even slightly crosses him. He may have a sense of guilt or sin of which he is unconscious, and may temporarily rid himself of his burden of guilt or sin by asserting that someone else whom he sues is a wrongdoer who has infringed his legal rights. Thwarted impulses of divers kinds may obtain an outlet in litigation. The court fight gives an outlet to "combat feelings."[2] The extreme,

[1] Some aspects of it have been suggestively explored. See Bok, *I, Too, Nicodemus* (1946); Goitein, *Primitive Ordeal and Modern Law* (1923); West, "A Psychological Theory of Law," in the volume *Interpretations of Modern Legal Philosophies* (1947) 707, 773, 780.

[2] See Smith, "Components of Proof in Legal Proceedings," 51 *Yale L.J.* (1942) 537, 575: "In trial by battle we see the primitive concept of letting the best man win by 'might and main,' using all the strength and means at his command short of actual foul play. This combat aspect of litigation has psychological connotations running deeper than self vindication of one's cause by valor or might. It expresses the animosity factor in litigation, the desire to be at one's assailant and 'have it out.' Later

pathological instance is the "litigious paranoiac" who uses trumped-up claims—in the validity of which he comes to believe—to assuage a "persecution complex." And, this side the extreme pathologue, there are many others eager to seek in litigation a solace for their inner disturbances.

Consequently, lawsuits are by no means limited to situations in which legal rights are dubious. Some men enjoy litigating and will institute litigation although their lawyers correctly tell them they have little or no chance of success. Havighurst[3] criticizes "the view that it is well that the field of uncertainty in legal relationship is relatively small because uncertainty causes disputes." For "disputes," he says, "are seldom caused by legal uncertainty. They occur when there is a conflict of interests which good manners and the desire for peace and good will are incapable of resolving. Ordinarily, in such a situation there will be some uncertainty either of law or of fact which calls for litigation, if the amount involved makes it worth while and a compromise cannot be worked out. This is eminently proper. There should be an opportunity for parties to let off steam without resorting to a breach of the peace. Also in the great bulk of dealings where no dispute occurs, there are to be found the materials for a law-suit if the parties wished to fight. All lawyers know the litigious client, and his cases are usually just as good as any others. On the other hand, legal certainty does not allay disputes if parties become irritable. A person who feels he has been wronged, yet finds he does not even have a law-suit, is more apt to prolong the dispute by resorting to extra-legal retaliation, than one who is told he may have a case. To the extent that unsocial persons are deterred from conduct injurious to others by the knowledge that they will be accountable by law, legal certainty is of some value in preventing disputes. But for persons so disposed, the lack of obscurity in the law usually merely makes it necessary either to obscure the facts, their property or themselves." This reference to obscuring "the facts" brings us back to our old theme that the certainty of the legal rules does not ensure certainty of decisions, that inaccurate testimony, if believed, will often circumvent the clearest of rules.

---

we see the more primitive arrangement giving way to combat by proxy in the form of bilateral litigation. Each party still fends for himself under rules of diligence but aided by a lawyer as his paid champion. The law suit here still retains a dual character, on the one hand being a means of settling disputes with approximate justice, and on the other a sublimation mechanism for combat feelings and expression of grudges."

[3] Book Review, 32 *Ill. L. Rev.* (1937) 383, 384.

Most things have many uses. Just as the mouth is employed for eating, breathing, talking and kissing, so the courts, primarily designed for the peaceable settlement of disputes, have developed multiple functions, some of them undesirable. A man without a bona fide claim may dishonestly employ a law-suit as a coercive weapon: So to speak, he shoves a law-suit in another's ribs as if it were a revolver. Litigation may be a "racket." An unscrupulous man may get away with one of several crooked ways to win a law-suit: He may kill or kidnap or intimidate or bribe hostile witnesses; bribe a judge or a juror or his adversary's lawyer; forge documents favorable to him, or secrete or destroy papers which are unfavorable; introduce false testimony. The courts, whose basic function is promotion of peace, may thus serve as aids in waging unjust private warfare. A law-suit may give a physiologically weak man a means of unfairly coercing a strong one; lacking physical force of his own, the weaker is able, if he wins by perjury, to enlist society's force, through a court order against his opponent.

The inclination to litigate is not a constant. It may vary with age, social class, nationality, and with the subject matter of the dispute. Also, the desires of a litigant may change as the suit progresses. Moreover, the motivations of one party to a suit may differ from those of the other party.

Goitein suggests that the ceremonial of the court-room contest, with its vestiges of the ancient ordeal, have immense emotional value for litigants. That may be true for some men. The formal court process we now employ does sometimes yield emotional satisfaction to a litigant which he would not receive from a decision based on a less formal but more accurate determination of the facts. So, too, in criminal prosecutions: The public, it is said, demands vengeance in a murder case; perhaps often it does; perhaps, also, it emotionally craves a decisional process which includes some ceremonial rites.

In spite of all the foregoing, I surmise that, by and large, most litigants do want the courts to discover the true facts in their cases.

2

There is a category of disputes for which the courts seem poorly designed: When two businessmen dispute about a breach of a contract, often neither of them wants vindication, or to assuage a feeling of injustice. What they may want is a speedy sensible readjustment of their relations, so that they can resume or maintain their usual mutual business transactions. Because of the difficulties of precise ascertainment by a court of the actual past facts out of which their dispute arose, it may well be that the best mode of settling it is not a court decision in a law-suit but arbitration in which the disputants agree to abide by the decision of the arbitrators.[4] Such is the conclusion of Sir Frederick William Eggleston. In a recent article, he writes: "With regard to the trial of pure questions of fact, I am of opinion that the results are so much a matter of chance that arbitration is the best procedure. This of course saves nothing if the arbitration simply follows the procedure of a court. The only arbitration," he says, "which is of any value is a submission to a single arbitrator with a direction that he shall investigate the case in his own way, getting his facts in whatever way he thinks right."[5]

Since, generally speaking, arbitrators are not bound to apply legal rules, the fact that, increasingly, businessmen resort to arbitration throws some doubt on the conventional notion, to which I previously referred, that precise legal rules are primarily needed in the realm of business, that they supply a certainty and stability which men of business must have, that "the commercial world" demands such rules "because no one . . . engages in complex commercial undertakings trusting to" decisions resting on uncertain exercise of "discretion." Paradoxically, arbitration, with its freedom to disregard the legal rules, seems to function best in dealing with business disputes and not with those disputes which arise from angry personal feelings—where, on the whole, legal certainty has been said to be as of far less importance. One suggested explanation of this paradox is that businessmen who arbitrate have less interest in the legal rules than in the customs of their trade, which they feel will receive more attention from arbitrators acquainted with those trade customs than from the courts.[6] That explanation does not wholly satisfy, since arbitrators can, and sometimes do, ignore those customs.

[4] See Radin, *Law as Logic and Experience* (1940) passim.

[5] "Experience teaches," says Dean Sturges, "that an arbitral adjustment of a business dispute leaves the parties susceptible to further business dealings. What is more significant, the use of future-dispute [i.e., arbitration] clauses [in contracts] often induces the parties to resolve their own misunderstandings before they require a formal arbitration."

[6] When businessmen choose arbitration, in part, they do so because court trials often involve more delay and expense; because of the exclusionary rules employed by courts which often shut out important evidence in trials; because juries are too much swayed by prejudice; and because, in many arbitrations, the arbitrators are men well acquainted with the usages of the particular trade or business of the disputants.

XXVIII. THE UNBLINDFOLDING OF JUSTICE

THE subject of arbitration brings to mind a notable legal feature of two cultures which highly valued that device—the ancient Greek and the Chinese cultures. Both have stressed, as an avowed aim, the individualization of cases.

I have hinted several times in previous chapters that such should be the aim of our own legal system, i.e., that our trial courts, having done everything practical to approximate the actual facts of particular cases, should view them with the purpose of doing justice by giving consideration to their unique aspects.[1] I shall now more directly pursue that idea, after a brief survey of Greek and Chinese practices.

In the Athens of Aristotle's day, most non-criminal suits began as arbitrations, and became contentious litigation only if the parties refused to accept the decisions of the arbitrators. In the light of this practice, Aristotle significantly discusses the differences between "legal" and "equitable" justice. (1) "Legal justice," he said, rests on "arithmetical" equality. According to such justice, "it makes no difference whether it is a good or bad man" who has violated a legal rule; "the law looks only to the distinctive character of the injury, and treats the parties as equal. . . ." (2) But the "equitable," although also justice, is a "correction of legal justice," a "better" kind. "The equitable man . . . is no stickler for his rights in a strict sense, but takes less than his share though he has the law on his side. . . . Equity bids us to be merciful to the weakness of human nature . . . ; not to consider . . . this or that detail so much as the whole story.[2] It bids us . . . to settle by negotiation and not by force; to prefer arbitration to litigation—for an arbitrator goes by the equity of a case, a judge by the strict law, and arbitration was invented with the express purpose of securing full power for equity." Here was a defense not only of negotiation and arbitration

1 I grant that that aim must fail to the extent that trial courts are unable to get at the actual facts. To that extent, individualization of cases will be artificial.

2 Compare this with my discussion of the "gestalt" in trial-court decisions.

but of individualization of cases, of a relaxation of legal rules to meet the unique circumstances of each particular case.

In actual practice in ancient Athens, even if arbitration failed, and a case went (as most cases, if litigated, finally did) to a "popular" court consisting of a large multitude of judges (whom moderns sometimes call "jurors"), nevertheless "equity" played a large role. For the Greeks openly recognized (as Aristotle's writings show) that these judges had no obligation strictly to apply the legal rules, that they could and frequently did use the rules only as general guides, with full allowance for the unique facts. "In the Greek administration of law," wrote Wigmore, "the emphasis was less on the strict law than on the general justice of the case."

No doubt this system had some of the disadvantages of our own jury system, since the Greek judges in the popular courts returned something like our general verdicts. However, most Greek "jurors," unlike ours, were constantly in court and were fairly well acquainted with the legal rules. The indications are that their avowed method of individualizing cases, and the absence of any rigid doctrine of following the precedents, produced excellent results.[3]

Many modern students, however, have denigrated the Greek legal system, comparing it unfavorably with that of Rome which they picture as having desirably evolved an elaborate network of legal rules and principles. Typical is the comment by Sir Henry Maine:[4] "There are two special dangers to which law and society which is held together by law, appear to be liable in their infancy. One of them is that law may be too rapidly developed. This occurred with the codes of the more progressive Greek communities, which disembarrassed themselves with astonishing facility from cumbrous forms of procedure and needless terms of art, and soon ceased to attach any superstitious value to rigid rules and prescriptions. It was not for the ultimate advantage of mankind that they did so, though the immediate benefit conferred on their citizens may have been considerable. One of the rarest qualities of national character [here referring to Rome] is the capacity for applying and working out the law as such, at the cost of constant miscarriages

[3] See, e.g., Vinagradoff, 2 *Historical Jurisprudence* (1922) 7-11, 78-79, 145; Calhoun, "The Greek Legal City," 24 *Col. L. Rev.* (1924) 154; Calhoun, *Greek Legal Science* (1944).

[4] For not dissimilar estimates of the Greek system, see quotations in Bonner and Smith, 2 *Administration of Justice from Homer to Aristotle* (1938) 288; Simpson and Stone, 1 *Law and Society* (1948) 168 note; Wigmore, 1 *Panorama of the World's Legal Systems* (1928) 358-59, 364.

of abstract justice, without at the same time losing the hope or the wish that law may be conformed to a higher ideal. The Greek intellect, with all its nobility and elasticity, was quite unable to confine itself within the strait waistcoat of a legal formula; and, if we may judge them by the popular courts of Athens, of whose working we possess accurate knowledge, the Greek tribunals exhibited the strongest tendency to confound law and fact. The remains of the Orators and the forensic commonplaces preserved by Aristotle in his Treatise on Rhetoric, show that questions of pure law were constantly argued on every consideration which could possibly influence the mind of the judges. No durable system of jurisprudence could be produced in this way. A community which never hesitated to relax rules of written law whenever they stood in the way of an ideally perfect decision on the facts of particular cases, would only, if it bequeathed any body of judicial principles to posterity, bequeath one consisting of the ideas of right and wrong which happened to be prevalent at the time. Such jurisprudence [unlike the Roman] would contain no framework to which the more advanced conceptions of subsequent ages could be fitted. . . ."[5]

What a remarkable attitude Maine voices! He grants that the Greeks "never hesitated to relax" legal rules "whenever they stood in the way" of just decisions "on the facts of particular cases." He grants, too, that "the immediate benefit [conferred] on their citizens may have been considerable." But he criticizes the Greeks because, bent on justice in particular cases, they bequeathed no "body of judicial principles to posterity." Surely it is strange that those Greeks, from whom we have acquired many of our most precious political and philosophic ideas, and the foundations of our natural sciences, should be regarded as backward legally.[6] I suggest that in concerning themselves with the considerable benefit to their citizens rather than in contriving rules to benefit posterity, they showed that they were enlightened in the legal realm as elsewhere. I suggest that we have much to learn from the Greek view of the judicial process.

Parenthetically, comments such as Maine's on the Roman legal system ascribe to it a completeness which more recent scholars say it did not possess.[7] Like ours, too, the Roman system, since it unavoidably

[5] Maine, *Ancient Law* (3d. Am. ed. 1885) 72-73.

[6] Wigmore's comments on the Greek system echo Maine's. This is the more remarkable in the light (1) of Wigmore's laudation (discussed earlier) of our jury system because jurors secretly circumvent the legal rules and (2) his discussion of the Chinese system.

[7] See, e.g., Schulz, *Principles of Roman Law* (1936); Schulz, *Roman Legal Science* (1946). The Romans used arbitration extensively.

involved trial-court fact-finding,[8] of course, individualized; but, like ours, it did not admit, as openly as did the Greeks, that the unique aspects of cases were thus operative. Nor is it true that the Greeks bequeathed nothing of value, legally, to posterity: Aristotle's discussion of the "equitable" interpretation of statutes seemingly affected the Roman lawyers; through Aquinas, it was imported into England in the 16th century, and thence came to America.[9]

The Chinese legal system [10] bears some striking resemblances to the ancient Greek. In China, thanks apparently to the influence of Confucius, litigation has generally been regarded as virtually immoral. The parties to a dispute are expected to settle it, out of court, by negotiation or arbitration. If a case does come to court, the judge must first endeavor to bring about a fair settlement. If his efforts fail, he then, after hearing the evidence, seeks a just, ethical, result, employing the legal rules as but general guides, and individualizing his decision. Confucius (it is said) almost in so many words praised a government of wise and just men, and criticized a strict "government of laws." [11] For a period after Confucius, China tried a strict "government of laws," but that ideal was abandoned centuries ago, and even today has not again been actually adopted. Chinese judicial administration has had many faults, yet most observers consider that, on the whole, it has worked at least as well as ours.[12]

[8] The failure of Maine, in his discussion of the Roman legal system, to consider the effect of fact-finding on decisions is especially remarkable, since Maine is one of the few legal thinkers who has called attention to the nature of judicial fact-finding. See Maine, *Early History of Institutions* (1875) 48-50; Maine, Village Communities (4th ed. 1881) 311-12, 318; Frank, *If Men Were Angels* (1942) 116-17.

[9] For a brief description of this development, see my opinion in Usatore v. The Victoria, 172 F. (2d) 434, notes 11 to 16. It there appears that a great American judge, Learned Hand (who tells me that he has never carefully studied Aristotle) has expressed views which are a modernized paraphrase of that ancient Greek's thesis. See also Guiseppi v. Walling, 144 F. (2d) 608, 615-623, as to Aristotle's indirect influence on our Supreme Court.

[10] See, e.g., Wigmore, 1 *Panorama of the World's Legal Systems* (1928) Chapter IV; Hu Shi, Development of the Logical Method of Ancient China (1928); Latourette, *The Chinese, Their History and Culture* (3d ed. 1946); Lin Yutang, *My Country and My People* (1935); Lin Yutang, *The Importance of Living* (1937); Wu, *The Art of Law* (1936).

[11] I use the phrase "it is said" because much that has been ascribed to Confucius may be mythical. See Creel, "Sinism—a Clarification," 10 *J. of the History of Ideas* (1949) 135.

[12] I have given a most superficial sketch of Chinese judicial methods, a sketch which compresses many centuries of history of an alien culture. As to the dangers of glibness about China, see Wright, Book Review, 10 *J. of The History of Ideas* (1949) 143. My sketch is, however, based not only on reading published books but on dis-

Wigmore contrasts our occidental legal attitudes and the Chinese as follows: "The German jurist Puchta has concisely stated the antithesis between justice and law: 'The relationships of Rights are the relations of one man to another, and may be called legal relations. But the various human relationships do not enter, in their full extent, into the sphere of Right, because the legal notion of a person rests upon an abstraction and does not embrace the whole being of man. There must, therefore, occur much modification and subtraction before we reach the special relations which alone are involved in the idea of a Right. Thus, suppose a man has arisen from a protracted illness, and in order to pay the bill of his physician, to provide for the urgent wants of his family, due to his recent incapacity, and to procure the means of beginning business again, he goes to a well-disposed neighbor, whom he has helped in former times, and obtains a loan at the usual rate. How much of all this must we not leave out in order to ascertain the purely jural relation between the parties: Compare with this the case of the rich man who raises capital merely to add to his possessions by a new speculation, and consider the effort of abstraction which is required in order to assimiliate the resulting legal relations. And yet the legal relations in these two cases are identical.' For the Anglo-Saxon lawyer, accustomed as no other is to do homage to strict legal principle, as in and for itself the summum bonum of law, and to regard legal justice as manifesting itself only in a science of unbending rules, this quotation will indicate better than anything else, the vast gulf that is fixed between his own system and that which was indigenous to China. By making generalizations into hard-and-fast rules, by strictly eliminating in individual cases a variety of important moral considerations, the Anglo-Saxons have succeeded in creating a special type of justice. This tendency of theirs is so strong that English Equity, the one great effort to counteract it, has become in the end identical in these respects with the whole system. Yet there are peoples to whom this type of justice is utterly alien."

Wigmore has also described, similarly, the legal system in "old" Japan, explaining that it derived from the Chinese, so that his description is applicable to the latter. "It is," he says, "in Japan that we may find the extreme antithesis to the Anglo-Saxon conception of justice. Whether there is or not any practical lesson for us in studying this opposite type, is a question which we need not here take up. However

---

cussions with, and papers written by, some of my Chinese students at Yale Law School, one of whom served for several years as a trial judge in China.

this may be, the chief characteristic of Japanese justice, as distinguished from our own, may be said to be this tendency to consider all the circumstances of individual cases, to confide the relaxation of principles to judicial discretion, to balance the benefits and disadvantages of a given course, not for all time in a fixed rule, but anew in each instance —in short, to make justice personal, not impersonal. It would not be fair to infer from this that the courts of old Japan could have been no better than the tents of an Arab Sheikh, where justice came roughly and speedily, and the good sense of the tribunal was the only measure of equity. On the contrary, there was in Japan [13] a legal system, a body of clear and consistent rules, a collection of statutes and of binding precedents. But whether it be or not a mere mark of primitive legal development, there was always the disposition to take, as Puchta puts it, 'the whole being of man' into consideration, to arrange a given dispute in the most expedient way, to sacrifice legal principle to present expediency. . . . What the judge aimed at was general equity in each case."

2

Years ago, I suggested (à la Aristotle) that legal rules which, because of their generality, necessarily omit much, should, in their application to particular states of fact, be taken with a keen perception of their unexpressed qualifications. I went on to say that, in this sense, the rules might be considered "fictions," and that consequently, they should be dealt with as the courts deal with legal fictions when aware they are employing them. I noted that the courts have often said that legal fictions are "intended for the sake of justice" and should "not be permitted to work any wrong." The rules, I said, if applied without awareness, that (in the sense above noted) they are "fictional," do work harm. "They can," I continued, "be immensely useful and entirely harmless if used with complete recognition that they are but . . . convenient hypostatizations, provisional formulations, sign-posts, guides." [14]

However, I did not and do not now suggest that we should adopt the ancient Greek or the Chinese-Japanese judicial methods. But it is well to consider whether it would not be wise in part to emulate their approach. Would it not be better openly and candidly to confer on our courts the power to individualize cases rather than to retain our present mode of pretending that our courts lack that power while, in truth,

[13] In China, also.

[14] Frank, *Law and the Modern Mind* (1930) 167.

evasively, surreptitiously, they exercise it? Does not our method of sneaking in individualization through the back door smack of semi-hypocrisy? Is it desirable that our trial judges and juries do their jobs obliquely? Is not such evasiveness harmful to trial judges, jurors, and the litigants? Would it not be preferable to declare that, in our trial courts, legal rules, no matter how precisely worded, often do function only as general guides, to acknowledge that our courts often thus do individualize cases?

But what, then, of legal certainty? Schulz [15] notes that when we talk of such certainty, "the security of law," we do so "in a double sense of the term; in one sense it means the certainty that right will prevail in its struggle with wrong, in the other, certainty as to what is the law, its recognizable character and the predictability of the legal consequences entailed by a particular set of facts. If we assume a legal system under which decisions are made at the free discretion of the judge, but which ensures that the judge shall be an eminent, just, and entirely independent personality, then we have legal security in the first sense; it is certain that right will prevail, but there is no legal security in the second sense. If, on the other hand, the legal system is incorporated in detailed statute-books, but the judge is ignorant, corrupt, or dependent, there is certainty as to the law, but no certainty that it will prevail." And the same is true if he uses "free discretion," via the "facts," but that discretion is concealed.

3

I now turn to a somewhat fanciful idea: In a book I wrote nineteen years ago, I suggested that the quest for a practically unrealizable legal certainty might *partially* be explained by the carry-over into adult life of a hankering for the strict rules of the father which, in our kind of society, the young child cherishes as a means of procuring emotional stability.[16] Now it is notable that the Roman legal system—admired for its elaboration of rules and principles, and far less given to acknowledged, flexible, individualizing than the Greek system—arose in a society in which the power of the father (the patria potestas) was a dominant characteristic. In the maturity of Greek civilization, this power of the father had much diminished. I suggest that it is barely possible that, as a result, the role of the mother emerged as an influence

[15] *Principles of Roman Law* (1936) 258.

[16] See Frank, *Law and the Modern Mind* (1930; sixth printing with new preface, 1949). There (at p. 263) I suggested fourteen other partial explanations.

on Greek legal attitudes, so that equity, greater lenience, more attention to the "circumstances that alter cases" in the application of rules, became an accepted legal ideal. Perhaps, too, it is significant that Lin Yutang describes the Chinese "character" as essentially "feminine."

As I said, I admit that this is a somewhat fanciful idea. It lends itself to caricature. One might speak of the Mother-In-Law, or suggest that I am a victim of the "Mom-ism" described by Wylie, and that I have been overcome by Jolson's Mammy songs. Yet this idea may contain a grain of truth: The mother does symbolize "equity."

Think, for instance, of the role of Mary, the mother, in the 12th and 13th centuries, as pictured by Henry Adams:[17] "She alone represented Love. . . . The Trinity . . . must admit only one law. In that law, no human weakness or error could exist. . . . There was no crack and no cranny in the system, through which human frailty could hope for escape. One was forced from corner to corner by a remorseless logic until one fell helpless at Mary's feet. . . . Mary [was] the only court of equity capable of overruling strict law." Abelard wrote that "all of us who fear the wrath of the Judge, fly to the Judge's mother." The "mother," says Adams, "alone was human, imperfect, and could love; she alone was Diversity, . . . alone could represent whatever was not Unity; whatever was irregular, exceptional, outlawed; and this was the whole human race. . . . Her piety had no limit. . . . To her, every suppliant was a universe in itself, to be judged apart, on his own merits, by his love for her. . . ."[18]

To speak of "feminine" attributes is to speak glibly. For no one knows what are the innate, indelible, differences, in the thought-ways and emotional reactions, between the sexes. It seems impossible to doubt that they do exist, in view of the structural and functional differences physiologically: That I can neither bear nor nurse a child must have some effect on the way I think and feel. But the basic emotional divergences between men and women cannot, as yet, be adequately discerned, because custom and cultural influences have caused, and still cause, distinctions in the education of the sexes from early infancy.

[17] Adams, *Mont Saint-Michel and Chartres* (1905) Chapter 13.

[18] See Sandburg, *The People, Yes:* "Do you solemnly swear before the everliving God that the testimony you are about to give in this cause shall be the truth, the whole truth, and nothing but the truth?" "No, I don't. I can tell you what I saw and what I heard and I'll swear to that by the everliving God but the more I study about it the more sure I am that nobody but the everliving God knows the whole truth and if you summoned Christ as a witness in this case what He would tell you would burn your insides with the pity and the mystery of it."

Wherefore it is not improper to refer to "feminine" attitudes—remembering always that men also possess them in varying degrees.[19]

4

In 1884, Theodore Roosevelt, then 26 years of age, sneered at the legal profession as "especially fitted for 'the weaker sex.' " I think that the young Roosevelt was right in his conclusion, wrong in his attitude. For I believe that the judicial process is one of the best means worked out by human society for the adjustment of many of its difficulties. I believe also that flexibility, tact, and the understanding of people, are more important in the practice of the "law" than what has usually (but erroneously) been considered legal logic—the rigorous application of fixed legal principles. To what do these beliefs add up? To the conclusion that it is the so-called "feminine" attributes, rather than the so-called "masculine," that are essential in the task of administering justice.

How distasteful would have been that idea to most (not all) women who, about three or four decades ago, were winning their fight for admission to the law schools! They were known as feminists but were really masculinists—women who, consciously or unconsciously, wanted to be the counterpart of men. Logic, they believed, was, par excellence, a mark of maleness. Where better, they thought, could they use this masculine mental skill than in the practice of law? They were taken in by the then generally prevalent theory that the "law" contains an almost complete set of settled principles, and that, from these principles, the correct answers to all legal problems can be drawn—if only one be sufficiently logical.

Those prospective Portias should have heeded Mr. Justice Holmes. He had cautioned against the fallacious idea that "the only force at work in the law is logic." He wrote, as we saw,[20] that "the whole outline of the law . . . is the resultant of a conflict between logic and good sense—the one striving to carry fictions out to consistent results, the other restraining and at last overcoming that effort when the results become too manifestly unjust." Although he seemed to be inveighing against logic, he did not mean that legal thinking shouldn't be logical. He meant, as I have said, that this logic leads to error and injustice, if the principles on which it operates are deemed invariably precise and inflexible.

[19] See the suggestive, if erratic, writings of Weininger.
[20] See Chapter XIX.

But not for the feminist lawyers, this approach to their profession. Dogmatic, doctrinaire, they drove judges all but mad with their "logic." They failed to understand what was then sensed by many of their successful male competitors—and by a very few perceptive women lawyers—that the courts must often choose between alternative principles, must frequently modify old principles to meet novel and unanticipated circumstances, and must and do individualize cases. All this, the ultramannish women lawyers missed. They were absolutists. In short, they did not comprehend that a large part of a lawyer's or judge's job requires tact, rough-and-ready adjustment between clashing interests, finesse, intuition—in other words, the techniques ordinarily regarded as feminine.

Even as a young lawyer, I wanted to cry out to these women, "Be yourselves!" For I suspected that really womanly women—granted sufficient training of their capacities—could cope with and perhaps better their male competitors. I believed that they could effectively employ in court-rooms and law offices the insights women have traditionally used as wives and mothers in making life livable for their men, who tend too frequently to use over-precise abstractions, to distort life by over-simplifying it, to ignore gestalts.

Well, in the past decade or so, the law schools have been turning out, not feminists, but women lawyers—girls who don't want to be boys, who dress modishly, who don't scorn to be femininely attractive, who intend to have both marriage and a career—and generally do. And, to my satisfaction as a prophet, their batting average has been far higher than that of most of their predecessors.

You will perhaps recall the famous English judge who gave this advice to a newly-appointed member of the bench: "State your conclusions, but never your reasons. Your conclusions will probably be right; your reasons will usually be wrong." How often, to my youthful awe, had not my mother and sisters successfully used this device: "Let the reasons go hang." Women usually have a way of piercing to the core of the matter. To arrive at the "right" conclusions, and (unlike the younger English judge) with moderate adequacy to articulate the reasons—such a gestalt-like combination of intuition and logic produces the successful woman lawyer.

Holmes said, "The life of the law has not been logic; it has been experience." This sagacious comment the modern woman lawyer understands. She understands, too, that "law" is not a science but an art, the art of intelligent compromise. Just as father's stern disciplining of little Johnny is mitigated by mother's gentleness, so in our legal system individualization softens the asperities of over-rigid rules.

In the courts, as in the home, allowances must be made for extenuating circumstances, specific cases must be individualized. Behind the facade of abstractions, intelligent trial judges see the living human beings involved in law suits, feel the subtle human factors which distinguish one case from another. "The heart has reasons, which reason does not know," wrote Pascal. A man-dominated legal tradition often conceals those reasons of the heart, although actually they motivate many court decisions. Who can better comprehend those reasons than women?

I recently read an essay by a psychologist who insists that women's reasoning lacks "the element of consistency." Perhaps he is correct. But is that an altogether deplorable trait? Emerson called consistency the hobgoblin of little minds. That epigram has been much misapplied. Inconsistency, as such, is not to be prized. Consistency in argument is unquestionably a virtue. But the effort to make of the "law" a closed, static, and consistent system is neither desirable nor possible.

5

When moralists speak of an undesirably cold and inhumane code of ethics, they are wont to describe it as "legalistic." Genuine morality, writes Leon, "is not an affair of . . . rules"; only a "pharisaic" morality maintains that "hard cases make bad laws," and refuses to "concern itself with personality or individuality. Goodness is not expressible in a formula; and for acting rightly—that is, strictly speaking, for acting uniquely in each situation—there can be no rule any more than there can be one for producing original thought or art." Goodness requires "prosaic, unheroic patience and adaptation to the individual case and even something very like compromise or the scorned *via media*. . . ."[21] Moral principles, say Dewey and Tufts, if taken as "generalized points of view are of great use in surveying particular cases." But there is danger when they "become prescriptions," "something ready-made and fixed," not "cautionary directions" but "recipes."[22] Then the "moral life is reduced . . . to an elaborate formalism and legalism."[23]

[21] Leon, *The Ethics of Power* (1935) passim.

[22] It was the use of moral principles as "recipes" or fixed "rules," I had in mind when, in *Law and the Modern Mind* (1930) 260, I wrote: "Holmes has been telling us for fifty years that, in effect, the Golden Rule is that there is no Golden Rule."

[23] Dewey and Tufts, *Ethics* (2d ed. 1932) 304-08, 310-11.

Such condemnatory use by moralists of the words "legalistic" and "legalism," should induce some doubts about our judicial system, especially when we find a moralist, Brunner, pessimistically concluding that there can be "no truly just system of law," and that a judge, although convinced that a legal rule is unjust, must undeviatingly act in accord with it and render an unjust decision. Such a position about "legalism" implies that judges, to the extent that they over-emphasize rigid legal rules, are insufficiently ethical. Like Niebuhr, I am disturbed by such a "complacent acceptance of injustice." I am unwilling to believe that our judging must depart so far from mature notions of the ethical. Mercy, charity, compassionateness, respect for the unique attributes of the men and women who come before our trial courts—these would seem to be needed components of a civilized judicial process. I find some solace in the fact that, in spite of contrary pretensions, those are actual components of many decisions. But I ask myself why our judges must continue to do merciful justice by stealth.[24] I cannot believe that such stealthiness produces the soundest administration of justice.

6

In the Juvenile Court we have rejected such stealth. "The ingredients of this court's approach," says Lukas, "are understanding, sympathy, and unvarying resolve to unravel the relentless web of conditions which determine human behavior, whether it be a child's delinquency or a parent's neglect. . . . Some lawyers feel that the Childrens' Courts do not dispense uniform 'justice.' In thinking so, they overlook individual differences among people, and ignore the fact that the court endeavors to deal with these crucial differences rather than search for those similarities which, in other places, call for dispensing what is called 'even-handed justice.' . . . It is . . . impossible, just as it would be inadvisable, to lay down pre-fixed procedures to cope with these characteristics. The rule against the 'disintegrating erosion of particular exceptions' simply does not apply to these human problems."[25] Is it not possible that the techniques of the Juvenile Court could desirably, in some measure, be taken over by all our trial courts?

In fact, most of our trial courts do use such techniques when they

[24] When they do, they are victims of what Chesterton called "that miserable fear of being sentimental, which is the meanest of all the modern terrors."

[25] Lukas, in 3 *Record of the Ass'n. of the Bar of the City of New York* (1948) 331. Much the same can be said of Workmen's Compensation Commissions.

come to fixing the length and character of sentences of adult persons convicted of crimes. As the Supreme Court said a few months ago in Williams v. New York: "Both before and since the American colonies became a nation, courts in this country and in England practiced a policy under which a sentencing judge could exercise a wide discretion in the sources and types of evidence used to assist him in determining the kind and extent of punishment to be imposed within limits fixed by law. Out-of-court affidavits have been used frequently, and of course in the smaller communities sentencing judges naturally have in mind their knowledge of the personalities and backgrounds of convicted offenders. A recent manifestation of the historical latitude allowed sentencing judges appears in Rule 32 of the Federal Rules of Criminal Procedure. That rule provides for consideration by federal judges of reports made by probation officers containing information about a convicted defendant, including such information 'as may be helpful in imposing sentence or in granting probation or in the correctional treatment of the defendant. . . .' A sentencing judge . . . is not confined to the narrow issue of guilt. His task within fixed statutory or constitutional limits is to determine the type and extent of punishment after the issue of guilt has been determined. Highly relevant—if not essential—to his selection of an appropriate sentence is the possession of the fullest information possible concerning the defendant's life and characteristics. And modern concepts individualizing punishment have made it all the more necessary that a sentencing judge not be denied an opportunity to obtain pertinent information by a requirement of rigid adherence to restrictive rules of evidence properly applicable to the trial. . . . The belief no longer prevails that every offense in a like legal category calls for an identical punishment without regard to the past life and habits of a particular offender. . . . Under the practice of individualizing punishments, investigational techniques have been given an important role. Probation workers making reports of their investigations have not been trained to prosecute but to aid offenders. . . . And the modern probation report draws on information concerning every aspect of a defendant's life." Someday, when we have stopped importing into non-jury criminal trials those exclusionary evidence rules we maintain in jury trials (because of jury incompetence), and when we have trained trial judges whom we fully trust, we may perhaps provide that similar information—subject, of course, to cross-examination and rebuttal evidence—be made part of the testimony to aid the judges in determining guilt or innocence.

Our traditional image of Justice is a blindfolded goddess, who treats all persons alike, disregarding extenuating circumstances. "Lately," says George Boas, "Justice has been peeking from under her blindfold to distinguish between children and adults. . . . She is of course blamed occasionally for this, since she is no longer impartial; but in time, it will probably be the proud boast of her worshippers that she treats no two individuals alike" (i.e., that she mercifully individualizes in the spirit of the Aristotelian arbitrator's "equity").

Otherwise, Justice may provide an artificial or fictitious "equality before the law," an "arithmetical" equality which is cruel. The "spirit of justice," wrote Faguet, "when not joined with the spirit of kindness, is so dry and so cold that it is no better than a mania for equality and it can lead . . . as much to the suppression of the weak as to the desire to help them. . . . When one wants to know, not what maintains society, but how it must be improved . . . , it is to charity, to the spirit of devotion, to the spirit of brotherhood, that one must look. It is these which are the true duties, not only for the individual but for society itself; those are the principles which in their farthest consequences do not risk turning out to be the opposite of what they were." [26]

[26] Faguet, *Politicians and Moralists of the Nineteenth Century* (1899) 142-43.

XXIX. LEGAL CLASSICISM AND ROMANTICISM

"THE classic conception of justice is derived from Roman law, and shares its formal legalistic character," write Dewey and Tufts. The adjective "classic" opens up further vistas: Our conventional theory of the judicial process is in the "classical" tradition. The term "classical," originally used in aesthetic criticism, reflected Roman artistic standards which stressed the alleged need of rather rigid application of formal rules or "laws" in artistic creation. Indeed, these artistic "laws" were said to be primarily of a legal nature.

Dr. Samuel Johnson, a pronounced classicist, insisted that art should restrict itself to generic types, to the generalized. "The poet," he said, "does not number the streaks of the tulip, or describe the different shades in the verdure of a forest; he is to exhibit in his portraits of nature such prominent and striking features as recall the original to every mind; and must neglect the minute discriminations . . . for those characteristics which are alike obvious to vigilance and carelessness."[1] The classical tradition demands that poetry "speak a universal language," that art adhere to universal, uniform, uncomplicated patterns, to the least common denominator, to the generalized and abstract. Its keynote is standardization, uniformitarianism. The classical is ultra-rationalistic, striving to eliminate the irrational, the aberrant, the unique. It dwells on the typical, the recurrent, the invariant, the general.[2] It shudders at individual differences, regards them as disgustingly capricious and arbitrary.

Opposed to the classical is the "romantic." The word, paradoxically, stems from the word Rome, via the medieval popular "romances," so that "romantic" designated writings, and, subsequently, all artistic

[1] "Dr. Johnson's general powers of reasoning," wrote William Hazlitt, "overlaid his critical susceptibility. All his ideas were cast in a given mold, in a set form: they were made out by rule and system . . . Johnson's understanding dealt only in round numbers: the fractions were lost upon him . . . The shifting shapes of fancy, the rainbow hue of things, made no impression on him: he seized only on the permanent and tangible . . . He saw only the definite, the positive, and the . . . average forms of things, not their striking differences—their classes, not their degrees." Preface to Hazlitt, *Characters of Shakespeare's Plays* (1818).

[2] In this sense, mass-production machine products are classical.

products, which did not conform to the classical Roman canons. Later, not only in the arts but in other fields, "romanticism" came to mean the non-classical, the spontaneous, the original, the intuitive, the ecstatic, the exhilarating, the exuberant, the emotional, the individual, and, above all, the unique. It refuses to treat the individual as merely a representative of a type. The romantic tends to dwell on the non-rational, the personal, that which is uncommon and cannot be generalized. Its essence is diversity; it is diversitarian.

In 19th century Germany, in large part as a reaction to the rationalistic classical temper of the French Enlightenment, Romanticism reached its zenith, approaching madness at times. There was, among many of the German intelligentsia of that period, a deliberate pursuit of idiosyncrasy. Schiller, as a young man, looked "hospitably" on "even that little flowering of pleasure which finds its roots in madness." "From the romantic point of view," wrote A. W. Schlegel, "the abnormal species of literature also have their value—even the eccentric and monstrous—provided only that . . . they are really original." "It is precisely individuality," said Friederich Schlegel, "that is the original and eternal thing in man. . . . The cultivation and development of this individuality, as one's highest vocation, would be a divine egoism." Novalis declared, "The more personal, local, peculiar, of its own time, a poem is, the nearer it stands to the center of poetry." Says Lovejoy, "This, obviously was the polar opposite of the fundamental principle of the neo-classic aesthetic doctrine. This interpretation of the Romantic ideal suggested that the first and great commandment is: 'Be yourself, which is to say, be unique.'" Carried to an extreme, Romanticism issued in the solipsism of Stirner who glorified the "autocratic" personality which "recognizes nothing but itself. . . ."

This romantic mood spread in all directions, and notably in psychology. Although many writers of the Enlightment, such as Diderot and Voltaire, for instance, did not lack insight into the non-rational elements in human nature,[3] they did tend, relatively, to minimize the importance of the emotions. The Romanticists, on the other hand, dwelt on the irrational components of men. They studied hypnotism, the unconscious, the irreducibly individual, the singular, concrete, the particular, the specific, the unique.

This shift in emphasis, with its valuation of individual dignity, had, if not carried too far, important potentialities in the legal field. Un-

[3] As to Diderot, see Trilling, "Freud and Literature," reprinted in Schorer, Miles and McKenzie, *Criticism* (1948) 172.

fortunately, in Germany, the dominant theme, in political and social thinking, soon became not unique individuals but unique societies, the singularity of peoples, of nations—of the Germans. Thence developed that intense and vicious nationalism which culminated later in Nazism. As a consequence, the dignity of the unique individual was repudiated, was submerged in the dreadful worship of the German group "personality" with its unique "mission." [4]

In the legal field, this mystic folk-worship expressed itself in the German "historical school" which over-emphasized tradition, the past, the social heritage. And so the rich potentialities of the romantic movement for legal individualization were not realized.

But they can now be realized. That the Germans perverted this insight, that their misuse of the Romantic mood led to brutalitarian fascism, does not justify the not uncommon rejection of the valuable kernel in the romantic attitude.[5] Out of it, through its interest in the non-rational, has come, for example, much of the "new psychology" [6] which, wisely ("classically") utilized, can be immensely fruitful for our courts—in dealing with witnesses and litigants, and in self-understanding on the part of judges.

2

Maurois, writing of "the role of art in life and law," [7] and comparing the judge and the artist, voices the classical view. In the fine arts, he says, rhythm or pattern has the value of regulating, which is "reassuring because it makes prediction possible." The "real world" is disturbing, because of the "impossibility of knowing what is going to happen next." From the repetitious regularity of poetry or music, the audience obtains a satisfaction like that which the crying baby obtains when his mother soothes him by rocking. The soothed baby "knows . . . what is going to happen to him. He is soon sure that this . . . movement is regular; that he may rely upon it . . . ; and so presently the baby stops crying." The "recurrence of rhythm or rhyme" in a poem

[4] For this development, see e.g., Frank, *Fate and Freedom* (1945) 6-10.

[5] See Vierek, *Metapolitics* (1941) for such rejection. For support for the view I take here, see Friedmann, *Legal Theory* (1944) 405-06. See also Lovejoy, *The Great Chain of Being* (1936) 312: "The discovery of the intrinsic worth of diversity was . . ., with all of the perils latent in it, one of the great discoveries of the human mind; and the fact that it, like many other of his discoveries, has been turned by man to ruinous uses, is no evidence that it is in itself without value."

[6] For Freud's "romantic" background, see Trilling, *loc. cit.*

[7] An address before the Brandeis Law Society in 1945.

gives pleasure like that which "makes the baby, being rocked, smile." So, too, with music: the "unity of rhythm and repetition . . . makes reliable prediction possible. . . ." Art pleases because "reality, so confused, so terrifying, obeys certain laws under the magic power of the artist. . . . Similarly, a poem is beautiful when unruly passions have been made to accept the disciplines of poetry and rhyme." Art contrives "order" which "makes it possible to foresee the future." Maurois says, or implies, that "law" has the same function.

I cannot agree. In the first place, Maurois' conception of the function of the fine arts seems to me too limited, too classical, since it omits those art products which stress diversities, unruly particulars, unconquerable by form or rhythm, and those which aim to express disharmonies, disjunctions, uncertainties, the spirit of "wild" facts with "no stall or pigeon-hole."[8] Maurois' "aesthetics," which insists on soothing, resembles "anaesthetics." It prizes, regressively, an undue prolongation of emotional infancy.[9] Nor are the courts, properly, practitioners of an art to be used to "baby" men, to rock them into smiling. Such a conception of the judicial "mother role" I consider unwise. The trial courts do, indeed, deal with the "unruly." If they aim solely to make it "ruly," in order to make prediction possible, they miss one of their chief functions—understanding of the unique, in order to do justice.

3

Excessive classicism, with its excessive worship of abstractions, has its psychological roots in a morbid fear of particulars, of uniques. To "the man with the abstracting attitude," says Jung, "the world is filled with powerfully operating and therefore dangerous objects; these inspire him with fear, and with a consciousness of his own impotence: he withdraws himself from a too close contact with the world, thus to create those . . . formulae with which he hopes to gain the upper hand." Craving "fixed bounds," seeking a "negation . . . of irreconcilable diversities," by abstractions he "conjures impressions into a law-abiding form," and thereby "depotentiates" particulars, puts an end to their "tyrannical hold," their "threatening quality." Thus he strives to rob life of what are to him its dangerous spontaneities. His attempted use of abstractions wholly to "confine the changing and irregular within

[8] See Frank, *Fate and Freedom* (1945) 197-98, 235.

[9] Frank, *Law and the Modern Mind* (1930) 158 note.

law-abiding limits" is "at bottom a magical procedure. . . ." [10] He becomes intolerant of the diversities.[11]

Excessive classicism is excessive rationalism: Ignoring the non-rational (the "romantic"), rationalism becomes irrational rationalism. For to be thoroughly aware of the non-rational in human affairs (including judicial affairs) enables one better to cope with it—to treat the non-rational rationally. That is to say, the super-rationalist is fundamentally irrational.

But excessive romanticism, spurning rationality, denying all reality to generalizations, is also at fault. We should not, then, eject classicism from the judicial realm. The legal rules and principles will ever be indispensable as guides. But such "classicism" should be tempered by a recognized "romantic" respect in our courts for the unique individual. There is need, in our courts, for a conscious "piety towards the unique," [12] a piety which opposes an "individualism" that treats human beings as homogeneous units, and dwells, instead, on individuality.

As that "piety" seems to be the spirit of Chinese justice, it is of interest to note what Lin Yutang says of William James, who untiringly fought for such individuality.[13] "William James," he writes,[14] "was a Chinese in his keen awareness of life and the varieties of human experience, in his rebellion against mechanistic rationalism, his anxiety to keep thought constantly fluid, and his impatience with people who think they have discovered the one all-important, 'absolute' and universal truth and have enclosed it in a self-sufficient system. He was Chinese, too, in his insistence on the importance of the artist's sense of perceptual reality. . . . The philosopher is a man who holds his sensi-

[10] Jung, *Psychological Types* (1923) Chapter 7.

[11] See Dixon, *The Human Situation* (1937) passim.

The "classical" abstractionist is prone to use a "static logic," which, with its "hard-and-fast demarcation lines" and its "absolutistic unmodifiable judgments," breeds intolerance. See Bogoslovsky, *The Technique of Controversy* (1927) 255.

Bogoslovsky outlines a "dynamic logic" which regards all antitheses as "poles" or extreme limits of a "continuum." This dynamic logic has as its foundation the principle, "A is B and not B simultaneously," or "A is B to such and such degree and non-B to such and such degree." It thus differs from "static" logic ["classical" logic] which insists that always "A either is or is not B."

Bogoslovsky seems to maintain that, in every field, it will be possible to contrive "quantitative indices or scales," so that one can say "how much of B and of non-B exists in A." There he is over-sanguine, I think. I doubt whether we shall ever have scales which will enable us to measure nicely the degrees of mixed components of each human being's motivations.

[12] The phrase is Gide's.

[13] See Kallen, *William James and Henri Bergson* (1914).

[14] *The Importance of Living* (1937) 420-21.

bilities at the highest point of focus and watches the flux of life, ready to be forever surprised by newer and stranger paradoxes, inconsistencies and inexplicable exceptions to the rule." [15]

Trial judges have much to learn from James. He would not put up with either-or attitudes. He saw no sharp antithesis between reason and emotion. He wanted neither 100% classicism nor 100% romanticism, but a blend of both.[16] With his marked poetic insight, which made him the despair of sedate, "classical," psychologists, he went far in exploring the intricacies of the human mind. Judging, especially in trial courts, calls for such poetic insight.[17] For poetry, which involves synthetic imagination, gives "an inclusive understanding of situations" in a way that "analytic reason" cannot.[18] Judges would do well to heed Pascal who, a first-rate scientist and mathematician, had the sensibilities of a poet. "Those," he wrote, "who are accustomed to reason from principles, do not at all understand matters of feeling, seeking principles, and being unable to see at a glance. . . . Intuition is the part of judgment, mathematics of intellect. . . . Two extremes: to exclude reason, to admit reason only. . . . We know truth, not only by the reason, but also by the heart. . . . And reason must trust those intuitions of the heart. . . . " Pascal describes what might be called the "classicist's fallacy": to mistake men for "propositions." [19]

4

Classicism holds precious the "average" patterns of conduct, the "types" of human behavior. Most of those average patterns or types turn out, on close scrutiny, to be merely the conventions of some particular society. Yet so powerful is custom that most men have always regarded complete conformity to the customary patterns as a sign of normality, and have looked upon as abnormal or queer the persons

[15] Mrs. David Riesman notes that, as to many aspects of experience, we develop, when childhood recedes, "the amnesia of ever having experienced them"; but she differentiates "the artist": "He sees freshly in other than the conventional schemata of perception and so is able to capture the living quality." 6 Etc. (1949) 160.

[16] "One must know concrete instances first," he wrote, "for as Professor Agassiz used to say, no one can see farther into a generalization than just so far as one's previous acquaintance with particulars enables one to take it in."

[17] See Judge Bok's statements quoted in Chapter XII.

[18] Whicher in 16 *Amer. Scholar* (1947) 393.

[19] "This man," he said, "is a good mathematician. . . . He would take me for a proposition." Feibleman writes that "good intuition and reason lie in the psyche of the organism in layers, and hence . . . the intuitions of genuine rationalists (not dogmatists, mind you, who are simply bad rationalists) are safer guides to judgments and actions than the unprincipled, more irrational types of feeling." Feibleman, Book Review, 57 *Sewanee Rev.* (1949) 337, 340.

to whom any of the conventions seemed queer. Erich Fromm and David Riesman are now saying that, especially in our contemporary society, there is a too-ready acquiescence in the conventional, and a derision of the "queer"—born of fear—which puts our civilization in danger.

Riesman depicts most men of our time as "other-directed" or "radar-directed," possessed of an "irrational" craving for "indiscriminate approval," "losing their characterological defenses against the group and . . . sinking into ever-greater impotence," "surrendering their judgment to the market"; the "individual fails to . . . exercise freedom of choice even where he might safely do so" because he is "afraid of disobeying the subtle and unpermeable injunctions of the . . . group to which he looks for approval." With "a ritual of submergence in the group," men are easily manipulated; "psychic cravings for unity and consensus" create a situation "which modern dictators exploit."[20]

Fromm writes of the current "marketing orientation" of character in which each man experiences himself as a commodity for sale on the "personality market," with success dependent on "how nice a 'package' he is." There results an undue "sensitivity to the expectations of others," a loss of a "genuine feeling of identity." The "feeling of identity becomes as shaky as . . . self-esteem; it is constituted by the sum total of the roles one can play: 'I am as you desire me.' "[21] That "which is peculiar and unique" in men is becoming valueless. "The meaning which the word 'peculiar' has assumed is quite expressive of this attitude. Instead of denoting the greatest achievement of man—that of having developed his individuality—it has become almost synonymous with 'queer.' The word 'equality' has also changed its meaning. The idea that all men are created equal implied that all men had the same fundamental right to be considered ends in themselves and not as means. Today equality has become equivalent to 'interchangeability'; and is the very negation of individuality. Equality, instead of being the condition of each man's peculiarity, means the extinction of individuality, the 'selflessness' characteristic of the marketing orientation. Equality was conjunctive with difference, but it has become synon-

[20] Riesman's article in the volume, *Year of the Modern* (1949). Since the "patterns" of behavior are often set by the currently conventional stereotypes, it is of interest that Dr. Russell Myers (using a behavioristic vocabulary) says that "we take to be 'real' that to which we have developed relatively adaptive behavior patterns of response." 6 Etc. (1949) 169.

[21] Recall here that the word "person" originally derived from the word designating an actor's mask which represented a type. We seem to be in danger of reverting to that concept of "person."

ymous with 'in-difference.' . . . The marketing personality must be free of all individuality." As a consequence, we have "depersonalization . . . , emptiness, . . . automatization of the individual. . . , People are not able and cannot afford to be concerned with that which is unique and 'peculiar' in each other." They have "lost the sense of the significance and uniqueness of the individual." If so we continue, ours will be a sick society, since "the respect for life, that of others as well as our own, is the concomitant of the process of life and a condition of psychic health." [22]

Here is a strange and dangerous new "classicism," one which imposes on men what old Sir Thomas Browne termed "under-living themselves." We must learn to resist it.[23] Effective resistance, however, will not come from an immature "romanticism" which is but bondage to a compulsion to revolt, or from a "subservience of contradiction"—that sort of rebellion against the authority of the "average" which is no more free than slavishness to such authority.[24] In the courts, mature resistance to this new, menacing "classicism" calls for a more honest and openly acknowledged respect for each man's uniqueness, his "peculiarities."

5

There remains another defense of legal classicism which must now be considered: Paradoxically, we reduce our ignorance by temporarily ignoring—making ourselves ignorant of—the entirety of experience, and by concentrating ("classically," one might say) on selected portions of it. The success of the natural sciences, for instance, depends upon such deliberate, educated, "ignorance." But men err when, "classically," they forget to remember that the ignored portions still exist.

Each specialist group, when functioning as such, in the interest of its special concerns, creates its own sub-universe, its special province of experience, and sets up immigration laws which bar "alien" facts from entering. So, to a dentist, a man is a body surrounding his teeth; to an undertaker, a potential cadaver to be embalmed; to a cytologist, a collection of cells; to a painter, lines and colors and shadows; to a precinct-committeeman, a voter.

22 Fromm, *Man for Himself* (1947).

It should be noted that, in 1859, J. S. Mill, in his essay *On Liberty* had, in some detail, uttered warnings quite similar to those of Riesman and Fromm.

23 Note that "typical" is a synonym of "normal."

24 See Frank, *Law and the Modern Mind* (1930) 249-50. Said Pascal: "It is superstition to put one's hopes in formalities; but it is pride to be unwilling to submit to them."

Each specialist group, then, has its own limited perspectives, its unique "attentional attitude," its carved-out province with its special presuppositions or "quasi-realities." When functioning specialistically, it restricts itself to but a limited amount of the available complex of events. Only some of the entire "data" of the "natural world" does it regard as "relevant." As a consequence, because it abstracts from the whole of experience, it has its own "fictions" and conventions—what might be called its particularistic "just-so stories." It endows its "just-so stories," its sub-universe of fictions, with the "accent of reality." [25]

So it is with lawyers. Employing legal conventions—legal "just-so stories," built up by legal traditions—they circumscribe the field of the relevant, and, in their capacity as lawyers, dwell in a more or less artificial sub-universe of discourse. The lawyers' special province is "not peopled with human beings in their full humanity, but with types," i.e., with human beings only so far as they fit into legal categories.

Lawyers, however, in one respect differ from many other specialist groups. They must concern themselves with virtually all the activities of all other persons. They must work with all other groups in the attempt to compose disputes, clashes of interests. Lawyers are, in that sense, not specialists—but generalists. Nevertheless, they are often dominated by their peculiar professional conventions, their restricted attentional attitudes. To these restricted attitudes the lawyers and judges are prone to be excessively devoted. Many lawyers and judges resent intrusions into their "world" of those parts of "reality" which their traditional "just-so stories" treat as irrelevant.

"Even when brought into the most direct contact with reality," says Tourtoulon, "the judge reasons according to fiction. He recognizes certain human types, as well as certain economical and social facts. By his experience and by his reading he creates for himself an artificial world from which he cannot be drawn. Thus the chief effort of the lawyer is to adapt the facts to the schematic conception towards which the judge is inclined and by which alone he is enabled to form an idea of the reality." As I have indicated, however, that legal typology prevails, often, more in theory than in practice: Trial judges and juries do often break through the types and get at the individuals masked by the types. The "irrelevant" thus becomes secretly relevant. My plea

[25] See James, *Psychology* (1890) II, 291-95; 633-34, 638; Schuetz, "Multiple Realities," 5 *Phil. & Phenom. Research* (1945) 333; Frank, *Fate and Freedom* (1945) 183, 185-86, 311-28; Frank, "The Place of the Expert in a Democratic Society," 16 *Phil. of Science* (1949).

is that our trial courts should revise the "classical" theory to bring it into line with their "romantic" practices.

This the wiser physicians have always learned to do.[26] It "appears," said Aristotle, "that a physician does not regard health abstractedly, but regards the health . . . of a particular man, as he gives medicine to individuals." Classicism, which, since the era of Greek medicine, has recurrently sprung up in the medical art, is these days in ill repute. Dr. Crookshank deplores the notion that diseases are "Platonic realities" or "morbid entities" existing apart from sick individual persons. Most modern psychiatrists agree with Dr. William Alanson White in criticizing the method of classifying psychiatric symptoms "as separate and distinct affairs out of relation with any particular patient who may have manifested them," and in demanding attention to "the human problems involved in each [such] patient." Wisely, Saleilles attacked the "classical" theory of "criminal law" which he described as being "somewhat as if a physician were to maintain that there are only diseases and no patients." [27]

6

The ultra-classicist derides any degree of romanticism. If he is learned in the history of philosophy, he denounces it as "nominalism"—the name for the philosophic doctrine that abstractions or generalizations are mere words and lack "reality," that particulars alone are "real."

Nominalism is an invaluable antidote to the vice of ultra-classicism which—known in philosophic discourse as "realism"—regards abstractions as the solely "real," and particular things as mere "appearances." As such an antidote to "realist" snobbishness towards particulars, nominalism is indispensable. But, except as it thus red-flags the dangers of "realism," the nominalist's position, like that of the ultra-romanticist, is untenable.[28] For abstractions do express existing relations between

[26] See Frank, *Law and the Modern Mind* (1930) 209-10, 351-52.

[27] See Bok, *I Too, Nicodemus,* 319, 321, 323, 327, 330: "The better informed people become, the less patient they are of restrictions whose reason is not readily apparent to them, and the wisdom of legal rules, gathered from the stretch of experience, is beginning to break against the single rock of the case at hand. The law has been able to manage average behavior quite well, but if it is to manage unique behavior it must leave more room. . . . Those in its high places must be careful lest they forget people and remember only the machinery that governs them. . . ."

[28] It is a mistake to identify "nominalism" with the development of science and "realism" with conservatism. See McKeon, Book Review, 40 *Isis* (1949) 49, 53. Galileo, and many others who helped to initiate modern physics, were, in large part, "realists," Platonists. See, e.g., Frank, *Fate and Freedom* (1945) 100-04. Their "realism," however, did tend to create the dogmatic "religion of science." *ibid.*

particulars; in reality, as we experience it, we do find such relations, which are therefore "real."[29]

Ultra-romanticism is, indeed, nominalism applied to human beings. It is "individualism" run riot—or anarchism.[30] It sees no value or reality in the social relations of organized society. But social relations, too, are real; they inhere in man's nature. Excessive "realism," on the other hand, when applied to human beings is totalitarianism.[31] It overvalues the social relations, denies all value to the unique or individual characteristics of men, repels any and all "anarchistic" tendencies to some of which democracy furnishes outlets.[32]

The antithesis of the "individual" and "society"—made by both the nominalists (ultra-romanticists) and the "realists" (ultra-classicists)—is vicious. That dichotomy stems from faulty "either-or" thinking.[33] As John Dewey says, the words "individual" and "social" are adjectives. Both stand for traits of human beings, are "but two aspects of man in his actual existence . . . [The] 'social ties' do not inhere in 'individuals'; they inhere in human beings in their very humanity. . . . 'Individual' is as truly but an adjective as 'social.' Each word is a name for what is intrinsic in the constitution and development of human beings. . . . But 'individual' is commonly treated as if it were a noun, standing for an entity in itself. . . . Extend reflection beyond what is immediately

[29] Morris Cohen, in the legal realm, was given to throwing the word "nominalist" as a verbal brick-bat at those who, to his distress, pointed to the unconquerable "real" subjectivities in the trial of most particular lawsuits. But Cohen did write illuminatingly of the errors of nominalism. He warned against being "browbeaten by a word like 'reality,' which often represents nothing definite except a certain emotional afflatus. It ought to be clear that abstractions and universals exist in every situation in which individual things can be said to exist, and by the same evidence. If any statement like 'Smith is white and an honest man,' is true, whiteness, honesty, and manhood must exist as truly as Smith. Similarly, if it is true that one body is equal to, greater than, or less than another, then the relations of equality, greater than, or less than, exist just as truly as the bodies between which they hold. If the results of logical and mathematical reasoning are observed to hold true of nature, it seems more proper to say that nature is logical and mathematical than to suppose that logical and mathematical principles are just words having no meaning in nature, or that they have a dubious existence 'in the mind only' (the 'mind' being conceived as outside of nature). The difficulty that most people have in conceiving of the existence of universals is due to the tendency to *reify* all relations, i.e., to think of these relations or universals as if they were themselves additional things, instead of what they are defined to be, viz., qualities or relations of things. This shows itself in the naive question, 'Where do these universals exist?'—as if universals were particular entities occupying space. In brief, it seems that the actual procedure of natural . . . science demands the doctrine that universals do exist, but that they exist as universals, not as additional individual things."

[30] See Frank, *Fate and Freedom* (1945) 219 note 25.

[31] Plato, a totalitarian, was a philosophic "realist."

[32] See Frank, *Fate and Freedom* (1945) 203-05.

[33] *ibid.* 211-12.

obvious, and it is clear that the variety and scope of the connections for which the word social is a shorthand expression are the determining conditions of the kind of actuality achieved by capacities that are individual or differential."[34]

Legal nominalism (ultra-romanticism) is thus untenable. The legal rules—often crudely to be sure—symbolize social relations. The rules are attempted verbalizations of real similarities between different cases. But the danger is that those relations, those similarities, so verbalized, will be over-valued to the exclusion of the singularities of particular law suits. "Hypnotized by a label which emphasizes identities," I have said elsewhere, "we may be led to ignore differences. In all fields of thought this evil is encountered. Nowhere can it do more harm than in democratic government—and in democratic court-house government in particular. For, with its stress on uniformity, an abstraction or generalization tends to become totalitarian in its attitude toward uniqueness."[35]

7

Some sort of compromise there should be between judicial "classicism" and "romanticism." The mention of compromise angers the extremists, whether they be classicists or romantics. But life demands wise compromises, and notably in matters of government. Halifax, denounced as a political "Trimmer," adopted the name proudly. He ended his pamphlet, The Character of a Trimmer, published in 1684, with these words which, I think, hold enduring wisdom: "Our Trimmer, therefore, . . . thinketh fit to conclude with these assertions: That our climate is a Trimmer between that part of the world where men are roasted, and the other where they are frozen; . . . that our laws are Trimmers between the excesses of unbounded power and the extravagance of liberty not enough restrained; that true virtue hath ever been thought a Trimmer, and to have its dwelling in the middle between the two extremes; that even God Almighty Himself is divided between His two great attributes, His mercy and His justice. In such company, our Trimmer is not ashamed of his name, and willingly leaveth to the bold champions of either extreme, the honour of con-

[34] Dewey, "The Crisis in Human History," 1 *Commentary* (1946) 1. Helpful here is Bogoslovsky's "dynamic logic" in the light of which a paradox is "always something counter-balancing some one-sided attitude" resulting from the use of "static logic." The paradox of a "social individual" is thus explained.

[35] Guiseppi v. Walling, 144 F. (2d) 608, 619.

tending with no less adversaries than nature, religion, liberty, prudence, humanity and common sense." [36]

8

Traditional legal theory has another "classical" fault: It tends to look upon each man who comes before a court as if his character were unchanging and consistent. That conception is a fiction.[37] As no such man exists, that fiction, if taken as a truth, may at times be cruelly unjust in its deforming of reality.

Strangely enough, some modern psychologists have done much to fortify the belief in the reality of that fiction, by holding out, as a norm, the "integrated personality." The human "mind," these psychologists tell us, is pre-eminently a unifying, "integrating," implement; they picture the "self" as the unity which each man is or should be. The thoroughly "normal" man, they say, is a wholly integrated self.

That notion is unwise as an ideal, and false as a description.[38] Our ideal ought not to be the achievement of such integration. We should want each man to be a democracy of selves, with a moderate amount of dissent or inconsistency—anarchy—in his organization. The over-integrated man—like Hitler—is a totalitarian ideal. As a description, that conception of "integration" is clearly false. No man is a single "self." Each sane person has a host of selves, and they are never entirely unified, at one. In respect of judges, jurors, lawyers, witnesses or litigants, the "classical" (or totalitarian) idea of a man as a persistent and consistent unity will hamper the administration of justice.

Aristotle had balanced views on these subjects. He was neither ultra-classicist nor ultra-romanticist. Never did he look on man as an "individual" set over against "society." His conception of man as a social being has been a major contribution to sagacious thinking in occidental civilization.[39] Yet, as we saw, he dwelt on the un-wisdom of over-stressing "mathematical equality," on the value of individualization of cases.[40]

[36] Foxcroft, *Life and Letters of Sir George Saville, Bart., First Marquis of Halifax* (1898) II, 342.

[37] It may also be seen as an abstraction, just as, indeed, any "thing" is an abstraction. See Frank, *Fate and Freedom* (1945) 364 note 15, quotation from Brown.

[38] For development of this theme, from another viewpoint, see Frank, *Fate and Freedom* (1945) 208-10.

[39] Via Aquinas, this conception became an important ingredient of Catholic doctrine, expressed in modern times in the famous Encyclicals on social questions.

[40] John Dewey has never done full justice to Aristotle. See Randall, in the volume, *The Philosophy of John Dewey* (Schilpp ed., 1939) at 105. Perhaps in part on that account, Dewey's otherwise astute writings on matters legal have signally failed to face the problem of judicial fact-finding.

XXX. JUSTICE AND EMOTIONS

THE legal classicist's view seems to find expression in the slogan that we must have "a government of laws, and not of men." Correctly understood, that phrase is of inestimable value in a democracy. Correct understanding, however, requires a glance at the history of that phrase,[1] a history which shows it to be not as expressive of "classicism" as it sounds.

The phrase came to America through John Adams, later our second President, who immortalized it in the 1780 Constitution of Massachusetts. Adams knowingly took the phrase from the writings of a 17th century Englishman, Harrington, whom Adams greatly admired. Harrington, in turn, knowingly borrowed it from Aristotle. It will be worth our while to note what Aristotle had in mind. To do so, we must observe that Aristotle was reacting to the classical views of his former teacher, Plato.

In Plato's ideal state, which was an enlightened despotism, a few men of superior wisdom would govern, exercising the art of rational statesmanship based upon an exact science of government. Because this science, resembling mathematics as Plato conceived it, rested on principles independent of actual human experience, there would be no laws, in the ordinary sense, in Plato's ideal, scientifically governed, Republic, for such laws are experiential, a result of convention, and therefore not "scientific."[2] Referring to them as the "law," Plato derisively said that the law resembles a foolish physician who would prescribe inflexibly for his patient, regardless of alterations in the patient's

[1] This history is told in greater detail in Frank, *If Men Were Angels* (1942) Chapter 12.

[2] See Sabine, *A History of Political Theory* (1937) Chapters 3 and 4. "The exclusion of the law from the ideal state," says Sabine, "resulted from the twofold fact that statesmanship is defined as an art depending upon an exact science, and that this science is conceived, after the manner of mathematics, as a rational apprehension of the type of knowledge to which factual knowledge contributes nothing, or at least nothing beyond illustration." The "wisdom of the law is the wisdom of experience, feeling its way from precedent to precedent and never arriving at a very clear-cut knowledge of its principles. In short, it is quite different from what Plato conceived an art to be—the self-conscious application of scientifically ascertained causes to produce a clearly foreseen end. The problem was inherent in the contrast of nature and convention from which he started. For if the law belongs to convention . . . and cannot be ruled out as a factor in government, how can institutions ever be got on a rational basis where they are seen to realize the maximum natural good?"

condition. The "best thing," Plato declared, would be a government by the wisest man, "because the law does not perfectly comprehend what is best. The differences of men and actions, and the needless irregular movements of human beings, do not admit of any universal and simple rule. And no art whatsoever can lay down a rule which will last for all time . . . , but the law is always striving to make one. . . ." Rules are unable, he declared, "to provide exactly what is suitable for each particular case. . . . For how can the legislator sit at everyman's side all through his life, prescribing for him the exact particulars of his duty?"

But, as Plato grew older, he concluded that his ideal of government could not be put into practice. He reluctantly fell back on what he called the "second best"—a government of rigid and invariable laws or rules.[3] In his disappointment at the unattainability of his ideal, he thus went to the other extreme. His lengthy description in his book, *The Laws,* of the "second best" government contains no discussion of practicable means for day-to-day avoidance of the legal rigidities which he deplored.

Aristotle, with his common sense, and in the light of an extensive study of actual governments, rejected Plato's needlessly sharp antithesis between (1) a government, scientifically and flexibly administered by the wise man or men and (2) a government by inflexible rules. It is necessary, Aristotle said, to reconcile the desire for generality in the rules and the need for their adaptation to particular circumstances. He restated the problem thus: When there is government by one or a few (with no popular participation in government) then there is no differentiation between the functions of (a) enacting general rules and (b) making specific decisions each of which relates to a particular occasion, or affects a particular person. And the same, he says, is true in democracies when the populace, while acting in a legislative assembly, does not confine itself to the enactment of general rules, but also decides specific cases. The making of such specific decisions is not a proper legislative function. A government which thus conducts itself is not a government of laws but one of men.

The application of the general rules to particular cases should be left, said Aristotle, to judges or other designated officials. By their ascertainment of the facts of particular cases, and the adjustment of the rules to those facts, necessary flexibility can be procured. In that

[3] They could be amended, but until amended, they were to be largely inflexible.

way Aristotle substituted "both-and" thinking for Plato's "either-or" thinking.

Thus, while he remarks that "the rule of law is preferable to that of an individual," he notes, "There may indeed be cases which the law seems unable to determine. . . The law trains officers for this express purpose, and appoints them to determine matters, which are left undecided by it, to the best of their judgment. . . ." In a much-quoted sentence, Aristotle states: "He who bids the law rule, may be deemed to bid God and Reason rule, but he who bids man rule adds an element of the beast; for desire is a wild beast, and passion perverts the minds of rulers, even when they are the best of men. The law is reason unaffected by desire. . . ." But Aristotle quickly adds a qualification which those who quote him usually omit, i.e., that "there are some magistrates, for example judges, who have authority to decide matters which the law is unable to determine. . . . For matters of detail . . . cannot be included in legislation. Nor does anyone deny that the decision of such matters must be left to man. . . ."

And so, when we find set forth, in American state instruments, the slogan "a government of laws, and not of men," let us remember that its first author, Aristotle, was not talking of rigid, inflexible rules of law mechanically applied; he was referring to rules administered, by judges or other officers, selected to "determine matters, which are left undecided by" general rules, and to determine them "to the best of their judgment." Why? Because, "the decision of such matters" in particular cases "must be left to man." This was his conclusion, in spite of his complete awareness that men are fallible, that "passion must ever sway the heart of man," and that, in the courts, individualization is both unavoidable and desirable. Aristotle's conception of "a government of laws" contained both "classicism" and "romanticism."

2

In his great treatise on *Evidence,* Wigmore quotes with approval the following passage from an article, written in 1922, by George Alger (described by Wigmore as "a modern thinker who has never failed to voice accurately the best standards of his profession"): "Primitive law, the jurists tell us, was in all countries technical and formal. It dealt in ceremonies and procedures. Form came first, while justice lagged and came last. Perhaps it was the failure of law in old times to make approximation to justice that leaves to us two great figures of personal justice: Harun-al-Rashid, and Saint Louis. Down the ages they have come to us, each called by the same undying name, 'The Just.' In themselves, they unite the power of the law, and the will to do justice, not according to procedure long since gone and forgotten, but according to the Golden Rule. Under the big tree at Vincennes, history pictures to us Saint Louis dispensing the high justice, the middle justice, and the low, to those who flocked to him appealing for the righting of their wrongs. It pictures Harun as the protector of the poor, going about among his people, punishing the wrongdoer and giving justice to the oppressed. The Puritan, and later the Anglo-Saxon, ideal of justice resolutely supplanted the type which these historic figures embody. Ours was to be, as the ancient Charter of Massachusetts solemnly stated, a government 'of laws and not of men.' Laws should be made so that the people could read and understand them; so that standards should be set, which judges should follow and enforce. Personal justice, justice dependent alone or mainly upon the personal concept of right in the heart of the judge—a concept varying with the moral calibre of judges—was to be discarded. The law was to be, in the main, a book—enforced, to be sure, by a person, but in accordance with the book. The whole history of Law is the struggle for a working compromise between two ideals: Judicial discretion and the Saint-Louis ideal, on the one hand, and the letter law, superior to and binding upon the judge, and he its sworn servant, on the other. . . . However much the letter law extends its precedents, however much the statute law may seek to make the standards of law concrete and definite, there is an instinct in the soul of man which bids him look, not to the unending scrolls of the law, but to a Saint Louis and a Harun; to some good man whom he knows and respects, and has confidence in, more for his character than for his learning, however great. As society became complicated, this personal ideal grew so remote as to seem altogether lost in the mazes of the letter law. It never wholly disappeared . . . The question is this: How long will it be before the pendulum will swing to the other extreme—the demand for personal justice administered by the good man as a substitute for our endless barren wilderness of precedents in law and a maze of indigestible statutes? The final hope for democracy must be, not in its letter law, but in its leadership. The day must come when the people's trust must be less in law and more in men. In the last analysis, the main test that will determine the survival of democracy will be its capacity for the wise selection of men—men sufficient in character and wisdom to be trusted with the powers of the State."

Alger, I think puts the case altogether too much in terms of black or white, as one of purely impersonal versus purely personal justice. But his over-statement does focus attention on the irrepressible human need for considerable personalization of justice. We purport to impersonalize it. Our courts daily personalize it, nevertheless. The question is not whether we shall have such personalization but whether we shall have it out in the open, with the resultant opportunity to make it function as justly as possible.[4]

Our present method means that ordinarily our trial judges fool both themselves and the public about the real nature of much of the trial courts' task. Justice cannot best be achieved by such working in the dark. Today trial judges often talk "classically" but, half-consciously, act "romantically." It would seem wiser to authorize them, consciously and candidly, to combine the two.[5]

I confess that I am unable to tell just how this can and should be accomplished—just how our judicial system should be altered in order that our trial judges may be empowered to do knowingly and avowedly, with appropriate self-restraint, what now they frequently do without awareness on their part or that of the public. *A solution of that problem requires far more wisdom and imagination than I possess.* I merely repeat this vague, general suggestion:

Let us revise many (perhaps not all) of the substantive legal rules which are now worded in such a way that they create the illusion of excluding all judicial discretion. Let us reword them so that they will become on their face what in truth they now often are, i.e. but general guides for trial judges in deciding specific law suits. The "sovereignty" of the trial judge, now largely concealed, would be acknowledged. An upper court would have the power it now has on an appeal from a decision involving a rule which now expressly confers discretion on the trial judge; i.e. the upper court, in addition to correcting important procedural errors, would reverse for any "abuse" of discretion. *I confess that, when I write down that tentative suggestion I grow frightened, so strong in me is the traditional lawyer's attitude.* I say

[4] See Frank, *Law and The Modern Mind* (1930) 362.

[5] Suggestive here is the notion of bifocal vision. Compare Demos: "Government, recognizing the limitations of law as inevitably abstract, sets up courts of equity, with the function of taking individual and changing circumstances into account. Poetry is the court of equity for science. Conversely, philosophy and science . . . are needed curbs on the poetic mood, saving fancy from frenzy." Demos, "The Spectrum of Knowledge," 56 *Phil. Rev.* (1947) 237, 256.

to myself that under such a system there would be the utmost uncertainty, that men could not act in reliance on lawyers' advice as to what they may lawfully do. The answer is that which, in previous chapters, I have often given: Under our existing system, when litigation breaks out, the presence of the "unruly," the "constant inconstancy," in trial-court "fact-finding," causes that very same uncertainty. Only in appearance, not in reality, can men now usually rely with assurance on lawyers' advice based on precise legal rules. We now have, and will have even if we greatly improve our trial methods, that condition which led Judge Learned Hand to think of litigation as something to be dreaded almost as much as sickness or death. The rewording of many of the rules along the lines I suggest would not, then, increase legal uncertainty; it would but bring the uncertainty out into the open. And if coupled with adequate training of trial judges, it would make possible (but of course would not ensure) decisions which would be more just. I think that under such a revised system, intelligently contrived, the courts, at least to the same extent as at present, could and would protect any person shown actually to have relied upon a settled rule . . . But, I say once more, all this is vague and tentative.

3

When all is said and done, we must face the fact that judges are human. That should not dismay those of us who cherish democracy.[6] For in a democracy it is imperative never to forget that public offices are, of necessity, held by mere men, who, of course, have human foibles. It is only where government officials are deemed to be semi-divine that people have any excuse for ignoring the ineluctable personal factor in government. Wherefore the belief that government can ever consist of perfect creatures is alien to a democracy. That false belief constitutes the core of the philosophy of dictatorship; it is the basis of "personal government," in its most extreme and pernicious form. In a dictatorship, the effects on government of the all-too-human personalities of government officials is least open to discussion. The pretense that the personalities of those government officials known as judges are or can be anaesthetized does not relieve us of the evils which result from the abuse of judicial power. On the contrary, it increases those evils.

We have all, unfortunately, known or heard of judges who have

[6] In this section I have borrowed from my books, *If Men Were Angels,* Chapter 1, and *Law and the Modern Mind,* 138-39.

turned out to be corrupt. Experience discloses that those corrupt judges make the greatest pretense of the purely mechanical workings of the courts, through the application of the rules, when they decide cases. In their opinions and extra-judicial addresses, they never concede for an instant that judges are human, that the personality of the judge, his prejudices, predilections, and passions, have any effect on his decisions. Their judicial opinions, delivered from the bench, give a magnificent appearance of complete objectivity. Each of their decisions is made to appear to be the product of a mere logic machine, of purely logical reasoning in which the conclusion is reached by applying a precise legal rule, as to which there can be no question, to definite "facts," as to which there can be no doubt. And yet, when the real character of such a judge is exposed, then, behind that front—of dispassionate logic working on indubitable legal rules and an objective state of facts—we find gross dishonesty. Then we see that the judging process, in the case of his decisions, actually began with conclusions which were bought and paid for, and that the rules and the facts were deliberately chosen by him so as dishonestly to justify that predetermined, purchased, decision.

Much the same can be said of other undisclosed elements in decision-making, elements which are not venal. Those judges who are most dominated by the "perverting influences of their emotional natures" are often those who use most meticulously the language of compelling mechanical logic, who elaborately wrap about themselves the pretense of merely discovering and carrying out existing rules. If every judicial opinion were so worded as to contain, as clearly as possible, all the actual grounds of the decision, the tyrants, the bigots and the dishonest men on the bench would lose their disguises and become known for what they are.

Rules we must have.[7] They set limits to the discretion vested in our judges, but limits which, in many instances, can be imposed only by the judges themselves. The rules are a sort of legal machinery. But legal machinery will not suffice. The men who operate that machinery must be men keenly alive to their immense responsibilities to the citizens.

[7] "If Men were angels," it was said long ago in The Federalist, "no government would be necessary. If angels were to govern men, neither external nor internal controls on government would be necessary. In framing a government which is to be administered by men over men, the great difficulty lies in this: You must first enable the government to control the governed, and in the next place oblige it to control itself. A dependence on the people is, no doubt, the primary control on the government; but experience has taught mankind the necessity of auxiliary precautions."

We could not, if we would, get rid of emotions in the administration of justice. The best we can hope for is that the emotions of the trial judge will be sensitive, nicely balanced, subject to his own scrutiny. The honest, well-trained trial judge, with the completest possible knowledge of the character of his powers and of his own prejudices and weaknesses, is the best guaranty of justice. The wise course is to acknowledge the necessary existence of "personal element" and to act accordingly. Indeed, as Ehrlich puts it, this personal element "should not be tolerated as something unavoidable but should be gladly welcomed. For the one important desideratum is that (the judge's) personality must be great enough to be properly intrusted with such functions." [8] But we must not expect too much of any judge, however great, must not assume that he will cease to be a man and become an angel. "Man," said Pascal, "is neither angel nor brute, and the unfortunate thing is that he who would act the angel acts the brute."

Some persons, asking "Who will watch the watchman?" have suggested that a judge, fully cognizant of the real nature of his powers and of the operation of the "personal element" in his decisions, will necessarily be more prone to be arbitrary, knowing that he can effectively conceal his arbitrariness. That may be—it has been—a grave danger, when judges do not publicly admit that they have such powers. But contrast judges like, say, Marshall, Field and McReynolds, with those like, say, Learned Hand and Rifkind: The former, I think, were not at all ignorant of their powers. But, concealing what they did under a show of complete "objectivity," they often ruthlessly decided in accordance with their personal predilections. Judges Hand and Rifkind, however, alive to, and avowing, the true nature of the judging process, are far more demanding of themselves, far more given to critical self-scrutiny, far more cautious in the exercise of their authority.

4

I can most easily indicate what I do and do not mean in much that I have said by quoting the following passage from an opinion I de-

[8] See Bok, *Backbone of the Herring* (1941) 9: "It was in court that the conviction which later settled in him like fire deep in wood began to take form, that Justice has to do with the play of an enlightened personality within the boundaries of a system. He learned to trust his own personality. . . ."

livered several years ago on behalf of our court, in speaking of trial judges: [9]

"Democracy must, indeed, fail unless our courts try cases fairly, and there can be no fair trial before a judge lacking in impartiality and disinterestedness. If, however, 'bias' and 'partiality' be defined to mean the total absence of preconceptions in the mind of the judge, then no one has ever had a fair trial and no one ever will. The human mind, even at infancy, is no blank piece of paper. We are born with predispositions; and the process of education, formal and informal, creates attitudes in all men which affect them in judging situations, attitudes which precede reasoning in particular instances and which, therefore, by definition, are prejudices. Without acquired 'slants,' pre-conceptions, life could not go on. Every habit constitutes a pre-judgment; were those pre-judgments which we call habits absent in any person, were he obliged to treat every event as an unprecedented crisis, presenting a wholly new problem, he would go mad. Interests, points of view, preferences, are the essence of living. Only death yields complete dispassionateness, for such dispassionateness signifies utter indifference. 'To live is to have a vocation, and to have a vocation is to have an ethics or scheme of values, and to have a scheme of values is to have a point of view, and to have a point of view is to have a prejudice or bias. . . .' [10] An 'open mind,' in the sense of a mind containing no preconceptions whatever, would be a mind incapable of learning anything, would be that of an utterly emotionless human being, corresponding, roughly to the psychiatrist's description of the feeble-minded.

"More directly to the point, every human society has a multitude of established attitudes, unquestioned postulates. Cosmically, they may seem parochial prejudices, but many of them represent the community's most cherished values and ideals. Such social pre-conceptions, the 'value judgments' which members of any given society take for granted and use as the unspoken axioms of thinking, find their way into that society's legal system, become what has been termed 'the valuation system of the law.' The judge in our society owes a duty to act in accordance with those basic predilections inhering in our legal system (although, of course, he has the right, at times, to urge that some of them be modified or abandoned). The standard of dispassionateness obviously does not require the judge to rid himself of the unconscious influence of such social attitudes.

[9] In re J. P. Linahan & Co., 138 F. (2d) 650, 651-654.
[10] Burke, *Permanence and Change* (1936) 329.

"In addition to those acquired social value judgments, every judge, however, unavoidably has many idiosyncratic 'leanings of the mind,' uniquely personal prejudices . . . which may interfere with his fairness at a trial. He may be stimulated by unconscious sympathies for, or antipathies to, some of the witnesses, lawyers or parties in a case before him. As Josiah Royce observed, 'Oddities of feature or of complexion, slight physical variations from the customary, a strange dress, a scar, a too-steady look, a limp, a loud or deep voice, any of these peculiarities . . . may be, to one, an object of fascinated curiosity; to another . . . , an intense irritation, an object of violent antipathy.' In Ex Parte Chase, 43 Ala. 303, Judge Peters said he had 'known a popular judicial officer grow quite angry with a suitor in his court, and threaten him with imprisonment, for no ostensible reason, save the fact that he wore an overcoat made of wolf skins,' and spoke of 'prejudice, which may be swayed and controlled by the merest trifles—such as the toothache, the rheumatism, the gout, or a fit of indigestion, or even through the very means by which indigestion is frequently sought to be avoided. Trifles,' he added, 'however ridiculous, cease to be trifles when they may interfere with a safe administration of the law.'

"Frankly to recognize the existence of such prejudices is the part of wisdom. The conscientious judge will, as far as possible, make himself aware of his biases of this character, and, by that very self-knowledge, nullify their effect. Much harm is done by the myth that, merely by putting on a black robe, and taking the oath of office as a judge, a man ceases to be human and strips himself of all predilections, becomes a passionless thinking machine. The concealment of the human element in the judicial process allows that element to operate in an exaggerated manner; the sunlight of awareness has an antiseptic effect on prejudices. Freely avowing that he is a human being, the judge can, and should, through self-scrutiny, prevent the operation of this class of biases.

"But, just because [the trial judge's] fact-finding is based on his estimates of the witnesses, of their reliability as reporters of what they saw and heard, it is his duty, while listening to, and watching them, to form attitudes towards them. He must do his best to ascertain their motives, their biases, their dominating passions and interests, for only so can he judge of the accuracy of their narrations. He must also shrewdly observe the stratagems of the opposing lawyers, perceive their efforts to sway him by appeals to his predilections. He must cannily penetrate through the surface of their remarks to their real purposes and motives.

He has an official obligation to become prejudiced in that sense. Impartiality is not gullibility. Disinterestedness does not mean child-like innocence. If the judge did not form judgments of the actors in those court-house dramas called trials, he could never render decisions."

Lest you think I am extreme in my views, I quote from a recent statement by Lord Macmillan, a distinguished English judge: "The judicial mind," he said, "is subject to the laws of psychology like any other mind. . . . The judge . . . does not divest himself of humanity. He has sworn to do justice to all men without fear or favor, but . . . impartiality . . . does not imply that the judge's mind has become a mere machine to turn out decrees; the judge's mind remains a human instrument working as do other minds, though no doubt on specialized lines, and often characterized by individual traits of personality, engaging or the reverse."

XXXI. QUESTIONING SOME LEGAL AXIOMS

LONG words, or jargon unfamiliar to most persons, do not ordinarily aid communication. One may, too, surmise that often (not always) a man who understands an idea can state it in fairly simple terms. Too many writers identify profundity and obscurity.[1] Yet here I shall introduce a formidable-looking phrase—"non-Euclidean thinking." For in this book I have tried, in a modest way, to engage in such thinking.

The phrase, "non-Euclidean thinking," may frighten some readers. It shouldn't. It labels a simple, although revolutionary, idea which began in the field of mathematics and spread rapidly elsewhere. The story can be briefly told in homely language as follows:[2]

Euclid's system of geometry, accepted and used with great practical success for several thousand years, is based on some fundamental assertions, called axioms or "self-evident truths." From those "truths" the balance of that system is worked out logically, so that the system has self-consistency. Those axioms were considered "self-evident" because men deemed their opposites to be inconceivable. But the self-evidence of at least one of Euclid's axioms was questioned from time to time; its opposite was not inconceivable. In the 19th century, some brilliant mathematicians contrived systems of geometry which contra-

[1] Ivor Brown, in *Say the Word,* thus parodies the style of much current literary criticism: "Mr. X's failure to integrate his fundamentally nostalgic symbolism with the imperative demands of a personality essentially schizoid has provoked an anxiety neurosis resulting in an ideology irreconcilable with the over-all conditioning imposed by the managerial revolution's impact upon an inchoate capitalism. His constantly Narcissistic self-identification with all the traumata of his repressed diathesis has produced in his later writings a series of image-clusters which strikingly reveal a complete disassociation of his incipient Existentialism from his unconscious preoccupation with a subjective cognizance of reality."

Dobyns, in 35 *Am. Bar Ass'n. J.* (1949) 665, chides me for being pedantically obscure in one of my judicial opinions. My purpose there, which seems to have miscarried, was to be humorous.

[2] The story is told somewhat more elaborately in Frank, "Mr. Justice Holmes and Non-Euclidean Legal Thinking," 17 *Cornell L.Q.* (1932) 568, 572-78, 599-603, which contains a bibliography; see also Frank, *Fate and Freedom* (1945) 298-308, which also gives a bibliography.

dicted one or more of Euclid's axioms. These novel, "non-Euclidean," geometries were also perfectly logical and self-consistent. At first they were mere mathematical playthings, having no practical utility. But the work of Einstein showed that Euclidean geometry was, for some purposes, less useful, in explaining some facts observed by physical scientists, and in turning up new facts.

As a result, the notion of an axiom as a self-evident truth came into disrepute. Any axiom is now recognized as merely a possibly helpful assumption. One writer has said that the dethroning of the self-evident was like a change from an absolute monarchy to an ideal democracy in which the "self-evident truth," previously ruling by the divine right of the inconceivability of its opposite, was replaced by the "assumption," elected for its qualification to serve. For the position previously held by an old axiom, a rival new assumption may always be put forward as a candidate; it has an excellent chance of being elected if it can be shown to be better than the old. "Better" means this: From the new assumption there can be logically deduced a new body of propositions which is more serviceable than the body of propositions logically deducible from the displaced assumption.

"More serviceable" means—what? The history of natural science gives the answer. For (without talking of "non-Euclidean thinking") peaceful revolutions, displacing old assumptions, have often occurred in the natural sciences. Typical are the cases of Ptolemy's and Newton's systems of astronomy: For many centuries, Ptolemy's "self-evident" astronomical "truths," and the "laws" deduced therefrom, successfully reigned. But, as astronomical observations increased, those "laws" needed more and more elaborations and adjustments to make them jibe with the observed phenomena. The adjustments became exquisitely complicated, and the system awkward, cumbersome. Moreover, some astronomical observations made in the 17th century did not fit into the system even as adjusted. Then Newton, building on the work of Copernicus, Kepler and Galileo, contrived a new system which substituted some new "axioms" (or assumptions) for Ptolemy's. Newton's won out, for three reasons: It got rid of the complicated adjustments; with greater simplicity, the "laws" deduced from Newton's assumptions explained the observed facts; they also aided in the discovery and explanation of new facts. However, further observations did not jibe with Newton's "laws," except after complicated adjustments of those "laws." Then Einstein, using a non-Euclidean geometry, devised a new system, based on new assumptions, which did the job better than Newton's.[3]

The practical outcome of using non-Euclidean geometry brought out clearly the nature of such revolutions in thinking. Non-Euclidean thinking[4] is not a totally novel method. It is novel in that it consciously and deliberately employs a thought-method previously employed without full cognizance of its nature.[5] Briefly stated, this method has this significance: With respect to thinking in any field which—as distinguished from "pure" logic or "pure" mathematics—bears, directly or indirectly, on actual mundane happenings, a proposed new assumption (axiom) may be regarded as preferable to an old, if it has one or more of these attributes: (1) The thinking in that field is simplified, freed of complicated qualifications, yet is self-consistent. (2) The propositions deduced from the new assumption click more adequately with the observed phenomena. (3) Some of the deduced propositions lead to the discovery of phenomena theretofore undetected.[6]

2

Now apply the "non-Euclidean" method to traditional legal thinking, which rests upon "axioms" (i.e., assumptions), some of which are explicit, avowed, and some of which are not.[7] We may ask these questions: Does it contain any express or concealed assumptions which are defective because they do not jibe—directly, or by logical deductions—with what now happens (or can be made to happen) in courthouse government? If so, how can those assumptions be modified to make them adequate? Will the necessary modifications render those assumptions cumbersome? Are there alternative assumptions which more simply and adequately, and without lack of consistency, click, directly or

[3] Two important aspects of non-Euclidean thinking are pertinent here: (1) When a new assumption is elected, the old is not necessarily banished. Thus, even after Einstein, the Newtonian system is still allowed to hold office, but it now governs a more limited province of phenoma. So, too, Euclid's geometry, as a "natural geometry," is still alive and functioning but on a smaller scale. (2) A newly elected assumption may not hold office forever. Recall of "axioms" is now a well-established principle.

[4] Sometimes called "postulational" thinking.

[5] Some students say that Euclid knew that his axioms were mere assumptions. In other words, Euclid was not a Euclidean.

[6] For excellent examples of modern non-Euclidean thinking about "economics," see Clark, "The Socializing of Theoretical Economics," in his book, *A Preface to Economics* (1936); Polanyi, *The Great Transformation* (1944).

[7] In my article, "Mr. Justice Holmes and Non-Euclidean Legal Thinking," 17 *Cornell L.Q.* (1932) 568, I tried to show that Holmes initiated such questionings of traditional legal "axioms."

indirectly, with and explain the observed phenomena of courthouse government? Will those alternative assumptions help us in better coping with those observed phenomena? Will the alternatives aid in uncovering phenomena which have been overlooked?

Such questions I have been asking in this book. In the preceding chapters, I have raised doubts about the adequacy of several assumptions of traditional legal thinking, pointing out that, unless so qualified by exceptions as to be all but meaningless, they are out of line with courtroom happenings. I have also smoked out some concealed assumptions, and have attempted to disclose inconsistencies between them and those that are acknowledged. Here is a list of some of the old "axioms" I have thus discussed:

1. The "personal element" in the judicial process should not and usually does not have much effect on either legal rights or court decisions. Even if we admit that the "personalities" of witnesses, lawyers, jurors and judges do have considerable effect, we must disregard all elements of those "personalities" which are not fairly uniform.

2. The legal rules are the dominant factor in decision-making.

3. When those rules are precise, they ordinarily prevent litigation; and, if litigation does occur, it will be easy to predict the decisions.

4. Trial judges and juries have only the limited discretion conferred by the legal rules; they have no discretion when those rules are precise.

5. Decisions result from the application of legal rules to the actual facts involved in law-suits.

6. If the actual facts of two cases are the same, usually the decisions in those cases will be identical.

7. Trial courts usually discover the actual facts of cases; usually "the truth will out"; innocent men are hardly ever convicted; seldom does a man lose his property or his means of livelihood because of a court's mistaken notion of the facts.

8. The intense fighting method of conducting trials is the best aid in discovering those facts.

9. Effective criticism of most decisions is easy.

10. Upper courts can, and do, correct most of the mistakes of trial courts.

11. Upper courts are far more important than trial courts.

12. Less attention need be paid to the selection of trial judges than to that of upper-court judges.

13. Almost any man licensed to practice as a lawyer is qualified to be a trial judge.

14. Juries are better fact-finders than judges.

15. Juries are better at rule-making and rule-revising than judges.

16. It is desirable that juries should ignore any legal rules they deem undesirable.

17. In law-suits (whether or not tried by juries), legal rules relating to property and commercial transactions are precise and usually lead to predictable decisions.

18. Individualization of cases, if desirable, should be accomplished surreptitiously, not openly.

19. The method of following precedents, if properly used, ensures certainty and stability, supplies rules on which men can safely rely.

20. Trial courts, in fact finding, have little to do with the interpretation of statutes.

21. Non-lawyers should be deceived into believing that the results of the judicial process are more certain, regular, uniform and just than in truth they are or can be.

22. Law students should not be persuaded to observe at first-hand what goes on in trial courts and law offices.

23. The attempt to obtain legal certainty (i.e., predictability of decisions) is more important than the attempt to obtain just decisions of specific law suits.

I suggest that the reader ask himself whether the opposite of each of those old assumptions will not, directly or indirectly, click better with what can be observed in the legal realm, and, in some instances, call attention to ignored aspects of court-house doings. Consider here my tentative suggestion of the possible need of "four-dimensional" legal thinking.[8]

3

One major defect of the traditional legal assumptions is that those who use them mix up two attitudes: (a) "This is true." (b) "This should be true." The users, without knowing it, slide back and forth between saying, "This is what now happens in courts," and "This is what I would like to have happen in courts," between a description of the existent and a program for the future.

Of course, there is no reason why a person, dissatisfied with existing court-house doings, should not start with a program, founded on assumptions of the desirable, and logically deduce their consequences. He would then say: "Here are some assumptions I suggest. They are

[8] See Chapter XII.

not in accord with court-house actuality. But, if they could be made to exist, they would have results which are better than the present actualities. Here are the results which would ensue. And here is a program for actualizing those assumptions." Or he would begin the other way around, saying: "Suppose it were possible to have the kind of legal world I like (stating it). It does not now exist. Such a world would involve the actualization of some assumptions on which we do not now act. Here they are. To actualize those assumptions, and thereby bring such an altered legal world into existence, it is necessary to create new conditions, to institute some reforms. Here, then, are the reforms I propose."

I would call such assumptions "wish-assumptions" or "wish postulates" or "programmatic postulates." If you openly formulate your "wish assumptions," you can then be rigorously logical in working out their implications. You can painstakingly seek to learn what changes in the existing affairs are necessary conditions of the fulfilment of your wishes, your program for the future. But if you mix up your wishes and your is-es, your description and your program, you will probably be sloppy, inconsistent, timid and wavering. Why? Because you will have a half-conscious fear that what is implied in your assumptions will show up as a false description of presently existing occurrences. Indeed, one cause of your mixing up, "I wish this were so" and "It is now so," is precisely that you fear to face up to the fact that what you want does not now exist—and that it may be impossible to achieve. The fear of that disclosure will make you dogmatic. You will insist that your "wish assumptions" are "is assumptions," that they are self-evidently true in present fact. In short, you will practice magic.

If, however, you do separate your "wish assumptions" and your "is assumptions," you will at once improve the quality of your thinking. You will abandon self-evidence as a characteristic of any of your assumptions. You will be courageous in working out their implications. Your "is assumptions" you will recognize as suggested means for adequately formulating generalizations relative to observable court-house phenomena. Those generalizations may perhaps serve as guides in predicting concrete legal events—specific decisions of specific law suits. Or your generalizations may show, or tend to show, the impossibility of so predicting in most instances.[9] If your "is assumptions" do not square with observable court phenomena, you will be ready to modify or drop them. Since you know that they are mere assumptions, you

[9] This, of course, is my own perspective.

will follow up their logical implications without timidity, in order to discover their inadequacies as well as their adequacies.

And so, too, with your "wish assumptions," your programmatic assumptions. Recognizing them for what they are, you will not be hesitant in working them out with clarity, on paper, to their logical conclusions. You will not "invent hypotheses to explain facts that do not exist" and then "proceed to give false interpretations to facts that do exist."[10] Consistency and clarity you will then welcome, not dodge. And, beyond all else, you will see that accurate descriptions of existing phenomena are essential to the realization of your program. In that way you will acquire the habit of "sterilizing the instruments of research before undertaking surgical operations upon the body politic."[11]

4

I have done my best to keep separate my own two kinds of assumptions. Endeavoring honestly to describe the actualities of court-house activities, I have criticized some of them, and have proposed some reforms. For the reader's convenience, I here list some of those suggested reforms:

1. Reduce the excesses of the present fighting method of conducting trials:

   (a) Have the government accept more responsibility for seeing that all practically available, important, evidence is introduced at a trial of a civil suit.

   (b) Have trial judges play a more active part in examining witnesses.

   (c) Require court-room examination of witnesses to be more humane and intelligent.

   (d) Use non-partisan "testimonial experts," called by the judge, to testify concerning the detectible fallibilities of witnesses; circumspectly employ "lie-detectors."

   (e) Discard most of the exclusionary evidence rules.[12]

   (f) Provide liberal pre-trial "discovery" for defendants in criminal cases.

2. Reform legal education by moving it far closer to court-house and

[10] See Hogben, *The Nature of Living Matter* (1931) 114.

[11] *ibid.* 215.

[12] Not, however, the major privilege rules, especially those relating to self-incrimination and to evidence obtained by unlawful searches and seizures.

law-office actualities, largely through the use of the apprentice method of teaching.

3. Provide and require special education for future trial judges, such education to include intensive psychological self-exploration by each prospective trial judge.

4. Provide and require special education for future prosecutors which, among other things, will emphasize the obligation of a prosecutor to obtain and to bring out all important evidence, including that which favors the accused.

5. Provide and require special education for the police so that they will be unwilling to use the "third degree."

6. Have judges abandon their official robes, conduct trials less formally, and in general give up "robe-ism."

7. Require trial judges in all cases to publish special findings of fact.

8. Abandon jury trials except in major criminal cases.

9. At any rate, while we have the jury system, overhaul it:
   (a) Require fact-verdicts (special verdicts) in all jury trials.
   (b) Use informed "special" juries.
   (c) Educate men in the schools for jury service.

10. Encourage the openly disclosed individualization of law suits by trial judges; to that end, revise most of the legal rules so that they avowedly grant such individualizing power to trial judges, instead of achieving individualization surreptitiously as we now largely do.

11. Reduce the formality of appeals by permitting the trial judge to sit with the upper court on an appeal from his decision, but without a vote.

12. Have talking movies of trials.

13. Teach the non-lawyers to recognize that trial courts have more importance than upper courts.

5

I suggest those reforms most tentatively. No one person, I least of all, has the competence to contrive sane, practical, solutions of the problems I have posed. Such solutions must come from the concerted efforts of many of our ablest minds, and not exclusively lawyers' minds. I hope that this book will stimulate sound thinking about those problems which, as I believe I have shown, have too long been neglected.

There are persons who quarrel with the notion that improvements should be proposed tentatively. Those persons are either themselves one-hundred percenters, perfectionists, or believe that other men will refuse to adopt new ways not stridently and unequivocally proclaimed. They quote, "For if the trumpet gives an uncertain sound, who shall prepare himself to the battle?"

I dissent from those views. Too many battles have been won that lost wars. The sin of perfectionism is that it mutilates life by demanding the impossible. I grant that the positive perfectionist, who at least is forward moving, is preferable to the negative prefectionist—the man who objects to any change of the status quo, no matter how bad it is, unless the change will yield perfection.[13] But the 100% positive perfectionist, striving for the impossible, deludes his followers, many of whom will end up in despair. We should beware of what Johnson calls the "I.F.D. disease: from idealism to frustration to demoralization."[14] It is essential to remember Aristotle's warning to distinguish between the desirable and the possible. We should avoid suggestions, however delightful, which lack all practicality.

To be sure, that counsel may be used by the defeatist to dampen ardor, to discourage improvement; many a prized achievement has resulted from the efforts of men who have scaled the walls of the seemingly impossible, proving that a desirable, at which the defeatists had sneered, was a possible. Amos told Andy, during the Great Depression, that the "status quo" is "Latin for the fix we's in"; and enterprising men, despite the hootings of the pessimistic negative perfectionists, found a way out of that "fix." I do not, then, plump for timidity. I urge only that boldness be coupled with due recognition of feasibilities. I favor ardent "improvists," not perfectionists.

[13] See Frank, *If Men Were Angels* (1942) 136: "It has been too little observed that there are *two kinds of perfectionists.* The *positive perfectionist* is a man who insists that men must live up to his ideals even if they are impossible of attainment. He demands the impossible in conduct. He is impatient with anything short of absolute perfection. But this at least can be said in his favor: he is usually aggressive—forward moving—in his search for perfection. There is, also, however, the *negative perfectionist.* He is against any supposed novelty unless it will produce "absolute" perfection. He prefers whatever has existed, no matter how inadequate, unless it can be supplanted by a flawless substitute. And he tries to defeat any particular change by falsely charging that its proponents claim perfection. He erroneously reports them as saying, 'This new device will be absolutely perfect.' He ignores their qualifying adverbs and puts in their mouths words which they never uttered and ascribes to them attitudes which they never entertained, and asserts that they are 100 percenters, all-or-nothing fanatics, wild-eyed advocates of the impossible."

[14] Johnson, *People in Quandaries* (1946) 13-14, 16, says: "If your ideals or goals are too high, in the sense that they are . . . unrealistic, then you are likely to experience a sense of failure. . . . The sense of failure . . . tends to . . . blend into . . . generalized loss of interest in possible opportunities for achievement. . . . As your sense of failure deepens, you settle more and more into despondency."

We need a new kind of courage—the courage to face unconquerable imperfections in the solution of human problems.[15] Our human finiteness, which limits our knowledge, commits us to many uncertainties. The only absolute knowledge on which we can count is the knowledge that man's wisdom will never be absolute. That knowledge will eliminate much blundering.[16] But it will not enable us to elude our limitations.[17] We ought not, however, to be smug in our humility.[18]

It is true that, as to vast areas of experience, the human race is ignorant and will always remain largely so. For there are factors in the universe of which, because of our limited equipment, we shall always, almost surely, remain in darkness. Ignorance will therefore always play an important part in human affairs. But because our ignorance is and must be large, that is no reason why we should wallow in it, no reason why we should diminish our efforts to reduce the unknowable so far as possible.[19]

No truly intelligent person rejects the possibility of reducing uncertainty because it cannot be completely obliterated—just as no sane man will turn his back on all physicians merely because the flesh is heir to many diseases for which no cure has been, and in all likelihood will ever be, discovered by the medical profession. The perfectionist is not satisfied by any such intermediate position. But life is hard for the perfectionist, everywhere. The insane asylum, and not any part of the ordinary walks of life, is the place for those who demand complete freedom from all uncertainties. We are but mortal, and contingency is the essence of mortality. Only in the grave do we escape it. Almost

[15] Says Bridgman: "The individuals of the race will not be purged of fear until they are able to accept themselves and cease to look for salvation from without, and when the individuals of the race are purged of fear, society itself will lose its fear complexes and be able to tolerate free discussion of the imperfections and limitations of the tools that it uses and of the ideals that it follows."

J. S. Mill said that "when it is impossible to obtain good tools, the next best thing is to understand the defects of those we have."

[16] Morley, after quoting, "Ignorance remains the evil which it ever was, but something of the peace of certitude is gained in knowing the worst, and in having reconciled the mind to the endurance of it," adds, "Precisely, and what one would say of our own age is that it will not deliberately face this knowledge of the worst. So it misses the peace of certitude, and not only its peace, but the strength and coherency that follow strict acceptance of the worst, when it is after all the best within reach."

[17] See further, Frank, *Fate and Freedom* (1945) 336-337; Frank, Book Review, 15 *Un. of Chicago L. Rev.* (1948) 475-478.

[18] "Vanity," said Pascal, "is so rooted in the heart of man . . . that those who write against it want to have the glory of having written it well; and those who read it desire the glory of reading it. I who write this have perhaps this desire, and perhaps those who will read it."

[19] In this and the next few paragraphs, I am borrowing from my book, *If Men Were Angels* (1942) 137-138.

all thinking is based on mere probabilities, not on guarantees. Even the physicist today employs the concept of uncertainty or indeterminacy. To ask for absolute exactitude in any phase of government is absurd. "Every day, if not every year," said Mr. Justice Holmes, "we have to wager our salvation upon some prophecy based upon imperfect knowledge."

It has been said that the better is the enemy of the best. Sometimes, not always, that is true. But it is even more true that the all-or-nothing men, those who will have nothing new unless it is perfect, are the foes of improvement. If men had insisted that either they must fly with the skill of birds or not fly at all, aviation would be non-existent. Negative perfectionism has often retarded the use of valuable inventions. Robert Fulton's steamboat was called "Fulton's Folly." DeForest's efforts to launch the wireless telephone were laughed at by the Western Electric Co. Not so very long ago the chief engineers of a leading telephone company scoffed, before the American Institute of Engineers, at the automatic telephone.

Paradoxically, the calm acceptance of unavoidable imperfection improves our effectiveness. For such an admission rids us of an impossible task, and enables us to face the environment unburdened by a feeling of necessity to stretch our aims beyond their practically possible scope. By conceding the immense amount of our ignorance, we become more alert in detecting the detectable facts. To the extent that one goes to sleep in a dream of attainable perfection, he becomes the victim of uncertainties which he ignores and for which he therefore fails to allow. The courageous attitude of accepting uncertainties makes one's world picture more complex; life is disclosed as far more precarious and difficult to conciliate. But, just in proportion as we learn more about what was previously undetected, we reduce the dangers of being crushed by unobserved dangers. That is the paradox of wisdom: Insofar as we become mindful that life must be less perfect than we would like it to be, we approach nearer to perfection. The impossibility of reaching it does not justify indifference to the aim of constantly bettering man's lot.

XXXII. REASON AND UNREASON—IDEALS

BECAUSE I have stressed the difficulties caused by non-rational factors in the decisional process, I have been accused at times of being an advocate of anti-rationalism, of urging a "retreat from reason." Quite the opposite is true. I have a firm conviction that the province of reason will not be extended by false pretenses that it now extends further than it actually does. Anti-rationality can have no better disguise than fictitious rationality.

I am no foe of all that is not rational. The anti-rational and the non-rational are not co-extensive. To quote again Pascal's aphorism: "Two extremes: to exclude reason, and to admit reason only." Putting it more prosily, some reason and some non-reason are both "natural" and desirable components of human nature. Anti-reason is another matter. But we cannot cope with anti-rationality, reduce its scope so far as may be, if we refuse to grant that it exists. Some of those who dislike the anti-rational cry out in anger when, by an accurate description of present realities, its existence is exposed. They say to the describer, "You favor unreason. You have a program for opposing reason." Such a criticism is absurd. It confuses a description with a program. It is like saying of a physician who reports the prevalence of tuberculosis—for the purpose of inducing the public to reduce the causes of its ravages—that he favors that disease, hopes that its ravages will continue.[1]

There is an elightening parable in the following passage from a recent book on the human eye:[2] When a short-sighted person first wears glasses, he often complains, "I can't bear it. They make all my friends look ugly. They all have spots on their faces. And all the houses look so untidy and old. I don't like it. I don't want to see all that detail."

The authors of that book remark: "All one can say is that it is a pity such a patient was allowed to grow up so out of touch with reality, as this attitude of not wanting to see what is ugly may extend to one's attitude towards life and lead to shelving of responsibility." The desire

[1] Trilling remarks that Freud, in exposing the "night-side of life," did so with the aim of teaching how to control it.

[2] Mann and Pirie, *The Science of Seeing* (1946) 160-61.

to remain ignorant of the ugliness which creates problems is a "short-sighted" policy. It leads, in the case of the courts, to a shelving of responsibility for their needless shortcomings.

Radbruch, a foreign critic of contemporary American legal thinkers, says that the "realistic school" prefers "to dwell upon the human weaknesses of the judge" while "the sociological school lays stress upon the nobler motives of judicial decisions. . . ." He names me as the "most radical representative" of the "realists." His comment implies that such as I have little interest in the "nobler motives." I plead not guilty. My position involves no denigration of ideals, no opposition to constant efforts to promote judicial justice. On the contrary, I consider nothing more important about a man, be he a layman or judge, than his actual (not his pretended) ideals. But ideals are goals, to be won by hard striving; they will not be achieved by slothful men who merely mouth their ideals, who are satisfied with big talk of noble aims while they avert their gaze from painful actualities.

These are times of travail. Those of us who are incorrigible optimists believe that, one of these days, we shall have a sane, effective, world-organization and wiser methods of handling our domestic American affairs.[3] In the meantime, many troublesome global and national problems will press on us. But, while concerned with the macrocosm, we dare not overlook the microcosms, the more minute factors that loom large in the lives of individual men. Court-house ways are important among those factors. And they will be, as long as any sort of civilization endures. For that reason, I have thought it not undesirable to give the lay reader some notion of how our courts actually operate.

My attitude is precisely the opposite of that recently ascribed to judges by an English lawyer:[4] "A judge," he says, "is called upon to decide all kinds of hotly contested controversies; and this would be the most invidious of tasks if he could not 'cover up' behind a doctrine proclaiming to the world that in fact he has little or no personal discretion, and that he is compelled by ineluctable logic to the conclusions which he reaches." This lawyer concedes that "there is much room in the judicial process for the idiosyncracies of the particular judge to as-

[3] Several of my other writings, and my participation for years in government service in Washington, will go to show that I have not been without interest in those problems.

[4] Wade, "The Concept of Legal Certainty," 4 *Mod. L. Rev.* (1941) 183.

sert themselves." But he maintains that "the inherent uncertainty . . . should be concealed from the laymen," for the resultant delusion "will stop the public . . . from perceiving . . . defects in the legal system which they may be ill-qualified to judge." To my mind, such judicial concealment is pernicious and undemocratic to the last degree. John Q. Citizen should be told of the flaws in the workings of the courts, and should be taught how to become well-qualified to consider them—differentiating between inherent, ineradicable, difficulties in the administration of justice and those which are eradicable and should be eliminated. For, in a democracy, the courts belong not to the judges and the lawyers, but to the citizens.

INDEX

INDEX

[illegible] High School
Library

Frank, Jerome

345
F

Courts on Trial

10581

	DATE DUE		
FEB 26 '80			
JAN 27 '81			
MAR 31 '81			
MAR 10 '82			
MAR 01 1983			
MAR 18 1983			
APR 7 1986			